Lecture Notes in Computer Science 3833

Commenced Publication in 1973
Founding and Former Series Editors:
Gerhard Goos, Juris Hartmanis, and Jan van Leeuwen

Ki-Joune Li   Christelle Vangenot (Eds.)

Web and Wireless Geographical Information Systems

5th International Workshop, W2GIS 2005
Lausanne, Switzerland, December 15-16, 2005
Proceedings

 Springer

Volume Editors

Ki-Joune Li
Pusan National University, Department of Computer Science and Engineering
Kumjung-Gu, Pusan 609-735, South Korea
E-mail: lik@pnu.edu

Christelle Vangenot
EPFL, School of Computer and Communication Sciences, Database Laboratory
EPFL-IC-LBD, Station 14, 1015 Lausanne, Switzerland
E-mail: christelle.vangenot@epfl.ch

Library of Congress Control Number: 2005936807

CR Subject Classification (1998): H.2, H.3, H.4, H.5, C.2

ISSN   0302-9743
ISBN-10   3-540-30848-2 Springer Berlin Heidelberg New York
ISBN-13   978-3-540-30848-5 Springer Berlin Heidelberg New York

Springer is a part of Springer Science+Business Media

springeronline.com

© Springer-Verlag Berlin Heidelberg 2005
Printed in Germany

Typesetting: Camera-ready by author, data conversion by Scientific Publishing Services, Chennai, India
Printed on acid-free paper   SPIN: 11599289   06/3142   5 4 3 2 1 0

Preface

These proceedings contain the papers selected for presentation at the 5th edition of the International Workshop on Web and Wireless Geographical Information Systems, held in December 2005, in Lausanne, Switzerland. The aim of the series of annual W2GIS workshops is to provide an up-to-date review of advances on recent development and research results in the field of web and wireless geographical information systems. It follows the successful 2001, 2002, 2003, 2004 editions, held in Kyoto, Singapore, Rome and Seoul, respectively. It now represents a young but rapidly maturing research community.

In its 5th year, W2GIS reached new heights of recognition as a quality workshop for the dissemination and discussion on latest research and development achievements in the domain. The number of papers received for this workshop demonstrates the growing interest of the research community. There were 70 submissions from 17 countries, many of them of excellent quality and most of them very related to the topics of the workshop. Each paper receives three reviews. Based on these reviews, 25 papers were selected for presentation and inclusion in the proceedings. The accepted papers cover a wide range of topics from the Semantic Web, Web personalization, contextual representation and mapping to querying in mobile environments, to mobile networks and location-based services.

We had the privilege of having a distinguished invited talk "The next revolution: Peer-to-Peer discovery on mobile devices" by Ouri Wolfson, University of Illinois at Chicago, USA.

We wish to thank the authors that contributed to this workshop for the high quality of their papers and presentations and the support of Springer LNCS. We would also like to thank all the Program Committee members for the quality of their evaluations in spite of the high number of submissions. Finally, many thanks to the Steering Committee members for providing continuous advice.

October 2005

Ki-Joune Li
Christelle Vangenot

W2GIS 2005 Workshop Committee

Workshop Chairs

Ki-joune Li (Pusan National University, South Korea)
Christelle Vangenot (EPFL, Switzerland)

Steering Committee

Michela Bertolotto (University College Dublin, Ireland)
Christophe Claramunt (Naval Academy, France)
Bo Huang (University of Calgary, Canada)
Hui Lin (Chinese University of Hong Kong, China)
Stefano Spaccapietra (EPFL, Switzerland)

Program Committee

Masatoshi Arikawa (University of Tokyo, Japan)
Chaitan Baru (San Diego Supercomputer Center, USA)
Alain Bouju (University of La Rochelle, France)
Rolf A. de By (ITC, The Netherlands)
James Carswell (Dublin Institute of Technology, Ireland)
Nadine Cullot (University of Burgundy, France)
Matt Duckham (University of Melbourne, Australia)
Max Egenhofer (NCGIA, USA)
Mark Gahegan (Penn State, USA)
Francis Grin (EIVD, Switzerland)
Jihong Guan (Wuhan University, China)
Peter Guth (US Naval Academy, USA)
Christian S. Jensen (Aalborg University, Denmark)
Myoung Ah Kang (University of Clermont-Ferrand, France)
Menno-Jan Kraak (ITC, The Netherlands)
Yong-Jin Kwon (Hankuk Aviation University, South Korea)
Robert Laurini (INSA Lyon, France)
Michel Mainguenaud (INSA Rouen, France)
Yoshifumi Masunaga (Ochanomizu University, Japan)
Pedro R. Muro-Medrano (University of Zaragoza, Spain)
Enrico Nardelli (University of Rome "Tor Vergata", Italy)
Silvia Nittel (University of Maine, USA)
Beng C. Ooi (National University of Singapore, Singapore)

Dimitris Papadias (Hong Kong University of Science and Technology, Hong Kong, China)
Vasily V. Popovich (University of St Petersburg, Russia)
Shashi Shekhar (University of Minnesota, USA)
Markus Schneider (University of Florida, USA)
Katsumi Tanaka (Kyoto University, Japan)
Yufei Tao (City University of Hong Kong, Hong Kong, China)
George Taylor (University of Glamorgan, UK)
Jari Veijalainen (ITRI, University of Jyväskylä, Finland)
Agnès Voisard (Fraunhofer ISST and FU Berlin, Germany)
Robert Weibel (University of Zurich, Switzerland)
Stephan Winter (University of Melbourne, Australia)
Ouri Wolfson (University of Illinois at Chicago, USA)

External Reviewers

Pedro Alvarez (University of Zaragoza, Spain)
Spiridon Bakiras (Hong Kong University of Science and Technology, Hong Kong, China)
Ruben Bejar (University of Zaragoza, Spain)
Lin Dan (National University of Singapore, Singapore)
Hae-Kyong Kang (Pusan National University, South Korea)
Yutaka Kidawara (NICT, Japan)
Hua Lu (National University of Singapore, Singapore)
François Pinet (Cemagref Clermont-Ferrand, France)
Anastasiya Sotnykova (EPFL, Switzerland)
Kazutoshi Sumiya (University of Hyogo, Japan)
Taro Tezuka (Kyoto University, Japan)
Man Lung Yiu (University of Hong Kong, Hong Kong, China)
Shijun Yu (EPFL, Switzerland)
Javier Zarazaga-Soria (University of Zaragoza, Spain)

Sponsor

Korea Telematics Business Association, KOTBA
Point-I Co. Ltd.

Table of Contents

Mobile GIS and LBS

Mapping and Representation Issues in Web and Mobile GIS

Mobile Networks

Querying in a Mobile Environment

Context and Personalization Issues in Web and Mobile GIS

Web GIS

Modeling for Web and Mobile GIS

Development of an Embedded Spatial MMDBMS for Spatial Mobile Devices

Jae-Kwan Yun, Joung-Joon Kim, Dong-Suk Hong, and Ki-Joon Han[*]

School of Computer Science & Engineering, Konkuk University,
1, Hwayang-Dong, Gwangjin-Gu, Seoul 143-701, Korea
{jkyun, jjkim9, dshong, kjhan}@db.konkuk.ac.kr

Abstract. Recently, with the development of wireless communications and mobile computing, interest in mobile computing is rising. Mobile computing can be regarded as an environment where a user carries mobile devices and shares resources with a server via wireless communications. A mobile database, which can be used in the various fields, refers to a database used in these mobile devices. Especially, LBS which utilizes location information of users becomes an essential field of mobile computing. In order to support LBS in the mobile environment, there must be an Embedded Spatial MMDBMS that can efficiently manage large spatial data in spatial mobile devices. Therefore, in this paper, we developed an Embedded Spatial MMDBMS, extended from the HSQLDB which is an existing MMDBMS for PC, to manage spatial data efficiently in spatial mobile devices. The Embedded Spatial MMDBMS adopted the spatial data model proposed by ISO, provided the arithmetic coding method suitable for spatial data, and supported the efficient spatial index suitable for spatial mobile devices. In addition, the system offered the spatial data display capability and supported the data caching and synchronization capability between the Embedded Spatial MMDBMS and the GIS server.

1 Introduction

Today's development of information communication technologies is followed by extensive requirement of business affairs through mobile information devices that provide convenience and promptness in all industries. This trend is accompanied by exponential development of the mobile communication technologies for the wide spread of mobile devices throughout the world. The development of these mobile devices enabled the emergence of the mobile computing age that allows the public to access the desired information anywhere at any time[7,8,9]. Mobile database refers to the databases applied for these mobile devices. The applicable fields of the mobile database generally include insurance affairs, financial affairs, and medical affairs, but the LBS(Location Based Service) using the location information of the users through GIS has emerged to become an important new field of applications[2,9]. This paper particularly defines spatial mobile devices as the mobile devices that use spatial data for the LBS.

---

[*] Corresponding author.

K.-J. Li and C. Vangenot (Eds.): W2GIS 2005, LNCS 3833, pp. 1 – 10, 2005.

Spatial mobile devices currently use lower capacities of memories and processors than other PCs. Also, spatial mobile devices generally process data based on their own file systems. It may be convenient when processing small-sized data, but generates problems when managing the large-sized spatial data that increase everyday or processing the complex and varied spatial query. These existing problems can be solved by managing the spatial data using the Embedded MMDBMS(Main-Memory Database Management System) within the spatial mobile devices[8].

In this paper, we designed and implemented an Embedded Spatial MMDBMS that can manage the spatial data in spatial mobile devices by adding or extending a few functions within the HSQLDB, which is a main-memory DBMS. The added or extended functions include a arithmetic coding compression technique appropriated for spatial data types, spatial operators, and spatial data characteristics; a spatial index using the MBR compression or hashing technique suitable for the spatial mobile devices; and a data-caching function to improve the synchronized connection with the GIS server as well as the display function and communication function of the spatial mobile devices.

This paper starts with an introduction in Chapter 1 and examines the requirements of the Embedded Spatial MMDBMS for the spatial mobile devices and the HSQLDB in Chapter 2. Chapter 3 explains the structure and the functions of the Embedded Spatial MMDBMS in detail, and Chapter 4 states detailed descriptions of each module of the Embedded Spatial MMDBMS. Chapter 5 states performance tests. Lastly, Chapter 6 mentions the conclusion and possible future work.

2 Related Works

This chapter examines the requirements of the Embedded Spatial MMDBMS for the spatial mobile devices and the HSQLDB.

2.1 Requirements of the Embedded Spatial MMDBMS

The Embedded Spatial MMDBMS for the spatial mobile devices is applicable to the super-lightweight real-time DBMS technology field and requires a new technology to overcome the major weaknesses of the spatial mobile devices with low processing CPU and limited memory. Also, it is required to contain a spatial data conversion and synchronization system to convert the large-sized data of the central servers into the data compressed for the spatial mobile devices in order to process the GIS function that processes large-sized spatial data on the spatial mobile devices.

Additional functions include a spatial data filtering technique to convert the data into what is applicable to the spatial mobile devices; a mobile spatial index technique[1,2,4] to quickly search for the highly compressed data in the spatial mobile devices; and a map-caching technique[5] to enhance the display property of the data in the spatial mobile devices. The Embedded Spatial MMDBMS, in particular, should support the spatial data types and the spatial operators in order to support the spatial data efficiently[9].

2.2 The HSQLDB and Improvement of the HSQLDB

The HSQLDB is a memory-related DBMS created purely by the Java language[3]. The HSQLDB started out as the Hypersonic SQL project and was first distributed in 1988. Also, the HSQLDB development team was formed by a few developers of the Hypersonic SQL to distribute 1.7.2 version in July 2004. As the characteristics of the HSQLDB were composed purely in Java, the system is independent and supports the ANSI-92 SQL standards and JDBC interface. Also, it supports the B+-tree for fast searching and transaction and Outer Join/Inner Join for data integrity. It supports View and Trigger, ORDER BY, GROUP BY and HAVING, and provides COUNT, SUM, MIN, MAX and AVG functions. Especially, the user may create databases using the SQL script files.

This paper extended the HSQLDB into the Embedded Spatial MMDBMS for the spatial mobile devices to satisfy the requirements of Section 2.1. In other words, the spatial data types and spatial operator of the ISO/DIS 19107, the arithmetic coding compression technique and data caching functions for the spatial data in order to enhance the efficiency when importing/exporting spatial data to and from GIS servers, the synchronized connection function for GIS servers, and a spatial index for the spatial mobile devices that can use the MBR compression and hashing techniques for the fast searching of the spatial data suitable for the spatial mobile devices are added to the HSQLDB.

3 Design of the Embedded Spatial MMDBMS

This chapter explains the structure and the functions of the Embedded Spatial MMDBMS.

3.1 Structure of the Embedded Spatial MMDBMS

The Embedded Spatial MMDBMS that is developed in this paper is roughly divided into an interface manager, a display manager, a data-cache manager, a transaction manager, a spatial index manager, a data compression manager, an import/export manager, a query processing manager, and a synchronization manager. Figure 1 illustrates the overall structure of the Embedded Spatial MMDBMS.

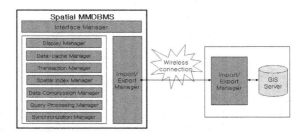

Fig. 1. Structure of the Embedded Spatial MMDBMS

The Import/Export Manager and the Data-cache Manager provide the spatial data exchange function between the Embedded Spatial MMDBMS and the GIS server. The Interface Manager and the Display Manager support functions for query input and result display for the users. The Data Compression Manager compresses the spatial data when importing/exporting the spatial data and the Query Processing Manager and the Transaction Manager examine, analyze and control the SQL queries. Also, the Synchronization Manager accords the spatial data from the Embedded Spatial MMDBMS and the GIS server, and the Spatial Index Manager provides spatial indexes for the spatial mobile devices.

3.2 Spatial Data Types and Operators

Table 1(a), (b) indicates the relationships of spatial data types and spatial operators between the ISO/DIS 19107 and the Embedded Spatial MMDBMS.

Table 1. Spatial Date Types and Spatial Operators

(a) Relationship of Spatial Data types (b) Relationship of Spatial operators

ISO/DIS 19107	Embedded Spatial MMDBMS
GM_Point	point
GM_LineSegment	simpleline
GM_Curve	polyline
GM_PolyhedralSurface	polygon
GM_Envelope	rectangle
GM_Circle	circle
GM_Polygon	hpolygon
GM_Complex	shape

ISO/DIS 19107	Embedded Spatial MMDBMS
contain	contain
buffer	cover
disjoint	disjoint
equals	equal
intersects	crossover
intersection	overlap
touch	touch
area	area
centroid	center
distance	distance
length	length
nearest	nearest
edges	edges
transform	translation
union	union
difference	difference
envelope	boundary

Table 2 indicates the definitions of the spatial operators of the Embedded Spatial MMDBMS. The spatial operators are composed of the topology and geometry operators.

Table 2. Definition of Spatial Operators

Spatial operator (topology operator)	Definition
operand1 **contain** operand2	Return TRUE if a first operand contains a second operand and intersection between these boundary values does not exist.
operand1 **cover** operand2	Return TRUE if a first operand contains a second operand and intersection between these boundary values exists.
operand1 **disjoint** operand2	Return TRUE if intersection between two operands does not exist.
operand1 **equal** operand2	Return TRUE if two operands is equal.
operand **touch** operand2	Return True if intersection between internal values of two operands doesn't exist and intersection between themselves exist.
Spatial operator (geometry operator)	Definition
area operand	Getting an area of a spatial object
center operand	Getting a center of gravity of a spatial object
operand1 **distance** operand2	Getting the minimum distance between two spatial objects
operand1 **direction** operand2	Getting the angle between straight line which connects center of gravity of spatial objects and axis of X.
length operand	Getting a length or a circumference of operand which is line or plane object type
edges operand	Getting nth sigh from operand which is polyline or polygon object type

3.3 Spatial Data Compression

This paper applied the arithmetic coding technique using the distance to the standard point based on the spatial data compression method. Generally, those taking the largest sizes in GIS are not Point or SimpleLine, but MultiLine or Polygon. This MultiLine or Polygon has clustered shapes for certain parts. Therefore, when calculating the distance based on the clustered MultiLine or Polygon, actual data of the standard point takes eight bytes, but the distances after that gradually display smaller integer values.

This paper improved the arithmetic coding technique to enhance the compression rate. The weakness of the existing arithmetic coding technique was the first coordinates of each unit could not reduce their sizes. Therefore, the improved arithmetic coding technique enhanced the compression rate by calculating the distance between the second units and the first units to reduce the integer values of the first coordinates of each unit. This method results in even higher compression rates when the units are concentrated in a certain region. Figure 2 shows an example of a spatial data compression using the improved arithmetic coding technique.

Fig. 2. Example of Spatial Data Compression

When -12.2309, which is the difference between 207068.9921, the X coordinate of the first Polygon, and 207081.223, that of the second Polygon, is expressed by the compression structure proposed in this paper, the values of the first coordinates that could not be reduced by the existing arithmetic coding technique can be reduced to enhance the compression rates even higher.

3.4 Spatial Index

In the realm of spatial efficiency, R*-tree uses less disk space when dividing and combining nodes to create a balanced tree. This characteristic of R*-tree makes it unsuitable for the memory systems with limited capacities. Also, CR-tree, the main-memory spatial index, uses the MBR compression technique. However, although the MBR compression technique using a quantitative method has high spatial efficiency, it is not suitable for the spatial mobile devices due to its low filtering efficiency. Therefore, this paper used a spatial index for spatial mobile devices using the MBR compression and hashing techniques that are efficient for simple displays and calculations of the spatial data of points and ranges, rather than using modified spatial data. The following formula (1) is the hashing functions used for the spatial index of the spatial mobile devices.

$$Hx(x) = \text{int}[(x - X\min)/(X\max - X\min) * Nx]$$
$$Hy(y) = \text{int}[(y - Y\min)/(Y\max - Y\min) * Ny]$$

(1)

In this formula (1), Xmax, Xmin, Ymax, and Ymin refer to the overall MBR and Nx, Ny the number of buckets on each axis. In case of overflows, the min and max values are replaced by the MBR of the bucket with the overflow to perform second hashing to maintain the consistency of the number of units contained in one bucket. The compression technique of the MBR, as presented in this paper, used the HMBR (Hybrid MBR) technique combining the RMBR (Relative MBR) and QMBR (Quantization MBR) techniques. The expression of HMBR involves expressing the lower left points as ordinary coordinates and the upper right points by sizes. This method adequately maintains the accuracy of the MBR and reduces the size of data. The performance test on several kinds of spatial indexes revealed that HMBR was superior to other several methods.

4   Implementations of the Embedded Spatial MMDBMS

This Chapter states detailed descriptions of each module of the Embedded Spatial MMDBMS.

4.1   Import/Export Manager and Data-Cache Manager

The Import/Export Manager provides the data exchange function between the Embedded Spatial MMDBMS and the GIS server using a wireless network socket, upon request, and the RSA(Rivest-Shamir-Adleman) encryption transmit function optionally. The Data-cache Manager performs two functions. First, for importing/exporting it first transmits the range questioned by the user and caches and receives the range that exceeds the questioned range by 30% in advance for the next question of the user. Second, it primarily displays the spatial and aspatial data on the memory range that exceeds the range displayed to the user by 30% and then displays what is requested by the user on the spatial mobile device.

4.2   Data Compression Manager and Query Processing Manager

The Data Compression Manager performs spatial data compression using the arithmetic coding technique to enhance the network efficiency of the importing/ exporting between the Embedded Spatial DBMS and the GIS server. The Query Processing Manager accepts the SQL query entered by the user from the Interface Manager to examine, analyze and control the SQL query statement and uses the spatial data types and spatial operators provided by the Embedded Spatial MMDBMS to process the searching, inserting, deleting and updating functions for the spatial data.

4.3   Transaction Manager and Display Manager

The Transaction Manager supports the COMMIT and ROLLBACK functions to guarantee the data integrity. That is, it provides the log.properties file recording the last system connection time, system version information, and the proper termination of the system and the log.script file recording the COMMITED SQL statements to support the data integrity. Also, it supports the restore function in case the system is improperly terminated. The Display Manager performs parsing of the spatial data received from the Data-cache Manager and converts them into the coordinate values suitable for the spatial mobile devices to display them on the screen.

4.4 Interface Manager and Spatial Index Manager

The Interface Manager accepts user's questions and zoom-in/zoom-out and pan the map displays. The Zoom-in/Zoom-out module expands/shrinks the map displays on the spatial mobile devices. The Zoom-in/Zoom-out module is composed of Zoom-In() and Zoom-Out() functions and creates questions to expand/shrink the spatial data to be displayed on the spatial mobile devices. The Fan module moves the map display displayed on the client's devices to all directions in east, west, north and south. The Fan module is composed of East(), West(), South() and North() functions and creates questions to move the displayed spatial data in all four directions.

The Spatial Index Manager uses hashing, a method of direct searching, to enhance the searching efficiency and provides spatial indexes for the spatial mobile devices using the MBR compression and hashing techniques with enhanced spatial efficiency achieved by the compressed MBR.

4.5 Synchronization Manager

The Synchronization Manager accords the data from the Embedded Spatial MMDBMS and the GIS server. The Synchronization Manager used a point-update synchronization method that supports two-way synchronization. The point-update synchronization method only renews the portion modified after the last synchronization, and the transaction LOCK is applied for the Embedded Spatial MMDBMS and the GIS server during the synchronization. Also, the recent data priority method was used to solve any crashing during the synchronization.

5 Performance Test

This Chapter states performance tests of the Embedded Spatial MMDBMS.

5.1 Performance Test Environment

This paper used the Java language as the development language of the system and ANT as the compile tool. In this paper, we used ZEUS as the GIS server and Compaq iPAQ 5450 as the spatial mobile device. Also, the Operating System used Personal Java 1.1 and Embedded Java 1.3 within Pocket PC 2002 and Embedded Linux environments. The Sequoia 2000 benchmarking data[4] and Seoul Gangdong-gu's building data are used as test data.

5.2 Data Compression Performance Test

The performance test on the arithmetic coding technique of the Compression Manager compared it to the zip compression for the compression rates and compression time on the spatial mobile devices. Table 3 and Table 4 display the performance test results in the compression rates and time of the arithmetic coding technique respectively.

Table 3. Compression Rates of the Arithmetic Coding Technique

Compression \ Data	Sequoia 2000 bench mark data	Gangdong-gu's building data
zip compression	15,135 KB	1,327 KB
Arithmetic coding technique	11,352 KB	996 KB

Table 4. Compression Time of the Arithmetic Coding Technique

Compression \ Data	Sequoia 2000 bench mark data	Gangdong-gu's building data
zip compression	19,578 ms	2,610 ms
Arithmetic coding technique	13,060 ms	1,739 ms

As shown in Table 3 and Table 4, the arithmetic coding technique has the compression rate improved by 25% and the compression time by 30% when compared to the zip compression.

5.3 Spatial Index Performance Test

The performance test of the Spatial Index Manager compared the sizes of dynamic hashing and indexes and the performances of spatial data insertion and search on the spatial mobile devices. Table 5 compares the index size between the spatial index and the dynamic hashing index applied to the Embedded Spatial MMDBMS.

Table 5. Sizes of Spatial Index

Index \ Data	Sequoia 2000 bench mark data	Gangdong-gu's building data
Spatial index	783 KB	96 KB
Dynamic hashing	624 KB	78 KB

As shown in Table 5, the index size of the spatial index applied to the Embedded Spatial MMDBMS is larger than that of the dynamic hashing index. Testing of the inserting and searching times of the spatial index and dynamic hashing revealed that the spatial index improved performances in inserting and searching times of the spatial data than the dynamic hashing by 25~30%, as shown in Table 6 and Table 7.

Table 6. Inserting Times of the Spatial Index

Index \ Data	Sequoia 2000 bench mark data	Gangdong-gu's building data
Spatial index	2136.5 ms	305.4 ms
Dynamic hashing	2847.3 ms	406.5 ms

Table 7. Searching Times of the Spatial Index

Data/Index	Query domain	PointQuery	Domain Query		
			0.1%	0.4%	1%
Gangdong-gu's building data	spatial index	6.6 ms	64.5 ms	101.8 ms	147.5 ms
	dynamic hashing	8.9 ms	87.0 ms	148.5 ms	210.7 ms
sequoia 2000 bench mark data	spatial index	46.8 ms	451.8 ms	782.9 ms	1103.0 ms
	dynamic hashing	63.1 ms	607.9 ms	1046.7 ms	1487.9 ms

5.4 Spatial MMDBMS Performance Test

The performance test of the Spatial MMDBMS compared the performances of spatial data insertion and search on the spatial MMDBMS and the file system of mobile devices.

The insert time of the spatial data is 35~40% larger than that of the file system of mobile devices. However, testing of the searching times of the spatial data revealed that the spatial MMDBMS improved performances in searching times of the spatial data than the file system of mobile devices by 55~60%, as shown in Table 8 and Table 9.

Table 8. Inserting Times of the Spatial Data

System / Data	sequoia 2000 bench mark data	Gangdong-gu's building data
File system of mobile devices	51102 ms	3454 ms
Spatial MMDBMS	85170 ms	5678 ms

Table 9. Inserting Times of the Spatial Data

Data/System	Query domain	PointQuery	Domain Query		
			0.1%	0.4%	1%
Gangdong-gu's building data	File system of mobile devices	12.6 ms	164.5 ms	501.8 ms	1147.5 ms
	Spatial MMDBMS	6.6 ms	105.0 ms	302.4 ms	684.2 ms
sequoia 2000 bench mark data	File system of mobile devices	74.1 ms	984.5 ms	3010.5 ms	6887.1 ms
	Spatial MMDBMS	38.5 ms	607.9 ms	1819.3 ms	4112.6 ms

6 Conclusions and Future Work

As the wireless Internet and mobile computing technology are developed and the mobile devices are popularized, the LBS is applied to more various fields. In order to process the large-sized spatial data faster and manage them effectively in the LBS, an Embedded Spatial MMDBMS that can manage the spatial data efficiently in the memory of the spatial mobile device is necessary.

This paper added spatial data types and spatial operators to support the spatial data necessary for the LBS and the arithmetic coding technique that is suitable for new spatial data to reduce the sizes of the spatial data when importing/exporting the spatial data between the Embedded Spatial MMDBMS and the GIS server for efficient importing/exporting of the spatial data within the HSQLDB, a memory-related DBMS. Spatial indexes using the MBR compression and hashing techniques suitable for the fast searching of the spatial data by the spatial mobile devices are also applied to HSQLDB. Overall, an Embedded Spatial MMDBMS that can manage the spatial data effectively on the spatial mobile devices by adding the display function and the data-caching function to enhance the communication performance with the GIS server was designed and presented in this paper. Possible future research subjects include a standardized synchronization method with many different kinds of GIS.

Acknowledgements

This research was supported by the MIC(Ministry of Information and Communication), Korea, under the ITRC(Information Technology Research Center) support program supervised by the IITA(Institute of Information Technology Assessment).

References

1. Greene, D.: An Implementation and Performance Analysis of Spatial Data Access Methods. IEEE Transaction on Knowledge and Data Engineering (1989) 606-615
2. Gueting, R. H.: An Introduction to Spatial Database Systems. The VLDB Journal (1994) 357-399
3. HSQLDB: http://hsqldb.sourceforge.net.
4. ISO TC/211: ISO 19107 Geographic Information - Spatial Schema. http://www.isotc211.org
5. Kim, K. H., Cha, S. K., and Kwon, K. J.: Optimizing Multidimensional Index Trees for Main Memory Access. Proc. of Int. Conf. on ACM SIGMOD (2001) 139-150
6. Lee, K. Y., Kim, D. O., Yun, J. K., and Han, K. J.: A Real-time Mobile GIS based on the HBR-tree. Proc. of the 33rd Int. Conf. on Computers & Industrial Engineering (2004)
7. Stonebreaker, M., Frew, J., Gardels, K., and Meredith, J.: The SEQUOIA 2000 Storage Benchmark. Proc. of Int. Conf. on ACM SIGMOD (1993) 2-11
8. Yun, J. K., Kim, D. O., and Han, K. J.: Development of a Real-Time Mobile GIS supporting the Open Location Service. Proc. of Geotec Event Conference (2003)
9. Yun, J. K., Zhang, Y. S., and Han, K. J.: Location Based Service for Mobile GIS. SIGDB Korean DataBase Research, Vol.18, No.1 (2002) 3-15

Design of Query Language for Location-Based Services

Jaiho Lee, Kyounghwan An, and Jonghyun Park

Telematics Research Group,
Telematics USN Research Division,
Electronics and Telecommunications Research Institute,
Daejeon, Korea
{snoopy, mobileguru, jhp}@etri.re.kr

Abstract. Recently, the need for LBS (Location Based Services) is increasing due to the widespread of mobile computing devices and positioning technologies. In LBS, there are many applications that need to manage moving objects (e.g. taxies, persons). The trajectories or the positions of moving objects are displayed on the map by using GIS. However, it is hard to use GIS or traditional relational database systems to manage moving objects. Modeling consistent information about the location of continuously moving objects and processing motion-specific queries is challenging problem. The previous studies suggested several query languages to retrieve moving objects. However, they do not propose DDL (Data Definition Language) and do not support full functions that are necessary. In this paper, we formally define a data model and data type for moving objects and propose MOQL (Moving Objects Query Language) which is a convenient interface and tool for developers. MOQL has the following features. First, it supports DDL to insert/delete/update the positions of moving objects. Second, it can be used to retrieve the trajectories of moving objects. Third, it defines several functions to manage spatial or temporal properties of moving objects.

1 Introduction

Location Based Services (LBS) are services that provide value added information using locations of things or people. The services are enabled by mobile devices, wireless communication, and positioning technologies based on mobile network or GPS. Since the infrastructures previously mentioned are wide spread already, LBS will be more prevalent in the future. The examples of LBS are a buddy finder service to find a location of a friend, a navigation service to provide routing information to a driver, L-commerce to advertise goods based on customer's location, and "E911" service for emergency calls.

In those applications, there are enormous numbers of "moving objects" to be managed and queried. Since the moving objects may report their locations frequently, a database system should be able to handle a huge number of updates and queries quickly. However, traditional disk resident relation DBMS cannot handle the updates and queries efficiently. Even more it does not support a query language specific to handling moving objects. It means application developer should concern all the things to update and retrieve the locations.

K.-J. Li and C. Vangenot (Eds.): W2GIS 2005, LNCS 3833, pp. 11 – 18, 2005.

The previous studies [1, 4, 6] on the query language about moving objects have the following problems. First, they do not provide DDL (Data Definition Language) specific to moving objects. Second, they do not provide proper update constructs to add or remove the part of the trajectories. Third, they do not provide full functionalities to retrieve moving objects.

In this paper, we solve the previous problems. We suggest new DDL syntax to support migration and purging, update constructs to update trajectories. We also classify and define several operators to manage the trajectories of moving objects. The suggested query language can make it easy to develop location based services.

The remainder of this paper is organized as follows. In section 2, we explain data model and data types for moving objects. In section 3, we present constructs and examples of the data definition language. In section 4, we propose several operators and examples of data manipulation language. Finally, we conclude with issues and further works.

2   Modeling Moving Objects

In the real world, moving objects like car or person show continuous movement. However, the continuous movement can not be represented in the database. Thus the movement should be sampled discretely and interpolated between sampled locations.

To design moving objects components that can be used in location-based database applications, we need more complex data structures and operations than those of general relational database applications. Since moving objects change the positions and shapes in temporal dimension, we should design temporal and spatial components first of all, and then moving objects. Also, we need to define new operations for manipulating and retrieving the moving objects in databases.

Geometry classes consist of Point, LineString, Polygon, GeometryCollection, Surface classes, and et al. UML modeling for geometry classes is borrowed from its of International Standard of Open GIS Consortium[7]. So, we abbreviate the detail description for geometry classes.

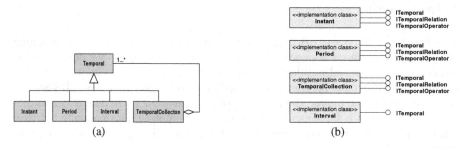

Fig. 1. Temporal Data Types (a) Temporal Class Hierarchy (b) Interface Diagram of Temporal Component

Fig. 1. shows a diagram of temporal classes. Temporal classes consist of Period, Interval, Instant, and TemporalCollection classes as shown in Figure 3(a). These classes have ITemporal, ITemporalRelation, and ITmporalOperator Interfaces as shown in Figure 3(b).

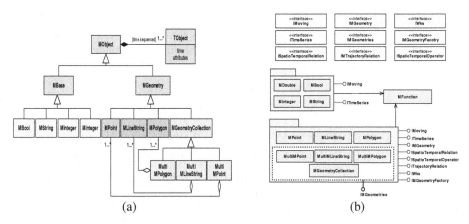

Fig. 2. Moving Objects Data Types : (a) Moving Objects Class Hierarchy (b) Interface Diagram of Moving Objects Component

Fig. 2 shows moving objects classes. Classes for moving objects consist of TObject, MObject, MBase, MGeometry classes, and et al. MObject is a super class of all moving object classes, and TObject is a unit element class for organizing moving objects such as a tuple of <geometry|instant> as shown in Fig. 2.

MBase is a super class for non-spatial moving object classes such as moving float, moving integer, moving string, and moving boolean. For example, moving float class can express a sequence of varying distances between two moving cellular phone users, such that [<5m|12:00pm>, <4.5m|12:01pm>, ...,<3.9m|12:10pm>]. MGeometry is a super class for spatial moving object classes such as moving point, moving linestring, moving polygon classes, and et al. The type MPoint is the most frequently used data types for modeling the moving objects. Cars can be modeled as a point at a specific time. As the time progresses, the time value and geographic coordinates are accumulated in MPoint such that [<(0.0)|12:00pm>, <(5,10)| 12:01pm>, ..., <(3,9)|12:10pm>]. The semantic of the other data types can be easily interpreted without confusion. To use these data types, the moving objects should report the time value and the geometry simultaneously.

3   Data Definition Language

To store the locations of the moving objects, database tables should be created. In this paper, several new syntactical constructs are suggested to create the moving objects table.

The overall syntax is similar to the traditional syntax. However, the developer should use the specific data type to the moving objects. If the purpose of the creation is to store the trajectories of the moving objects, new constructs like "MIGRATE" or "PURGE" could be used.

Trajectory of a moving object can't be stored in storage forever because new locations will continuously be appended. It is not efficient that so much of trajectories store all together. That brings lowering of performance of query processing. What's more, there's a weak possibility that old data was referenced. Therefore it is desirable that we discard old useless trajectories or preserve it in other system.

The "MIGRATE" means the trajectories migrate from one storage system to another according to the given condition. "PURGE" is similar to "MIGRATE". It means that the part of the trajectories should be removed when the given condition is met.

The following shows the syntax of DDL for the creation of the table.

CREATE TABLE *tablename*

({ColumnDefinition}[,......][,TableConstraints]

[, **MIGRATE** (TIME|SPACE) (MigrateConstraint)]

[, **PURGE** (TIME|SPACE) (PurgeConstraint)]);

Example 1 shows the creation of the table using "MIGRATE". The table taxi has the field called position, which is the MPOINT type. Also it maintains trajectories only for 30 days.

Example 1:

```
CREATE TABLE taxi
( id INT, position MPOINT, MIGRATE TIME 30 days);
```

Example 2 shows the creation of the table using "PURGE". The trajectories in the table car are automatically deleted when it exceeds 100MB. When the migration occurs, meta data should be maintained to notify users of the fact that there were trajectories but they were deleted.

Example 2:

```
CREATE TABLE car ( id INT, position MPOINT, PURGE SPACE
100MB);
```

4 Data Manipulation Language

4.1 Update Statement

The update is the most characteristic feature of the moving objects database. The following example shows the new construct "add" to update a trajectory of a moving object.

Example 3:

```
insert into taxi values (1, importfromwkt
('MPOINT(2005/04/01 12:00:01, 1, 1' ));

update taxi add position = importfromwkt
('MPOINT(2005/04/01 12:05:00,4,4)') where id=1;
```

First, a record representing a moving object should be inserted. After the insertion, the reported locations should be reflected in the database. The traditional SQL syntax of the update statement was to use a pair of update and set. However, we used "add" instead of "set" because the newly reported location does not replace whole trajectory but just appended at the end of the trajectory. In case of not maintaining the past trajectories, "set" construct can be used.

4.2 Retrieval Statement

Moving objects databases should support past, now, and future queries. However, storage structures and access methods are totally different among the past, now, and future queries. Moving objects database may not support all types of queries.

In the future queries, queries can contain MAY or MUST construct. "MAY" means query result may satisfy the query conditions while "MUST" means query result must satisfy the conditions.

According to the form of query result, queries can be classified into instantaneous query and continuous query. Instantaneous query is a query that is evaluated and returns a query result immediately. Continuous query is a query that runs during the specified time or infinitely. It returns query results whenever the conditions are satisfied. Continuous query can be canceled by the user explicitly. To express continuous query, constructs like "for", "interval" are necessary. The following shows the example of the continuous query. The first query runs for 1 hour and execute every 5 second.

Example 4:

```
SELECT * FROM taxi EXECUTE INTERVAL 5s FOR 1 hr;
```

To handle trajectories of moving objects, several types of operators are necessary. In this paper, we classified the necessary operators into 5 categories: mgeometry, moving, temporal relation, spatio-temporal relation, and trajectory relation functions. The functions are summarized in table 1. The other function that does not shown in table 2 is nearest neighbor function. It is one of the most important operators in LBS. Since the semantic is clear, we omit detailed description of the nearest neighbor function.

Table 1. Operators

Type	Operator Name
MGeometry	ENVELOPE, DIMENSION, ISEMPTY, ISSIMPLE
Moving	SNAPSHOT, SLICE, SNAPSHOTBYVALUE, SLICEBYVALUE, PROJECT, LIFETIME, SUBSEQUENCE, FIRSTSUBSEQUENCE, LASTSUBSEQUENCE
Temporal	UNION, INTERSECTION, DIFFERENCE, PRECEDES, OVERLAPS, CONTAINS, MEETS, EQUALS
Spatio-Temporal	EQUALS, DISJOINT, INTERSECTS, TOUCHES, CROSSES, WITHIN, RELATE
Trajectory	ENTERS, PASSES, MEETS, LEAVE, INSIDES

First, the semantic of the MGeometry functions are explained below.

- ENVELOPE(MGEOMETRY): returns minimum bounding box of the given trajectory
- DIMENSION(MGEOMETRY): returns dimension of the given trajectory
- ISEMPTY(MGEOMETRY): checks if the given trajectory is empty
- ISSIMPLE(MGEOMETRY): checks if the given trajectory is simple geometry

The following shows the example of the MGeometry function envelope. It returns minimum bounding box of the moving objects of which id is 1.

Example 5:

```
select envelope(position) from truck where id=1;
```

Second, the semantic of the moving functions are explained below.

- SNAPSHOT(MGEOMETRY, TEMPORAL): returns MGEOMETRY of the specified time
- SLICE(MGEOMETRY, TEMPORAL, TEMPORAL): returns MGEOMETRY of the given time period
- SNAPSHOTBYVALUE(MGEOMETRY, GEOMETRY): returns the time that has the same geometry with the given input geometry
- SLICEBYVALUE(MGEOMETRY, GEOMETRY, GEOMETRY): returns the time period that contains the input geometries
- PROJECT(MGEOMETRY): returns the geometry which is the projection of the MGEOMETRY into x, y plane
- LIFETIME(MGEOMETRY): returns the lifetime of the moving object
- SUBSEQUENCE(MGEOMETRY, INT, INT): returns MGEOMETRY from the first index to the second index
- FIRSTSUBSEQUENCE(MGEOMETRY, INT): returns MGEOMETRY from the oldest to the given index
- LASTSUBSEQUENCE(MGEOMETRY, INT): returns MGEOMETRY from the latest to the given index

The following shows the example of the moving function slice. It returns trajectory of the moving objects of which id is 5 from '2004/01/01 12:00:03' to the current.

Example 6:

```
select slice(position, '2004/01/01 12:00:03' , CURRENT)
from car where id=5;
```

Third, the semantic of the temporal functions are explained below.

- UNION(TEMPORAL, TEMPORAL): returns the union of the input temporal values
- INTERSECTION(TEMPORAL, TEMPORAL): returns the intersection of the input temporal values
- DIFFERENCE(TEMPORAL, TEMPORAL): returns the difference of the input temporal values
- PRECEDES(TEMPORAL, TEMPORAL): checks if the first input precedes the second
- OVERLAPS(TEMPORAL, TEMPORAL): checks if the first input overlaps the second
- CONTAINS(TEMPORAL, TEMPORAL): checks if the first input contains the second
- MEETS(TEMPORAL, TEMPORAL): checks if the first input time meets the second at the end
- EQUALS(TEMPORAL, TEMPORAL): checks if the first input value is equals to the second value

The following shows the example of the temporal function intersection. It returns the intersection of the two input time.

Example 7:

```
select id, intersection(lifetime(position),'2004/1/1
01:03:00,2004/1/8 12:20:00') from taxi where id < 10;
```

Fourth, the semantic of the spatio-temporal functions are explained below. The several operators have the same name and semantic with the temporal operators.

- UNION, INTERSECTION, DIFFERENCE: the same semantic with the temporal operators
- BUFFER(MGEOMETRY, INT): returns the buffering of the input MGEOMETRY by int value
- SYMDIFFERENCE(MGEOMETRY, MGEOMETRY): returns the symmetric difference of the two input values
- DISTANCE(MGEOMETRY, MGEOMETRY): returns the distances between two input values
- WITHIN, DISJOINT, EQUALS, INTERSECTS, TOUCHES, OVERLAPS, CROSSES: similar to the spatial operators of the OpenGIS[7]

The following shows the example of the spatio-temporal function overlaps. It returns the changes of the topological relation.

Example 8:

```
select id from taxi where overlaps(position,
importfromwkt('MPOLYGON((2004/01/01 12:00:05,
10,10,1500,10,1500,1500,10,1500,10,10),(2004/01/01
12:30:05,10,10,1500,10,1500,1500,10,1500,10,10))')) =
1;
```

Finally, the semantic of the trajectory functions are explained in [2]. The semantic of the operators are composed of several spatio-temporal operators.

The following shows the example of the trajectory function pass. It checks if the trajectory passes through the given MPOLYGON.

Example 9:

```
select id from taxi where passes( position,
importfromwkt('MPOLYGON((2004/01/01 02:28:10,627
870,645 870,645 887,627 887,627 870) , (2004/01/01
02:30:10,627 870,645 870,645 887,627 887,627
870))'))=1;
```

5   Conclusions

In this paper, we proposed the data types, DDL, DML for the moving objects database. The suggested data types can express location or trajectories. The DDL can define moving objects specific field and can specify the condition for the migration and purge. The DML are classified into 5 categories. It provides several operators to manage the trajectories of the moving objects. By using our proposed query languages, much of the burden of the developer is relieved. Our future work is to implement the query language and to invent efficient query processing algorithms.

References

1. R. H. Guting, M. H. Bohlen, M. Erwig, C. S. Jensen, N. A. L. M. Schneider, and M. Vazir-giannis, "A Foundation for Representing and Querying Moving Objects," In ACM-Transactions on Database Systems Journal, pp.1-42, 2000
2. D. Pfoser, C. S. Jensen, and Y. Theodoridis, "Novel approaches in query processing for moving objects," Proc. of Int'l Conf. on Very Large Data Bases, pp. 395-406, 2000
3. S. Saltenis, C. S. Jensen, S.T. Leutenegger, and M. A. Lopez, "Indexing the positions of continuously moving objects," Proc. of the ACM SIGMOD Int'l Conf. on Management of Data, pp. 331-342, 2000
4. A. P. Sistla, O. Wolfson, S. Chamberlain, and S. Dao, "Modeling and Querying Moving Objects," In Proc. of the International Conference on Data Engineering, pp.422-432, 1997
5. G. Trajcevski1, O. Wolfson, F. Zhang, and S. Chamberlain, "The Geometry of Uncertainty in Moving Objects Databases," in EDBT 2002, LNCS 2287, pp. 233-250, 2002
6. O. Wolfson, S. Chamberlain, K. Kalpakis, and Y. Yesha, "Modeling Moving Objects for Location Based Services," in IMWS 2001, LNCS 2538, pp. 46-58, 2002
7. Jong-Yun Lee, " Integrating Spatial and Temporal Relationship Operators into SQL3 for Historical Data Management", in ETRI Journal, vol.24, no.3, June 2002, pp.226-238.
8. OpenGIS, http://www.opengis.org

Towards a Taxonomy of Location Based Services

Kostas Gratsias[1,2], Elias Frentzos[1], Vasilis Delis[2], and Yannis Theodoridis[1,2]

[1] Department of Informatics, University of Piraeus,
80 Karaoli-Dimitriou St, GR-18534 Piraeus, Greece
{gratsias, efrentzo, ytheod}@unipi.gr
http://isl.cs.unipi.gr/db
[2] Research and Academic Computer Technology Institute,
11 Akteou St & Poulopoulou St, GR-11851 Athens, Greece
{gratsias, delis, ytheod}@cti.gr

Abstract. Location-based services (LBS) constitute an emerging application domain involving spatio-temporal databases. In this paper, i) we propose a classification of LBS, depending on whether the user (query object) and the data objects are moving or not and ii) we provide algorithms for the efficient support of real applications, for every class. We also survey recent work in query processing for the proposed LBS algorithms and sketch open issues for future research.

Keywords: location based services, moving objects, spatiotemporal databases.

1 Introduction

The rapid growth of mobile devices, such as mobile phones and Personal Digital Assistants (PDAs) has contributed to the development of an emerging class of e-services, the so-called Location-Based Services (LBS). An LBS provides information relevant to the spatial location of a receiver. LBS constitute an innovative technological field which influences the way that people organize their activities, promising great business opportunities for telecommunications, advertising, tourism, etc. [10].

From a database perspective, LBS have combined most of the existing research results in the spatial and spatiotemporal database domain regarding indexing [4, 14] and query processing [1, 5, 13, 17, 18]. They have also indicated some open research issues such as the processing of forecasting queries (determining future positions of moving points), the support for continuous location change in query processing techniques [8], knowledge discovery from data collected via LBS, etc.

In this paper, we propose a novel classification of LBS based on whether the involved objects are stationary or mobile (Section 2) and provide indicative examples of applications as well as sketch algorithms for their efficient support (Section 3), for each class. In Section 4 we review the related literature and briefly discuss implementation issues for such query processing. Relevant open problems are also mentioned. Finally, Section 5 concludes the paper giving hints for future work.

K.-J. Li and C. Vangenot (Eds.): W2GIS 2005, LNCS 3833, pp. 19–30, 2005.

2 LBS Taxonomy

From a query processing point of view, the data structures and algorithms required to support queries involved in LBS depend on the mobility of the user. For a stationary user, the execution of a nearest neighbor query over a set of spatial objects (without taking into consideration any network constraints) could be sufficiently supported by a simple R-tree [4] and a classic nearest neighbor algorithm [13, 5]. However, such algorithms are not applicable in the case of a mobile user who wishes to be informed about the nearest point of interest at any time of his/her movement. Continuous nearest neighbor searching techniques that can efficiently support this type of service are presented in [18].

Likewise, let us consider services where the user asks for information about continuously moving objects; finding a cab is a good example. The efficient support of such queries entails indexing the moving objects (including future positions) by an appropriate structure (for example the TPR-tree [14]) and the use of a suitable nearest neighbor algorithm, such as the one presented in [1].

So, one could extend these thoughts and fully classify LBS according to the mobility of the user (query object) and the data objects. Four classes are identified which are presented in Table 1 along with indicative application examples. These examples are further described in the following section.

Table 1. LBS Classification

Query Object Data Object	Stationary (S)	Mobile (M)
Stationary (S)	*What-is-around* *Routing* *Find-the-nearest*	*Guide-me*
Mobile (M)	*Find-me*	*Get-together*

The novelty of the proposed classification stands on the fact that database query processing is the driving wheel behind our approach. As we will further discuss in subsequent sections, whether involving mobility or not in a service offered by an LBS system adds new and very interesting processing issues. On the other hand, other classification approaches that can be found in the literature either target on kinds of LBS applications [9] or present core services with respect to interoperability [10].

3 Fundamental LBS and Algorithms

In this section we describe six representative services that cover all S and M combinations that appear in Table 1: the former three address the (naïve) S-S category while the latter three uncover interesting issues of the (more advanced) S-M, M-S and M-M categories. Due to space constraints, we provide the corresponding high-level algorithmic descriptions of the latter three services only.

Some definitions: Let $G(V, E)$ be the directed graph that represents the underlying road network on which objects are moving. So, the vertices (nodes) V of G correspond to junctions while its edges E represent road segments. We can apply movement constraints for some (blocked) edges. Let S denote this subset of the edges. Each edge is associated with two weights (distance metrics), the length of the corresponding road segment and the average time required to travel through that segment, respectively. Finally let L denote all the landmark (point of interest) types and Q denote the set of all objects whose type belongs to L (i.e. pairs of the form *<object_id, object_type>*).

3.1 Both (Query and Data) Objects Are Stationary

The first three services belong to the S-S category, where both query and data objects are stationary. Although they are algorithmically simple, they constitute an LBS core upon which most of the rest are based.

What-is-around
The simplest service is the one that retrieves and displays the location of every landmark being in a circular[1] area (P, d), where P is the location of the user (or simply a point of interest – POI) and d is a selected distance. This service assumes a storage containing all the existing types of landmarks (POIs). The input of the corresponding algorithm for "*what-is-around*" consists of the point P, the radius d and the set LT (indicating the preference on object types, e.g. 'gas-station' and 'ATM') which is a subset of L. The algorithm returns the set $Q' \subseteq Q$ of all objects inside the circular area (P, d) whose type belongs in LT.

Routing
This service provides the optimal route between a departure and a destination point, P and Q, respectively, using the minimal network distance or minimal traveled time as the optimization criterion. The input of this service includes the graph G, the set of constraints S, the coordinates[2] of P and Q and a flag f that specifies the optimization criterion. The algorithm is based on the *Routing* function, which will be described in Section 4.

Find-the-Nearest
This service retrieves the k nearest landmarks (POIs). For example, "*find the two restaurants that are closest to my current location*" or "*find the nearest café to the railway station*". The underlying algorithm takes as input the graph G, the subset of landmarks of interest LT and a query point P (for example, calling user's current

---

[1] Alternative to circle, a rectangular or a more complex shape could be used to be the 'window' of the query.

[2] Finding the shortest path between two arbitrary points that lie on two edges, rather than between two nodes of a graph, is a slightly more involved operation. It depends on whether the particular road segments are bidirectional and the data structure that implements the graph. In the worst case it requires the calculation of four shortest paths, for the four pair combinations among the nodes of the corresponding edges. The distance between the point lying on the edge and the end-nodes must also be computed.

location). Using the *Net_k_Nearest_Neighbor* routine (described in Section 4), the system returns the set of points $Q' \subseteq Q$, which are the k nearest to P members of Q and their type belongs to *LT*. Once more, any of the two distance metrics can be applied.

3.2 Involving Mobility

The services presented in this section belong to the S-M, M-S or M-M category, where at least one part (query and/or data objects) is mobile. In contrast to the previously discussed services, these ones involve advanced graph and trajectory management routines, a fact that makes their development really attractive from the perspective of moving object database management.

Find-me
The provision of the *Find-me* type of services is fundamental for a commercial LBS platform. The scenario is the following (Fig.1): after receiving an emergency call, the system routes the k (in Fig.1, $k = 3$) nearest mobile first-aid units (U_2, U_3, U_4) to the location of the calling user (point P), who is periodically informed about the condition of his request (for example, he/she receives messages of the form *"The ambulance is 1 Km away"*).

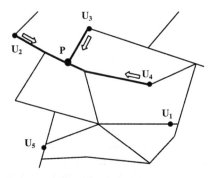

Fig. 1. Find-me example

In this service the query object (user) remains stationary, while the data objects (first-aid units) are mobile and their locations are automatically being recorded as they approach the calling user.

Obviously, this service can be implemented as a combination of *Find_the_nearest* and *Routing* presented in Section 3.1. The input of the proposed algorithm, which is illustrated in Fig.2, includes:

- the graph G along with the set of movement constraints S,
- the location P of the calling user,
- the set of ids of the mobile units $U = \{U_1, ..., U_N\}$,
- a distance threshold $\delta \geq 0$, which defines the minimum distance between the user and a mobile unit below which the unit is supposed to have reached the user,

- a time delay *dt* between subsequent notifications of a user about the state of his request, and finally,
- the parameter *k*.

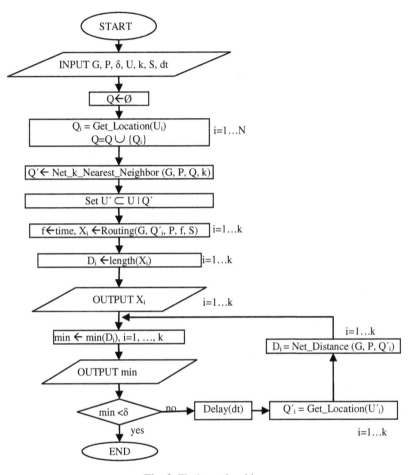

Fig. 2. Find-me algorithm

Guide-me

An extension of the (static) *Routing* described above is the so-called *Guide-me* service (an example of which is illustrated in Fig. 3): Likewise, the system determines the best route between a departure and a destination point (*P* and *Q* respectively). Simultaneously, the system keeps track of the user's movement towards the destination point and allows him/her to deviate from the 'optimal' route, as long as the user's location does not fall out of a predefined safe area (buffer) built around this route. The user is notified of his/her deviation every time he/she crosses out of the buffer's border and he/she is given the option of re-routing from that current location (point *P'*).

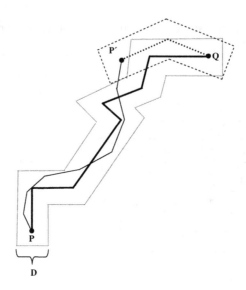

Fig. 3. Guide-me example

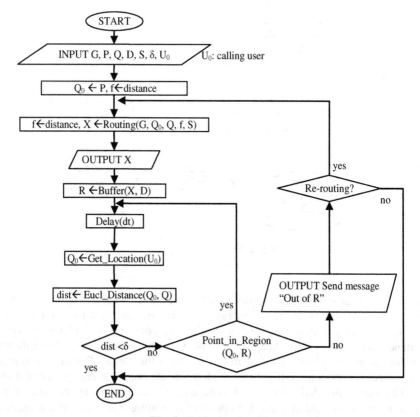

Fig. 4. Guide-me algorithm

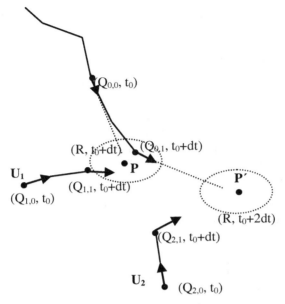

Fig. 5. Get-together example

The input of *Guide-me* algorithm is the following:

- the graph G along with the set of movement constraints S,
- the departure and destination points, respectively P and Q
- the id of the calling user, U_0
- the distance D, which defines the buffer width
- the distance threshold δ (as in the previous algorithm)

As illustrated in Fig.4, *Guide-me* computes the (dynamically updated) path between the user's current location and Q.

Get-together

With this service a moving user U_0 invites other users U_i, $i = 1, 2, ..., N$ (let us assume, members of a community), also moving in the same area, to converge at a meeting point not-known in advance. This point is periodically (every dt seconds) calculated by the system based on the future projection of the calling user's trajectory. This query falls in the M-M category, which is algorithmically the most complicated one.[3]

As an example of *Get-together*, consider Fig.5, where the calling user U_0 is at (the spatiotemporal) location $(Q_{0,0}, t_0)$ and moves towards the direction shown. The invited users U_1 and U_2 are located at $(Q_{1,0}, t_0)$ and $(Q_{2,0}, t_0)$ respectively. The system predicts that by the time t_0+dt U_0 will most probably be at location P and therefore routes U_1 and U_2 towards P. Eventually, at t_0+dt the (recorded) location of U_0 is $(Q_{0,1}, t_0+dt)$. Likewise, the system projects the trajectory of U_0 to the future time t_0+2dt, predicting that at that time U_0 will be at P', so it routes the rest of the users accordingly. The

---

[3] Ericsson offers a simplified and static version of this service, called *'Seek-your-friends'*, where all U_0 and U_i are stationary [15].

algorithm terminates when the distance between U_0 and each U_i becomes smaller than a predefined threshold δ; then, the system informs all that they have practically converged to the same location.

The input of the *Get-together* algorithm, which is illustrated in Fig.6, consists of:

- the graph G along with the set of movement constraints S and the distance/time flag f,
- the distance D, which defines a proximity are of users to be invited,
- the set $U = \{U_1, ..., U_N\}$ of ids of the called users,
- a distance threshold δ which defines the minimum distance (i.e. the convergence criterion) between U_0 and each U_i, and
- a time delay dt

The algorithm returns a set of (dynamically updated) paths between each U_i and the periodically predicted location of U_0.

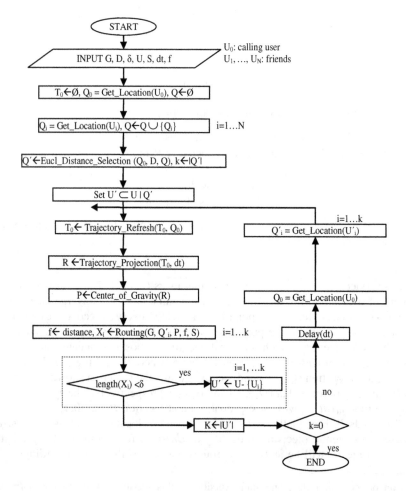

Fig. 6. Get-together algorithm

4 Query Processing Issues

In this section we summarize the routines involved in the implementation of the algorithms of Section 3. These routines can be classified into four main types: computational geometry operations, graph operations, trajectory operations and adaptive LBS operations; they are summarized in Table 2.

Computational geometry operations provide solutions to simple problems and are usually included in the relevant functionality of GIS or DBMS providing spatial data handling. More details on computational geometry algorithms can be found in [12].

Graph operations can be further classified into i) routing queries and ii) nearest neighbor (NN) queries. Calculating shortest paths in graphs is a well studied problem (see for example the Dijkstra [2] and the Bellman Ford [6] algorithms). The k-NN problem has been in the core of spatial and spatiotemporal database research during the last decade. Initially, the proposed k-NN algorithms focused on Euclidean space [13, 5]. Papadias et al. [11] presented the first comprehensive approach for query processing in spatial network databases in which data and query points are stationary and proposed several novel algorithms for k-NN, range, closest pairs and distance join queries. The proposed in [11] k-NN algorithm can be utilized for the implementation of the *Net_k_Nearest_Neighbor* operation used in the *Find-the-nearest* and *Find-me* services. A k-NN algorithm for the case of moving query and data points, the movement of which is constrained on a road network, is presented in [7].

Among the trajectory operations, *Trajectory_Projection* appears to be the most interesting to be further discussed. This routine estimates the future location of a moving object by projecting its trajectory to a future time t_0+dt. Such a computation requires some extra knowledge such as the velocity and the direction of each object. Although several methods have been proposed for processing and indexing the current and future location of objects moving without network constraints [14, 19], the problem of predicting the position of an object moving in a network (Fig.7) still remains open. The *Trajectory_Projection* routine is a step towards this direction, as it calculates a set of possible future locations (points Q_1, Q_2). Furthermore, instead of considering only object's current position (point P) (as the proposed in the literature methods do), an efficient *Trajectory_Projection* makes use of a trace (of dynamic length) of the trajectory for the estimation of the object's future location (thus the point Q_3 is excluded due to the direction of the trajectory of the moving object).

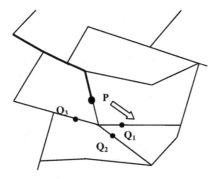

Fig. 7. Example of Trajectory Projection

Table 2. LBS Routines

Notations: Qs: Set of Points, D: Distance, R: Polygonal Region, G: Network Graph, P,Q: Points, f: Minimization criterion, S: Set of Network Constraints, X: Path	
Computational geometry operations	
Eucl_Distance_Selection (Qs, P, D)	Returns the set of points Qs', $Qs' \subseteq Qs$, located inside the circular area (P, D)
Length(X)	Returns the length of a path X
Eucl_Distance(P, Q)	Calculates the Euclidean distance D between the points P and Q
Point_in_Region(R, P)	Checks whether a point P is located inside a region R
Center_of_Gravity(Qs)	Calculates the centre of gravity of a set of points Qs
Buffer(X, D)	Builds a buffer of width D around a path X
Graph operations	
Routing(G, P, Q, f, S)	Finds the best route on a graph G between a departure point P and a destination point Q, considering the set of constraints S and the minimization criterion f (minimal network distance or minimal traveled time)
Net_Distance(G, P, Q)	Calculates the network distance on a graph G between the points P and Q
Traveled_Time(G, X)	Calculates the time required to move through a path X of graph G
Net_k_Nearest_Neighbor (G, Q, P, k)	Returns the k points of the set Q nearest (with respect to network distance on G) to a point P.
Trajectory operations	
Get_Trajectory(U)	Returns the trajectory of user U stored in a data file
Trajectory_Refresh(T, Q)	Adds (spatiotemporal) point Q to the existing trajectory T of an object
Trajectory_Projection (T, dt)	Projects the trajectory T of a moving object to the future time $now+dt$. In particular, considering the existing trajectory of the object as well as the direction in which it moves, this operation computes the set R of all the potential point locations of that object at $now+dt$.
Adaptive LBS operations	
Get_Location(U)	Returns the coordinates (x, y) of the current location of object U (assumes some positioning technology)

Finally, regarding the last type of LBS operations, it involves *Get_Location*, which returns the current location of a moving object. This can be easily developed with the utilization of current or emerging positioning technologies, such as TDOA (Time Difference Of Arrival) and GPS (Global Positioning System) [15, 3].

5 Conclusions

In this paper we present the first, to the best of our knowledge, attempt of classifying LBS from a stationary vs. mobile object perspective. For each LBS class, we describe representative examples of potentially useful services, focusing on the query processing requirements that arise.

It has become evident that several of the involved operations can be supported by existing commercial DBMS and GIS while some others require special data structures and query processing algorithms. Another important conclusion is that, as indicated in [16], the efficient handling of a new 'first-class' datatype, namely, the *trajectory*, poses new functional requirements for GIS and DBMS in terms of storage, indexing and query processing. It seems that commercial systems have still a long way to go.

Future continuation of this work focuses on open research issues, such as future trajectory projections.

Acknowledgements

Research partially supported by FP6/IST Programme of the European Union under the GeoPKDD project (2005-08) and EPAN Programme of the General Secretariat for Research and Technology of Greece under the NGLBS project (2004-06).

References

1. Benetis, R., Jensen, C., Karciauskas, G., and Saltenis, S., Nearest Neighbor and Reverse Nearest Neighbor Queries for Moving Objects. *Proceedings of IDEAS Symposium*, 2002.
2. Dijkstra, E. W., A note on two problems in connexion with graphs, *Numerische Mathematik*, vol 1, pp. 269-271, 1959.
3. Davies, N., et al., Using and Determining Location in a Context-Sensitive Tour Guide, IEEE Computer, vol. 34(8), pp. 35-41, 2001.
4. Guttman, A.: R-Trees: a dynamic index structure for spatial searching. *Proceedings of ACM SIGMOD Conference*, 1984.
5. Hjaltason, G., and Samet, H., Distance Browsing in Spatial Databases, *ACM Transactions in Database Systems*, vol. 24(2), pp. 265-318, 1999.
6. Johnson, D., B., Efficient algorithms for shortest paths in sparse networks, *Journal of the ACM*, vol. 24(1), pp. 1-13, 1977.
7. Jensen, C., Kolar, J., Pedersen, T., and Timko, I., Nearest Neighbor Queries in Road Networks, *Proceedings of ACM-GIS Symposium*, 2003.
8. Jensen, C., Christensen, A., Pedersen, T., Pfoser, D., Saltenis, S. and Tryfona, N., Location-Based Services: A Database Perspective. *Proceedings of Scandinavian GIS*, 2001.

9. Lopez, X., The Future of GIS: Real-time, Mission Critical, Location Services. *Proceedings of Cambridge Conference*, 2003.
10. Open GIS Consortium, OpenGIS® Location Services (OpenLS): Core Services. Available at http://www.opengis.org.
11. Papadias, D., Zhang, J., Mamoulis, N., and Tao, Y., Query Processing in Spatial Network Databases, *Proceedings of VLDB Conference*, 2003.
12. Preparata, F., Shamos, M. *Computational Geometry, An Introduction*, Springer-Verlag, New York, 1985.
13. Roussopoulos, N., Kelley, S., and Vincent, F., Nearest Neighbor Queries, *Proceedings of ACM SIGMOD Conference,* 1995.
14. Saltenis, S., Jensen, C. S., Leutenegger, S., and Lopez, M., Indexing the Positions of Continuously Moving Objects, *Proceedings of ACM SIGMOD Conference*, 2000.
15. Swedberg, G., Ericsson's Mobile Location Solution, *Ericsson Review*, vol. 4, 1999.
16. Theodoridis, Y., Ten Benchmark Queries for Location Based Services, *The Computer Journal*, vol. 46(6), pp.713-725, 2003.
17. Tayeb, J., Ulusoy, O., and Wolfson, O., A Quadtree-Based Dynamic Attribute Indexing Method, *The Computer Journal*, vol. 41(3), pp. 185-200, 1998.
18. Tao, Y., Papadias, D., and Shen, Q., Continuous Nearest Neighbor Search, *Proceedings of VLDB Conference*, 2002.
19. Tao Y., Papadias D., Sun J., The TPR*-Tree: An Optimized Spatio-Temporal Access Method for Predictive Queries, *Proceedings of VLDB Conference*, 2003.

Refined Route Instructions Using Topological Stages of Closeness

Markus Wuersch[1] and David Caduff[2]

[1] Intelligent Spatial Technologies, Target Technology Center,
20 Godfrey Drive, Orono, ME 04473
markus@i-spatialtech.com
[2] Department of Geography, University of Zurich – Irchel,
Winterthurerstr. 190, CH-8057 Zurich, Switzerland
caduff@geo.unizh.ch

Abstract. In pedestrian navigation, navigators are free to choose any passable way. Because of this characteristic, accurate route instructions are important when navigating from waypoint to waypoint. In this paper, a theoretical framework is described for dealing with position uncertainty in pedestrian guiding systems. Stages of closeness are defined based on the topological relation between the navigator and a waypoint. These stages of closeness allow for refining route instructions and, therefore, leading to more accurate navigation and increased efficiency of the system.

Keywords: mobile, wireless GIS, pedestrian navigation, route instruction.

1 Introduction

Routes for car navigation are confined to street networks and any instruction given to navigators is always with reference to the underlying network. The ride from Boston to New York, for instance, takes place on the different types of street networks. This system has many constraints associated with it (e.g., lanes, entrances, exits, etc.) and rules (e.g, speed limits, one ways, etc). These rules and constraints, together with the street network provide a forgiving system with regard to user and data inaccuracies. As long as route instructions are not given too late, user location and data inaccuracies do not deter drivers from their chosen route.

Pedestrian navigation, however, is not confined to a network of streets, but includes all passable areas, such as walkways, squares, and open areas, within or outside buildings. The property of being a decision point is not specific to junctions anymore, but becomes a property associated with the actual position of the pedestrian as pedestrians are free to choose their own path, get on and off street networks anywhere and anytime (with exceptions of bridges, walls, etc), take shortcuts, or cross squares. Hence, we define a path for pedestrians as consisting of *waypoints*. Waypoints differ from traditional decision points, such as junctions, as they are not part of the street network, but demarcate points that the navigator passes, independent of the

K.-J. Li and C. Vangenot (Eds.): W2GIS 2005, LNCS 3833, pp. 31–41, 2005.
© Springer-Verlag Berlin Heidelberg 2005

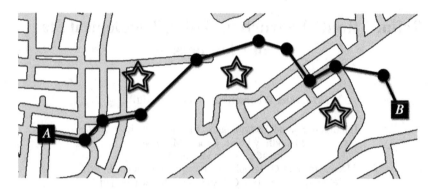

Fig. 1. Example of a tour indicating the way between start (A) and destination (B) and passing by several attractions along the route. The path consists of waypoints that are not necessarily attached to the underlying route network.

underlying structure (i.e., street, square, walkway). For the sake of simplicity, we confine the extent of this paper to the description of the route in terms of route instructions for a given path, and not to the generation of the route itself. An example of such a route is illustrated in Figure 1.

Because of the complexity of pedestrian navigation, it is important to provide route instructions at each point along the way. Examples of applications that require this kind of route instructions are GPS-based tourist guides that describe routes with attractions, such as sightseeing tours or museum guides. Such route instructions are preferably given 'just in time', that is, not too late, but also not too early. In cases where instructions are given too early, navigators might choose the wrong path, while late instructions may result in overshooting, both cases requiring extra instructions and corrections.

The goal of this paper is to provide route instructions that are more accurate under consideration of inaccuracies of the navigator's position and the location of the waypoint. A qualitative measure of how close a navigator is to the next waypoint is defined. Based on this qualitative measure, the route instructions are refined, resulting in

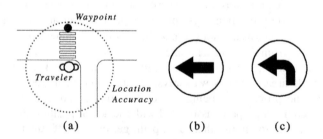

Fig. 2. (a) An example of a tourist navigating along a route; (b) simple route instruction; (c) refined route instruction

more accurate and more intuitive navigation. For example, Figure 2a shows a tourist navigating along a chosen route from one waypoint to the other. Because of an inaccurate location determining method, the next waypoint is selected before the user actually gets to it. Figure 2b shows a visual instruction given at the user's location. If no other instructions are given, the user most likely will turn left without actually reaching the waypoint across the street. Figure 2c shows a refined visual instruction given at the same location. This instruction represents the current situation more accurately. It combines instructions on how to reach the next waypoint as well as how to continue when that waypoint is reached, i.e., go straight and then turn left.

2 Related Work

Wayfinding can be categorized in planning a route and following a route. The two main research areas are: 1) research that aims at shedding light on the question of how humans actually find their way (Arthur & Passini, 1992; Hollands, Patla, & Vickers, 2002; Iachini &Logie,2003; Werner, Krieg-Brückner, Mallot, Schweizer, & Freksa, 1997), and 2) research that aims at supporting humans in the activity of finding the way (Haklay, O'Sullivan, Thurstain-Goodwin, & Schelhorn, 2001; Kray, Laakso, Elting, & Coors, 2003; Tversky & Lee, 1999). The research topics in the second category include analysis of the characteristics of good route instructions in general (Lovelace, Hegarty, & Montello, 1999), specific aspects of car navigation systems (Burnett, 1998), and investigations on how to provide route instructions to pedestrians (Altai, 2001; May, Ross, Bayer, & Tarkiainen, 2003).

Another emerging aspect of route instructions is the uncertainty derived from different sources, i.e., data, sensors, etc. The first model that attempts to consider uncertainty in the navigation process is Chown's PLAN model (1999), which is basically an extension of Kuiper's TOUR model (1979). Busquets (2003) uses fuzzy set theory to model imprecision in robot navigation, which allows improving the robot's navigation. Finally, Duckham, Kulik, and Worboys (2003) address the problem of delivering location-based services to an agent under imprecision.

The approach followed in this paper complements research on supporting humans and other agents in following a route under constraints. However, unlike most research in this field, we do not assume an underlying street network that can be referenced, but rather assume a series of waypoints that define a path. The path may follow segments of streets or walkways, but may also cross these. This assumption requires a different approach to describing routes and a different handling of uncertainty, which we will explain in the following sections.

3 Approach

The route we use in our approach consists of a sequence of waypoints. In order to generate refined instructions for navigation, it is crucial to know how close the navigator is to the next waypoint. Consider the example of a tourist in the process of following a predefined route as illustrated in Figure 3. In the vicinity of the next way-point, the visual instructions will still guide the user to the next waypoint while giving an indication of where to go once that waypoint is reached. When the user has reached a waypoint, i.e., is very close to the waypoint, the given visual instruction is not refined and simply points the user in the direction of the next waypoint.

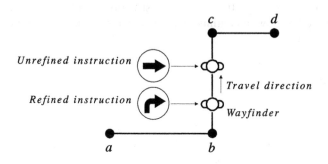

Fig. 3. Example of a tourist moving from waypoint b to waypoint c and the according instructions

In this example, we used *vicinity* and *closeness* to describe the navigator's location in relation to the location of the waypoint. Hence, the conclusion is that the key to provide refined instructions is to determine different stages of closeness of the naviga-tor with respect to the upcoming waypoint. Once such stages are defined, refined instructions can be given based on each stage. The remainder of this paper describes the following tasks:

1. Definition of a data model of the navigator's location and the waypoints, including location accuracies and the waypoint's accuracy or decision area.
2. Analysis of possible relations between a navigator's location and the location of a waypoint.
3. Analysis of navigator's movement towards a waypoint and definition of stages of closeness along such a trajectory.
4. Example of refinements of route instructions based on stages of closeness in 3.

4   The Data Model

Lists are a natural mechanism for representing ordered sets of elements, such as way-points along a route. A list of a route L_r consists of a set of n ordered waypoints $\{wp_1, wp_2, ..., wp_n\}$. The navigator N travels along the route by moving from waypoint to waypoint. We will use the same data type for both, navigator and waypoints. The data type used has a central point in two-dimensional space (x, y) called *pivot*, and a circle with radius r around this point, which describes the positional accuracy or the waypoints decision area. This data type is conceptually similar to a Spatially Extended Point (SEP) (Lee and Flewelling 2004) except that the region around the pivot is always circular We will use the term Circular Spatially Extended Point (CSEP) to refer to the data type associated with navigator and waypoint (Figure 4).

CSEP	
x	x-value of pivot
y	y-value of pivot
r	position accuracy/decision area (radius of circle)

Fig. 4. CSEP Data type for navigator and waypoint.

5   Topological Relations Between a Navigator and a Waypoint

The relation of a navigator's location to the location of a waypoint can be described qualitatively or quantitatively. A quantitative approach defines different relations based on metric distance thresholds. In order to define these metric thresholds, qualitative measures are applied and, therefore, we only analyze qualitative, binary, topological relations between a user's location and a waypoint.

5.1   16-Intersection Model

Egenhofer and Herring (1990a, 1990b) formalized the topology of binary relations between two geographic features using point-set topological relations. Lee and Flewelling (2004) further described binary topological relations between a region and a SEP. Here we describe the topological relations between two CSEPs. Any such relation can be described with the 16-intersection model (Equation1). The 4x4-matrix defines the possible topological relations between a navigator A and waypoint B based on their parts, i.e. pivot $A^\bullet$ interior A°, boundary $A\partial$ and exterior A^-.

$$relation(A,B) = \begin{pmatrix} A^\circ \cap B^\circ & A^\circ \cap B\partial & A^\circ \cap B^- & A^\circ \cap B^\bullet \\ A\partial \cap B^\circ & A\partial \cap B\partial & A\partial \cap B^- & A\partial \cap B^\bullet \\ A^- \cap B^\circ & A^- \cap B\partial & A^- \cap B^- & A^- \cap B^\bullet \\ A^\bullet \cap B^\circ & A^\bullet \cap B\partial & A^\bullet \cap B^- & A^\bullet \cap B^\bullet \end{pmatrix} \tag{1}$$

Theoretically, the 16-intersection matrix can have 16^2 possible combinations of empty (∅) and non-empty (¬∅) fields. The top left three columns and rows, however, describe the intersections between the two circles around each pivot, resulting in only eight possible topological relations (Egenhofer and Herring, 1990b). Further, a pivot is a one-dimensional geometric object and, therefore, can intersect only one other element (exterior, boundary, or interior) at once. These constraints in addition to the constraints given by the data type lead to 26 possible topological relations between two CSEPs (Figure 5).

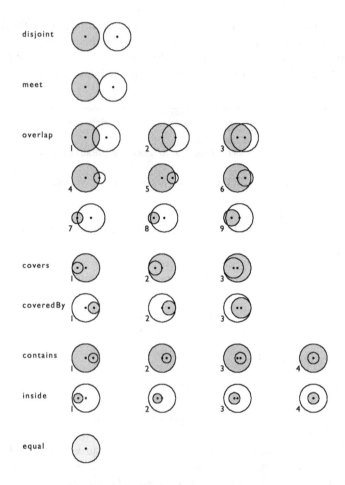

Fig. 5. 26 possible topological relations between two CSEPs ordered by the topological relation between the two circles around their pivot

6   Stages of Closeness Between Two CSEPs

This section orders the topological relations based on the distance between the two pivots. In a first step, we qualitatively describe the relative distance between two CSEPs as a function of their radiuses. Using this description does not allow a distinctive order across all 26 topological relations and, therefore, in the second step, the topological relations are grouped into collections where the two CSEPs maintain their sizes. In the third step, we then order the topological relations within each group by distance. For example: group B contains all topological relations where $R_B = \frac{1}{2}R_A$.

6.1 Relative Distance Between Two CSEPs

The distance between two CSEPs is defined as the distance between the two pivots. Rather than expressing the distance in quantitative terms, we express the distance d between two CSEPs as a function of their radiuses $f(R_A, R_B)$ (Table 1). In addition, where possible, we express the radius R_B of CSEP B as a function of the radius R_A of CSEP A.

Table 1. Comparison of the length of the two radiuses and the distance between the two pivots in terms of the radiuses for each topological relation

Topological Relation	Distance $d_{A,B}=f(R_A, R_B)$	Radius $R_B=f(R_A)$
disjoint	$> (R_A + R_B)$	Any
meet	$= (R_A + R_B)$	Any
overlap 1	$> R_A$ AND $> R_B$ AND $< (R_A + R_B)$	Any
overlap 2	$= R_A$ AND $= R_B$	$= R_A$
overlap 3	$< R_A$ AND $< R_B$	$> \frac{1}{2} R_A$ AND $< 2* R_A$
overlap 4	$= R_A$ AND $> R_B$	$< R_A$
overlap 5	$< R_A$ AND $> \frac{1}{2} R_A$ AND $> R_B$	$< R_A$
overlap 6	$< R_A$ AND $= R_B$ R_A AND $> \frac{1}{2} R_A$	$< R_A$ AND $> \frac{1}{2} R_A$
overlap 7	$> R_A$ AND $= R_B$	$> R_A$
overlap 8	$> R_A$ AND $< R_B$	$> R_A$
overlap 9	$= R_A$ AND $< R_B$ AND $> \frac{1}{2} R_B$	$> R_A$ AND $< 2*R_A$
covers 1	$< R_A$ AND $> \frac{1}{2} R_A$ OR $< R_A$ AND $> R_B$	$< \frac{1}{2} R_A$
covers 2	$= \frac{1}{2} R_A$ AND $= R_B$	$= \frac{1}{2} R_A$
covers 3	$< \frac{1}{2} R_A$ AND $< R_B$	$> \frac{1}{2} R_A$ AND $< R_A$
coveredBy 1	$> R_A$ AND $> \frac{1}{2} R_B$ AND $< R_B$	$> 2*R_A$
coveredBy 2	$= R_A$ AND $= \frac{1}{2} R_B$	$= 2*R_A$
coveredBy 3	$< R_A$ AND $< \frac{1}{2} R_B$	$< 2*R_A$ AND $> R_A$
contains 1	$< R_A$ AND $> R_B$	$< \frac{1}{2} R_A$
contains 2	$< \frac{1}{2} R_A$ AND $= R_B$	$< \frac{1}{2} R_A$
contains 3	$< \frac{1}{2} R_A$ AND $< R_B$	$< R_A$
contains 4	0	$< R_A$
inside 1	$> R_A$ AND $< R_B$	$> 2*R_A$
inside 2	$= R_A$ AND $< \frac{1}{2} R_B$	$> 2*R_A$
inside 3	$< R_A$ AND $< \frac{1}{2} R_B$	$> R_A$
inside 4	0	$> R_A$
equal	0	$= R_A$

6.2 Groups of Topological Relations with Consistent Sizes of Each CSEP

The different sizes of CSEPs amongst the 26 topological relations in Figure 5 make it impossible to plausibly define stages of closeness throughout all 26 topological relations. For this reason, the topological relations are grouped based on the size of their CSEPs' radiuses (Table 2). Each CSEP in a group maintains its size through all topological relations in that group.

Table 2. Groups of topological relations with consistent sizes of R_A and R_B

Group	Size of Radius B	Topological Relations
A	$0 < R_B < \frac{1}{2}R_A$	disjoint, meet, overlap 1, 4, 5, covers 1, contains 1, 2, 3, 4
B	$R_B = \frac{1}{2}R_A$	disjoint, meet, overlap 1, 4, 5, covers 2, contains 3, 4
C	$\frac{1}{2}R_A < R_B < R_A$	disjoint, meet, overlap 1, 3, 4, 5, 6, covers 3, contains 3, 4
D	$R_B = R_A$	disjoint, meet, overlap 1, 2, 3, equal
E	$R_A < R_B < 2R_A$	disjoint, meet, overlap 1, 3, 7, 8, 9, coveredBy 3, inside 3, 4
F	$R_B = 2R_A$	disjoint, meet, overlap 1, 7, 8, coveredBy 2, inside 3, 4
G	$2R_A < R_B$	disjoint, meet, overlap 1, 7, 8, coveredBy 1, inside 1, 2, 3, 4

6.3   Stages of Closeness for Groups of Topological Relations

Each group in Table 2 can be ordered by the distance between the two CSEPs using Table 1. For example: the disjoint topological relation clearly represents a situation where two CSEPs are further apart than the inside relation, whereas the overlap relation is somewhere in-between disjoint and inside. Table 3 shows the 26 topological relations between two CSEPs ordered by groups and by closeness. There are 8 degrees of closeness, except for group D, which has only six. For group D, however, the topological relations are matched with the topological relations in other groups that have the same distance between the pivots. Column five is therefore empty. We see that column one, two, and three are the same in every group. Column eight is consistent in that it only contains the topological relations where the two pivots coincide. Columns four and six contain all the topological relations where the distance between the pivots is the radius of R_A or R_B. The table is consistent as well in that any topological relation is in only one column. From this property we can conclude that it is possible to reason about the degree of closeness independent of its group in Table 2.

Table 3. The 26 topological relations ordered by groups and closeness (1=farthest, 8=closest)

Grou p	Stages of Closeness							
	1	2	3	4	5	6	7	8
A	disjoint	meet	overlap 1	overlap 4	overlap 5, covers 1, contains 1	contains 2	contains 3	contains 4
B	disjoint	meet	overlap 1	overlap 4	overlap 5	covers 2	contains 3	contains 4
C	disjoint	meet	overlap 1	overlap 4	overlap 5	overlap 6	overlap 3, covers 3, contains 3	contains 4
D	disjoint	meet	overlap 1	overlap 2		overlap 2	overlap 3	equal
E	disjoint	meet	overlap 1	overlap 7	overlap 8	overlap 9	overlap 3, inside 3, coveredBy 3	inside 4
F	disjoint	meet	overlap 1	overlap 7	overlap 8	coveredBy 2	inside 3	inside 4
G	disjoint	meet	overlap-1	overlap 7	overlap 8, coveredBy 1, inside 1	inside 2	inside 3	inside 4

7 Refined Route Instructions

The theoretical framework for the refinement of route instructions derived in this paper can be applied for various types of guidance systems. In the following sections we describe the principle of refining routes instructions based on the example of a GPS-based tour guiding system. The range of applications, however, is not limited to this example, but applies for all route guiding systems that exhibit some degree of uncertainty.

7.1 Application Example: A GPS-Based Tour Guide

Let's assume a predefined list of waypoints that describes a sightseeing tour and leads tourists through a region containing a set of attractions alike Figure 1. The waypoints define a route that passes by the attractions, while the circles around the waypoints represent the accuracy of the waypoint's position. Alternatively, these circles could indicate the region within which the guiding system may provide simple instructions to the tourist, without the risk of misleading the tourist. The instructions are provided by the means of a GPS-based guiding device that uses arrows as instructions. Specifically, the guiding system uses straight arrows as unrefined instructions and bent arrows as refined instruction (Figure 6). Directional change is derived from the predefined route for each waypoint and indicated by adjusting the arrow showing the consecutive way accordingly.

A bent arrow is used when a wayfinder is approaching a waypoint. In this situation, the tip of the arrow is already pointing towards the next waypoint, while the end of the arrow is still pointing towards the upcoming waypoint. This visual instruction represents the situation in the real world closer than an unrefined instruction, i.e., "go straight and then turn right".

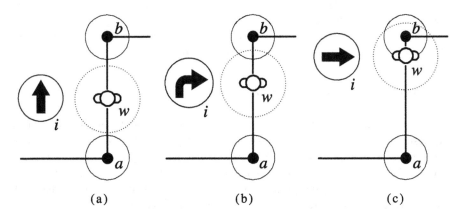

(a)   (b)   (c)

Fig. 6. A wayfinder w navigating between waypoint a and b by following the instruction i. (a) A straight arrow is used for an unrefined instruction. This representation is mapped to the stage of closeness 1. (b) Refined routing instructions that map to the stages of closeness 2 to 5. (c) The stages of closeness 6 to 8 show again a straight arrow.

The guiding system continuously updates the navigator's position and accuracy, determines the type of relation between navigator and waypoints, and adjusts the display accordingly. The adjustment of the display is based on a lookup table that maps the spatial configuration between navigator and waypoint to the corresponding representation on the screen. An example of such a mapping is shown in Figure 6. The mapping between the stages of closeness and the visual instructions can be adjusted for each route. For example, the visual instruction in Figure 6b could not be shown until the stage of closeness 4. This shift guides the wayfinder more closely along the route. On the other hand, mapping the stage of closeness 4 to Figure 6c gives a wayfinder more freedom in following a route.

7.2 Discussion

Guiding systems typically use the distance between wayfinder and waypoint as leading criteria. Based on these factors, the position for the next instructions is calculated and the instruction generated. This approach works well for network-based navigation (i.e., streets, etc.), because the positional uncertainty of the wayfinder is compensated by the clear definition of the road segments that can be followed, and by distinct waypoints, i.e., intersections of the street network. For routes that do not exhibit such structures, however, the instructions need to be refined. In the approach presented in this paper, we base this refinement on topological stages of closeness. The main benefit of this approach is that it considers positional uncertainty when determining the next instruction.

Another benefit of the approach is the higher granularity (8 stages of closeness) of potential route instructions. From a topological point of view, the traditional approach uses a CSEP for the waypoint (position and radial distance) and a point to derive the instructions, which limits the number of stages of closeness to 4 (i.e., the number of possible topological relations between a point and a CSEP). Instead of treating the position of the wayfinder as a simple point, we base our model on a CSEP. This approach increases the number of possible stages of closeness to 8, which results in higher granularity of possible route instructions (independent of the representation of the instructions) and finally increased accuracy and reliability of the guiding system.

8 Summary and Future Work

In this paper we provide a theoretical framework for dealing with position uncertainty in pedestrian guiding systems. We have defined stages of closeness based on topological relation between two CSEPs representing navigator and waypoint. These stages of closeness allow providing refined route instructions, which ultimately results in increased efficiency of the system. Our approach is especially helpful in areas with poor GPS reception or where location determination yields accuracies below average.

Future work will extend the stages of closeness with relations between a CSEP (navigator) and a SEP (waypoint area). Using a SEP allows to more accurately model an area around a waypoint such as a town square. A prototype implementation based on the principles described in this paper along performance analysis will also be part of future work.

References

Altai, J. (2001). *GIS-gestützte Entwicklung eines Fussgänger-Routings vor dem Hintergrund der Raumwahrnehmung von Füssgängern in der Stadt.* Unpublished Diplomarbeit, Universität Stuttgart, Stuttgart.

Arthur, P., & Passini, R. (1992). *Wayfinding: People, Signs, and Architecture.* Oakville, Ontario, Canada: Focus Strategic Communications Inc.

Burnett, G. E. (November 1998). *"Turn right at the King's Head" Driver's Requirements for Route Guidance Information.* Unpublished PhD Thesis, Loughborough University.

Busquets, D., Sierra, C., & Màntaras, R. L. d. (2003). A Mulitagent Approach to Qualitative Landmark-Based Navigation. *Autonomous Robots, 15*, 129-154.

Chown, E. (1999). Making predicitions in an uncertain world: Environmental and cognitive maps. *Adaptive Behavior, 7*(1).

Duckham, M., Kulik, L., & Worboys, M. (2003). Imprecise Navigation. *GeoInformatica, 7*(2), 79-94.

Egenhofer, M. and Herring, J. (1990a) A Mathematical Framework for the Definition of Topological Relationships. Fourth International Symposium on Spatial Data Handling, Zurich, Switzerland,.

Egenhofer, M. and Herring, J. (1990b) Categorizing Binary Topological Relations Between Regions, Lines, and Points in Geographic Databases. Technical Report, Department of Surveying Engineering, University of Maine,.

Haklay, M., O'Sullivan, D., Thurstain-Goodwin, M., & Schelhorn, T. (2001). "So go down town": Simulating Pedestrian Movement in Town Centres. *Environment and Planning B, 28*(3), 343-359.

Hollands, M. A., Patla, A. E., & Vickers, J. N. (2002). "Look where you're going!": Gaze Behaviour associated with maintaining and changing the direction of locomotion. *Exp Brain Res, 143*, 221-230.

Iachini, T., & Logie, R. H. (2003). The Role of Perspective in Locating Position in a Real-World, Unfamiliar Environment. *Applied Cognitive Psychology, 17*(6), 715-732.

Kray, C., Laakso, K., Elting, C., & Coors, V. (2003, 12-15 January). *Presenting Route Instructions on Mobile Devices.* Paper presented at the International Conference on Intelligent User Interfaces - IUI'03, Miami, FL, USA.

Kuipers, B. (1979). *Commonsense knowledge of space: learning from experience.* Paper presented at the AAAI-79, Seattle.

Lee, B. and Flewelling, D. (2004) Spatial Organicism: Relations between a Region and a Spatially Extended Point. GIScience 2004, Extended Abstracts and Poster Summaries.

Lovelace, K. L., Hegarty, M., & Montello, d. R. (1999). *Elements of Good Route Directions in Familiar and Unfamiliar Environments.* Paper presented at the Inernational Conference COSIT'99, Stade, Germany.

May, A. J., Ross, T., Bayer, S. H., & Tarkiainen, M. J. (2003). Pedestrian Navigation Aids: Information Requirements and Design Principles. *Personal Ubiquitous Computing, 7*, 331-338.

Tversky, B., & Lee, P. U. (1999). *Pictorial and Verbal Tools for Conveying Route Directions.* Paper presented at the International Conference on Spatial Information Theory: Cognitive and Computational Foundations of Geographic Information Science, COSIT.

Werner, S., Krieg-Brückner, B., Mallot, H. A., Schweizer, K., & Freksa, C. (1997). Spatial Cognition: The Role of Landmark, Route, and Survey Knowledge in Human and Robot Navigation. *Informatik 1997*(Informatik aktuell), 41-50.

An Increment Based Model for Multi-resolution Geodata Management in a Mobile System

Jean-Michel Follin[1,2], Alain Bouju[1], Frédéric Bertrand[1], and Arunas Stockus[1]

[1] Laboratoire L3i Informatique, Image, Interaction,
Université de La Rochelle
[2] École Supérieure des Géometres et Topographes,
Conservatoire National des Arts et Metiers, Le Mans
jean-michel.follin@esgt.cnam.fr
{alain.bouju, ...}@univ-lr.fr

Abstract. We propose a model for management of vector multiresolution geodata in a client-server framework which takes into account constraints related to mobile context (limitations of storage and transfer rate). The amount of data exchanged between client and server can be minimized by reusing data already available on the client side with the concept of "increment". An increment corresponds to a sequence of operations allowing the reconstruction of an object in one resolution from the same object in another resolution available in the client's cache.

Keywords: Multi-resolution, Generalization, Geographical information, Client Server, Objects Cache, Increment.

Introduction

We consider a mobile Geographic Information System (GIS) which relies on standard and wide-spread technologies like Global Positioning System (GPS), mobile computing devices and wireless communications. Its main functions are related to the navigation of mobile users and their access to spatial information through a web mapping application. The management of users requests and the transfert and visualization of spatial vector data are considered as key operations.

Needs of multi-resolution data in such an embedded navigation application are obvious: for example, detailed information are required in town center, and generalized data are sufficient on highway.

We propose a Level of Detail (LoD) approach for the management of multi-resolution geodata [1]. The purpose of our visualization system is to minimize the amount of data exchanged between client and server with the concept of increment. Increments allow to rebuild required LoD representations of objects from LoD representations of the same objects already available on the client side. In this way the volume of transferred data can be reduced. The principles of data management and transfer model have been introduced in [2]. Here we give the formal and complete presentation of our concepts of LoD object and increment.

K.-J. Li and C. Vangenot (Eds.): W2GIS 2005, LNCS 3833, pp. 42–53, 2005.

1 General Framework of Mobile GIS

1.1 System Overview

We consider a mobile system organized following a client-server architecture. The *client* manages data visualization, user requests and communication with a data server. The *server* manages both data and access to data sources.

The system uses standard technologies: Global Positioning System (*GPS*) for real-time location of mobile users, mobile computing devices, like Personal Digital Assistants (*PDA*) or hand-held PC, for visualization of geographic information by the client and cellular phones (with communication standards like GPRS[1] and UMTS[2]) for client-server communication.

We have to take into account possible constraints of mobile GIS related to wireless communications (weakness and instability of data transfer) and to mobile devices (calculation power, storage capacity and display size). The amount of data exchanged between client and server has to be minimized in our system [3].

1.2 Related Works and Adopted Approach

Solutions for providing mobile user with multi-resolution data are often based on combined use of standards Geographic Markup Language (GML) and Scalable Vector Graphics (SVG) with Real-Time Generalization (RTG) approach [4]. An approach which combines LoD representations for some feature classes and RTG for others is proposed in [5].

Other solutions to transfer data through a limited bandwidth channel is a progressive transmission of vector data brought up by [6] and [7]. Such streaming approaches are adopted with progressive meshes for the simplification of triangulated surfaces [8], "elementary generalization operators" (EGO's) for the simplification of cartographic objects [9]. In [10], Douglas-Peucker algorithm of polyline simplification (see section 2.2) has been adapted to incremental data transmission for web and mobile devices.

More globally, [11] has proposed to use different gradual changes in order to get a visually continuous generalization of a map: moving, rotating, morphing, fading and appearing.

In these progressive data transmission methods, the process of increment production is linked to those of generalization. Consequently their scope is limited to derivation oriented strategies (where different levels of detail are derived from one base data set by applying a generalization process). Our method could be applied to representation-oriented approaches (where maps with different fixed defined scales are stored in one database) because increments are computed from existing datasets. Furthermore, in these approaches, only data refinement is considered and no formalism for data reuse is proposed.

We propose a general framework that considers LoD and incremental data in a mobile system. The approach where "each object has multiple, interconnected representations", one for each resolution where it exists, has been chosen [12].

---

[1] General Packet Radio Service.
[2] Universal Mobile Telecommunications System.

We suppose that we have several layers of data at various LoDs which respect certain conditions (defined in section 2.1). All layers are served from a single and topologically consistent source. We use the spaghetti model for data storage and management.

Data and data transfer models are presented in [3]. They have been extended to multi-resolution data through a LoD approach combined with the use of increments that allows the real time reconstruction of object representations [2].

1.3   Data Model

In this section, we define a multiresolution data model adapted to limitations of mobile context. Data organization is based on the traditional definition of a geographic map: objects are grouped into layers and a sequence of layers forms a map [3, 13]. As representations of objects vary according to the level of detail, we consider different LoD objects grouped into different LoD layers. Increments allow to navigate through these different LoD objects and in this way to reuse available LoD representations on the client-side. In order to reduce volume of transferred data from server to client, they are sent rather than LoD object if their size is less important.

Layer, Map and Object. A *layer* is a collection of objects associated with a description of their attributes. Each layer corresponds to a specific theme (e.g. transportation network or buildings). Layers could be decomposed in different LoD layers according to the scale of representation.

A *map* is a succession of layers at a scale grouping objects according to their thematic. We consider distinct finite sets: $\mathcal{L} = \{l_1, l_2, \ldots\}$ domain of layers, $\mathcal{A} = \{a_1, a_2, \ldots\}$ set of attributes names, $\Gamma = \{\gamma_1, \gamma_2, \ldots\}$ domain of attributes values, $\mathcal{S} =]e_{min}, \ldots, e_{max}]$ domain of scales for which the map is defined (with $1 \leq e_{min} < e_{max}$), $\mathcal{I}$ domain of valid scales intervals such that $\mathcal{I} = \mathcal{S} \times \mathcal{S}$ (i.e. $\mathcal{I} = \{]e_{min}, e_1], \ldots,]e_n, e_{max}]\}$) and $\mathcal{L}^{lod}$ domain of LoD layers (see below).

A map M can be defined as a couple $M = (L^{lod}, \Sigma)$ where:

- $L^{lod} = \{l_1^a, \ldots, l_i^b, \ldots, l_n^c\}$ stands for a finite suite of LoD layers in $\mathcal{L}^{lod}$ such that each LoD layer of $\mathcal{L}^{lod}$ is a representation of a layer of $\mathcal{L}$ at a specific scale interval of $\mathcal{I}$,
- Σ is a set of attributes definitions $(a, l^i \to \Gamma)$ where $a \in \mathcal{A}$ and $l^i \in L^{lod}$. It defines that a LoD layer l^i has an attribute a_i which takes its values from domain Γ. This value is assigned at map level because it is defined in relation with semantic resolution.

It defines the schema of a map (i.e. its syntax). The *instance* of a map is formed of objects whose content respects the definition of map (i.e. its semantic).

An *object* entity is defined by the quadruple (o, t, g, γ) where:

- o: unique identifier,
- t: timestamp value (last modification time),

- g: geographical location modelled by one among six two dimensional geo-graphical objects of spatial domain $\mathcal{G}$: Point, Polyline or Region for connected objects, and MultiPoint, MultiLine and MultiRegion for not connected ones,
- γ: alphanumeric values $\gamma = \gamma_1, \gamma_2, \ldots, \gamma_n$ accessed through the set of object's attributes $a = a_1, a_2, \ldots, a_n$ (for example, the name of a street). Those values must respect the attribute definition of corresponding layer.

Descriptions of layers and objects must be decomposed in different LoD descriptions adapted to the scale. The concept of increment allows to navigate between these different LoD representations.

LoD Layer, LoD Object and Increment. A *LoD layer* l^i is a representation at level of detail i of thematic data of l. LoD layers of a layer l correspond to the definitions of objects in the scale ranges where they are represented. Indeed, each layer of $\mathcal{L}$ can be represented at different scales intervals corresponding to different LoDs. So a layer l_i can be seen as a serie of n LoD layers:

$$l_i = \{l_i^1, \ldots, l_i^n\}$$

LoD objects included in LoD layers can be matched (i.e. can be linked) between the two or more consecutive levels where they are represented. The *matching configuration* corresponds to the number of matched LoD representations of same real world entities (when objects are represented at two different LoDs). In [14] three different matching cases are distinguished:

- 1:1 spatial entity matching case where 1 LoD representation of an object is mapped to 1 representation of the same object at different LoD,
- 1:n matching case where 1 LoD representation is matched to a composite entity representing the same real-world objects set at a different LoD,
- n:m matching case that can be seen as a matching case of cluster object.

In this work we consider the 1:1 matching case. The linking is based on identifier o of the object's different representations.

A *LoD representation* or *LoD object* corresponds to a version of object o defined for a level of detail i (in adequation with a scale interval from $\mathcal{I}$). Indeed object geometry g and alphanumeric information γ can take various values g^i and γ^i according to the level i where o is represented. In the following, the geometry of object will be more specifically considered. The identifier o and timestamp t of object are not expected to vary in different LoDs because the matching between LoD representations is based on o and modification of object o must be propagated to each of its LoD representations (and its value t must be updated). The representation of an object o at the LoD i, i.e. such that $o.g = g^i$, will be noted o^i in order to simplify notations.

The below described concept of increment is mainly applied to polylines, i.e. LoD objects such that $o^i.g = P^i$ for each level of detail i where o is represented.

A *polyline* P is defined as a sequence of vertices $\{V_1, \ldots, V_n\}$ such that each couple (V_i, V_{i+1}) defines a segment $[V_i, V_{i+1}]$.

As we deal with multiple representations of same polylines, we use the following definition: a *vertex* V_i^j is a vertex V at index i of a polyline P^j. For example, a polyline is represented at two LoDs in figure 1: one can see that vertices of P^n with indexes 1, 4 and 5, i.e. V_1^n, V_4^n and V_5^n, have the same coordinates that vertices of P^{n+1} with indexes 1, 2 and 3, i.e. V_1^{n+1}, V_2^{n+1} and V_3^{n+1}.

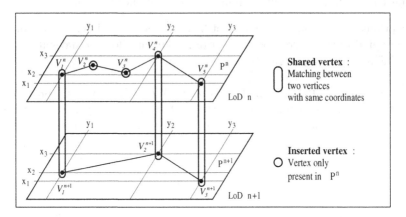

Fig. 1. Vertices of two matched LoD representations of the same polyline

We define the vertices which have the same coordinates, i.e. are matched, in two LoD representations P^n and P^{n+1} as *shared (or matched) vertices*. By considering two matched representations P^n and P^{n+1}, if V_i^n is matched to V_j^{n+1}, this vertices matching will be noted $V_{i,j}^{n,n+1}$. It is defined by a couple:

$$V_{i,j}^{n,n+1} = (V_i^n, V_j^{n+1})$$

The set of matched vertices noted V' is used by functions of increment creation and polyline reconstruction (cf. section 2.3).

An increment allows to perform changes on LoD object o^n in order to rebuild its representation o^{n-1} or o^{n+1}.

An *increment point* corresponds to a couple (op_i, V_i^j) where a LoD operator op_i is combined with a manipulated vertex V_i^j.

An *increment* is defined as a sequence of increment points. The increment allowing transition from o^n to o^{n+1} (resp. o^{n-1}) will be noted $Inc(o, n \rightarrow n+1)$ (resp. $Inc(o, n \rightarrow n-1)$).

We note V_{inc} an ordered list of increments points (described in section 2.2). Four LoD operators are considered:

- *insert*: puts a vertex V which is only present in the most detailed polyline P^{n-1} at index i of the less detailed one P^n during a transition from LoD n to LoD $n - 1$ (noted $n \rightarrow n - 1$). It manipulates the index and coordinates of a vertex.
- *keep*: keeps a vertex V^n shared by P^n and P^{n+1} at index i of P^n,
- *remove*: removes a vertex V^n only present at index i of P^n,

- *move*: changes the coordinates of a vertex V in a polyline P^n. It manipulates index and coordinates shifts of a vertex for a given transition $n \rightarrow n - 1$ or $n \rightarrow n + 1$.

Operators *keep* and *remove* are used during a transition $n \rightarrow n + 1$ and manipulate only the vertex index.

For a transition $m \rightarrow n$ of a polyline P^j the expression of an increment is:

$$Inc(o, m \rightarrow n) = \{(op_1, V_1^j), \ldots, (op_i, V_i^j), \ldots, (op_p, V_p^j)\}$$

such that each couple $(op_i, V_i^j) \in \mathcal{V}_{inc}$.

Each increment point (op_i, V_i^j) has an *encoding cost* (or *size*) C_{op_i} representing the number of bytes used to encode a vertex V_i^j and an operation op_i. This cost depends on the vertex part manipulated by the operator (index only or both index and coordinates). The total encoding cost C_{Inc} of an increment corresponds to the sum of costs of its increment points, and thus to the time it will take to transfer it from a server to the client:

$$C_{Inc} = \sum_{i=1}^{p} C_{op_i}$$

Increments act in a similar manner as EGO's defined in [9]. But the EGO's are used to achieve a continuous generalization while avoiding popping effect whereas LoD operators are used in order to reduce the amount of exchanged data by reusing LoD representations of available objects.

The above described different concepts are used during client-server transfer of data.

Transfer Models. In [3], three schemas of data transfer between client and server have been defined in order to reduce the amount of exchanged data (a query is considered as a window bounding the data that need to be visualized by the user):

- The *simple communication mode* where all queries are executed on the server and every query result is entirely transmitted to the client ;
- The *two-step communication schema* where all queries are still executed on the server but the client maintains data cache and can reuse already received objects ;
- In *pre-computed answer mode*, the client can execute some queries locally without connection to the server.

In [2], we have proposed a general transfer model of multi-scale data based on communication with a pre-computed answer. Multi-scale data transfer is performed in order to reuse data already locally available at a LoD different from requested one. Thus, local processing of LoD objects can be made as the answer to a client request of transition between a LoD m to a LoD n representation (zoom in or out). It can also be made each time that required data are covered

by data available at another LoD (during a pan operation or as a consequence
of the user's displacement).

This data transfer model is decomposed in four steps:

1. Local search of the identifiers of objects reusable at the same and different
   layers,
2. Sending of a request to the server including identifiers of the same and different layers, completed by two sets of identifiers: objects available at queried
   level n and objects O^m exclusively available at source level m,
3. Sending by the server of an answer which mainly includes (if there is no data
   update) missing objects at both LoDs and increments set $Inc(O^m, m \rightarrow n)$
   allowing reuse of objects O^m only available in level m and required for level n,
4. Rebuilding of missing LoD n objects from same objects O^m available at level
   m and $Inc(O^m, m \rightarrow n)$.

Efficiency of our model for reducing the amount of transferred data is presented
in [1].

2   An Incremental Strategy for Management of Multi-resolution Geodata

2.1   Conditions for Incremental Strategy

If LoD n objects set O^n is required on the client-side then transfer from the
server and use of an increment $Inc(O^m, m \rightarrow n)$ rather than transfer of O^n
depends on a significant reduction of the size of the first compared with the size
of the second. Furthermore objects must be shared between O^m and O^n and
conditions on these objects' geometries must be observed.

Shared Objects. Condition on the presence of objects O' shared by two LoDs
can be verified: function of generalization is surjective and consequently each
element of the generalized set O^{n+1} has at least one originating object in the
source set O^n [15]. Objects O^{n+1} correspond to selected and simplified objects
from O^n ($O^{n+1} \subseteq O^n$).

Conditions on Objects Geometries. For shared objects of O', LoD representations o^m and o^n must have a set V' of shared vertices (see section 1.3).
Otherwise, more detailed representation P^1 must necessary contain more vertices than less detailed one P^2. We call the number of vertices of a polyline its
geometry size.

Reduction of Data Volume. Use of increments in a mobile context has to
be justified by a less important size of increments $Inc(O^m, m \rightarrow n)$ than LoD
representations of objects O^n. It is expected to be more efficient to transfer
only increments than to download "entire" LoD representations [1]. Reduction
of data volume is evaluated with increment cost C_{Inc}. Incremental strategy relies
on manipulation of geometric parts of an object's LoD m representation, i.e. its
vertices, in order to rebuild its LoD n one. This reconstruction is made through
increments points.

2.2   Increments Points

We have defined in the section 1.3 an increment point as a couple (op_i, V_i^j) where an operator op_i is combined with a manipulated vertex V_i^j.

Types of increments points grouped in an increment $Inc(o, n \rightarrow n + 1)$ or $Inc(o, n + 1 \rightarrow n)$ depend on the generalization processes involved in the derivation of o^{n+1} from o^n.

Simplification of a polyline with the classic Douglas-Peucker algorithm (and with all similar "vertex sub-sampling" algorithms) removes some vertices of o^n in order to get o^{n+1} [16]. Moreover, vertices can be moved between o^n and o^{n+1} for example in order to respect topological relations with neighboring objects.

As we consider polylines generalized with simplification and displacement operators, resulting dataset respects the conditions on objects geometries (section 2.1).

Different sets of increments points may be distinguished by comparing two LoD representations of the same object:

- set $\mathcal{V}_i$ of inserted vertices is used for a refinement transition $n \rightarrow n - 1$. It corresponds to the vertices only present in the more detailed representation of the object. An increment point of $\mathcal{V}_i$ is defined as a couple $(insert, V_i^{n-1})$.
- sets $\mathcal{V}_k$ and $\mathcal{V}_r$ of vertices respectively selected for conservation and suppression are used for a generalization transition $n \rightarrow n + 1$.
  - set $\mathcal{V}_k$ of kept vertices corresponds to the set of shared vertices between the two LoD representations (i.e. vertices from V'). An increment point of $\mathcal{V}_k$ is defined as a couple $(keep, V_i^n)$.
  - set $\mathcal{V}_r$ of removed vertices corresponds to the set of inserted ones (i.e. vertices from $\mathcal{V}_i$). An increment point of $\mathcal{V}_r$ is defined as a couple $(remove, V^n)$.
- and set $\mathcal{V}_m$ is used either for a $n \rightarrow n-1$ transition or for a $n \rightarrow n+1$ one. It corresponds to the set of vertices moved between two LoD representations. An increment point of $\mathcal{V}_m$ is defined as a couple $(move, V_i^n)$.

All increments points are grouped in a tuple noted $\mathcal{V}_{inc}$, such that:

$$\mathcal{V}_{inc} = \{\mathcal{V}_i, \mathcal{V}_k, \mathcal{V}_r, \mathcal{V}_m\}$$

Different increments vertices are illustrated in figure 2. They are combined in refinement and generalization increments: refinement increments $Inc(P, n \rightarrow n - 1)$ are constituted of $\mathcal{V}_i$ and $\mathcal{V}_m$, and generalization increments $Inc(P, n \rightarrow n+1)$ are composed of increments points from $\mathcal{V}_k$, $\mathcal{V}_r$ and $\mathcal{V}_m$.

2.3   Functions Involved in Incremental Strategy

Types of Functions. Two types of functions are distinguished in incremental strategy: those for creation of increments from two LoD representations of the same object o and those for reconstruction of the LoD representation of an object from another LoD representation of the same object and the corresponding increment.

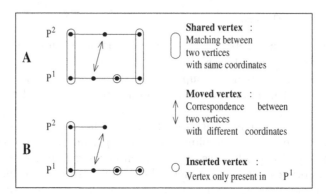

Fig. 2. Different configurations of LoD representations of polylines in 1-dimensional space

Increment creation functions correspond to mappings from $\mathcal{G} \times \mathcal{G}$ to $\mathcal{V}_{inc}$. Two functions are considered:

- d to create the generalization increment: $d(o^n, o^{n+1}) = Inc(o, n \to n + 1)$,
- i to create the refinement increment: $i(o^n, o^{n-1}) = Inc(o, n \to n - 1)$.

The produced increment is used by a reconstruction function which allows a transition from LoD m representation to LoD n one of an object o or dataset O. Once an increment has been transferred from a server to the client, it can be used with available LoD object to reconstruct a coarser or more detailed version of that object.

Reconstruction functions correspond to mappings from $\mathcal{G} \times \mathcal{V}_{inc}$ to $\mathcal{G}$. Two functions are identified:

- g to rebuild a coarser version: $g(o^n, Inc(o, n \to n + 1)) = o^{n+1}$,
- r to rebuild a more detailed version: $r(o^n, Inc(o, n \to n - 1)) = o^{n-1}$.

Increment creation functions rely on the use of shared vertices.

Refinement and Generalization Increments. In descriptions of the different increments we consider two representations P^n and P^{n+1}, such that: $P^n = \{V_1^n, \ldots, V_a^n\}$ and $P^{n+1} = \{V_1^{n+1}, \ldots, V_b^{n+1}\}$.

Refinement increments and Creation function i
In the creation of refinement increment $Inc(P, n \to n - 1)$, set V' of shared vertices can be used to determine the "pivots" from which increments sets $\mathcal{V}_m$ and $\mathcal{V}_i$ are computed. Our algorithm for operation i is the following:

1. Computing of shared vertices set V' between two LoDs P^n and P^{n+1} of the same polyline.
2. Creation of increments by considering couples of successive matching of V', $V_{i,e}^{n,n+1}$ and $V_{j,f}^{n,n+1}$. For each vertex of P^n in interval $]V_i^n, V_j^n[$ if there exists a "corresponding" vertex on P^{n+1} in interval $]V_e^{n+1}, V_f^{n+1}[$ then it is a moved vertex otherwise it is an inserted one (there is no corresponding point).

Reconstruction function r
By browsing the increments vertices V_{inc} from $Inc(P, n \rightarrow n - 1)$, each corresponding vertex of P^n is either moved, or the corresponding vertex of P^{n-1} is inserted.

Generalization increments and Creation function d
In the creation of generalization increment $Inc(P, n \rightarrow n+1)$, two sets of vertices must be computed: the set V' of shared vertices and the set V_i of inserted ones, such that $V_i = P^n - P^{n+1}$.

If the number of shared vertices $|V'|$ is lower than the number of inserted ones $|V_i|$, i.e. if $|V'| < |V_i|$ (with $|V_i| = a - b$), we mark indexes of vertices of V' to conserve, otherwise we mark indexes of vertices of V_i to remove. In both cases the set V_m of moved vertices is computed.

Reconstruction function g
By browsing the increments vertices V_{inc} from $Inc(P, n \rightarrow n + 1)$, each corresponding vertex of P^n is either moved, or selected (for conservation or removal).

2.4 Practical Aspects

The presented functions are used in our management and transfer models.

The creation functions are performed on the server side in order to compute increment sets between two datasets at consecutive levels of detail in a generalization direction and in a refinement one. All increments are stored on the server and recomputed if data are updated. They are transferred to a client for reusing data available in its cache. The reconstruction functions are finally applied on the client side to create the instances of objects by reusing the available LoD representations.

Three LoD layers representing the transportation network of La Rochelle have been produced by generalization in order to be adapted to an incremental management of data (cf. 2.2).

Experimentations have been made by simulating navigation (with both pan and zoom operations) of a mobile user with three GPS routes from 7,82 to 32,7 kilometers (i.e. three sets of coordinates collected at regular time steps with a car equipped with GPS). We have computed the volume of data (in bytes) exchanged between client and server in the cases of strategies with and without reuse. In the case of strategy with reuse, four sets can be transferred:

- increments for reuse objects which respect the condition on data volume reduction (cf. section 2.1), i.e. the major part of matched objects,
- objects which not respect the condition (because there is too much details to add or remove),
- identifiers of *identical* objects, i.e. objects which not have been modified by generalization processes and must be kept in a generalization direction,
- not shared objects (cf. section 2.1) in a refinement direction.

In the case of strategy without reuse, set of all requested objects is send.

On average, our incremental strategy allows a reduction of transferred data from around 6 to 15% (for more details, see [1]). Those results depend on both routes configurations and numbers of zooms.

More globally, we can compute the gain to reuse an entire layer in order to get a more detailed version or a more generalized one of the same layer. The observed gains vary from 8 to 15 % in the refinement direction and from 70 to 80 % in the generalization one. Importance of the gain mainly depends on the proportion of shared and reusable objects between the sets of data at different resolutions.

3   Conclusion and Outlook

In this paper we propose principles for the management of multi-resolution geo-data in a mobile system. They are based on a LoD approach where concepts of layer and object are extended to different LoD representations. The core of this framework is the concept of increment: it allows to perform changes on an object representation at some LoD in order to rebuild its geometry at a different LoD. It can be adapted to the required direction of transition (generalization or refinement) by using only useful part of manipulated vertices. In this way it allows to reduce data transfer between server and client each time that requested data are covered by data available at a different LoD (during a zoom operation or as a consequence of the user's displacement).

We expect to extend this framework to attributes values γ of object and to generalize the concept of increment to all geometries from $\mathcal{G}$. Furthermore integration of 1:n and n:n matching cases is another direction for future works. This strategy could be applied to LoD datasets coming from different sources: matching operators should be defined in order to make such datasets adapted.

Acknowledgment

This research was partially founded by the Communauté d'Agglomération of the city of La Rochelle, France.

References

1. Follin, J.M.: Gestion incrémentale de données multi-résolutions dans un système mobile de visualisation d'informations géographiques. Phd thesis, Universit de La Rochelle (2004)
2. Follin, J.M., A. Bouju, F.B., Boursier, P.: Multi-resolution extension for transmission of geodata in a mobile context. Computers & Geosciences **31** (2005) 179–188
3. Stockus, A.: Accés à des bases de données spatiales dans un environnement client-serveur : Application à un système de navigation embarqué. PhD thesis, University of La Rochelle, L3i research laboratory (2002)
4. Lehto, L., Kilpelinen, T.: Generalizing XML-encoded spatial data on the web. In: Proceedings of 20th International Cartographic Conference. Volume 4., Beijing (China) (2001) 2390–2396

5. Cecconi, A.: Integration of cartographic generalization and multi-scale databases for enhanced web mapping. PhD thesis, University of Zurich (2003)
6. Bertolotto, M., Egenhofer, M.J.: Progressive transmission of vector map data over the world wide web. GeoInformatica **5** (2001) 345–373
7. Buttenfield, B.: Transmitting vector geospatial data across the internet. In: Proceedings of the Second International Conference on Geographic Information Science, Boulder, Colorado (USA), Springer-Verlag (2002) 51–64
8. Hoppe, H.: Progressive meshes. In SIGGRAPH, A., ed.: Proceedings of SIGGRAPH 96. Annual Conference Series, New Orleans (USA) (1996) 99–108
9. Sester, M., Brenner, C.: Continuous generalization for fast and smooth visualization on small displays. In: International Archives of Photogrammetry and Remote Sensing. Volume 34., Istanbul (Turquie), ISPRS (2004)
10. Zhou, M., Bertolotto, M.: Implementation of progressive vector transmission using a new data structure and a modified RDP algorithm. In: the proceedings of GIS Research UK, 12th Annual Conference. (2004) 69–72
11. Kreveld, M.v.: Smooth generalization for continuous zooming. In: Proceedings of 20th International Cartographic Conference, Beijing (China) (2001) 2180–2185
12. Spaccapietra, S., Parent, C., Vangenot, C.: GIS Databases: From Multiscale to MultiRepresentation. In: Abstraction, Reformulation, and Approximation. (2000)
13. Tomlinson, R.: An Introduction to the Geographic Information System of the Canada Land Inventory. Departement of Forestry and Rural Development, Ottawa, Canada (1967)
14. Ai, T., van Oosterom, P.: A map generalization model based on algebra mapping transformation. In: Proceedings of the Ninth ACM International Symposium on Advances in geographic information systems, Atlanta (USA), ACM Press (2001) 21–27
15. Bobzien, M., Morgenstern, D.: Abstracting and formalizing model generalization. In: 5th ICA Workshop on Progress in Automated Map Generalization, Paris (France) (2003)
16. Saalfeld, A.: Topologically consistent line simplification with the douglas-peucker algorithm. Cartography and Geographic Information Science **26** (1999) 7–18

Efficiently Generating Multiple Representations for Web Mapping[*]

Min Zhou and Michela Bertolotto

Department of Computer Science,
University College Dublin,
Belfield, Dublin 4, Ireland
{Min.Zhou, Michela.Bertolotto}@ucd.ie

Abstract. Line simplification is the most commonly used operation in map generalisation. In many commercial Geographic Information Systems (GIS), line simplification is performed by applying the classical Ramer-Douglas-Peucker (RDP) algorithm. However, such an algorithm has the drawback of not guaranteeing the preservation of topological consistency. This requires a posteriori checks to ensure that unwanted intersections introduced by the application of the algorithm get rectified. To overcome this problem, Saalfeld proposed a modification of the classical RDP algorithm based on the fact that, while generalising a polyline, conflicts can only occur with vertices of other polylines that lie within its convex hull. In this paper we propose an improvement to Saalfeld's algorithm to detect possible self-intersections of a simplified polyline more efficiently. This improves the performance especially when generalising very large datasets. Nevertheless, the processing time is still not acceptable for real-time web mapping. Therefore, we have integrated our algorithm into a web mapping system that pre-computes a sequence of topologically consistent map representations, stores them on the server, and transmits them progressively upon request. We present experimental results of the performance of the algorithm as well as results of the transmission system.

1 Introduction

With the popularity of the Internet, the need arose to allow for diverse geo-spatial data and analysis tools to be downloaded for public and commercial use. Although several systems have been developed, web mapping still suffers from limited functionality and slow transmission. A possible solution to the latter problem relies on applying progressive transmission of more refined versions of the same map starting with a coarse one. This is useful in many applications where full detail is not required. These versions can be generated by applying map generalisation techniques [21]. The process of map generalisation involves complex cartographic knowledge and is time consuming [5][20][21][25]. Its real time application is not possible yet.

---

[*] The support of the Informatics Research Initiative of Enterprise Ireland is gratefully acknowledged.

K.-J. Li and C. Vangenot (Eds.): W2GIS 2005, LNCS 3833, pp. 54–65, 2005.

An alternative consists of pre-computing the different versions, storing the sequence on the server, and transmitting more detailed versions progressively upon request [1][2][3] [8][23][24]. Based on this approach, we have developed a system for progressively transmitting multiple representations of large vector datasets across networks.

As the majority of features in a map are represented by polylines (line features, boundaries of polygons, etc.), line simplification is used to generate the less detailed representations. Many algorithms for line simplification have been developed and applied in commercial systems [7][9][10][14][15][18]. Most proposed algorithms treat each polyline as an isolated feature and simplify it individually. As a consequence, inconsistencies may be introduced to the simplified map dataset. These include:

- Self-intersections: a simplified polyline intersects itself;
- Intersections: a simplified polyline intersects other polylines;
- Topological inconsistencies: a feature (point or line) lies on a different side with respect to a polyline after simplification.

Adding consistency checks to existing line simplification algorithms allows to guarantee that the final result does not contain self-intersections, other intersections or topological inconsistencies. de Berg *et al.* [6] combined existing algorithms [4] [7][10][14][15][17][18] to propose a contextual approach for line simplification on planar subdivisions, where the context for a polyline is represented by other polylines as well as point features. Such an approach guarantees consistency but is computationally expensive (i.e., $O (n(n+m)log\ n)$, where n is the number of vertices of the polyline and m is the number of external features). Wu and Marquez proposed a self-intersection preventing line simplification algorithm [22]. However, other intersections and topological inconsistencies can still occur. Saalfeld [19] proposed a topologically consistent line simplification method by adding parity checks to the terminating condition in the classical RDP algorithm [7][18]. This algorithm has been very successful and has been used by other researchers [3][24]. We developed a new Self-Crossing-Preventing (SCP) line simplification algorithm based on Saalfeld's algorithm. Such an algorithm detects more efficiently the potential self-intersections of simplified polylines. In case when no self-intersection occurs the algorithm prevents the unnecessary calculation of Saalfeld's parity checks. This improvement is particularly significant when very large datasets are being handled. Nevertheless, the processing time is still not acceptable for real-time web mapping. Therefore, we have integrated our algorithm into a web mapping system that pre-computes a sequence of topologically consistent map representations and transmits them progressively in order of increasing detail.

The remainder of this paper is organised as follows. Section 2 describes the classical RDP algorithm and Saalfeld's algorithm upon which our algorithm is based. Section 3 proposes our new SCP line simplification algorithm. Sections 4 and 5 evaluate the SCP algorithm and our progressive transmission system. Finally Section 6 presents some conclusions.

2 Background

The classical RDP algorithm [7][18] is acknowledged as the most visually effective line simplification algorithm in GIS, digital image processing and computational geometry [9]. Such an algorithm simplifies each individual polyline by recursively splitting it at the vertex with the maximum distance from the segment connecting the endpoints of the polyline. This is repeated until the maximum distance is less than a tolerance value, i.e., a pre-determined threshold distance (see the pseudocode in Algorithm 1).

Algorithm 1. The classical RDP algorithm

```
RDPSimplify(P, i, j, t) simplifies polyline P with
vertices V_i, V_{i+1}, ... V_{j-1}, V_j
Where
t is a pre-defined tolerance value;
//Initialise output vertex set V with start and end
//vertices V_i, V_j of P
V = {V_i, V_j};

RDPSimplify(P, i, j, t);
Output V;

RDPSimplify(P, i, j, t)
{
    if (j > i + 1)
    {
        Find vertex V_k with maximum distance (dist) from seg-
ment V_iV_j;
        if (dist > t)
        {
            Add V_k to output vertex set V;
            RDPSimplify(P, i, k, t);
            RDPSimplify(P, k, j, t);
        }
    }
}
```

As polylines are considered individually, self-intersections, other intersections and topological inconsistencies may be introduced during simplification [11][19][21]. Simplification of coastlines provides a very good scenario to show that applying the RDP algorithm can cause inconsistencies. For example, Fig. 1(b) shows that a simplified coastline (drawn in solid stroke) intersects with itself and with a simplified road while the original dataset (Fig 1(a)) did not contain any intersection. Furthermore islands have jumped inland after simplification of the coastline.

Hershberger and Snoeyink developed an algorithm that builds and maintains the convex hull of a polyline to improve the worst case complexity of the classical RDP algorithm from $O(n^2)$ to $O(n \log n)$, where n is the number of vertices of the polyline [9]. The convex hull of a polyline is the boundary of the smallest polygon containing the vertices of the polyline such that the segments connecting any two of these vertices are completely contained inside the polygon. Saalfeld noted that the convex hull is much more useful as a tool to efficiently detect potential inconsistencies of simplified polylines [19]. He indicated that conflicts could only occur when isolated point features or vertices of other lines lie within the convex hull of the line being simplified. He proved that in order to guarantee that no self-intersections, no intersections and topological inconsistencies occur, it is sufficient to calculate the parity check value of each such vertex as supplement condition to terminate the recursive application of the RDP algorithm.

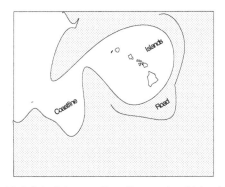 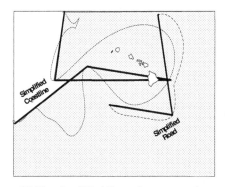

(a) Original dataset: Coastline, road and islands   (b) The simplified linear features are drawn in solid stroke

Fig. 1. The RDP algorithm may produce inconsistencies

The parity check value of a vertex can be initially calculated by projecting a ray from the vertex in any direction and counting the number of intersections both with the line and with the segment connecting the start and end vertices of the line. If the sum of all intersections is even (including zero), the parity check value of the vertex is positive otherwise it is negative. The parity value of these vertices should be dynamically reversed if they are within the triangle formed by the splitting vertex, the start and end vertices of the simplified line. The classical RDP algorithm is continually applied until no vertex has a negative parity check value (see Algorithm 2).

The primary difference between the classical RDP algorithm and Saalfeld's algorithm is that the latter adds parity checks to the condition for terminating the recursive application of the classical RDP algorithm. Saalfeld's algorithm guarantees that no self-intersections, no intersections with other polylines and no topological inconsistencies are introduced.

Note that vertices of other polylines that lie in the convex hull of a polyline are checked only once to prevent intersections and maintain topological consistency. Vertices of a subpolyline that lie in the convex hull of another subpolyline are checked repeatedly to prevent from self-intersections to be introduced as the polyline is recursively subdivided. The detection of self-intersections plays a key role for efficient implementation. Even though Saalfeld [19] proposed an efficient strategy to

Algorithm 2. Saalfeld's algorithm

```
SaalfeldSimplify(P, i, j, CH, t) simplifies polyline P with
vertices Vᵢ, Vᵢ₊₁, ... Vⱼ₋₁, Vⱼ by preserving
consistency
Where
t is a pre-defined tolerance value;
//CH is a set of points on the convex hull of a
//polyline and is initialised to the convex hull of P
CH = constructCH(P, i, j);
//Parity identifies whether a parity value is
//negative and is initialised to a positive value
parity = 1;
start = true;
//Initialise output vertex set V with start and end
//vertices Vᵢ, Vⱼ of P
V = {Vᵢ, Vⱼ};

SaalfeldSimplify(P, i, j, CH, t);
Output V;

SaalfeldSimplify(P, i, j, CH, t);
{
   If (j > i + 1)
   {
    Find vertex Vₖ with maximum distance (dist) from segment
VᵢVⱼ;
     If (start)
     {
        Identify the vertices of other polylines and
         point features that lie within the convex hull
         of P;
        Compute parity check values for these vertices
         and point features;
        If (any parity check value is negative)
           parity = -1;
        start = false;
     }
     else
     {
        Identify the vertices of one subpolyline that lie
         within the convex hull of another subpolyline;
        Compute parity check values for these vertices;
        If (any parity check value is negative)
           parity = -1;
     }
     If (dist > t or parity < 0)
     {
        Add Vₖ to the output vertex set V;
        Reverse parity value for the vertices and point
         features within triangle ΔVᵢVⱼVₖ;
        If (any parity check value is negative)
           parity = -1;
        CH= constructCH(P, i, k);
        SaalfeldSimplify(P, i, k, CH, t);
        CH= constructCH(P, k, j);
        SaalfeldSimplify(P, k, j, CH, t);
     }
  }
}
```

construct the convex hull of a polyline used for detecting potential inconsistencies including the case of self-intersection, our approach provides a further improvement to efficiently detect potential self-intersections of polylines. In order to focus on the difference between Saalfeld's algorithm and the SCP algorithm (described in the next section), we do not outline details on how to compute a convex hull for a polyline. We just assume that Saalfeld's algorithm and the SCP algorithm use the same convex hull algorithm as a subalgorithm.

3   A New Self-crossing-Preventing Algorithm

The RDP algorithm recursively replaces a polyline with two subpolylines by selecting a split vertex as the vertex with maximum distance from the segment connecting the two endpoints of the original polyline. Self-intersections may only occur with vertices of a subpolyline that lie within the convex hull of another subpolyline [19]. In fact a "newly introduced" subpolyline is treated in the same way as an independent polyline by performing parity checks to guarantee that the simplified polyline has no self-intersection.

Note that each splitting vertex causes the replacement of the convex hull of a polyline with two possibly overlapping sub convex hulls. The two corresponding subpolylines may intersect only if their convex hulls are overlapping. Subpolylines do not intersect if their convex hulls are not overlapping. We are able to determine very easily if the two convex hulls of subpolylines are overlapping by checking whether the endpoint of either of the two edges of convex hulls of subpolylines incident at the split vertex lies in the convex hull of the other subpolyline. This is because the two sub convex hulls share the splitting vertex and they are convex polygons.

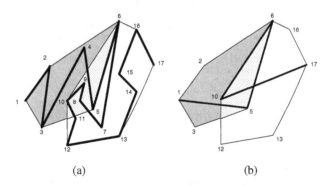

(a)   (b)

Fig. 2. Self-intersection occurs only when the convex hulls of subpolylines are overlapping

Our new SCP algorithm adds this check as a condition for calculating parity checks to prevent self-intersections. In other words, if the convex hulls of subpolylines are not overlapping there is no need to apply parity checks. Fig. 2(a) shows an example of a polyline with 17 vertices (drawn in solid stroke) being simplified. The split vertex

Algorithm 3. The SCP algorithm

```
SCPSimplify(P, i, j, CH, t) simplifies polyline P with vertices
V_i, V_{i+1}, ... V_{j-1}, V_j
Where
t is a pre-defined tolerance value;
//CH is a set of points on the convex hull of a
//polyline and is initialised to the convex hull of P
CH = constructCH(P, i, j);
//Parity identifies whether a parity check value is
//negative and is initialised to a positive value
parity = 1;
start = true;
//Initialise output vertex set with start and end
//vertices V_i, V_j of P
V = {V_i, V_j};

SCPSimplify (P, i, j, CH, t);
Output V;

SCPSimplify (P, i, j, CH, t)
{
    If (j > i + 1)
    {
        Find vertex V_k with maximum distance (dist) from
        segment V_iV_j;
        If (start)
        {
          Identify the vertices of other polylines and
          point features that lie within the convex hull
          of P;
          Compute parity check values for these vertices
          and point features;
          If (any parity check value is negative)
            parity = -1;
          start = false;
        }
        If (the endpoint of either of two edges of
            convex hulls of subpolylines incident at
            the splitting vertex is contained in the
            convex hull of the other subpolyline)
          {
            Identify the vertices of one subpolyline
            that lie within the convex hull of
              another subpolyline;
            Compute parity check values for these
            vertices;
            If (any parity check value is negative)
              parity = -1;
          }
        If (dist > t or parity < 0)
          {
            Add V_k to the output vertex set V;
            Reverse parity check values for the vertices
             and point features within triangle ΔV_iV_jV_k;
            If (any parity value is negative)
                parity = -1;
            CH= constructCH(P, i, k);
            SCPSimplify (P, i, k, CH, t);
            CH= constructCH(P, k, j);
            SCPSimplify (P, k, j, CH, t);
          }
    }
}
```

is vertex 6 and the two subpolylines are $P_{1,6}$ and $P_{6,17}$. The convex hulls of these subpolylines are overlapping. This is checked by verifying if either vertex 10 is contained in the convex hull for $P_{1,6}$ or vertex 5 is contained in the convex hull for $P_{6,17}$ (Fig. 2(a)). By further applying the RDP algorithm, we eliminate vertices 2, 3, 4, 7, 8, 9, 11, 12, 13, 14, 15 and 16 and the simplified polyline with vertices 1, 5, 6, 10 and 17 is self-intersecting (Fig. 2(b)). The pseudocode for the new algorithm is illustrated in the following where the condition highlighted in bold represents the additional check.

4 Performance Evaluation

We have evaluated the SCP algorithm and compared it to the performance of Saalfeld's algorithm in terms of efficiency using a real world dataset. The dataset describing Arapahoe county, Colorado, USA from the US Census Bureau TIGER/Line data files was initially loaded into a database [26]. Arapahoe county is represented by 33054 lines. These lines are composed of 73761 points. The experiments were performed on a 1.6 GHz CPU processor with 2 GB memory.

We applied the SCP algorithm and Saalfeld's algorithm respectively to generalise the dataset describing Arapahoe county with tolerance values of 16 and 8 meters. Table 1 shows the percentage (with respect to the original dataset) of points contained in each of the two coarser representations extracted. Table 2 shows that the SCP algorithm performs more efficiently with both tolerance values. Note that the SCP algorithm performs proportionally better when the tolerance value is smaller. Using the same tolerance values, the difference between the two algorithms varies between approximately 32 to 35 seconds. The SCP algorithm is 7% faster than Saalfeld's algorithm (on average).

Table 1. Datasets after applying line simplification with specified tolerance values

Tolerance	Number of points	Percentage of points
16	53662	72.8%
8	64468	87.4%
0(full detail)	73761	100%

Table 2. Comparison of CPU times for datasets with 2 different tolerance values

Tolerance (m)	CPU time (second)	
	SCP algorithm	Saalfeld's algorithm
16	444.2	479
8	438.8	470

5 Progressive Transmission

Even though the SCP algorithm improves the efficiency of performance in topologically consistent line simplification, the processing time still limits its application for online web mapping. However, it has been adapted in our system to pre-compute topologically consistent multiple representations corresponding to different Levels of Detail (LoDs) from a fully detailed map (details in [24]). Such multiple representations are stored in the server. The coarsest LoD is represented by Layer0 and subsequent layers by increasing numbers. Multiple representations are then progressively transmitted from the server to the client on demand.

Our system uses a distributed three-tier client-server architecture which includes a client, an application server, and a map server. Different clients can connect to the application server via networks simultaneously. All communications between a client and the map server are conducted through the application server (see Fig. 3). Our system has been implemented using the Java programming language. As Java is platform independent, our applications can be easily run on any platform without any changes or recompilation required.

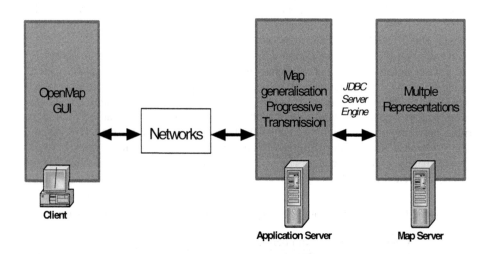

Fig. 3. Three-tier client server architecture

The client is connected to the server via Local Area Networks (LANs). The response time is the transmission time from server to client over the network. We consider two cases in transmission: (1) transmit a fully detailed map in one step and (2) progressively transmit simplified maps stored in layers.

The experiments were performed on a 1.6 GHz CPU processor with 2 GB memory for the server and a 2.4 GHz CPU processor with 512 MB memory for the client (details in Table 3).

Table 3. Hardware configurations

	CPU	Memory	OS
Server	1.6 GHz Laptop	2 GB	WindowsXP
Client	2.4 GHz Laptop	512 MB	WindowsXP

Table 4 Average response time for transmission via LANs at the speed of 100Mbps

	Seconds
Layer 0	10
Layer 1	6
Layer 2	9
Total	25
One step	24

In Table 4, the results show that progressive transmission across the LANs takes place in a reasonable amount of time. Users can start working with a coarser version of the map downloaded from the server within half time and request finer versions gradually until an acceptable version is obtained. Furthermore we expect that frequently, the time of transmission would be reduced as the users would not need to download all layers to get the requested information. Our system reduces risk of network failure: if a network failure occurs during data transmission, users need request to re-download a smaller map rather than the fully detailed map.

6 Conclusions

Progressive transmission can be used as an effective solution to the exchange of large vector datasets for online web mapping. As generating topologically consistent multiple representations is critical for the exchange in progressive transmission systems, selecting the right algorithm for generating the different representations plays an important role. Our system relies on line simplification for generalising a fully detailed map into a sequence of maps at different LoDs.

The line simplification process has been well studied in cartographic generalisation [12][13][16]. A number of line simplification algorithms have been developed and used in practice. The main problem with these algorithms consisted of not guaranteeing the preservation of consistency. Such a problem has been solved by Saalfeld [19]. Self-crossing and other topological inconsistencies are prevented when applying Saalfeld's algorithm. We have improved such an algorithm by providing an efficient self-crossing-preventing check. Our SCP algorithm adds a simple test to detect possible self-intersections as a condition to applying Saalfeld's parity checks. Such a test on the endpoints of the two initial edges of the convex hulls of the subpolylines either shows a possible self-intersection or rules it out. Experimental results show that our SCP algorithm is efficient in terms of time complexity and scalable to large datasets. We have applied our SCP algorithm to generate multiple representations which were deployed for progressive transmission. An initial evaluation of the transmission system shows good results. A more extensive evaluation is ongoing.

Acknowledgement

The authors would like to thank Prof. Alan Saalfeld of The Ohio State University for his helpful suggestions.

References

1. Bertolotto, M., Egenhofer, M.: Progressive Vector Transmission, In Proceedings of ACMGIS99, Kansas City, MO, (1999), 152-157.
2. Bertolotto, M., Egenhofer, M.: Progressive Transmission of Vector Map Data over the World Wide Web, *GeoInformatica* - An International Journal on Advances of Computer Science for Geographic Information Systems, Vol. 5 (4), Kluwer Academic Publishers, (2001), 345-373.
3. Buttenfield, B.P.: Transmitting Vector Geospatial Data across the Internet, In Proceedings of GIScience 2002, Lecture Notes in Computer Science, Vol. 2478, Springer-Verlag, Berlin, (2002), 51-64.
4. Chan, W.S., Chin, F.: Approximation of Polygonal Curves with Minimum Number of Line Segments. In Proceedings of 3rd ISAAC'92, Lecture Notes in Computer Science, (1993), 762: 378-387.
5. Cecconi, A., Weibel, R.: Map Generalisation for On-demand Web Mapping, In: GIScience 2000, Savannah, Georgia, (2000), 302-304.
6. de Berg, M., van Kreveld, M., Schirra, S.: A New Approach to Subdivision Simplification. In ACMS/ASPRS Annual Convention and Exposition, (1995), volume 4: 79-88.
7. Douglas, D.H., Peucker, T.K.: Algorithms for the Reduction of the Number of Points Required Representing a Digitised Line or Its Character. The Canadian Cartographer, (1973), Vol. 10 (2): 112-123.
8. Han, Q., Bertolotto, M.: Prototype for Progressive Vector Transmission within an Oracle Spatial Environment, In Proceedings of GIS Research UK, 11th Annual Conference, (2003).
9. Hershberger, J., Snoeyink, J.: Speeding Up the Douglas-Peucker Line Simplification Algorithm. In Proceedings of 5th Symp on Data Handling, (1992), 134-143.
10. Imai. H., Iri, M.: Polygonal Approximations of A Curve – Formulations and Algorithms. In: G.T. Toussaint (Ed.), Computational Morphology, Elsevier Science Publishers, (1988): 71-86.
11. Johnston, M.R., Scott, C.D., Gibb, R.G.: Problems Arising From A Simple GIS Generalisation Algorithm. In Proceedings of 11th Annual Collloquium of the Spatial Information Research Centre, (1999), 191-199.
12. McMaster, R.: Automated Line Generalisation. Cartographica,, Vol.24, No. 2, (1987).
13. McMaster, R., Shea, K.S.: Generalisation in Digital Cartography. Association of American Geographers, Washington DC, (1992).
14. Melkman, A.: On-line Construction of the Convex Hull of a Simple Polyline. *Information Processing Letters*, 25, (1987).
15. Melzkman, A., O'Rourke, J.: On Polygon Chain Approximation. G.T. Toussaint (Ed.), *Computational Morphology*, Elsevier Science Publishers, (1988), 87-95.
16. Muller, J-C.: Automated Line Generalisation. Cartography and Geographic Information Systems, 17(2), (1990).
17. Preparata F.P., Shamos, M.I.: Computational Geometry – an introduction. Springer-Verlag, New York (1985).
18. Ramer, U.: An Iterative Procedure for the Polygonal Approximation of Plane Curves. Computer Vision Graphics and Image Processing, (1972), Vol. 1, 244-256.
19. Saalfeld, A.: Topologically Consistent Line Simplification with the Douglas-Peucker Algorithm. Cartography and GIS, Vol. 26 (1), (1999).
20. van Kreveld, M.: Smooth Generalisation for Continuous Zooming, in: `Proceedings of the ICA', Beijing, China, (2001) .

21. Weibel, R., Dutton, G.: Generalising Spatial Data and Dealing with Multiple Representations. Geographical Information Systems: Principles, Techniques, Management and Applications, Second Edition. Cambridge, GeoInformation International, (1999), 125-155.
22. Wu, S.T., Marquez, M.R.G.: A Non-self-intersection Douglas-Peucker Algorithm. In Proceedings of the Sixteenth Brazilian Symposium on Computer Graphics and Image Processing, IEEE, (2003), 60-66.
23. Yang, B.S., Purves, R.S., Weibel, R.: Implementation of progressive transmission algorithms for vector map data in web-based visualization, International Archives of Photogrammetry and Remote Sensing, Istanbul, Turkey, (2004).
24. Zhou, M., Bertolotto, M.: Exchanging Generalised Maps across the Internet, In Proceedings of Knowledge-based Intelligent Information & Engineering Systems 2004, Lecture Notes in Artificial Intelligent, Vol. 3214, Springer-Verlag, (2004), 425-431.
25. Zhou, X., Krumm-Heller, A., Gaede, V.: Generalisation of spatial data for web presentation. In Proceedings of the 2nd Asia Pacific Web Conference (APWeb'99), Computer Science Research, Education and Application Press, (1999), 115-122.
26. Tiger/Line files dataset: http://www.census.gov/geo/www/tiger. Accessed 15 June 2005.

A Framework for Dynamic Updates of Map Data in Mobile Devices

Hae-Kyong Kang[1] and Ki-Joune Li[2]

[1] Department of GIS
[2] Department of Computer Science and Engineering,
Pusan National University, Pusan 609-735, South Korea
{hkkang, lik}@pnu.edu

Abstract. Stored map services in mobile devices are being commercialized for mobile and wireless environment such as cellular phones. In order to ensure the quality and accuracy of map, the update on the source map must be reflected automatically to mobile devices. Due to the expensive communication cost and lack of hardware capacity of mobile devices, we should find a compromising solution between the transmission of an entire map and the transmission of only update logs to mobile devices. The transmission of the completely processed whole map results in an expensive communication cost, while simple transfer of update logs requires a large amount of processing to maintain geometric and topological consistency between multiple LODs(Level of Details). In this paper, we first propose a framework of update mechanism in mobile environments where the map data is stored on each mobile device. This framework provides an efficient strategy for processing an update and its propagation to multiple LODs without an expensive cost of communication and large amount of processing at mobile devices. Secondly, several methods are introduced to maintain topological consistency between LODs depending on the type of generalization operators. Finally, we propose an extended SVG(Simple Vector Graphics) to be used as a transfer format of update message to mobile devices.

1   Introduction

With the recent progress of mobile devices, it becomes possible to store a certain volume of map data on a mobile device such as cellular phones or PDAs. For example, several commercial services are being provided for LBS and telematics applications with road map data stored on cellular phones. In order to maintain the accuracy and quality of map stored on mobile devices, the map data must be up to date. If updates take place on the source map databases, they must be transferred and reflected on every mobile devices, where the source map databases are managed by a server. We should carefully consider several points to efficiently handle the update of map data on the server and mobile devices.

The map data distributed into a server and a large number of mobile devices has several important characteristics differing from the conventional distributed

K.-J. Li and C. Vangenot (Eds.): W2GIS 2005, LNCS 3833, pp. 66–77, 2005.

databases for several reasons. First, the updates for map services take place only at the server side, while they can occur at several sites in conventional distributed database systems. This difference makes the update management of map services simple. The second difference comes from the communication cost. For example, the cost of communication between the server and cellular phones is to be paid by subscribers, and becomes a crucial factor. Therefore, we should reduce the size of communication between the map data server and mobile devices. The third difference is the limited hardware capacity and battery of mobile devices. It means that a large amount of processing for updates in a mobile device may be critical.

A tradeoff relationship is found between the communication cost and processing overhead in mobile devices. If we try to reduce the communication cost, it often results in an increase of computing in a mobile device, and vice versa. Suppose that an update on an object occurs on the source map. Then it must be propagated to correspondent objects on levels of details(LOD) derived from the source map and to other objects, which are not even derived from the udpated source objects, to maintain the topological consistency between several LODs. On one hand, a mobile device is however not capable of processing updates and the propagation due to its lack of hardware capacity. On the other hand, it is too expensive to transfer the entire map to mobile devices, after the server has completely processed the updates and propagations.

In this paper, we make a contribution to find a compromising solution between these contradicting requirements. First, we will propose the framework for updating mechanism of a system under development, called MobiMap, which is a system consisting of a map server and mobile devices to provide mobile map services. Second, we propose methods to process the propagations of an update to several LODs for maintaining the consistency between LODs. Third, we propose an extension of SVG(Scaleable Vector Graphics) describing udpate objects so that mobile devices can receive the updated objects with the extended SVG by reducing the amount of communication for transferring the updates to mobile devices.

This paper is organized as follows. In section 2, we will present the motivation of our research and the related work. The framework for processing updates and their propagations in our MobiMap system will be presented in section 3. In the subsequent section, several methods are to be proposed for maintaining topological consistency between LODs according to generalization operators. In section 5, we will propose an extension of SVG, which is to be used as a message format of update reports from the server to mobile devices. Finally, we will conclude this paper in section 6.

2 Motivations and Related Work

The map stored on a mobile device consists of several LODs. Thus, an update of the source map implies not only the modification of an object but also the propagation of updates to the corresponding objects of different LODs. Further-

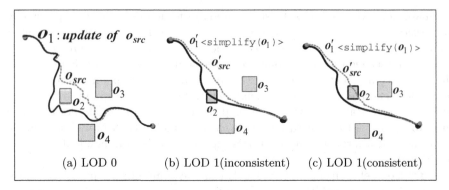

(a) LOD 0   (b) LOD 1(inconsistent)   (c) LOD 1(consistent)

Fig. 1. Topological consistency for line simplification

more, its neighboring objects may need to modify to maintain the topological consistency between LODs.

Figure 1 explains the processing of an update on the source map. In the application area like navigation, the landmarks on the roads are extremely important and the topological relationships between roads and landmarks are crucial to drivers. An updated object o_1 is not intersect with o_2 on the source map (LOD_0) as depicted by figure 1(a), while they are intersect on LOD_1 as figure 1(b), which is a generalized map from LOD_0. Because this topological inconsistency is critical, it must be corrected as shown by figure 1(c) to ensure the topological consistency between roads and landmarks. Consequently, a simplification of an object on the source map results in not only an simplification of an object on LOD_1 but also several modification of its neighboring objects. In order to process an update and its propagation to other LODs, two approaches may be possible as follows,

- **Transfer of map data:** The processing for updates and its propagations to LODs are carried out at the server side and the map data modified is transferred to mobile devices by this approach. However, it results in an expensive communication cost for transferring a large amount of data. The price for transferring 1M bytes data to a cellular phone is approximately US$50, which is not negligible.
- **Transfer of update logs:** According to this approach, we transfer only update log data to mobile devices. It is evident that the communication cost is greatly reduced by this approach. However each mobile device should process the update and its propagations to several LODs, which are a large amount of overhead to a small device like cellular phone. And this processing requires a lot of energy as well.

However, these two approaches are not feasible since each approach focuses on only one of two requirements contradicting, which are the reductions of communication cost versus the processing overhead of mobile devices. Therefore both of the approaches fail to satisfy the two requirements. In this paper, we focus on a compromise between the two opposite requirements.

The basic issue of this paper is related with how to process an update and its propagation to multiple LODs to ensure geometric and topological consistency. A number of work has been done to maintain the consistency between multi-scale or multiple LOD spatial databases. But few of them deal with the topological consistency except [5, 6, 15]. Several methods have been proposed for maintaining topological consistency depending on the operation type of generalization. In [6], a method to assess the topological integrity has been proposed for aggregation operator. A similar work has been carried out for collapse operator in [13]. J. Sharma has proposed a method to ensure topological integrity for line simplification operator in [5]. These work provide a theoretical background of our study and development of our MobiMAP manager.

3   Update Framework of MobiMap Manager

In this section, we present the framework of update mechanism designed for MobiMAP Manager, which is under development by our research team. The main focus in designing the framework is on how to reduce the communication cost as well as processing overhead of mobile devices. The framework is shown by figure 2, where an update and its propagation to multiple LODs are processed as follows.

- **step 1 : update on LOD_0**
  An update is processed in the source database (LOD_0).
- **step 2 : geometric propagation on LOD_n**
  The server stores all LODs. The corresponding objects in different LODs are updated by using generalization operators such as line simplification, collapse, and aggregation operations[9].
- **step 3 : handling consistency**
  This step consists of the two sub tasks, which are assessment of topological consistency and correction of inconsistency.
  a. assessment of topological consistency: For each LOD derived from LOD_0, neighboring objects are checked to assess topological consistency with LOD_0. The methods for assessment of topological consistency [5, 6, 13] will be explained in the next section.
  b. topological propagation on LOD_n: If any topological inconsistency is found at a LOD, the neighboring objects must be corrected to ensure the consistency with LOD_0. The correction methods are discussed in [10, 14].
- **step 4 : transfer of updates to each mobile device**
  After having found the updates on each LOD, the server transfers the update request to each mobile device in extended SVG, which will be explained in section 5.
- **step 5 : updates on mobile devices**
  The updates received from the server with an extended SVG format are to be reflected on a mobile device. The updates in an extended SVG format replace the old objects in original SVG files by *Update handler*.

Because hardward capacity of mobile devices are limited, we should consider the way to reduce the processing overhead on mobile devices. Therefore, our MobiMAP Manager generate updated LOD_n using a mobile device on a server-side, instead of generating it on a mobile device. We will discuss more details about this step 3(assessment of topological consistency) in the next section 4.

When MobiMAP Manager derives an updated LOD_n, it stores an udpate log. By reference the update log, updated objects of LOD_n are converted to an extended SVG format. It reduces the cummunication cost because the extended SVG format includes updated objects, instead of entire objects. In the section 5, the extended SVG schema and step 4 will be explained.

4   Checking Topological Consistency Between LODs

If an update takes place on the source map LOD_0, it must be propagated to other LODs, which are generalized from LOD_0. As we have seen in the previous sections, the propagation includes not only geometric generalizations, but also assessment of topological consistency, which differs depending on the type of geometric generalizations. In this section, we will present the assessment methods for three geometric generalizations - line simplification, collapse, and aggrega-

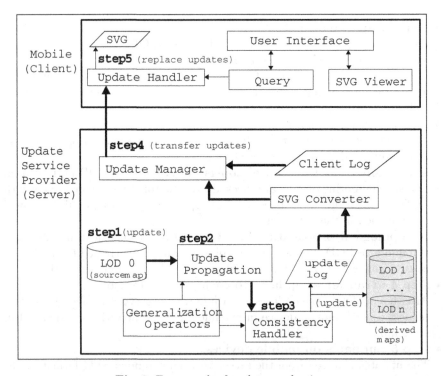

Fig. 2. Framework of update mechanism

tion. These assessment methods are implemented in the `consistency handler`
in figure 2.

4.1   Topological Consistency for Line Simplification

By line simplification, we can remove vertices of less importance from a line with
a large number of vertices. The most popular algorithm of line simplification is
proposed by Douglas and Peuker[2]. There is an one-to-one mapping between
the original line and the simplified line, the difference between LOD_0 and other
LODs is only found in geometric properties. It means that the topology in LOD_0
should be preserved in other LODs. If a different topology is found in two LODs,
they are considered as topologically inconsistent.

In figure 1, we already showed an examples of topological consistency for
line simplification. In addition, figure 3 shows an another example. In figure 3,
o_{src} in LOD_0 is an original line object and o_1 is the updated object from o_{src}.
o''_{src} in LOD_2 are the simplified objects from o_{src} in LOD_0. o''_1 in LOD_2 are the
simplified objects from o_1 in LOD_0.

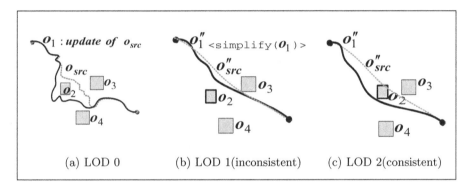

(a) LOD 0   (b) LOD 1(inconsistent)   (c) LOD 2(consistent)

Fig. 3. Directional Consistency for Line-Simplification

We observe that o_2 is at the south-west of o''_1 in LOD_1 as shown in figure 3(b),
while o_2 is at the north-east of o_1 in LOD_0 as figure 3(a). Thus, a topological
difference is found in LOD_1. In order to maintain the topological consistency,
we must correct o'' or move o_2 like figure 3(c) so that the topologies in LOD_0
and LOD_1 be identical.

We observe that o_2 is placed on the left side of o'_1 in LOD_1 as shown in figure
3(b), while o_2 is on the right side of o'_1 in LOD_0. A topological mismatch is found
and it must be corrected by moving o_2. In order to maintain the topological
consistency, we must correct o' or move o_2 like figure 3(c) so that the topologies
in LOD_0 and LOD_1 be identical.

A similar case is found in figure 1. In both cases, we observe that an update of
a line object results in at least two modifications. The detail algorithm to assess
the topological inconsistency is presented in [5] and the correction methods are
proposed by [10, 14].

4.2   Topological Consistency for Collapse

Collapse operator reduces the dimension of a spatial object, for example, from polygon to point. But in some cases, it is impossible to maintain the same topology. For example, if a polygon a containing another polygon b is collapsed to a point a', a' does no longer contain b. Consequently the topological consistency does not imply merely identical topology. For this reason, the assessment of topological consistency for a `collapse` operation is a little more complicated than `line-simplification`.

Figure 4 shows how to assess topological consistency between multiple LODs. Initially, we have map data of roads on LOD_0 and LOD_1, where roads on LOD_0 are collapsed to lines as shown by figure 4(a). Then, several road facilities are inserted into the map of LOD_0. All of facilities intersect with road polygons on LOD_0 as figure 4(b)-B1, while there are non-intersect facilities with road polygon on LOD_1 as shown by figure 4(b)-B2.

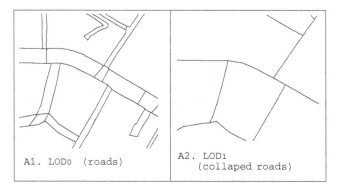

A1. LOD0 (roads)   A2. LOD1
                               (collaped roads)

(a) original and derived road maps

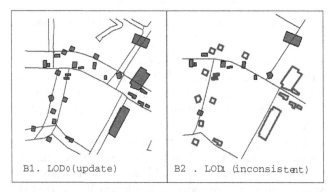

B1. LOD0(update)   B2 . LOD1 (inconsistent)

(b) detection of inconsistent relations(white polygons) after update(insert) of new facilities into LOD_0

Fig. 4. Topological Consistency for Collapse

In this figure, the topologies between roads and facilities marked as a black polygon are consistent with the topologies on LOD_0, even though the topologies on LOD_0 and LOD_1 are not identical each other. However, it is evident that the topologies between roads and facilities with white polygons are inconsistent with the topologies on LOD_0. Consequently these objects should be displaced so that they intersect with road polygons.

In [13, 16], a formal model is proposed to define the consistent topological correspondence between databases of multiple scales. The propagation method is also proposed to correct topologically inconsistent objects by [10, 14].

4.3   Topological Consistency for Aggregation

Aggregation operator merges a set of objects satisfying predefined condition into a new object. For this reason, the topology of the original objects must be carefully considered for assessing the topological consistency between LODs. If an update occurs to an object on LOD_0, which is aggregated to an object in LOD_1, the aggregated object in LOD_1 must be re-aggregated taking the update

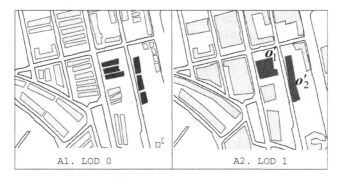

(a) original and derived maps

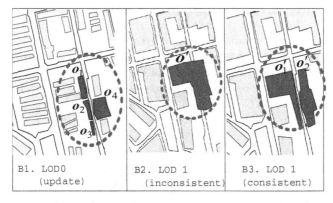

(b) update of the original map and its propagation results

Fig. 5. Topological Consistency for Aggregation

into account. Moreover, the topology on LOD_0 must be respected during the re-aggregation process as shown by figure 5.

In figure 5(a) shows the initial states of LOD_0 and LOD_1, where the polygons in figure 5(a)-A2 are created by aggregation of objects on LOD_0. Then new three objects o_1, o_2, and o_3 are inserted into LOD_0 and the shapes of o_4 and road are changed as shown by figure 5(b)-B1.

In the process of update propagation, a new aggregated object o' on LOD_1 is computed from updated objects on LOD_0 as depicted by figure 5(b)-B2. But since the topology between the new aggregated object and road on LOD_1 differs from LOD_0, the topology of LOD_1 is considered as inconsistent. In order to make it consistent, the aggregation must be re-computed as shown by figure 5(b)-B3. The derivation method of topology for aggregation is proposed [6], and it can be used to recompute the aggregation with updated or newly inserted objects.

5   Extending SVG to Transfer Updates to Mobile Devices

As we described in the section 1, we should reduce the size of map data for saving communication cost. Therefore, we transfer the updated parts of map to mobile devices, instead of replacing entire map. In this section, we will propose an update schema based on SVG(Scalable Vector Graphics)[17] to describe the updated parts. The udpate schema is generated by **update manager** on the server in figure 2.

The update schema consists of several tags to describe an update type, an identifier of an updated object and a new geometry. The diagram for the update schema is illustrated by figure 6.

In figure 6, the **SVG** element indicates the beginning of a SVG document, and consists of **g** elements. Each **g** element represents transform conditions for coordinate systems, or describes updated data with an attribute **id**. Each **id** corresponds a map layer, for instance, *RoadFacilityPolygon*.

When the attribute **id** is specified in the **g** element, upate types have to be indicated. Depending on the types of update, different attributes are included in the update schema. For example, updated geometries is needed for **insert** and **update** types of update, but it is not needed for **delete**. Each udpate type has attribute **Date** describing the time stamp of the update transfer.

Udpated geometry is specified by core attributes of a SVG document such as **path**. An example of a SVG extension in figure 6 shows insert of new obejcts into *RoadFacilityPolygon*, modification of two objects on *Agg_Building*, and delete of several objects on *EDUSRC*.

This SVG document is to be interpreted by an update handler(2) of MobiMap in mobile device rather than directly displayed by a SVG viewer, since it contains only the updated part of the entire map. The update handler of a mobile device must replace the old data by the new ones in the update document to build new map data. But this processing does not result in an overhead of mobile device, since it includes only searching by id and simple replacement operations.

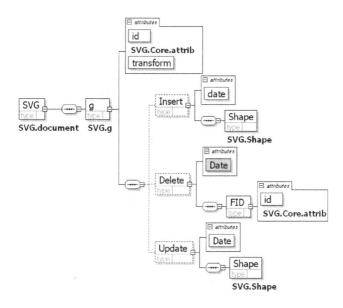

```
<?xml version="1.0"?>
<svg xmlns:xlink="http://www.w3.org/1999/xlink" x="0" y="0" width="100%" heigh
 <style type="text/css">
  .style-RoadFacilityPolygon-0 {fill:RGB(199,107,240);fill-opacity:1;stroke:RGB(
  .style-Agg-Building-0 {fill:RGB(160,191,156);fill-opacity:1;stroke:RGB(0,0,0);s
  .style-EDUSRC-0 {fill:RGB(222,85,110);fill-opacity:1;stroke:RGB(0,0,0);stroke-
 </style>
 <g transform="matrix(1 0 0 -1 0 857111.936 )">
 <g id="RoadFacilityPolygon">
    <insert date="2005 07 25 11:00"> <!-- Example : insert geometry-->
       <path id="RoadFacilityPolygon_f90" class="style-RoadFacilityPolygon-0
       <path id="RoadFacilityPolygon_f91" class="style-RoadFacilityPolygon-0
       <path id="RoadFacilityPolygon_f92" class="style-RoadFacilityPolygon-0
    </insert>
 </g>
 <g id="Agg_Building">
    <update date="2005 07 25 11:30"><!-- Example : update geometry-->
       <path id="Agg_Building_f2" class="style-Agg-Building-0" d="M 198741.3
       <path id="Agg_Building_f3" class="style-Agg-Building-0" d="M 199594.2
    </update>
 </g>
 <g id="EDUSRC">
    <delete date="2005 07 25 11:22"> <!-- Example : delete objects -->
       <fid id="EDUSRC_f110" />
       <fid id="EDUSRC_f111"/>
        ...
```

Fig. 6. Update schema and example

6   Conclusion

With the recent progress of mobile devices, stored map services begin to be commercialized for cellular phone and PDA. In order to ensure the quality and accuracy of map, the updates on the source map must be automatically reflected to mobile devices. However, the expensive communication cost and lack of hardware capacity of mobile devices are important constraints in dealing with the updates. It implies that we should find a compromising solution between the transmission of the entire map and the transmission of only update logs to mobile devices. The transmission of completely processed map results in an expensive communication cost, while simple transfer of update logs requires a large amount of processing to maintain geometric and topological consistency between multiple LODs. Therefore, we proposed a way to transfer udpated objects with SVG documents, neither the entire map nor update logs.

This paper has three contributions. First, we propose a framework of update mechanism in mobile environments where the map data is stored on each mobile device. This framework provides an efficient strategy for processing an update and its propagation to multiple LODs without an expensive cost of communication and large amount of processing at mobile devices. Second, several methods are introduced to maintain topological consistency between LODs depending on the type of generalization operators. The third contribution is the extended SVG to be used as a transfer format of update message to mobile devices.

References

1. M. J. Egenhofer and H. Herring, *Categorizing Binary Topological Relations Between Regions, Lines, and Points in Geographic Databases*, Technical Report, Department of Surveying Engineering, University of Maine, 1990.
2. R. B. McMaster, and K. S. Shea, Generalization in Digital Cartography. Association of American Geographers, 72-28, 1992.
3. M. Egenhofer, *Evaluating Inconsistencies Among multiple Representations*, Proc. 6th international Symposium on Spatial Data Handling, 902-920, 1994.
4. T. Kilpelainen, T. Saarjakoski, *Incremental Generalization for Multiple Representations of Geographical Objects*, GIS and Generalization : Methodology and Practice, Muller, J. P. Lagrange, R. Weibel(editors), Taylor & Francis, 1995.
5. J. Sharma, *Integrated Spatial Reasoning in Geographic Information Systems: Combining Topology and Direction"*, Ph.D Thesis, The Graduate School of Spatial Information Science and Engineering, University of Maine, 1996.
6. N. Tryfona and M. J. Egenhofer, *Consistency among Parts and Aggregates: A Computational Model*, Transactions in GIS, 1(3):189-206, 1997.
7. J. A. C. Paiva, *Topological Consistency in Geographic Databases With Multiple Representations*, Ph. D. Thesis, University of Maine, 1998, http://library.umaine.edu/theses/pdf/paiva.pdf.
8. A. Belussi, M. Negri, and G. Pelagatti, *An integrity constraints driven system for updating spatial databases*, ACM-GIS, 121-128, 2000.
9. Kang H., Do S., and Li K., 2001: Model-Oriented Generalization Rules. Proc.(in CD) ESRI User Conference, San Diego, USA, July.

10. A. Ruas, *Generalization of Updated Data(in the context of multiple representation)*, ISPRS/ICA, 2002.
11. Z. Guo, S. Zhou, Z. Xu, and A. Zhou, *G2ST: A Novel Method to Transform GML to SVG*, ACM-GIS, 161-168, 2003.
12. S. Balley, C. Parent, and S. Spaccapietra, *Modelling geographic data with multiple representation*, International Journal of Geographical Information Science, 18(4):327-352, 2004
13. H. Kang, T. Kim, and K. Li, *Topological Consistency for Collapse Operation in Multi-scale Databases*, Proc. 1st Workshop on Conceptual Modeling for Geographic Information Systems in Conjunction with ER2004, Lecture Notes in Computer Science 3289, Springer-Verlag, 91-102, 2004.
14. C. Duchene, *The CartACom model: a generalisation model for taking relational constraints into account*, Proc. 6th ICA Workshop on progress in automated map generalisation, Leicester, 2004, http://aci.ign.fr/Leicester/paper/duchene-v2-ICAWorkshop.pdf
15. H. Kang, J. Moon and K. Li, *Data Update Across Multi-Scale Databases*, Proc. of the 12th International Conference on Geoinformatics, 2004
16. H. Kang, and K. Li, *Assessing Topological Consistency for Collapse Operation in Generalization of Spatial Databases*, In Reviewing by the 2st Workshop on Conceptual Modeling for Geographic Information Systems in Conjunction with ER2005.
17. W3G, Scalable Vector Graphics(SVG) 1.1 Specification, W3C Recommendation, 2003.

Geo-Enabling Spatially Relevant Data for Mobile Information Use and Visualisation

Alistair J. Edwardes[1], Dirk Burghardt[1], Eduardo Dias[2],
Ross S. Purves[1], and Robert Weibel[1]

[1] Department of Geography, University of Zurich,
Winterthurerstrasse 190, 8057 Zurich (Switzerland)
{aje, burg, rsp, weibel}@geo.unizh.ch
http://www.geo.unizh.ch/gis
[2] Spatial Information Laboratory,
Free University Amsterdam
edias@feweb.vu.nl

Abstract. This paper addresses the methodological issues of developing and visualising added value geo-enabled content for mobile information systems. The research was carried out under the framework of WebPark, an EC-IST R&D project that developed a location aware application for nature/protected areas. The evaluation of existing information sources – tourism information, research data, and multimedia content – revealed that the tourism information and multimedia content analysed did not have an active geographic component and the geographic research data (e.g. animal counts/observations) had a clear mismatch as regards the visitors' information needs. Therefore, different types of data processing were developed and performed in order to render existing information sources useful for location-based services. Data preparation also included building hierarchical data structures (quadtrees and hierarchical stream ordering). The paper shows how these data structures are exploited to facilitate real-time generalisation in order to efficiently present thematic point data on portable devices. Finally, three key lessons for geo-enabling location-based services are presented.

Keywords: mobile information services, LBS, environmental information, geo-enabling, location modelling, visualisation, hierarchical data structures, tessellations, real-time cartographic generalisation.

1 Introduction

Protected areas are created, in the main, with the primary aim of conserving natural and cultural heritage and secondly in order to support the leisure and tourism industry. In this regard, delivering environmental education is a major task for most protected areas [10]. Mobile technology is becoming increasingly available and its usage more and more widespread [4] and mobile internet devices with geo-location capabilities may create an opportunity for delivering such education and information to visitors of protected areas. Location-based services (LBS) deliver information specifically customised to the user's location and, on occasion, context of use [1] and as such can

K.-J. Li and C. Vangenot (Eds.): W2GIS 2005, LNCS 3833, pp. 78–92, 2005.

play a role in helping visitors to protected areas (e.g. national or regional parks) achieve full awareness of the richness of the surrounding natural and cultural resources and contribute to environmentally friendly visits. However, although the technology is mature enough to deploy mobile and context- aware applications, much of the data available is not ready to be used in such applications.

In this paper we address a set of issues encountered in making diverse and heterogeneous data resources accessible as value-added, geo-enabled content for mobile information services. These entail a range of challenges both in terms of how geographic information is modelled and represented and, how it can be best be delivered to enhance exploration and understanding.

2 Context of Research

This paper builds on experiences made in WebPark, a European IST project that developed a series of location-based services for users of protected areas (for information and sample pictures of the system, see www.webparkservices.info). The services are based on wireless technology and available for mobile smart phones and PDAs. The prototype system was developed at two partner sites, the Swiss National Park (SNP) and the Wadden Sea Islands (NL), and tested with real visitors [1]. The system includes the following features:

- automatic location of a user on a map (via GPS);
- points of interest (POI) search, both spatially and using free text;
- access to fauna and flora information, including multimedia data;
- context-aware retrieval of information, respecting visitors' spatial behaviour and personal preferences;
- dynamic mapping of retrieved information including real-time map generalisation;
- the ability for visitors to add their own geographic data as 'geographical bookmarks'; and
- location-sensitive warnings (e.g. areas with increased protection level).

The system uses wireless communication between the server and mobile devices (PDAs) with client side caching ensuring a continuous visitor experience when coverage is lost.

3 Evaluation of Environmental and Geographic Information

Many authorities for protected areas are responsible for the collection and dissemination of information about their natural and cultural assets. Mobile information services can support such responsibilities by providing channels through which to access data holdings in geographically meaningful ways. Whilst the technology to allow this is relatively advanced, a problem remains in that most data resources help by such organisations are generally not in a state in which they can be made readily available. The reasons for this are well illustrated through the framework of Raper *et al.* [19] for evaluating geographic information (GI). This model distinguishes between components of GI that are representational, at the levels of ontology, modelling and system, and communicative, at the levels of relevance, exploration, commodfication and management. Table 1 uses this framework to describe the issues related to existing data resources encountered in the WebPark project.

Table 1. Data considerations within the evaluation framework of Raper *et al.* [19]

Component	Level	Issues for available data holdings
Representational	Ontological	Entities were represented within data holdings using differing abstractions, classifications and taxonomies for similar or related information.
	Modelling	Diverse spatial and aspatial (e.g. multimedia) data models were employed amongst different data resources, with few or no geo-referencing relationships between them.
	System	A wide variety of data formats and media were used to store data (e.g. CD-ROMs, databases, documents).
Communicative	Relevance	Data had been collected for assorted dedicated purposes, for example research or inventory, and were generally mismatched to the information needs of ordinary LBS users [10].
	Exploration	Data were not structured or indexed in ways that made them easily adaptable to location- or other context based exploration. Data models were ill-suited for supporting readability, comprehension and visualisation, for example through multiple representations, generalizations or hierarchical abstractions
	Commodification	Data were not organised in chunks easily distinguishable as information products. Copyright issues related to using data within information services had usually not been considered.
	Management	Data holdings were largely decentralised and often purchased or produced for one-off purposes making management and update difficult.

Addressing these issues called for a series of information processing and management strategies. Here, we focus specifically on those related to data transformations.

4   Overview of Data Transformation and Management

The WebPark system and related processes can be simplistically viewed as a publishing tool that allows intense information sharing of local knowledge with visitors to the park. In order to provide true added value for the visitors, the information available plays a crucial role. Hence, GI and multimedia content needed to be adapted or created in order to meet the required accuracy and expectations of the visitor.

The GI content needed for the WebPark service can be divided into '**background**' and '**foreground**' information. Typical background GI consists of topographic base map data e.g. roads, paths, coastlines, water features and boundaries; false colour imagery classified by land cover; terrain information and public service and safety information. By contrast, foreground GI contains processed and interpreted GI and multimedia such as animal distributions, POIs, flowers in blossom and up-to-date photographs and other multimedia information.

In order to prepare GI content for WebPark, an extension to the ETL (Extract, Transform, Load [25]) process was defined. Fig. 1 illustrates the extended process.

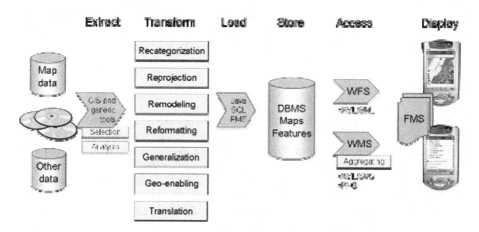

Fig. 1. Data processing flow in WebPark

The workflow can be considered as a linear process starting with the determination of available datasets (information audit) and ending with the display of information to visitors through extraction of data from its original storage medium, transformation to cope with the specified data model, and loading into a relational database. The extraction step also involves the analysis of the data in order to select a spatially and semantically relevant subset. The selected data is then transformed through a set of operations necessary to harmonise and standardise the data according to the WebPark data model. Depending on the individual dataset's these will include:

- Recategorization – harmonizing the conceptualization of entities into a single domain ontology.
- Reprojection – reprojecting spatial data into a common spatial reference system.
- Remodelling – mapping the different sources' data models into a WebPark one that allows access in a context- and location-sensitive way.
- Reformatting – converting the heterogeneous data formats (mime-types) for multimedia native content into the formats understood by the WebPark components.
- (Model) generalization – applying geometric processes such as line filtering, aggregating features that are too small or defined with semantics that are too detailed.
- Geo-enabling – creating associations between spatial and aspatial data
- Translation - Information is in English, French, German, Italian and Dutch.

Most of these steps can be easily mapped to the framework of Raper [19] shown in Table 1. For example, model generalization improves readability and comprehension of mapping and thus can be considered as improving the communicative experience of exploration.

The processing steps that are methodologically most demanding and interesting are recategorization, generalization, remodeling and geo-enabling. Recategorization is beyond the scope of this paper, but is described in [12]. (Model) generalization entails filtering and aggregating geometric as well as semantic information detail in a controlled fashion [26]. Different levels of detail are generated for the background data that can be associated with different target map scales. As the required procedures are relatively standard in GIS, they will not be discussed further. For a similar approach, see [6]. Remodelling and geo-enabling will be described in detail in sections 5 and 6, respectively. For more details on the other processing steps, see [9].

5 Remodelling

LBS primarily communicate information though two modes [12]; by answering questions about phenomena related to a user's context [1] and by answering questions about the contexts of phenomena. Questions about a user's context (e.g. location and time of year) might be termed *what* questions, for example "What animals can be found here at the moment?" Those about the contexts of other phenomena might be termed *where* or *when* questions, for example "Where can eagles be found?" Questions relating to the phenomena, such as, "Why do we see more eagles near mountain ridges?", are answered secondarily, by attributing the phenomena (e.g. with multimedia) and by providing inter-connections between them, for instance with hyperlinks, map layering or detailed ontological models [3].

Depending on the nature of the phenomenon, answering the two types of primary question can require different spatial data models in order to relate it to the user's context and for presentation of spatial distribution. Using the terminology of Maceachren ([16] pp. 59-60), for *discrete* and particularly *abrupt* phenomena such as points-of-interest or real-time incidents, a single point-based model can be used, for example using distance to relate the user's location to the phenomena. If the instances of the phenomena are numerous, for example where they are *discrete* and *smooth*, presenting them may also require real-time generalization (described in section 11 using the example of deer observation data).

More *continuous* phenomena, such as density of animal observations, exhibiting relatively complex patterns of spatial variation may need separate models with areas being used to relate the phenomena to the locations in the database [15] and a different cartographic model for presentation. In these cases, the cartographic content tends to be relatively static, e.g. seasonal animal distributions, and can be treated in a similar way to background data, using precomputed model generalization to control data volume and the level of geometric and semantic detail.

Remodeling thus seeks on the one hand, to unify the diverse data models of the various data sources and, on the other, to re-structure the data into models that can be used to answer the two primary types of questions. Such operations can be considered to first require consideration of the modeling of the data in the context of representation, and secondly to enhance the possibilities for exploration in the context of communication, as described in Table 1.

This section mainly deals with remodeling to relate the spatial occurrence of different phenomena to the location of a user. A process termed 'location modeling' [21].

5.1 Remodelling Wildlife Information

The main purpose of remodelling in WebPark was to allow a user to pose wildlife questions about their current situation. Achieving this requires a model of the user's location to which the spatial occurrences of plants and animals can be related.

It is possible to model location in different ways; geometrically, symbolically and semantically [14]. WebPark used a geometric model where locations could be the user's current position or locations that could be indexed with respect to their current position such as topographic features and the spaces over which activities are performed, e.g. visibility regions and navigable regions. Wildlife phenomena were then associated to these locations.

Data about spatial occurrences of wildlife were found to have been captured in a variety of ways and using different types of geometry. For example, they might relate the entity to the geography influencing its spatial variation or behaviour, e.g. home ranges or habitats, or they might relate them to the units used for recording direct experiences e.g. field observations, sections of path, census areas or areas delimited by expert knowledge. Mapping the phenomena onto the location model is thus essentially an intersection operation between the different geometry types. Table 2 illustrates this using a simple model of vector data intersections. These operations are performed either at query time in the case of point-point associations or the association is stored through an index related to the relevant object.

Table 2. Associating models of location and spatial occurrence geometrically

Phenomena / User		Point e.g. observation	Line e.g. river section	Area e.g. habitat zone
Point	e.g. user's position	Distance, proximity	Buffer intersection	Containment and zone adjacency
Line	e.g. path	Buffer intersection or shortest path	Incidence or Hausdorff proximity	Intersection
Area	e.g. visibility region	Containment and region hierarchy	Intersection	Overlap or intersection

The approach implies that the location model can be defined completely independent of the phenomena, with the advantage that the time needed to search for information relevant to a user's location is considerably reduced. However, this assumption is in fact too restrictive. To some extent, the user's context is created both through their interaction with the phenomena they are interested in [11] and to the size and behaviour of the entity. For example, large animals are usually very wary of people but their size means they can be observed from some distance using a telescope or binoculars; hence a location model of visibility can consider large regions. Small birds, even if tame, can only be observed at quite close proximity. This necessitates a model of visibility covering a much smaller extent.   Fig. 2 illustrates the generation of areas representing visibility regions in the mountainous terrain of the SNP for observing large animals such as ungulates. This involved computing the drainage morphology for stream channels at different stream orders [14]. The resulting hierarchy of regions gives an approximation of the area visible from a point at different scales. The approach has similarities with that of Schlieder *et al.* [21] who also considering a hierarchical view of space for location modelling. The visibility regions were subsequently intersected with forest stands to take into account visual obstruction from vegetation.

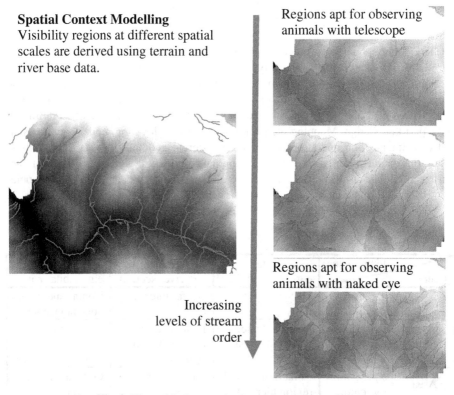

Spatial Context Modelling
Visibility regions at different spatial scales are derived using terrain and river base data.

Regions apt for observing animals with telescope

Regions apt for observing animals with naked eye

Increasing levels of stream order

Fig. 2. Hierarchical stream basins and visibility regions

A similar operation was carried out to associate path segments with song bird occurrence. A habitat preference model for song birds [13] was overlain with buffered path segments. Each path segment was then attributed with song birds whose habitat preference intersected with their visibility buffer.

6   Geo-Enabling

One of the main conclusions of the initial information audit was that there was a clear mismatch between the information currently provided by the park and the visitor information needs [1],[10]. Most of the questions from visitors had a high spatial component (e.g. "What animals can I see around me?", "Can I have a picnic here?") but much of the most suitable information (e.g. the multimedia and documentation) was not geo-referenced. Information with a spatial component had generally been captured for research purposes and was not structured in a way that was relevant to the visitors' information needs. A fundamental issue was how to make these data fit for the purpose in an LBS. Geo-enabling is therefore an example of improving the relevance of information communicated to users within the context of Table 1.

6.1   Geo-Enabling Multimedia

Various sources of information, well fitted to visitors needs, were available as multimedia in digital form. For example, the SNP produces an interactive CD-ROM containing over 800 high-quality photographs as well as detailed texts, videos and sounds. Part of the richness of these resources is the numerous hyperlinks amongst the different pieces of information providing the ability for users to explore questions related to particular phenomena. A particular challenge was to design a model that would both ensure information was spatially explorable and that these interconnections amongst pieces of information were maintained. Researchers on the GUIDE project [7] identified a similar problem. Their solution was to support separate information models for locations, containing places of interest and connections to travel between them, and for media, containing hyperlinked cultural and historical multimedia. The two models were then linked through the identities of places they had in common. This solution worked well for them because their primary interest was with places, with the system guiding their users between these. Thus their location model and entity ontology could to large degree be treated as the same thing. Our problem differed in that the entities of interest were wildlife and not inherently spatial phenomena. Hence different representations were need for entities and their locations. Our own solution was therefore to directly enrich the model of wildlife entities, with hyperlinks referencing the identities of related entities. Therefore, the entities became the main data chunks, around which other services could be commodified (see Table 1). This model is illustrated in Fig. 3.

The first step in this work was to recategorize data using an ontological mapping, such that, for example information about "bearded vultures" and information about "bartgeyer" were considered to relate to the same feature. The second step was associating these features with appropriate locations as described previously – thus for example bearded vultures might be associated with a path in terms of an area over which they were visible, but also with a point location used as a release site for a reintroduction programme. Finally, the entity description was enriched with links to appropriate multimedia and with links to associated features. Thus on querying for "What is near me?", a user might be informed that golden eagles (entity) and marmots (entity) were often seen in this area. On clicking on information about marmots, point locations of individual marmot sightings (location) could be displayed.

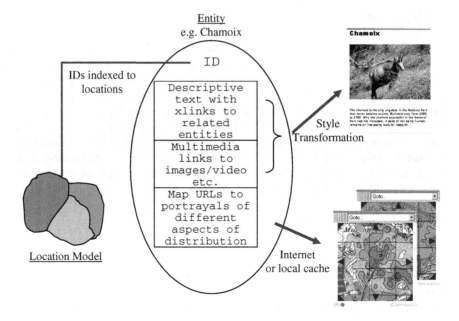

Fig. 3 Information model for WebPark

Associated with these marmot sightings are multimedia describing marmots, and since golden eagles predate on marmots a link to the golden eagle entity. Using this model it was possible to have entities that were; non-geographic but still available to through system (e.g. general rules of the park, history), semi-geographic being spatially indexed to locations according to expert knowledge but having no mappable distributions, and geographic being both locatable and mapped.

7 Design Considerations for Visualization

In LBS information reduction is an important issue, for three main reasons. First, network bandwidth and client computational power impose limitations on the amount of information that can usefully be transmitted and processed. Second, the small screen size and resolution of portable devices imposes restrictions on the information content and density that can be portrayed in order to maintain the readability of visualisations. Thirdly, user interactions can result in rapidly changing portrayals (and associated levels of detail), for example through *ad hoc* querying or changes in location.

The first limitation is addressed in WebPark through a variety of techniques to minimise transmission of extraneous data. For example, where mapping is independent of location and user interaction is limited, e.g. topographic background maps, model generalisation as previously described is used in conjunction with client-side caching.

Developing methods to counter the second and third limitations is more demanding. While the detail of the (static) background data layers can be tailored to the small screen size during model generalisation and stored in a multiresolution database containing the right levels of detail for the target map scales, the portrayal of foreground data cannot be pre-computed and requires client-side, real-time processing since the foreground thematic data which is to be visualised is usually retrieved as the result of a specific *ad hoc* query and therefore can not be known in advance and pre-compiled in a map. Methods addressing these issues have at their core attempts to enhance explorative communication by support readability and comprehension through, potentially, multiple representations (Table 1).

One example of data requiring such an approach are smoothly varying, discrete data such as those described in section 5. For instance, ungulate observations as shown in Fig. 4 are numerous and vary rapidly in density over space. Any representation of such points should meet three underlying constraints:

- the visualizations should be cartographically acceptable;
- any generalization operations should be performed in 'real-time, that is, the user's wait for a response should be minimal; and
- the visualizations should maintain meaningful spatial and thematic relationships.

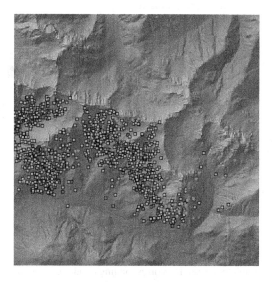

Fig. 4. Individual ungulate observations

Since the data we are dealing with are simple point data, a minimal set of cartographic constraints is sufficient to maximize legibility on small devices:

- minimum symbol size should maintain legibility – a common value is 5 pixels [22]; and
- symbols should not be allowed to overlap or touch.

7.1 Using Spatial Tessellations for Real Time Map Generalization

Many approaches exist to generalizing and transforming point data [8][18]. Our approach to this problem is based on the notion of hierarchical spatial tessellations. Quadtrees [20] have been widely used in both computer graphics [5] and GIS [24] to index and allow rapid traversal and retrieval of data. Here we use the quadtree to make decisions on the number of objects to display. Moving vertically through a quadtree can be considered analogous to zooming, whilst moving horizontally between nodes is comparable to panning. Each node contains a count of the number of objects existing within the block it represents. The count at the nodes for the current zoom level is used to generate a visualisation using simple selection and exaggeration rules (Fig. 5, lower part). The quadtree tessellates space until every point is assigned to a separate block. When zooming a level is chosen that meets a minimum acceptable symbol size criterion.

The upper part of Fig. 5 illustrates the results of zooming/generalisation through the quadtree, where maximum symbol size is constant, and symbol size is a function of the number of observations. Symbols are also displaced, within the quadtree block, toward the centre of gravity of the block's observations.

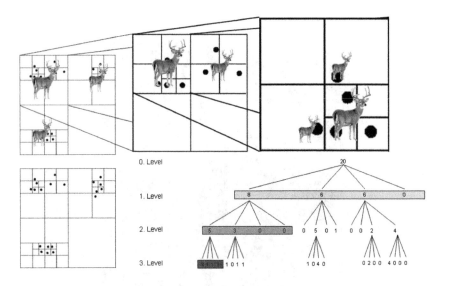

Fig. 5. Lower part: Example point set and corresponding quadtree (note the count stored at each node). Upper part: Successive generalisations of deer observations.

The quadtree provides an efficient implementation which allows the application of simple rules to generalize thematic point data for panning and zooming whilst meeting basic cartographic constraints. However, points are aggregated according to an arbitrary quadtree block, with no consideration given to the distribution of points either with respect to other points (i.e. point density) or relationships with other underlying variables (i.e. the position of a point within a landscape) [18].

7.2 Using Catchment Order in Tessellation

In Section 6 the use of hierarchically ordered catchment areas, based on stream orders to spatially index locational data was discussed. The main reason for using such an index was a hypothesized link between visibility and catchments.

Here we postulate a relationship between deer and the landscape. Deer in mountainous terrain may be unable or have difficulty to cross steep ridges, and thus individuals in one valley may be more likely to have some relationship with each other than spatially nearer deer in separate valleys. We therefore once again tessellate the point dataset in Fig. 5 using Strahler ordering and watersheds [23], but do not on this occasion time apply the mask of forested areas.

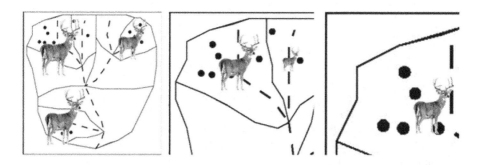

Fig. 6. Idealized Stahler stream ordering and tessellation using catchments at three levels showing progressive levels of zoom

An idealized example of such a tessellation is shown in Fig. 6. Fig. 7 shows a comparison between generalizations for the third level in a hierarchy based on the point data shown in Fig. 4. Here, the difference between the two images is striking and

Fig. 7. Comparison of hierarchical generalisation techniques using quadtree (left) and hierarchical stream ordering and associated catchments (right)

demonstrates the importance of using a geographically relevant unit of aggregation to tessellate space [17]. It is important to point out, that in this case, the link between catchments and ungulates is hypothetical.

8 Conclusions

This paper reported on lessons learned in making environmental data available through LBS, using the WebPark project as an exemplar. The paper focused on representation and communication of geographic information and some of the steps required in order to enhance these components of GI. In particular the paper described the steps necessary to model locational information and an approach to real time generalization whilst maintaining geographic relationships.

Although the paper describes a single project, some important general lessons can be drawn, which have in general not been considered by the bulk of previous research focused on predominantly point based representations of the world (in an LBS context).

The first key lesson, described in section 3, is that environmental data are not commonly found in a form that is fit for the purpose of an LBS – a lesson with resonance to [7]. Typically, the data have been collected with an alternative purpose in mind and the process, and most importantly the effort required, to transform them for use in an LBS is non trivial.

The second lesson, encountered in sections 5 and 6, is that not all locational data and relationships are best represented as points. Dependent on the context and location of use multiple representations of the users' location and related phenomena may be appropriate, providing a rich and diverse set of potential query types and possibilities for interaction and understanding.

The final lesson, highlighted in section 7.2, is simple. Don't forget the geography. Environmental data rarely, if ever, exist in isolation and thus transformations must consider how to preserve geographically important relationships. This in turn requires us to consider how best we can explore data in order to identify such relationships and requires support from domain experts.

Acknowledgements

The authors gratefully acknowledge the support of the WebPark team (www.webparkservices.info - Geodan Mobile Solutions, EADS Systèmes & Information, City University London, Laboratório Nacional de Engenharia Civil, and the Swiss National Park), the European Commission for supporting the WebPark research (Project Number IST-2000-31041) and the Swiss State Sectretariat of Education and Research (SER) in relation to this project (BBW Nr. 01.0187-1). Eduardo Dias would like to thank the support from the Portuguese National Science Foundation (FCT/MCT) under the PhD grant SFRH/BD/12758/2003. The WebPark system continues to be developed and marketed through a spin-off company Camineo (www.camineo.com).

References

[1] Abderhalden, W., Krug, K.: Visitor Monitoring in the Swiss National Park – Towards Appropriate Information for the Wireless Consumer. Proc. 10th Int. Conf. on Information Technology and Travel & Tourism, ENTER 2003, Helsinki, 29-31 January, 2003.

[2] Abowd, G., Dey, A., Brown, P., Davies, N., Smith, M. and Steggles, P.:, Towards a Better Understanding of Context and Context-Awareness, in H-W. Gellersen, ed.,'Lecture Notes In Computer Science', Springer-Verlag, London, UK, pp. 304-307. 1999

[3] Agarwal, P.: 'Ontological considerations in GIScience', *International Journal of Geographical Information Science* 19(5), 501-536. 2005

[4] Barnes, S.: The Mobile Commerce Value Chain: Analysis and Future Developments. International Journal of Information Management 22, pp. 91-108, 2002.

[5] Berman, D., Bartell, J.T., and Salesin, D.: Multiresolution painting and composition, in 'Computer Graphics; Proceedings of SIGGRAPH'94', pp. 85-90.1994

[6] Cecconi, A., Galanda, M.: Adaptive Zooming in Web Cartography. Computer Graphics Forum, 21, pp. 787-799, 2002.

[7] Cheverst, K., Davies, N., Mitchell, K. and Friday, A.: Experiences of developing and deploying a context-aware tourist guide: the GUIDE project, in 'Proceedings of the 6th annual international conference on Mobile computing and networking (MobiCom '00)', ACM Press, New York, NY, USA, pp. 20--31. 2000

[8] de Berg, M., Bose, P., Cheong, O., Morin P.: On Simplifying Dot Maps. Computational Geometry, 27, pp. 43-62, 2004.

[9] Dias, E., Edwardes, A. J.: Information Flows in Nature Areas – Information Needs and Data supply for Location-based Services in Nature Areas. Proceedings GISPlanet 2005, Lisbon (CD-ROM), 2005.

[10] Dias, E.; Beinat, E. and Scholten, H.: Effects of Mobile Information Sharing in Natural Parks. Proceedings of ENVIROINFO 2004 vol. 2, 18th International Conference Informatics for Environmental Protection. Tricorne Editions, Geneva, pp. 11-25, 2004.

[11] Dourish, P.:'What we talk about when we talk about context', *Personal Ubiquitous Computing.* 8(1), 19-30. 2004.

[12] Edwardes, A., Burghardt, D., Weibel, R.: WebPark – Location Based Services for Species Search in Recreation Areas. In Proceedings of the 21st International Cartographic Conference (Durban: ICC), CD-ROM, 2003.

[13] Filli, F., Haller, R., Moritzi, M., Negri, M., Obrecht, J.-M., Robin, K., and Schuster, R.: 'Die Singvögel im Schweizerischen Nationalpark: Verbreitung anhand GIS-gestützter Habitatmodell', Jahresbericht der Naturforschenden Gesellschaft Graubünden, Chur, Band 109, S.47-90, 2000.

[14] Hu, H. & Lee, D.:,Semantic Location Modeling for Location Navigation in Mobile Environment, in 'Proceedings of the 2004 IEEE International Conference on Mobile Data Management (MDM'04)', pp. 52-61. 2004

[15] Jose, R., Moreira, A., Rodrigues, H. and Davies, N.: 'The AROUND architecture for dynamic location-based services', *Mobile Networks and Applications* 8(4), 377--387. 2003

[16] MacEachren, A.M.: *Some Truth with Maps: A primer on symbolization and design,* Association of American Geographers, Washington D. C.. 1994

[17] Openshaw, S. and Alvandies, S.: Applying geocomputation to the analysis of spatial distributions, In Goodchild M Longley P, eds.,'Geograhpic Information Systems: Principles, Techniques, Management and Applications', John Wiley and Sons Inc, New York, pp. 267--282. 1999

[18] O'Sullivan, D., Unwin, D.J.: Geographic Information Analysis (John Wiley), 2003.

[19] Raper, J., Dykes, J., Wood, J., Mountain, D., Krause, A. and Rhind, D.: 'A framework for evaluating geographical information', *Journal of information science* 28(2), 39--50. 2002

[20] Samet, H.: Applications of spatial data structures (Addison-Wesley: New York), 1990.

[21] Schlieder, C., Vögele, T. and Werner, A.: Location modeling for intentional behavior in spatial partonomies, In Proceedings of Ubicomp 2001: Workshop on "Location Modeling for Ubiquitous Computing", pp. 63--70. 2001

[22] SSC: Topographic Maps – Map Graphics and Generalization. Cartographic Publication Series, Vol. 17 (Swiss Society of Cartography: Bern), CD-ROM, 2005.

[23] Summerfield, M.A.: Global Geomorphology (Longman: London), 1991.

[24] Timpf, S.: Cartographic objects in a multi-scale data structure, *in* M. Craglia & H. Couclelis, ed., 'Geographic Information Research: bridging the Atlantic', Taylor & Francis, 1997.

[25] Vassiliadis, P., Simitsis, A. and Skiadopoulos, S.: Conceptual modeling for ETL processes, Proceedings of the 5th ACM international workshop on Data Warehousing and OLAP. ACM Press, New York, NY, USA, 2002.

[26] Weibel, R.: Generalization of Spatial Data – Principles and Selected Algorithms. In: van Kreveld, M., Nievergelt, J., Roos, T., Widmayer, P. (eds.): Algorithmic Foundations of Geographic Information Systems. Lecture Notes in Computer Science, Vol. 1340, Springer Verlag, Berlin et al., 99-152, 1997.

The Self-relocating Index Scheme for Telematics GIS[*]

Duksung Lim[1], Bonghee Hong[2], and Daesoo Cho[3]

[1] Division of Computer Information Technology, Yeungjin College,
#218, Bokhyun-dong, Buk-gu, Taegu, 702-721, Korea
junsung@yjc.ac.kr
[2] Department of Computer Engineering, Pusan National University,
Jangjeon-dong, Geumjeong-gu, Busan, 609-735, Korea
bhhong@pusan.ac.kr
[3] School of Internet Engineering, Dongseo University,
Jurye2-dong, Sasang-gu, Busan 617-716, Korea
dscho@dongseo.ac.kr

Abstract. The history management of vehicles is important in telematics applications. To process queries for history data, trajectories, we generally use trajectory-preserving index schemes based on the trajectory preservation property. This property means that a leaf node only contains segments belonging to a particular trajectory, regardless of the spatiotemporal locality of segments. The sacrifice of spatiotemporal locality, however, causes the index to increase the dead space of MBBs of non-leaf nodes and the overlap between the MBBs of nodes. Therefore, an index scheme for trajectories shows good performance with trajectory-based queries, but not with coordinate-based queries, such as range queries. We propose a new index scheme that improves the performance of range queries without reducing performance with trajectory-based queries. In the new index scheme using the *entry relocation strategy*, two entries in different nodes are exchanged to minimize the dead spaces of the MBBs of the corresponding nodes.

1 Introduction

In telematics applications for vehicles such as bus, taxi, and airplane, indexing of history data has become increasingly important. In moving-object databases for telematics applications, history data of moving objects are usually mapped to trajectories. Several types of spatiotemporal queries are processed against a database of those trajectories[5]. To improve the performance of these queries, an efficient indexing scheme for continuously moving objects is required.

Indexing schemes for trajectories should be able to answer efficiently not only *range queries* of the form, "Report all objects located within a specific area during a given time period", but also *combined queries* of the form, "What were the trajectories of objects for the next hour after they left a specific area in a specific time interval?" Combined queries are composed of the selection of trajectories (range

---

[*] This work was supported by the Regional Research Centers Program(Research Center for Logistics Information Technology), granted by the Korean Ministry of Education & Human Resources Development.

queries) and the extraction of sub-trajectories (navigational queries). Indexing structures could be implemented differently according to the intended query types.

R-tree variants, such as the 3D R-tree[4] and the MV3R-tree[2], are often called *locality-based indexing schemes,* because the R-tree structure inherently has a hierarchy based on spatiotemporal locality. Therefore, while they generally show good performance in range queries, the factor of locality in R-tree variants leads to a large number of node accesses in combined queries.

To enhance the performance of combined queries, *trajectory-preserving indexing schemes,* such as the TB-tree[5] and the OP-tree[1], were devised. These schemes have the trajectory preservation property that a leaf node only contains segments belonging to one trajectory, regardless of the spatiotemporal locality of the segments. As a result of this property, the TB-tree shows better performance with combined queries than locality-based indexing schemes. However, the processing cost for range queries increases in the TB-tree because of the dead-space problem described in detail in Section 2.

Table 1. Related indexing schemes (italic) and research scope of this paper (grayed)

Types of Indexing Schemes	Query Performance (Relative)		Examples
	Range Queries	**Combined Queries**	
Locality-based indexing schemes	*Good*	*Bad*	*3D R-tree, MV3R-tree, ...*
Trajectory-Preserving indexing scheme	*Bad*	*Good*	*TB-tree, OP-tree*
Self Relocating indexing scheme (our approach)	Better than *Trajectory-Preserving indexing scheme*	Better than *Locality-based indexing schemes*	*SRTB-tree*

Table 1 gives a brief summary of previous work related to indexing schemes for trajectories of moving objects, and describes the research scope of our work. The purpose of this paper is to enhance trajectory-preserving indexing schemes to improve the performance of range queries without any performance deterioration in combined queries.

The motivation of our work is that the MBBs of non-leaf nodes in trajectory-preserving indexing schemes have a large number of dead spaces, which cause the poor performance of range query processing. We have reduced this problem by revising trajectory-preserving indexing schemes using the entry relocation strategy. The key idea of this strategy is that two entries in different nodes are exchanged to minimize dead spaces in the MBBs of the corresponding nodes. Most research on indexing schemes focuses on how to minimize MBB enlargement when inserting entries, but our approach focuses on how to maximize the reduction in MBB size by exchanging inserted entries.

In this paper, we propose *the self relocating trajectory bundled tree(SRTB-tree),* which is used as the relocation method to minimize dead spaces in the MBBs of non-leaf nodes. We also propose algorithms for this index scheme, and present performance studies to compare new index scheme with legacy index schemes under a varying set of spatiotemporal queries.

Our performance tests show that the SRTB-tree outperforms the TB-tree for range queries. Additionally, with this index scheme, the TB-tree performance is maintained for trajectory-based queries.

The rest of the paper is organized as follows. Section 2 defines the problem of the trajectory preserving index scheme. Section 3 presents the SRTB-tree using the ER(entry relocation) strategy for minimizing dead spaces in the MBBs of the nodes. Section 4 shows the results of performance evaluation of the proposed index scheme. Finally, we summarize our contributions and provide suggestions for future work in Section 5.

2 Problem Descriptions

In this section, we examine the *dead-space problem* in trajectory preserving index schemes such as the TB-tree and the OP-tree. These indices inherently have dead spaces in both leaf nodes and non-leaf nodes. In this paper, the dead space is defined to be the extra area covered by the MBB of a node with respect to the area covered by MBBs of entries. In Fig. 1, we depict dead spaces for a moving object O_1, where the capacity of a node is three.

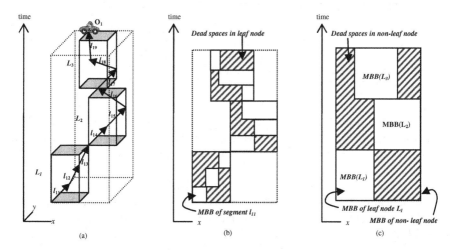

Fig. 1. Movements of a moving object O_1 and dead spaces. (a) MBBs of nodes; the subscript of each line segment shows the temporal order on the insertion. (b) Dead spaces of leaf nodes containing three line segments each in the x, t plane. (c) Dead spaces of a non-leaf node containing three leaf nodes R_1, R_2, and R_3 in the x, t plane.

There is no room to devise methods for decreasing dead spaces in leaf nodes because the trajectory-preserving indexing scheme strictly preserves trajectories in leaf nodes. We are therefore concerned with the dead-space problem in non-leaf nodes.

The dead-space problem in the trajectory-preserving indexing scheme results from the way entries are added to the non-leaf nodes. When a leaf node in the trajectory-preserving indexing scheme can accept no more entries, the index creates at least two elements: a new leaf node and an entry in a non-leaf node indicating the new node. A property of the entry in the non-leaf node is that it is stored in the most recent non-leaf node. That is, entries in non-leaf nodes are stored in order of creation time. Entries in non-leaf nodes at the same level are thus sorted by creation time.

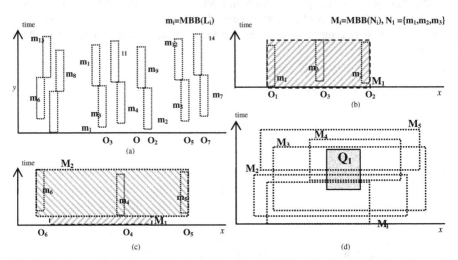

Fig. 2. Overlaps and dead spaces in non-leaf nodes. (a) MBBs of leaf nodes L_i when inserted in temporal order (b) the MBB M_1 of the non-leaf node N_1 created first contains m_1, m_2, and m_3 (c) the MBB M_2 of the second created non-leaf node N_2 containing m_4, m_5, and m_6 (d) Query Region Q_1 and MBBs of non-leaf nodes containing leaf nodes.

Assume line segments have been inserted in numerical order. Fig. 2 shows MBBs(m_1–m_{14}) of leaf nodes for moving objects O_1–O_7 in the TB-tree. Leaf nodes were created in insertion order regardless of spatial locality, and MBBs(M_1–M_5) of non-leaf nodes were also created in insertion order.

Fig. 2(d) shows the query region Q_1 and the MBBs(M_1–M_5) of the non-leaf nodes containing leaf nodes L_1–L_{14}. These MBBs have large amounts of dead space as well as high overlaps. In our example Fig. 2(d), to process query range Q_1, we must access all non-leaf nodes.

3   The Self-relocating Trajectory Bundled Tree

The SRTB-tree has two properties. One is a trajectory preserving property which a leaf node has entries with same trajectory ID and nodes with same trajectory is connected. The other is a self relocating property to minimize dead spaces and overlaps between non-leaf nodes.

The first property is common in trajectory preserving index scheme such as the TB-tree and the OP-tree. The structure of an entry in leaf nodes consists of segment ID, MBB, and direction. The leaf node has trajectory ID, entries, left node pointer, right node pointer. Because a leaf node has sub-trajectories with same trajectory ID, leaf node stores a trajectory ID. The left/right node pointer indicates a node with previous/next sub-trajectories. This structure of leaf nodes is useful for processing navigational queries.

For the second property, our basic idea is to exchange entries between non-leaf nodes that have large dead spaces and high overlaps of MBBs. Fig. 3(a) shows the index structure when line segments were inserted in numeric order. The non-leaf node N_1 has entries for leaf nodes L_1, L_2, and L_3, while the non-leaf node N_2 has entries for L_4, L_5, and L_6. Because M_1 is contained by M_2 in the x axis, the overlap between two leaf nodes is very high. In addition, M_2 has a large dead space.

Because m_6 in Fig. 3(a) has low spatial locality in the non-leaf node N_2, we could exchange m_6 with m_2 in the non-leaf node N_1. Fig. 3(b) shows a tree sample created by relocating entries to minimize dead space. The consequence is that there is no overlap between non-leaf nodes N_1 and N_2, and dead spaces are smaller than those in Fig. 3(a).

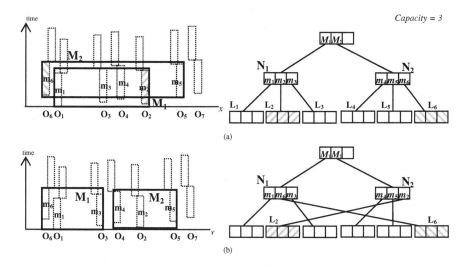

Fig. 3. Overlap and dead space in non-leaf nodes. (a) MBBs and the structure of nodes when inserted in temporal order. (b) MBBs and the structure of nodes after entry relocation.

3.1 Insertion Algorithm

The insertion process is based on the top-down procedure known from the TB-tree and the R-tree. But, methods for relocating entries in non-leaf nodes and searching the leaf node inserting new entry are considerably different.

Algorithm Insert(N,E)

I1 [Find position for new entry] Set N to be the root node. Invoke *FindNode(N,L)* to select a leaf node L in which to place E.

I2 [Add entry to leaf node] If L has room for another

entry to insert E. Otherwise make a new leaf node LL containing E.

I3 [Propagate change upward] Invoke *AdjustTree(L,LL)*.

I4[Grow tree taller] If a new node is created in depth 0, create a new root whose children are the two resulting node.

Algorithm FindNode(N,E)

F1 [Leaf check] If N is a leaf with same trajectory ID and right pointer is null, return N. If right pointer is not null, return right most leaf node N using right pointer in the leaf node.

F2 [Choose Subtree] If N is not a leaf, let {F} be the entry in N whose MBB is overlapped E.

F3 [Descent until a leaf node is reached] Set N to be the child node pointed to by each F and repeat from F1.

Algorithm AdjustTree(N,NN)

A1 [Check if done] If N is the root and NN is not null, create new root. If N is the root and NN is null, stop.

A2 [Relocating Check] If N is a non-leaf node and fixed (no more insertion are possible), Invoke *RelocatingEntry(N)*, and Adjust MBBs of affected node.

A3 [Adjust MBB] Let P be the parent node of N, and let E_N be N's entry in P. Adjust the MBB of E_N so that it tightly encloses all entry in N.

A4 [Move up to next level] Set N=P and NN=PP if new node is created. Repeat from A2.

RelocatingEntry is described in the following section.

3.2 Entry Relocation Algorithm

Entries are exchanged in two nodes called an event node and a target node. In this section we propose three methods to select target nodes. A target node containing entries to be exchanged should be overlapped with an event node. From this property we define a *candidate node* that satisfies the following: the node's level is the same as that of the event node, the node overlaps with the event node, and the node's MBB is fixed: The MBB of the node to be full is no more expansion because no more entry is inserted.

3.2.1 Exhaustive Method

The most straightforward way to minimize dead spaces with overlapped nodes is to exchange entries until no more shrinkage of dead spaces occurs. This method repeats the following four steps. First, find candidate nodes that overlap with an event node. Next, generate all possible groupings that can be created by exchanging one entry in the event node with one entry in each candidate node. Third, choose the grouping that offers minimum dead spaces. Finally, exchange those entries. However, the number of all possible groupings is k^2M^3 in the worst case, where k is the number of nodes overlapping with the event node, and M is the value of the fan-out for a non-leaf node. If page size is 1k and each entry consists of a pair of x, y, t and child node pointer, a typical value for M is 35, so the number of possible relocation cases is very large. We implemented the exhaustive algorithm to use as a standard for comparison with other algorithms, but it was too slow to use with large node sizes.

Algorithm Relocating Entry(N)

E1 [Find Candidate Nodes] Find candidate nodes {C$_i$} that overlap with an event node N. Stop if no candidate node is found.

E2 [Select Target Node] Select a target node T containing an entry E$_i$ that could maximally reduce dead spaces by exchanging with an entry E$_j$ in node N. (E$_i$∈T, E$_j$∈N, T∈{C$_i$}). Stop if no target node is found.

E3 [Exchange Entries] Exchange entry E$_i$ with entry E$_j$ in nodes T and N. Repeat from E2

3.2.2 Entry Relocation Method Based on Largest Dead Space

This method attempts to find the most wasteful dead space, but is not guaranteed to minimize dead spaces in all nodes.

The algorithm picks candidate nodes that overlap an event node at the same level. The cost is $n\log n$ to find candidate nodes (S1). Unlike the exhaustive method, this method chooses one target node to exchange entries with the event node (S2).

The condition for selecting a target node is that dead spaces are maximally reduced by exchanging entries. To achieve minimum dead spaces in both nodes, we use a quadratic-cost algorithm in the R*-tree [6].

```
Algorithm Relocating Entry In Highest Dead Spaces(N)

S1 [Find Candidate Nodes] Find candidate nodes {Cᵢ}
that overlap with an event node N. Stop if no
candidate node is found.

S2 [Select Target Node] Select target node T
containing an entry Eᵢ that could maximally reduce
dead spaces by exchanging entries Eⱼ in node N. Stop
if no target node is found.

S3 [Exchange Entries] Exchange entries Eᵢ with Eⱼ in
nodes T and N.
```

3.2.3 Entry Relocation Method Based on Highest Overlap

This method is almost identical to the second method but uses the most overlapped node as a target node. The overlap is the critical factor in minimizing node accesses in range queries. This method directly shrinks overlaps between nodes whereas the second method decreases the source of overlaps.

```
Algorithm Relocating Entry In Highest Overlaps(N)

O1 [Find Candidate Nodes] Find candidate nodes {Cᵢ}
that overlap with an event node N. Stop if no
candidate node is found.

O2 [Select Target Node] Select the target node T that
has the highest overlap with the event node N in
candidate nodes {Cᵢ}.

O3 [Exchange Entries] Exchange entries Eᵢ with Eⱼ in
nodes T and N.
```

4 Performance Comparison

In this section, we compare three index schemes: the R*-tree, the TB-tree, and the SRTB-tree with three methods, using a variety of sets of data and queries. The performance studies were conducted using C# implementations. For the parameters in the experiments, we have chosen the page size for leaf and non-leaf nodes to be 1024 bytes. With this page size, the fan-out for all methods is 31 for leaf nodes and 35 for non-leaf nodes. For fair comparison, no buffer mechanism is used.

Because of the lack of real data for trajectories, our performance study consists of experiments on synthetic datasets. We utilized the GSTD generator [7] of spatio-temporal datasets to create trajectories of moving objects under various distributions.

In our performance study, the parameters of the generator were given the following values. The initial distribution of points was Gaussian. The movement of points was always ruled by a random distribution, thus achieving an unbiased spread of the points in the workspace. The number of different possible snapshots was held constant at 1000. Finally, we used datasets for line segments that consisted of two consecutive points, and the number of moving objects varied between 10 and 2000, resulting in datasets consisting of between 10 K and 2000 K entries.

4.1 Query Performance

Range queries are important for spatial data as well as spatiotemporal data. In this section, we compare five methods for processing range queries. As already mentioned, we used datasets ranging from 10 to 2000 moving objects. We used three sets of query windows with a range of 5%, 10%, and 20% of the total range with respect to each dimension, or 0.125%, 0.1%, and 0.8% of the total space. Each query set included 1000 query windows.

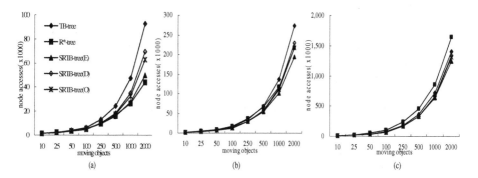

Fig. 4. Range queries: varying range (a) 5%, (b) 10%, and (c) 20% in each dimension

Fig. 4 shows the number of total node accesses for the various range queries and datasets. For various numbers of moving objects, the patterns for the three methods for the SRTB-tree, SRTB-tree(Exhaustive), SRTB-tree(highest Dead space), and SRTB-tree(highest Overlap) are similar. For large range queries, the Exhaustive method shows superior performance over the other methods. Moreover, we drew the following conclusions.

- Reducing dead spaces is more efficient for a small number of trajectories than a large number of trajectories.
- Reducing overlaps is more efficient for a large number of trajectories than a small number of trajectories.
- The critical factor for small range queries is the spatiotemporal locality, whereas the temporal ordering is more critical for large range queries.

In the performance studies for time-slice queries(Fig. 5), we chose 10%, 50%, and 100% of the respective range in each spatial dimension. This corresponds to three sets, each comprising 1000 individual queries. For each set of queries with spatial constraints, the TB-tree shows poor performance. In addition, as a spatial range increases, the trend is for the differences in performance for five methods to decrease. This is why we did not consider spatial constraints for queries with 100% spatial range.

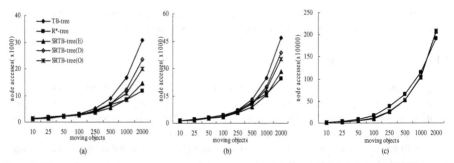

Fig. 5. Time-slice queries: varying spatial range (a) 10%, (b) 50%, and (c) 100% in each dimension

Performance results (Fig. 6) for combined queries show that all methods except for the R*-tree have similar performance. Three methods for relocating entries cause no deterioration of trajectory-related queries.

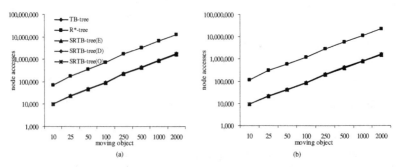

Fig. 6. Combined queries: (a) 5% inner–10% outer range and (b) 5% inner–20% outer range in total dimension

5   Conclusions and Future Work

The indexing scheme for trajectory-related queries must process classical range and time-slice queries efficiently, as well as navigational queries. However, it has poor performance in range and time-slice queries because the index scheme has a large amount of dead space.

This paper addresses the problem of dead spaces in non-leaf nodes resulting from creating nodes in insertion order to preserve trajectories. To minimize dead spaces, we propose the SRTB-tree with three entry relocation methods that shrink the MBBs of non-leaf nodes. This is accomplished by exchanging entries in an event node with entries in target nodes. Most research on indexing structures focuses on minimizing the enlargement of MBBs of nodes while inserting data, but our approach is to maximize the shrinkage of the MBBs when they have become fixed.

The main technical contribution of this paper is summarized below. We have developed the index scheme using the entry relocation strategy to reduce dead spaces in non-leaf nodes as follows:

1. We have defined the dead space problem in trajectory preserving index schemes.
2. We have defined relocation methods that identify entries to exchange: exhaustive, highest dead space, and highest overlap.

Although the SRTB-tree based on the entry relocation strategy improves the performance of range and time-slice queries in trajectory-preserving indexing schemes, the problem of indexing of trajectories with constraints remains unsolved. We are currently developing a spatiotemporal indexing scheme for static objects and moving objects with RFID.

References

1. Hongjun Zhu, Jianwen Su, Oscar H. Ibarra: Trajectory queries and octagons in moving object databases. In Proc. of CIKM (2002) 413–421
2. Yufei Tao, Dimitris Papadias: MV3R-Tree: A Spatio-Temporal Access Method for Timestamp and Interval Queries. In Proc. of VLDB (2001) 431–440
3. Anil Kumar, Vassilis J. Tsotras, and Christos Faloutsos: Designing Access Methods for Bitemporal Databases. TKDE Vol.10 No.1 (1998) 1–20
4. Antonin Guttman: R-Trees: A Dynamic Index Structure for Spatial Searching. In Proc. of SIGMOD (1984) 47–57
5. Dieter Pfoser, Christian S. Jensen, and Yannis Theodoridis: Novel Approaches in Query Processing for Moving Object Trajectories. In Proc. of VLDB (2000) 395–406
6. N. Beckmann and H. P. Kriegel: The R*-tree: An Efficient and Robust Access Method for Points and Rectangles. In Proc. of ACM SIGMOD (1990) 332–331
7. Theodoridis, Y., Silva, R., and Nascimento, M, "On the Generation of Spatiotemporal Datasets", In Proc. of the 6th Int'l Symposium on Spatial Databases, pp. 147–164, 1999.
8. Michael F.Worboys, "GIS: A Computing Perspective", Taylor & Francis, 1995.

Location Polling Algorithm for Alerting Service Based on Location

Byung-Ik Ahn[1], Sung-Bong Yang[1], Heui-Chae Jin[2], and Jin-Yul Lee[3]

[1] Dept. of Computer Science, Yonsei Univ. 126-749 Seoul, Korea
biahn@pointi.com, yang@cs.yonsei.ac.kr
http://algo.yonsei.ac.kr
[2] Dept. of E-Business, Cheonan Univ. 330-704 Cheonan, Korea
hcjin@paran.com
[3] LBS Lab., POINT-I Co, Ltd., 135-080 Seoul, Korea
jinylee@pointi.com

Abstract. Location Alerting Service is a push service that informs users whether predefined conditions be satisfied based on periodic acquisitions of location data from mobile terminals for several purposes such as safety. Polling the location of terminal is one of the basic functional requirements of this service. In this paper, an analysis of the location polling technique will be given, we will propose an efficient location polling algorithm and present the results of experiments with this algorithm.

1 Introduction

Location Alerting Service is a service that notifies users through SMS or provides a specific service that already has been defined by the users in the case of event such as entering, being and outing occurring in a specific region or established territory by monitoring the location of terminal users in the mobile communication network[1][2].

Location Alerting Service is a very personalized push type service. As for the examples of such service, there are Location Advertising Service, L-Commerce, Location Meeting/Matching Service, Polluted Area Alerting Service, Disaster Sensing Service, and Distribution Control Service.

An important technique of such location alerting service is either concerned about which method the location generation equipment uses or about scheduling for location acquisition. In relation to the type of location generation equipment, whether the location determination equipment is a server or a terminal becomes an issue and in relation to the scheduling for location acquisition, kind of method used in determining the location of mobile terminal either periodically or by calculation within the established time becomes an issue. Generally, the location determination equipment inspects and reports trigger condition by determining the location at the server or terminal at a fixed interval, for example, every five minutes, regardless of each method. However, a system that has large number of users, such as mobile communication, causes excessive location determination, and ultimately increases the network load.

Therefore, this paper will examine techniques that could accurately perceive and report trigger conditions while reducing the number of position acquisition by

K.-J. Li and C. Vangenot (Eds.): W2GIS 2005, LNCS 3833, pp. 104–114, 2005.

dynamically changing the position acquisition period and based on such examination, will present and evaluate an algorithm of efficient location determination method for alerting service. Section 2 examines location polling technique and method for alert service and Section 3 derives strengths, weaknesses and problems of location polling method and techniques. Section 4 develops a new AlertPoint algorithm based on the existing problems and Section 5 evaluates this method through an experiment.

2 Location Polling Technique and Method

A tracking technique for the location of mobile terminal in the location alerting service is the location polling technique. Location polling technique is divided into network polling technique(server polling technique) and intelligent polling technique (terminal polling technique) based on whether the location determination agent is a server or terminal in accordance with the location determination method. Server polling technique uses determination method of Cell-ID, TOQQ, AOA, TDOA, E-OTD and MS-Assisted GPS, and terminal determination technique uses determination method of MS-Based GPS and S-GPS[8][9].

2.1 Server Location Polling Technique

Server location polling technique is a technique that polls the location information using the internal server of mobile communication and wireless network. A method that uses MSC/HLR (Mobile Station Center / Home Location Register)[1] and a method that uses location acquisition polling server have been used to materialize the existing location alerting service[4]. The method that uses MSC/HLR is a method of acquiring location from the process of shifting the location of terminal user to HLR through sensing the update of VLR (Visitor Location Register). This requires a change of software directly on MSC/HLR. The method that uses position acquisition polling server is a method that acquires the location of user through requests to MSC and MPC of mobile communication companies by dynamically scheduling the interval of position acquisition time. The former of these two methods possesses a security level that is difficult for an ordinary service company to approach and also has the problem of having to directly adjust MSC/HLR. On the other side, the latter method is easily accomplished through a contract with each communication network company. Consequently, majority of existing location alerting service applies the latter model.

Location polling server is composed of location acquisition model engine, location request scheduler and alerting engine. The location acquisition interface is the standard for location request/reply between the location polling server and wireless mobile communication and mobile RAN network and is designated as MLP(Mobile Location Protocol) in the case of mobile communication network. Push interface is the standard for alerting engine to transmit messages. The location acquisition model engine is an important factor that calculates the location acquisition time intervals through algorithm. The location request scheduler schedules all of the calculated location acquisition time intervals. Lastly, the alerting engine inspects the trigger conditions with the location information of the mobile terminal and alerts through the push interface when satisfied. This paper describes a location acquisition model, which is an important technology of location acquisition model engine.

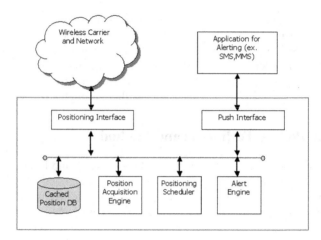

Fig. 1. Structure of Server Location Polling Service

2.2   Terminal Location Polling Technique

Terminal location polling technique is a method that could be applied to MS-based GPS and S-GPS determination techniques. This technique allows possible location determination by the terminal itself based on the initial information and data communication occurs between the server and the terminal to attempt synchronization with the sever when it diverges from the established threshold or satisfies the optional conditions. The attempt of synchronization between the server and terminal is a process of synchronizing the conditions calculated based on the territory of spatial trigger requested from the server to the terminal. Reliability on sensing the event occurring at the time when the trigger conditions have been satisfied can be acquired through such synchronization. Since this technique does not use the network determination method, there is an advantage of not having to consider the network load from the determination, but also possesses a disadvantage where network load communication for attempting synchronization exists. The greatest weakness is not being able to load GPS chip of high accuracy due to the function of mobile terminal and many of the mobile terminal don't mount GPS chip.

As shown in Figure 2, there exist Location Assistant of the terminal, Location Cash Database of the server, Tracking Module and Alerting Engine in the terminal location polling server and is divided into Synchronization Interface between Location Assistant and Tracking Module and Push Interface between Alerting Engine and Alerting Application. Location Assistant of the terminal carries out location determination and obtains present geographical location information of the terminal by communicating with artificial satellite and also evaluates conditions for synchronization with the server and communicates with the server. Tracking Module of the server calculates and transmits new condition to the terminal based on the location information obtained from the terminal. Alerting Engine evaluates trigger condition based on location information and transmits message to Alerting Application.

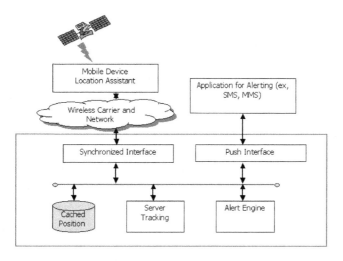

Fig. 2. Structure of Terminal Location Polling Service

3   Examples of Position Acquisition Method and Service

3.1   Position Acquisition Model

When storing location information of the terminal or acquiring location information, Position Acquisition Model aims to decrease overhead on network load and communication cost by requesting location information on the mobile communication network and LBS platform and reducing the number of acquisition within the range of not reducing the reliability of the location information.

Position Acquisition Model is classified into a method that does not request unnecessary location information by analyzing mobile pattern and a method that dynamically reduces the number of inquiries on location information by appropriately adjusting the intervals of location acquisition time. The flowing methods are being used[6][7][10].

Static Acquisition Model. Acquires location by setting the position acquisition time at regular intervals

Distance-Based Acquisition Model. Adjusts position acquisition time interval through changes in amount of distance based on standard distance

Respective Distance-Based Acquisition Model. Adjusts position acquisition time interval through differences in the standard distance of each terminal user and continuous condition changes of the terminal location

Group-Based Acquisition Model. Adjusts position acquisition time interval based on the amount of change in MBR(Minimum Boundary Rectangle) to the recent distance

Predict-Based Acquisition Model. Adjusts position acquisition time interval by predicting the next mobile location through a verified prediction model using direction and speed, which are the mobile information of terminal users in the past

Dynamic Acquisition Model. Operates the same with Static Acquisition Model but adjusts position acquisition time interval from system load

Among the position acquisition models, Static Acquisition Model, Distance-based Acquisition Model, Respective Distance-based Acquisition Model, and Group-based Acquisition Model are designed to minimize the number of position acquisition and maximize perception rate of event occurrence by adjusting position acquisition time interval based on important parameter of each model. However, on the other hand, Predict-based Acquisition Model and Dynamic Acquisition Model are models that stabilize the system by appropriately adjusting or apportioning time intervals from system load.

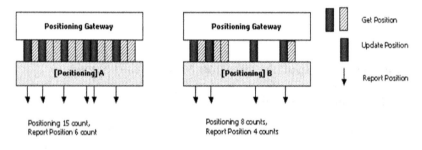

Fig. 3. Concept of Position Acquisition Model

Position Acquisition Model generally used up until now is Static Acquisition Model. It is a method that carries out location determination of mobile terminal at a fixed interval of time. The number of position acquisition is 144 times in 10 minute intervals based on 24 hour standard and it corresponds to 140 million times if service request for total of 1 million people. Such would cause network traffic and reduce economical adequacy of provided service. Therefore, the purpose of location polling technique is to perceive a significant point of time when event will occur to provide service with the minimum number of position acquisition.

The minimum number of position acquisition and the event perception rate are closely related to one another. In other words, as the number of position acquisition increases within a specific time, the period of position acquisition reduces and then causes more accurate perception of the point of time when the event would occur. However, this brings decline in the function of overall system with the load increase of mobile communication network. On the other side, when the number of position acquisition decreases, the perception rate for event occurrence reduces and causes decrease in the reliability of service. Thus, it is necessary to minimize the number of position acquisition within the range where the perception rate of event occurrence could be trusted.

3.2 Service Examples

WaveAlert Model. WaveMarket uses a method that supports the search for nearest alert request through Scheduler that adjusts position acquisition time by calculating MATT (Minimum Alert Triggering Time) and EAUT (Earliest Available Update Time) and territory division grouping of alert request area[3]. MATT is a future time value acquired from dividing the calculated distance (Euclid distance, Shortest Path distance, etc.) from the position of terminal user to the user's aimed location by the calculated maximum speed. EAUT is a renewal time with reception for the data acquired from request to renew a new MATT. In such case, previously acquired data is disregarded. In other words, as shown in Figure 4, the location data determined from the time between EAUT and MATT is valid and such data is used in the renewal of next MATT or EAUT.

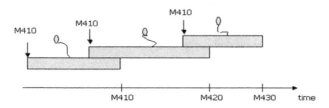

Fig. 4. Concept of MATT & EAUT

This solution has an outstanding function in the number of minimum position acquisition and event perception rate. On the other side, there is a disadvantage of high calculation cost of the software since algorithm for regional division of alert request is complex. As a solution to such problem, WaveAlert realizes division algorithm with hardware.

Cell ID Synchronization Location Polling Technique. Cell ID Synchronization Location Polling Technique is a method that minimizes the system load of mobile communication network by distinguishing a point of polling time on its own using location assistant software and receiving trigger assistant information from the trigger server by expanding the function of mobile terminal[4]. There is an advantage of minimizing the network load by carrying out precise position acquisition through mobile communication network when it exists in Cell ID list once the Location Assistant software within the terminal is transmitted to currently communicated Cell ID by transmitting base station Cell ID information, which includes Alert Zone, to the terminal. However, Cell ID has the network load where the server has to transmit Cell ID of alert zone to the terminal when a new alert request is received and needs support in the hardware part of the terminal equipment in order to bring the communicated base station ID, which is Cell ID. Moreover, Location Assistant software must exist in memory. The most important disadvantage is the fact that the number of precise position acquisition increases only when the zone that includes the registered Cell ID in the terminal is large or numerous cell IDs exist.

Update Policy Synchronization Location Polling Technique. Update Policy Synchronization Location Poling Technique has the server transmit update policy to the terminal and the terminal acquires position using GPS determination technique at a fixed time interval at the time of initial operation. The acquired position continues with the position acquisition at a fixed interval of time if it does not satisfy the server and the synchronized update policy. There are distance-based policy, vector-based policy, and street network-based policy and they differ accordingly to each service circumstances. The strength of this technique is the relatively great reduction in network load from the updated polices but with the burden on the terminal from the continuous location determination and the consumers' tendency to refuse, it can't be applied as a location polling technique for alert serve in a vast range of zones.

4 AlertPoint Location Polling Algorithm

AlertPoint adjusts the position acquisition time based on Distance-Ratio based Acquisition Model that bases on moving distance ratio and proposes algorithm for insert process of grouping and new request for one to multiple requests.

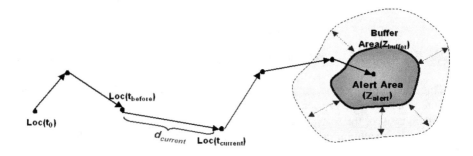

Fig. 5. Entering the Alert Zone

Set α is the ratio of distance ($d_{current}$) of current time ($t_{current}$) and before time (t_{before}) to distance (d_{before}) of before time (t_{before}) and former time (t_0).

When $0 < \alpha < 1$, position acquisition time (t_{next}) increases by Δt ($1/\alpha \times t_{unit}$)
and $\alpha \geq 1$, position acquisition time (t_{next}) decreases by Δt ($\alpha \times t_{unit}$).

This technique is similar to the concept of Respective Distance-based Acquisition Model but it carries out dynamic time adjustment and controls the infinitely increasing Δt by calculating static valid time section accordingly to the distance with the Buffer Zone for high perception rate of event occurrence. Moreover, the grouping process from alert request reduces the number of position acquisition by distinguishing whether or not to carry out the position acquisition for the alert request. As shown in Figure 6, when the location of terminal user is included in the Buffer Zone, time adjustment is set as the time value to minimize the possibility of the user's location getting out of the alert zone.

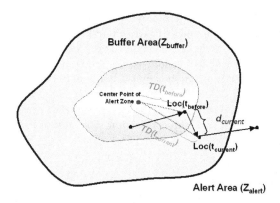

Fig. 6. Leaving the Alert Zone

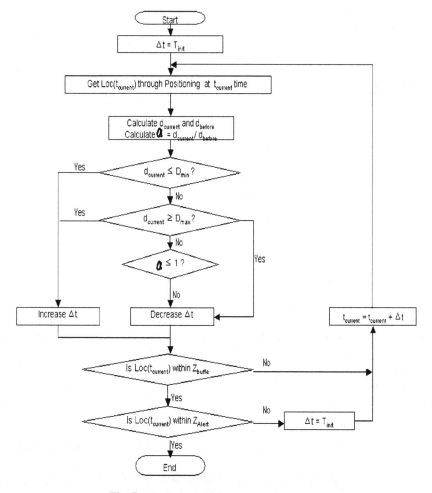

Fig. 7. AlertPoint Position Acquisition Model

Figure 7 shows a diagram of AlertPoint's Position Acquisition Model. When the ratio of moving distance used to obtain the time interval of position acquisition is very dramatic, the value comes out to be very large. This problem is resolved by adjusting the minimal moving distance (D_{min}) and maximum moving distance (D_{max}) by searching for the minimum error in position acquisition through the mobile communication network and the distance affected by base station.

AlertPoint Solution supports the grouping process of alert request. Accordingly, it reduces the number of position acquisition from unconditional position acquisition when a new request is inserted.

5   Experiment and Test

1,000 sample data have been generated for the performance test on data distribution per moving distance on AlertPoint. The alert zone entering of this data is 95% and the alert zone non-entering is 5%. 16 hours of location data has been traced.

As for the characteristic of the data, 50% was the case (for instance, housewives, students, office workers) that repeatedly stop and move at 2-3 locations, 25% was the case that continuously move to various locations after making stops, 15% was the case that move to various locations without long stop and 10% was the case that move to a wide zone without any stop.

The following Figure 8 shows the speed distribution of the sample group.

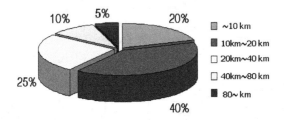

Fig. 8. Mobility Distribution of Sample Group

Let's experiment the optimal performance function by setting the standard radius of Alert Zone to be 1 km and using 5 minutes for Tmin, which is generally used in such experiment. Find the optimal value from the test and Vmax values of 20, 40, 50, 60, 70, 80, 90, 100, 120 Km when the Buffer Size is 1, 2, 3, 4, 5, 6 Km.

The evaluation of the overall function at this time is set as,

Performance =   (Total number of Alert engine location inquiry× 100)/total number of periodically location inquiry (5 minutes)

and   Alert Event Perception Rate is

Alert Event = (Total number of Final Alert Request(100)/Total number of Alerting Request.

The results of experiment in accordance with each variable are shown by Figure 9 and 10.

data Set	Buffer size (km)	TIME_MIN (min)	TIME_MAX (min)	V_MAX (km/h)	Total Number of Positioing by Alert Engine	Total number of Positioning by Static Engine (5 min)	Alerting count	The average of Positioing rate	catching rate of Alerting	Total Performance
1000	6.0	5	60	80	57,038	130,003	919	47.91%	91.90%	43.87%
1000	5.0	5	60	80	53,485	130,463	910	44.97%	91.00%	41.00%
1000	4.0	5	60	80	50,200	131,249	892	42.17%	89.20%	38.25%
1000	3.0	5	60	80	46,410	132,558	867	38.82%	86.70%	35.01%
1000	2.0	5	60	80	42,529	135,005	819	35.26%	81.90%	31.50%
1000	1.0	5	60	80	39,430	137,964	755	32.29%	75.50%	28.58%

Fig. 9. Alert Event and Performance by Buffer Size

data Set	Buffer size (km)	TIME_MIN (min)	TIME_MAX (min)	V_MAX (km/h)	Total Number of Positioing by Alert Engine	Total number of Positioning by Static Engine (5 min)	Alerting count	The average of Positioing rate	catching rate of Alerting	Total Performance
1000	5.0	5	60	120	56,565	130,473	912	47.33%	91.20%	43.35%
1000	5.0	5	60	100	55,416	130,410	911	46.49%	91.10%	42.49%
1000	5.0	5	60	90	54,489	130,165	918	45.78%	91.80%	41.86%
1000	5.0	5	60	80	53,485	130,463	910	44.97%	91.00%	41.00%
1000	5.0	5	60	70	52,315	131,200	901	44.00%	90.10%	39.87%
1000	5.0	5	60	60	51,411	130,723	908	43.34%	90.80%	39.33%
1000	5.0	5	60	50	49,415	130,778	909	41.76%	90.90%	37.79%
1000	5.0	5	60	40	47,048	130,529	912	39.96%	91.72%	36.04%
1000	5.0	5	60	20	41,065	130,472	908	35.12%	91.41%	31.47%

Fig. 10. Alert Event and Performance from Vmax Change

According to the result of this experiment, it has been verified that Alerting Event Perception Rate demonstrates over 95% of performance in most cases while improving the performance by reducing the number of location inquiry for alert by over 60% in general.

The result advices that using AlertPoint method, which could perceive 95% of event, is efficient if the importance of alert is not especially an urgent matter. Moreover, AlertPoint method has been recognized that it can be used appropriately in the reduction of network load when a large number of mobile terminal users request location alert since it can overcome the weakness of fixed time interval method of Static Acquisition Model, which has been generally used up until now.

6 Conclusion

Location-based Alerting Service has been developing as diversified and advanced personal service based on accurate location determination with the advancement of wireless determination method and the improvement in terminal performance. Consequently, the number of subscribers using the wireless network will increase and the wireless network load will gradually increase as well. Accordingly, mutual comparative evaluation between the reduction in the number of location determination and the reliability of service was necessary for the purpose of minimizing the network load.

This paper aims to use more efficient location polling method by analyzing location polling technique and presenting a new method to resolve problems. The location polling method presented in the paper proposes a method of appropriate scheduling and does not fall behind Static Acquisition Model, which has been developed previously and used up until now, in performance such as location inquiry and Alert Event Perception. If there is a gradual increase in the use of location-based service and the necessity of alerting service, AlertPoint method seems efficient in managing the system and the network load.

References

1. Ki Jun Han. : Standardization and Research Development of Location-Based Service (LBS). Informationization Policy Volume 10, 4th Edition (2003)
2. Korea IT Industry Promotion Agency. : "Location-Based Service (LBS)", Software Market News of Korea IT Industry Promotion Agency (2003)
3. WaveMarket Incorporated. : A System that Provides Alert-Based Service to Base Stations from Wireless Communication Network. Korea's Public Patent Notification, Application # 10-2004-700651 (2004)
4. Min, K. W., Cho, D. S.: Moving Object Position Acquisition Technique for LBS. Thesis Magazine Vol.1 (2003) of Korea Information Processing Society
5. Yun, J. K., Kim, D. O. & Han. K. J.: Development of Real-Time Mobile GIS supporting the open Location Service. Proc. of Geotec Event Conference.(2003)
6. Dieter Pfoser, Christian S. Jensen. : Capturing the Uncertainty of Moving-Object Representations. SSD (1999) pp.111-132
7. Ouri Wolfson, S. Chamberlain, S. Dao, L. Jiang, G. Mendez. : Cost and Imprecision in Modeling the Position of Moving Objects. Proceedings of the Fourteenth International Conference on Data Engineering (ICDE14) (1998)
8. OGC. : OpenGIS Location Services (OpenLS): Core Services, (2004)
9. Green, J., Betti, D. & Davison, J. : Mobile Location Services: Market Strategies, White Paper. , Ovum, (2000)
10. A. Prasad Sistla, Ouri Wolfson, Sam Chamberlain, Son Dao. : Querying the Uncertain Position of Moving Objects. Temporal Databases, Dagstuhl (1997) 310-337
11. T-S. Yeh, B. de Cambray. : Modeling Highly Variable Spatio-Temporal Data. PRiSM TR, 1994/50(1994)
12. Guttman, : A.:R-trees: a Dynamic Index Structure for Spatial Searching. In Proceedings of the ACM-SIGMOD Conference on the Management of Data, pp. 47-57(1984)
13. Luca Forlizzi, Ralf Hartmut Guting, Enrico Nardelli, Markus Schneider. : A Data Model and Data Structures for Moving Objects Databases. SIGMOD Conference (2000) 319-330
14. 3GPP : TS 23.271 V 6.7.0 chapter 9.5, (2004)
15. Yufei Tao, Dimitris Papadias. : Efficient Historical R-trees. IEEE SSDBM, (2001)
16. Yannis Theodoridis, Michael Vazirgiannis, Timos Sellis. : Spatio-Temporal Indexing for Large Multimedia Applications. ICMCS (1996)
17. Dieter Pfoser, Christian S.Jensen, Yannis Theodoridis. : Novel Approaches to the Indexing of Moving Object Trajectories. VLDB (2000)
18. Dieter Pfoser, Yannis Theodoridis, and Christian S. Jensen. : Indexing Trajectories of Moving Point Objects. CHOROCHRONOS Technical Report CH-99-03. (1999)

A Design of Telematics Application Framework on Ubiquitous Sensor Networks

Eunkyu Lee[1], Minsoo Kim[1], Byung Tae Jang[1], and Myoung Ho Kim[2]

[1] Telematics.USN Research Division, ETRI
161, Kajeong-dong, Yuseong-gu, Daejeon, Republic of Korea
{ekyulee, minsoo, jbt}@etri.re.kr
[2] Korea Advanced Institute of Science and Technology
373-1, Guseong-dong, Yuseong-gu, Daejeon, Republic of Korea
mhkim@dbserver.kaist.ac.kr

Abstract. In this paper, we introduce new types of Telematics services for a convergence of Telematics and USN technology and explain several requirements needed for those services. Then, we propose a Telematics application framework that can satisfy those requirements of a real-time service, a reliable data acquisition, and an efficient query processing. The framework is composed of Telematics sensor nodes, Telematics service station, and Telematics vehicle that can provide users with reliable and real-time traffic safety services. Also, we present important issues and solutions that can be applied to an implementation of the framework; In-network spatial query processing, vehicle location determination, and real-time and reliable routing protocol. It is expected that this framework can be helpful for the future Telematics services as a standard model when ubiquitous computing society is pervasively activated.

1 Introduction

Over the past few years, a great deal of attention in network communities has been directed towards making ubiquitous sensor networks (USN) feasible in real world applications [1][2]. USN is differentiated from other wireless networks in that they consist of large number of autonomous nodes that are capable of collecting and processing any information from all surroundings. However, USN also has problems of limited computation, limited wireless communication, and limited battery power. These constraints of sensor nodes lead to a quite different view of software systems for USN, compared with those for traditional wireless networks [3][4]. Many researchers have tried to process given sets of sensing data as power efficiently as possible using new USN technology such as In-network query processing [4][5][6][7]. In addition to development core USN technologies, many researchers also have tried to find out the new paradigm of services where the USN technologies are integrated with other industrial fields such as vehicle transportation, wild environment, distribution network, and so on [1][2][8].

In this paper, we are concerned with a new paradigm of services and especially focus on Telematics service issues expected that they will be one of the

K.-J. Li and C. Vangenot (Eds.): W2GIS 2005, LNCS 3833, pp. 115–128, 2005.

killer applications of USN. For these issues, we propose Telematics service models based on USN, Telematics application framework for realizing the service models, and core technological solutions for implementing the framework. As the service models, we especially propose some future services such as *Intersection Collision Avoidance, Vehicle Location Determination, On-Road Warning Notice, Traffic Information Analysis and Vehicle-to-Vehicle Communication,* which are concerned with traffic safety. And we show a detailed design of the Telematics application framework composed of Telematics sensor node, Telematics service station, and Telematics vehicle. The end, several core technologies needed to implement the framework are introduced. Concretely, In-network spatial query processing, vehicle location determination, and real-time and reliable routing protocol technologies are newly proposed based on USN. The second section introduces an overview of Telematics and USN environment from a technological view of point, and the third section proposes a Telematics application framework that includes service models, its requirements, and the detailed system design. The fourth section discusses implementation issues of the proposed framework, and the last section shows our conclusion and future works.

2   Overview of Telematics and USN Technology

We begin with an overview of some recent Telematics and USN technology and dis-cuss a convergence of Telematics and USN technology expected to have a powerful influence on the future Telematics services. Telematics, a compound word of 'Telecommunication' and 'Informatics', is a vehicular portal service that is capable of sup-porting the emergency rescue, the car navigation, the remote vehicular diagnosis, the Internet, the e-mail, the video-conferencing, the movie, the shopping, and the stock transaction. In order to achieve these complicated services, it is necessary for many types of technologies such as GIS, LBS, ITS, wireless communication, and vehicle to be integrated systematically. Recently, Telematics technologies have been under development in several fields: (1) communication, (2) location determination, (3) inter-operability, and (4) infrastructure. A communication field sets the goal at wireless broadband that integrates various wireless communication methods of CDMA, WCDMA, WLAN, DMB, and WiBro and IVC (Inter Vehicle Communication) [9]. A location determination field is developing a new location positioning method expected to work well even at a GPS signal blockage area by using sensor nodes. An interoperability field is developing an open standard service protocol between client and server and standard platforms for Telematics client and server. Lastly, an infra-structure field is constructing Telematics Testbed that can test, verify, and authenticate all kinds of Telematics technologies.

USN is an ordinary service environment where tiny sensor nodes are randomly deployed around a target area and sense surrounding values, and a base station utilizes such ubiquitous information [10]. A distinguished feature of the sensor network com-pared with a general communication network is its automatic collection of distantly scattered information. In other words, sensor nodes can acquire surrounding data and transmit their sensing data toward a base station through their neighbors based on a predetermined automatic mechanism, and then a user can access to the replica data-base to create a new service. A great number of researches on USN have currently studied in the fields of hardware, operating system, communication, middleware, and application. Recent researches on a hardware platform focus on technology to be able to efficiently handle energy as well as data sensing, processing, and communication of a sensor node [8][11][12]. In case of an operating system, there are many researches about embedded and tiny OS that can manage limited resources of a sensor node [13][14]. In case of a communication and networking, one of the most active research areas is an energy efficiency problem in the classified layer of physical, data link, network, and application [15][16][17][18]. Middleware researches include interoperability be-tween different types of sensor nodes, security, time synchronization, and software deployment and update. There have been countless endeavors in both Telematics and sensor networks area respectively to improve their technologies. However, there have been few works related to convergence of these two different areas. The intuitive prospect of the convergence might be a smart and automatic driving where a human tells his car a destination and then the car drives the destination by itself. Even though this scenario seems to be so simple, a story behind its technological interconnection is too complicated to complete its full architecture by the recent years. In this paper, we are interested in the convergence issue of Telematics service and USN technology. In other words, we will represent our service models, requirements, and system design for this convergence.

3 Telematics Application Framework Based on USN

In this section, we propose our possible Telematics service models based on USN environment, focusing on traffic safety system and we represent our considerations and requirements that should be needed for the service models. And then, we design a Telematics application framework that considers those requirements.

3.1 Telematics Service Models Based on USN

There has been few service models proposed for Telematics application using USN technology. In this subsection, we discuss how the sensor networks technology can be applied to Telematics services, and then especially propose the new paradigm of service models focusing on a traffic safety system. A traffic safety system can help drivers by collecting traffic and vehicle information such as a location, speed, and direction and providing them with drivers using sensor nodes deployed on roads and related facilities of traffic light and street light. It is expected that these services may be great value when ubiquitous computing technology is pervasively activated.

Fig. 1 shows examples of possible service models for a traffic safety system where sensor networks technologies are used: *"Intersection Collision Avoidance"*,

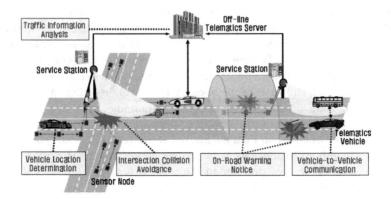

Fig. 1. Telematics Service Models for a Traffic Safety System based on USN

"Vehicle Location Determination", *"On-Road Warning Notice"*, *"Traffic Information Analysis"*, and *"Vehicle-to-Vehicle Communication"*. These services basically assume an infrastructure containing sensor nodes installed on roads, communication between sensor nodes, a service station collecting sensing data and providing services, and a vehicle equipped with Telematics terminal.

Intersection Collision Avoidance (ICA). ICA service model assumes that sensor nodes are adequately deployed near a intersection, a powerful service station is installed at the center of a intersection, for example at a traffic light or a street light, and Telematics vehicle with wireless communication capability moves over roads. At the first step of ICA service, sensor nodes that are some distant from the center of a intersection previously acquire information of vehicles approaching to the intersection in all directions and then sensor nodes forward the acquired information to a service station. The information holds location, speed, and time for each vehicle. At the second step, the service station collects lots of raw data from sensor nodes, transforms the raw data into a customized data, and broadcasts the customized data to all vehicles that are approaching to the intersection in all directions in real-time. At the last step, Telematics terminal of each vehicle estimates a collision probability at the intersection by comparing the broadcasted message with its location, speed, and time and previously notifies a warning message to driver, when an accident is expected. Fig. 2 shows a basic scenario for ICA service model. This scenario can be changeable into various models depending on an average complexity of intersection, a performance of service station, wireless communication circumstance, and so on.

Vehicle Location Determination (VLD). For moving vehicles, VLD service is to provide more accurate and real-time location determination function using sensor nodes than that using GPS. With sensor nodes deployed on a road, it is possible not only to measure high accurate and real-time location information of moving vehicles, but also to extract accumulated trajectory information of

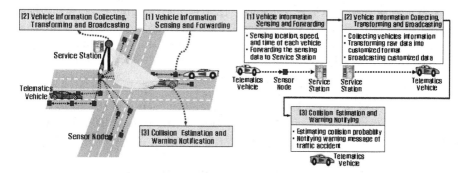

Fig. 2. A Scenario for "Intersection Collision Avoidance" Service

those vehicles. The trajectory information can be extracted by managing distributed location information stored at sensor nodes and service stations. That location and trajectory information may be utilized as main information for other Telematics applications such as Vehicle Relationship Management (VRM) and Seamless LBS.

On-Road Warning Notice (OWN). There exist many unexpected accidents on a road. For example, we used to facing unavoidable circumstances at a tunnel inside, above a bridge, and a highway. OWN service can solve these problems by notifying invisible and unexpected risks in advance. In case of a traffic tunnel or bridge, OWN service works on an environment where sensor nodes are deployed through a tunnel or bridge, a service station is located at an entrance to the tunnel or bridge, and Telematics vehicles are approaching to the tunnel or bridge. Sensor nodes acquire road circumstance information such as freezing, flooding, breakage, dropped goods, pedestrians from the tunnel or bridge, and transmit these information to the service station after verifying them. Then the service station broadcasts the received information to Telematics vehicles before they enter into the tunnel or bridge.

Traffic Information Analysis (TIA). ICA, VLD, and OWN, described in previous service models, are kinds of on-line services, where they work on real-time road environment that vehicles are moving. On the other hand, TIA is a kind of off-line service which analyzes accumulated information in an off-line Telematics server. A service station basically performs on-line services and periodically transmits its accumulated information such as location, speed, time, ID of vehicle and traffic signal data to the Telematics server. With the received data, the server can survey various wide-ranging traffic statistical values of traffic density, point speed, accident rate, and so on. The server even can analyze traffic accidents on intersections so as to find out the exact cause and source of that accident. We expect that this kind of service may be adequately applicable to CRM of insurance companies.

Vehicle-to-Vehicle Communication (V2VC). Two other vehicles can directly communicate with each other in order to share their information by adapting a mobile ad hoc network technology that enables neighbors between those vehicles to forward the data as a network router. Also, it could use intermittent sensor nodes through which data travels when there are few neighboring vehicles to transmit data between those vehicles. This service has advantages that can provide real-time information detected by vehicle on road and can assure connections among vehicles by using sensor networks. For example, when a car accident happened in a highway and the front vehicle detected the accident, the vehicle can transmit the accident information to the rear vehicles using both vehicular networks and sensor networks.

3.2   Requirements for Telematics Application Framework

In this subsection, we represent on properties about Telematics data and services on USN environment that should be considered when designing our Telematics Application Framework.

Real-Time and On-Line Processing of Telematics Services. Real-time and on-line processing is an inherent and very crucial property in a traffic safety service. If on-line Telematics data acquired from roads are sent to a Telematics server connected through internet, the server processes a service using the on-line data, and then a result are given back to vehicles, it is impossible to meet real-time requirements for traffic safety services such as ICA, OWN and V2VC. Therefore, we propose a new framework including Telematics service station instead of an external Telematics server and Telematics vehicle for an on-line analysis. The service station, as a kind of base station on wireless sensor networks, is a powerful system to be able to process real-time and on-line services, where its power is permanently supplied and it is generally placed at a road facility. The Telematics vehicle means Telematics terminal that is capable of communicating with sensor nodes and a service station, and directly performing on-line service in a client.

Reliable Telematics Data Acquisition. As another requirement that should be satisfied with a traffic safety service, there is reliability for acquired data from roads and vehicles. This requirement is very important in that reliability for a traffic safety service totally depends on the reliability for raw data. Existing sensor node specifications, however, do not satisfy the requirement that should quickly and accurately acquire Telematics data such as location, speed, direction, and time of vehicles and unexpected road circumstances. So, we propose a newly designed Telematics sensor node as a solution for that problem. Our proposed Telematics sensor node is a kind of smart sensor device equipped with sensing, computing, communication, and power module, and its main functionality is acquiring Telematics data rapidly and accurately. We will explain more details about it in the subsection 3.3.

Efficient Telematics Data Management. When acquiring Telematics data, we need sort of storage manager for an efficient Telematics data management.

The storage manager should be able to handle a continuously transmitted Telematics data without errors and with rapidity. Moreover, in order to manage location data of moving vehicles in sensor networks, spatial database requirement is also required on sensor networks. Sensor networks database technology generally sets a goal at an efficient query processing that minimizes communication cost for data stored at distributed sensor nodes. Recently, many researchers have tried to efficiently process a query using In-network query processing mechanism. This mechanism is a general way to minimize communication cost by filtering out un-necessary data as in approximated aggregation with quality guarantee [19] and increasing path sharing in Tiny AGgregation(TAG) [20] and Clustered AGgregation(CAG) [21] using tree-based routing and Directed Diffusion [17] using data-centric routing. In our framework, we especially propose In-network spatial query processing mechanism for the spatial issues on sensor networks.

3.3 The Framework

The constraints of real-time service, reliable data acquisition, and efficient query processing have to be inevitably considered when designing the Telematics application framework. Fig. 3 shows our framework that is composed of three parts: Telematics sensor node; Telematics service station; and Telematics vehicle.

In the framework, Telematics sensor node should be able to acquire vehicle, road, and road facility information such as location, speed, time, traffic signal, and accident. Telematics data acquisition component handles this function in the framework. How-ever, it is difficult to detect accurate and reliable informa-

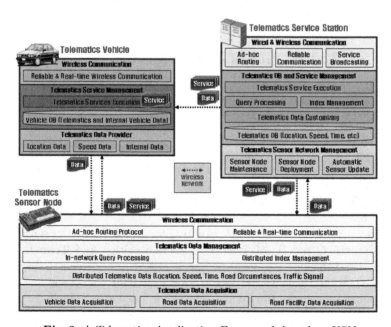

Fig. 3. A Telematics Application Framework based on USN

tion from lots of and high speedy vehicles. And, it is more difficult to detect exact location information within an error bound of 1m from moving vehicles. In the section 4, we show how USN technology could be used to measure locations of moving vehicles. Secondly, it should be able to execute an energy and time-efficient query using In-network query processing and distributed indexing techniques. For efficient query processing for spatial data such as vehicle location, we especially propose new In-network spatial query process-ing mechanism and distributed spatial indexing method cooperatively working with sensor nodes and service station. Lastly, it has to support reliable and real-time wire-less communication including ad-hoc routing protocol. Telematics service station should be able to manage a lifecycle of sensor nodes for monitoring their lifetime, config-ure a topology of sensor nodes for routing mechanism, and support an automatic S/W update of sensor nodes for constructing an adaptive framework. Secondly, it should be able to customize, store, and transmit the streamed sensor data in real-time and with reliability. Lastly, it, also, has to support wireless communi-cation capability like the sensor node. In the section 4, we propose new ad-hoc routing protocol that meets real-time and reliable property for the framework. Main functions required for Telematics vehicle are communication with sensor nodes and service stations when it moves or stops and service provision to users by analyzing transmitted data. This means there should be a smart Telemat-ics terminal in a vehicle, containing a wireless communication and a processing module. In addition, it should contain a sensing module that can provide nodes with its information such as location, speed, and time. For example, the vehicle might be equipped with a RFID reader to detect its location information from a tag that is installed into node. The basic working process of our framework for traffic safety services can be expressed as follows.

Framework. Working Process of the Telematics Application Framework.

Input : Service query(Q) of Telematics vehicle and Telematics data(D) of sensor nodes

Output : Service result(R) in Telematics vehicle

1. **Acquire** raw Telematics data of D from near circumstances, and **Reduce** D to $D_v = \{d_T | \forall d_T \in D$ in time T and $d_{T+1} \in D$ in time $T+1$ such that $d_T = d_{T+1}\}$ in Telematics sensor nodes
2. **Store** D_v at Telematics sensor nodes or **Send** D_v to Telematics service station
3. In Telematics service station, **Perform** Q for D_v of Telematics sensor nodes or **Perform** Q for D_v of Telematics service station and **Transmit** R to Telematics vehicle
4. **Send** D_v from Telematics service station to Telematics vehicle
5. In Telematics vehicle, **Perform** Q for D_v of Telematics vehicle

As you see above working process, the performance of our framework depends on the acquisition and reduction process for D, i.e., Step 1, and In-network query execution process for D_v of sensor nodes, i.e., Step 3. In the next section, we will discuss several issues for the performance improvement in detail.

4 Implementation Issues of Telematics Application Framework

As described in 3.3, this section presents implementation issues of the Telematics application framework. In-network spatial query processing, new location determination, and real-time and reliable routing protocol methods are proposed.

4.1 In-Network Spatial Query Processing

It is expected that many applications of USN will involve queries that combine sens-ing data with spatial data. Therefore, with rapid progress in the USN technology, spatial querying over sensor networks to retrieve spatial information about an area of interest is becoming more important. Prior researches, however, have focused on query processing for simple sensing data and have not considered spatial issues such as spatial relationships between sensing data and spatial data in USN. In recent years, new research directions towards spatial querying over USN are emerging [7][22].

A user may issue a query that retrieves spatial information such as location of vehicle and sensor nodes. If the spatial query is issued at the service station, it is disseminated into sensor networks when all data are stored at sensor nodes. As each sensor hears the query, it must decide whether the query applies locally and needs to be transmitted to its children in the routing tree. If the spatial query does not apply at a particular node, the entire sub-tree rooted at that node can be excluded from the query, where the costs for query dissemination, query execution, result forwarding across several nodes could be saved. Our challenge is to determine when a node and its children nodes do not need participate in a particular spatial query. For the challenge, we propose geographical routing tree(GRT) that is an index over location of sensor nodes that can be used to process a spatial query. However, unlike traditional indexing methods, the GRT is distributed on sensor networks. So, each node stores distributed indexing information (generally MBR) representing an entire range of locations be-neath each of its children. When a query with a spatial predicate P is given to a node n, n checks to see if there is an overlap between P and n's indexing information(MBR). If so, it executes the query and forwards the query to its children, and if not so, the query is not executed at n and is not forwarded to its children. The proposed GRT is an effective adaptation of R-tree [23] to a distributed version over sensor networks [19]. Basic algorithm of GRT building begins from a base station and ends to all sensor nodes. A base station floods children selection message to search for neighbor nodes and selects the searched neighbor nodes as its children. For each child, the children selection message is repeatedly propagated to search for next level children nodes. This children selection process is recursively performed until all sensor nodes are participated in GRT. And all

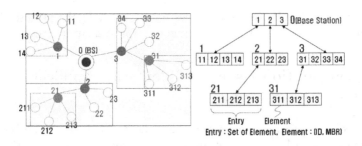

Fig. 4. A GRT Example. Gray circles mean intermediate parent nodes.

parent nodes hold ID and MBR of children at an indexing page. Fig. 4 shows a GRT example over locations of sensor nodes. As shown in Fig. 4, building of the basic GRT is so simple and straightforward. However, there will be many kinds of advanced GRT by changing children selection method using various heuristics that minimize overlapped MBR with intermediate nodes. We do not present the advanced heuristic GRT in this paper. The advanced work will be done as the future work of "Efficient In-network spatial query process-ing".The basic GRT has several distinctive features that are able to preserve network connection from base station to all nodes, to provide an efficient geographical routing method over sensor network, but not to maintain a balanced property of R-tree. More-over, the GRT that adapts a distributed indexing mechanism over sensor networks can be used in a peer-to-peer query processing and an efficient In-network spatial join processing using local indexing information stored at each sensor node. An In-network spatial query processing mechanism using the GRT is the same as R-tree mechanism composed of a filtering phase and refinement phase. It is a little different for GRT to perform the filtering phase over distributed sensor nodes, compared with R-tree.

4.2   Vehicle Location Determination Based on USN

Vehicle location is indispensable for Telematics applications. So, it is significant to develop technology of location determination with high accuracy. For a loca-tion de-termination, a GPS is mostly used, but it has wide error bounds more than $10m$. Moreover, its signals are too weak to go through hindrance such as tunnels and buildings, which result in a signal blockage area or even data distor-tion. Therefore, we propose a new location determination method that is more accurate than GPS and is possible everywhere without signal blockage areas.

The new location determination basically uses sensor nodes that are installed at road and Telematics terminal. In detail, each sensor node contains an RFID tag with accurate location information (previously measured) and each Telem-atics terminal contains an RFID reader being capable of communicating with the tag. Our location determination mechanism using the tag and reader is very simple, because we can directly get a location of the tag as a vehicle location whenever the communication is established between the tag and reader. It is, however, more difficult to implement the new method in the real world. It may

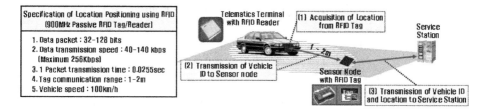

Fig. 5. Specifications and Operational Mechanism of Location Determination using RFID

cause many difficult requirements such that it should be able to satisfy a specific error bound of location ($2m$ in our service) and to measure a location from a high speedy vehicle (in maximum 100 km/h in our service). For these requirements, we adopted how to install sensor nodes with the tag at each traffic lane of road and how to attach the reader outside of the vehicle. Fig. 5 shows our detailed specification and its operational mechanism.

4.3   Real-Time and Reliable Routing Protocol

In terms of a data communication, this paper defines a Telematics Sensor Communication Network (TSCN) consisting of three elementary object types: Telematics sensor nodes, Telematics service station, and Telematics vehicles. Its outstanding characteristic is the number of the types that participates in the communication, which distinguishes the TSCN from traditional wireless networks generally having a provider and a consumer: $< server,\ client >$, $< sink,\ node >$, $< peer,\ peer >$. Even though the complexity may cause the network messy due to a huge amount of disordered packets, it can give the network a chance to have multi-purposeful achievement simultaneously like reliability, real time property, energy efficiency, quality of service, etc. In order to achieve reliable and real-time property, this paper proposes a context-aware routing protocol where a network topology for routing can be configured according to the combination of context models of network objects.

When deployed, each object identifies its own context model based on the condition that is determined by a few criteria. The criteria determining a context model in and object are its Position, Information Content, Functionality, Mobility, and Energy Constraint. A Position indicates an each object type that can be a Telematics sensor node, a Telematics service station, or a Telematics vehicle. The second criterion is kinds of data where the object handles, Information Content. Packets traveling in a TSCN are classified into two groups: raw data such as sensor readings and service data reproduced by analyzing and customizing the raw data. In addition, an action of an object that includes acquisition, provision, or usage as well as sending, receiving, or forwarding data can be a criterion of Functionality. The next one is Mobility of an object. In our framework, intuitively only Telematics vehicle has mobility, however, a recent technology is now considering mobile sensor nodes and service station. The

Table 1. Criteria for Context-aware Routing

Criteria	Position	Information details	Functionality	Mobility	Energy constraint
Details	– Telematics sensor node – Telematics service station – Telematics vehicle	– Raw data – Service data	– Send – Receive – Forward – Acquisition – Provision – Usage	– High mobility – Low mobility – No mobility	– High – Medium – Low

last criterion is Energy Constraint that is currently one of the most active research areas. This must play an important role in a context model because an energy condition in an object has an effect on the routing topology. The criteria stated are listed in Table 1. After the identification of objects, an initial routing topology is configured. The primary mechanism of the configuration is a path reservation where data can go through the optimized routing path that supports a reliable transmission in an expected time period. The network environment is changed by such service operations that Telematics sensor nodes acquire road information, Telematics vehicles join in or leave from the TSCN, and Telematics service stations provide various services. This makes the network reconfigure its routing topology to maintain the optimized routing path by rearranging context models of objects that it contains.

5   Conclusion and Future Works

We think the convergence will have a great synergy effect on future Telematics services based on USN. Especially, we think the convergence is more important for traffic safety services which require real-time and reliable property. However, there have been few works related to convergence of Telematics service and USN technology. So, firstly, we proposed possible Telematics service models related to a traffic safety system. Speaking in detail, we proposed various kinds of services such as ICA, VLD, OWN, TIA, and V2VC that can help drivers by collecting traffic and vehicle information on road environment using USN technology. Secondly, for the service models, we proposed a Telematics Application Framework that has following features: (1) it can provide users with real-time and on-line services on a road environment; (2) it can acquire Telematics data with reliability from roads and vehicles using sensor nodes; and (3) it can efficiently process continuously transmitted Telematics data without error and within the allowed time in a distributed management. The framework is composed of Telematics sensor node, Telematics service station, and Telematics vehicle. The sensor node acquires on-line traffic data, executes an energy and time efficient query, and transmits traffic data and query results with reliable wireless communication. The service station manages a lifecycle of sensor nodes, configure a topology of sensor nodes, and process services for a streamed sensor data in real-time. The vehicle provides sensor nodes with its information and executes services using Telematics terminal. And we proposed several technological solutions for efficiently implementing the framework. Concretely, we proposed (1) In-network spatial query processing that can process a spatial query on sensor networks environment with GRT (of a distributed indexing method), (2) vehicle location determination that can measure a vehicle location within 1m error bound, that is moving with high speed, and (3) real-time and reliable routing protocol that is based on a context-aware routing.

Summarizing our work, we presented the Telematics service models based on USN, designed the Telematics application framework for the service models, and proposed several technological solutions for practically implementing the framework in this paper. We think this framework can be practically applied to real world Telematics applications using USN technologies as a standard model. As the future work, we are planning to implement a simulation of the framework for the verification and test of its performance, and then we are planning to construct a real prototype and test it on road environment.

References

1. A. Mainwaring, J. Polastre, R. Szewczyk, and D. Culler.: Wireless Sensor Networks for Habitat Monitoring. ACM, Sensor Networks and Applications, 2002
2. A. Cerpa, J. Elson, D. Estri, L. Girod, M. Hamilton, and J. Zhao.: Habit Monitoring: Application Driver for Wireless Communications Technology. ACM SIG-COMM'2001
3. S. Madden and M.J. Franklin.: Fjording the stream: An Architecture for Queries over Streaming Sensor Data. ICDE'2002
4. Y. Yao and J. Gehrke.: The Cougar Approach to In-network Query Processing in Sensor Networks. SIGMOD'2002
5. S. Madden, M.J. Franklin, and J.M.Hellerstein.: The Design of Acquisitional Query Processor for Sensor Networks. ACM Sensys'2003
6. J. Gehrke and S.Madden.: Query Processing in Sensor Networks. Pervasive Computing'2004
7. Murat Demirbas, Hakan Fehatosmanoglu.: Peer-to-Peer Spatial Queries in Sensor Networks. P2P'2003
8. C. Sadler, P. Zhang, M. Martonosi, and S. Lyon.: Hardware Design Experiences in ZebraNet. ACM Sensys, Nov. 2004.
9. Woo Yong Han, Oh Cheon Kwon, Jong Hyun Park, and Ji-Hoon Kang.: A Gateway and Framework for Telematics Systems Independent on Mobile Networks. ETRI Journal, Vol. 27, NO. 1, February 2005
10. I.F. Akyildiz, W. Su, Y. Sankarasubramaniam, and E. Cayirci.: A Survey on Sensor Networks. IEEE Communication Magazine, Aug. 2002.
11. Mote system. http://www.xbow.com/
12. Nano-24. http://www.octacomm.co.kr/

13. TinyOS. http://www.tinyos.net/
14. Nano Qplus. http://www.qplus.or.kr/
15. A. Woo and D. Culler.: A Transmission Control Scheme for Media Access in Sensor Networks. MobiCom 2001, July 2001
16. K. Sohrabi, J. Gao, V. Ailawadhi, and G.J. Pottie.: Protocols for Self-Organization of a Wireless Sensor Network. IEEE Personal Communications, Vol. 7, No. 5, Oct. 2000
17. C. Intanagonwiwat, R. Govindan, and D. Estrin.: Directed Diffusion: A Scalable and Robust Communication Paradigm for Sensor Networks. MobiCom 2000
18. W.R. Heinzelman, A. Chandrakasan, and H. Balakrishnan.: Energy-Efficient Communication Protocol for Wireless Microsensor Networks. Hawaii Intl. Conf. on System Sciences, Jan. 2000
19. A. Deligiannakis, Y.Kotidis, and N.Roussopoulos.: Hierarchical In-Network Data Aggregation with Quality Guarantees. Proc. EDBT'2004, LNCS 2992, PP.658-675
20. Samuel R. Madden, Michael J. Franklin, Joseph M. Hellerstein, and Wei Hong.: TAG: Tiny AGgregation Service for Ad-Hoc Sensor Networks. OSDI'2002
21. Sunhee Yoon and Cyrus Shahabi.: Exploiting Spatial Correlation Towards an Energy Efficient Clustered AGgregation Technique (CAG). ICC'2005
22. Mehdi Sharifzadeh, Cyrus Shahabi.: Supporting Spatial Aggregation in Sensor Network Databases. GIS'2004
23. Guttman, A.: R-Trees: A Dynamic Index Structure for Spatial Searching. SIGMOD'1984

Resource Discovery Using Spatio-temporal Information in Mobile Ad-Hoc Networks[*]

Ouri Wolfson[1], Bo Xu[1], Huabei Yin[1], and Naphtali Rishe[2]

[1] Department of Computer Science, University of Illinois at Chicago
{wolfson, boxu, hyin}@cs.uic.edu
[2] High Performance Database Research Center, Florida International University
rishe@fiu.edu

Abstract. In this paper we examine the benefit of reports about resources in mobile ad-hoc networks. Each disseminated report represents information about a spatio-temporal event, such as the availability of a parking slot or a cab request. Reports are disseminated by a peer-to-peer broadcast paradigm, in which an object periodically broadcasts the reports it carries to encountered objects. We evaluate the value of resource information in terms of how much time is saved when using the information to discover resources, compared to the case when the information is not used.

1 Introduction

A few recent papers augment routing protocols of mobile ad-hoc networks (MANET) in order to enable discovery of physical resources (see [9, 12]). However, the existing work does not distinguish between competitive and non-competitive resources. A competitive resource is used in an exclusive style, that is, it can be used by at most one consumer at any point in time. For example, a parking slot can be used by a single vehicle at a time, a taxi-cab request can be satisfied by a single cab, and a cab can satisfy a single request at a time. Thus parking slots, cab-customers, and cabs are competitive resources. In contrast, a non-competitive resource is used in a shareable style, that is, it can be used by more than one consumer at any point in time, for example, gas stations and traffic conditions.

In this paper, we consider discovery of competitive physical resources in a MANET, and conduct a comparative study of alternatives. One contribution is to quantify the benefit of using resource-discovery information. We define this benefit to be the (resource-discovery-time-without-information) minus (resource-discovery-time-with-information). As far as we know, this benefit has not been quantified previously. Our experiments show that by using resource-discovery information disseminated via a MANET the resource discovery time can be cut by as much as 70%.

Another difference between existing literature and the present paper is the following. Existing literature on MANET's has studied resource discovery in a *pull* fashion. Specifically, a mobile node disseminates queries in a MANET, in which routing

---

[*] This research is supported by NSF Grants 0326284, 0330342, ITR- 0086144, 0513736, and 0209190.

K.-J. Li and C. Vangenot (Eds.): W2GIS 2005, LNCS 3833, pp. 129–142, 2005.
© Springer-Verlag Berlin Heidelberg 2005

protocols have been augmented and adapted for resource discovery. The nodes that have the queried resources will send the resource-information to the querying node.

However, in this paper we consider the *push* fashion, because the *pull* fashion can be inefficient, particularly in high mobility vehicular networks which are prone to frequent disconnection. In the *push* fashion, a resource periodically broadcasts resource-reports it produces to neighboring objects (i.e. objects that are within the wireless transmission range of the resource). These objects store the received reports in their local reports database. After that an object *o* periodically ranks the reports in its local reports database and broadcasts the top *M* reports to its neighboring objects. Thus resource-reports transitively spread out across objects. The reports are ranked by a relevance function that decreases the older the report gets, and the farther the reported resource is from *o*. We call this approach *peer-to-peer broadcast*, or *PPB*. PPB may seem like simple flooding, but the flooding is controlled by the relevance of reports which decays with distance and time. Consequently, the flooding is automatically limited to spatial and temporal proximity to the resource, similar to the behavior of an opportunistic peer-to-peer system (see [4]). Furthermore, our study shows that the performance of PPB, on disseminating useful resource information to consumers, is insensitive to the value of *M*. In other words, broadcasting only the top one report is as good as broadcasting the whole local reports database. This demonstrates that PPB is efficient in bandwidth consumption.

In Summary, This Paper Makes the Following Contributions. (1) It proposes a data model for representing physical resources, possibly having spatial and temporal characteristics. (2) It proposes the PPB method for disseminating resource-discovery information in MANET's. (3) It quantifies the value of resource-discovery information.

Before outlining the rest of the paper, let us observe that MANET resource discovery arises in many application domains including social networks, transportation, mobile electronic commerce, emergency response, and homeland security. For example, in a large professional, political, or social gathering, the technology is useful to automatically facilitate a face-to-face meeting based on matching profiles. In transportation, the PPB algorithm incorporated in navigational devices can be used to disseminate to other similarly-equipped vehicles information about relevant resources such as free parking slots, traffic jams and slowdowns, available taxicabs, and ride sharing opportunities. In mobile electronic commerce, the PBB algorithm is useful to match buyers and sellers in a mall, or to disseminate information about a marketed product. In emergency response, the PPB algorithm can be used by first responders to support rescue efforts even when the fixed infrastructure is inoperative; it will match specific needs with expertise (e.g. burn victim and dermatologist), and help locate victims. In homeland security, sensors mounted on neighboring containers can communicate and transitively relay alerts to remote check-points.

The rest of the paper is organized as follows. Section 2 develops the data model. Section 3 discusses resource discovery in PPB. Section 4 evaluates the benefit of using resource information in PPB. Section 5 discusses relevant work and section 6 concludes the paper.

2 The Model

In our system, there is a single type of spatio-temporal resources, such as parking slots, car accidents (reports about such resources provide traffic-jam information), taxi-cab requests, ride-sharing invitations, or demands of expertise in disaster situations, and so on. These resources are spatial in the sense that they are tied to a location, and are temporal in the sense that they are valid or available only for a limited time-duration. We assume that resources are located at points in two-dimensional geospace. The state of each resource alternates between *valid* (i.e. available) and *invalid*. The period of time during which the resource is valid is called the *valid duration*. For example, the valid duration of the cab request resource is the time period since the request is issued, until the request is satisfied or canceled.

The validity of a resource R is indicated by its *validity report* (or *report* for short), denoted $a(R)$. The report may be produced by a sensor or a processor associated with the resource. Each report $a(R)$ contains three attributes, namely *resource-id*, *timestamp*, and *location*. Attribute resource-id is the identification of R that is unique among all the resources in the system. Timestamp indicates the time at which $a(R)$ is transmitted by R. Location indicates the location of R.

In addition to resources, the system consists of *moving objects*. At each point in time, a moving object o is either a *consumer* or a *broker*. o is a consumer if it is searching for a resource. o is a broker if it is not searching for a resource but is participating in PPB dissemination. Resources are used only by moving objects that are consumers. o has a *reports database* that stores the reports o has received. Moving objects and resources are collectively called *peers*.

Each report $a(R)$ has a relevance when it is received. The relevance of $a(R)$ to a moving object o is determined by the following spatio-temporal function.

Definition: The relevance of a report $a(R)$ to a consumer that receives it t time units after $a(R)$'s timestamp, and d distance units from the location of R is:

$$\mathrm{Rel}(a(R)) = e^{-\alpha \cdot t - \beta \cdot d} \quad (\alpha, \beta \geq 0) \tag{1}$$

α and β represent the decay factors of time and distance respectively. t represents the delay from the time when $a(R)$ is transmitted until $a(R)$ is received by the consumer, and is referred to as the *report delay*. We now show that for a competitive resource R, under some very reasonable conditions the relevance of a report $a(R)$ to a consumer o, as computed by Equation (1), equals to the probability that R is still valid when o reaches it.

Theorem 1: Assume that consumers arrive at a resource R according to a Poisson process with intensity λ. Let o be a consumer that moves at a constant speed v, and receives a report $a(R)$ t time units after $a(R)$'s timestamp, at distance d from the location of R. When $\alpha = \lambda$ and $\beta = \lambda / v$, $\mathrm{Rel}(a(R))$ as computed by (1) equals to the probability that R remains valid when o reaches it.

Proof Idea. Let t_0 be the timestamp of $a(R)$. According to the report transmission model, R is valid at t_0. Since consumers arrive at R according to a Poisson process with intensity λ, the probability that no other consumers reach R x time units after t_0 is $e^{-\lambda \cdot x}$. Observe that the consumer o will reach the resource $t+d/v$ time units after t_0, and thus the probability that R remains valid when o reaches it is $e^{-\lambda(t+d/v)}$, which equals to $\text{Rel}(a(R))$.

The theorem motivates our definition of the relevance function.

The relevance function we use in this paper is one example in which the relevance decays exponentially per time and distance. But there are other possible types of relevance functions in which other behaviors may be exhibited. Furthermore, other factors such as the travel direction with respect to the home of a resource, or the price of the resource, may be considered in the relevance function. However, in this paper we confine ourselves to time and distance alone.

3   Resource Discovery in PPB

In this section we first describe PPB in 3.1, and then, in 3.2 we discuss two resource-discovery strategies, one using resource-reports to discover resources, and another which does not do so.

3.1   PPB Dissemination

We assume that each peer participating in PPB is capable of communicating with the neighboring peers within a maximum of a few hundred meters, via for example, the 802.11 wireless technology. In addition, each peer is equipped with a GPS system so that (i) the peer knows its location at any point in time and (ii) the clock is synchronized among all the peers.

In the PPB dissemination, the resource-reports are periodically broadcast by resources to the moving objects that pass by, i.e. within transmission range. A report is broadcast only during the valid duration of the resource, and each report is timestamped with the broadcast time. Upon receiving new reports, a moving object o saves the new reports into its local reports database. Periodically, o sorts the reports in its local database according to their relevance, and broadcasts the top M reports. M is called the *broadcast size* and it is a parameter of the PPB algorithm.

For the rest of the subsection we discuss how the broadcast period used in PPB is determined. For the sake of simplicity we assume that all the moving objects in the system use the same broadcast size. Denote by w the broadcast period. w is chosen based on the analytical model introduced in [1]. This model gives the throughput[1] of the wireless channel in an 802.11 ad hoc network as:

$$Th = \frac{L \cdot (p \cdot e^{-p \cdot \lambda \cdot \pi \cdot r^2 \cdot (1+9 \cdot (2 \cdot L/\tau+1))})}{\tau + p \cdot (L+\tau)} \tag{2}$$

where L is the transmission time of the average broadcast message (which is proportional to the length of the message), τ is the length of the media-access time slot (20μs for 802.11b), p is the probability with which a node starts a broadcast at an arbitrary media-access time slot, λ is the average number of nodes per unit size of area, and r is the transmission range in meters. Observe that the broadcast probability p can be

---

[1] The throughput is defined to be the fraction of time in which the communication channel of a moving object is engaged in successful transmission of user data.

substituted by τ / w, because if every moving object broadcasts every w seconds, then for every moving object the broadcast probability at an arbitrary medium access time slot is τ / w. For example, if $w=5$ seconds and $\tau = 20\,\mu s$, then $p = \dfrac{20 \cdot 10^{-6}}{5} = 4 \cdot 10^{-6}$.

After substituting p by τ / w in Equation (2), if τ, L, λ, and r are fixed, then the throughput Th as a function of the broadcast period w is a bell curve. Thus there is a value of w that maximizes Th. Intuitively, when w is very big, then for a large fraction time the wireless channel is idle, and therefore the channel utilization is low. As the broadcast period decreases, the idle time decreases. But in the meantime the probability of collisions becomes higher, because the 802.11 broadcast does not use handshakes to avoid or detect collisions as unicast does. Thus there is a value of w that achieves the best tradeoff between the channel utilization and broadcast reliability. And this value is computed and used by the PPB algorithm.

Now we show that indeed, except for w, all the parameters of Equation (2) can be determined by a moving object. The object density λ can be determined by an object o in various ways. For example, each moving object periodically handshakes with each one of its neighbors and counts the number of neighbors, or o has a pre-loaded table in which each entry gives the object density at each geographic area at each time period (e.g. rush hour). The transmission time L can be computed as follows. Denote by S the size of a report in bytes, by b the transmission speed in bits per second (2Mbps for 802.11b), and by h the size of the MAC header of the broadcast message in bytes (47 for 802.11b). Then the transmission time L is $\frac{(S \cdot M + h) \cdot 8}{b}$. For example, if $S = 1000, M = 10, h = 47, b = 2 \times 10^{6}$, then $L \approx 40ms$.

Furthermore, the broadcast period w can be adjusted to parameterization of the bandwidth consumption. For example, a user may allocate only 10% of the available short-range bandwidth to resources-reports of the particular type (e.g. parking). The rest of the bandwidth may be dedicated to other resources, multimedia applications, etc. In this case, for determining the period w, the message transmission time L is computed with the broadcast size taken to be $10 \cdot M$ reports.

3.2 Resource-Discovery Strategies

In this subsection, we discuss two resource-discovery strategies for competitive resources; one does not use any reports, while the other one takes advantage of the reports of competitive resources.

Blind Search. The first competitive resource-discovery strategy is a naive one, called *blind search*, or BS. With this strategy, a consumer moves around the area where a resource of interest could possibly be located, and it takes possession of the first resource that is valid at the time when the consumer reaches it. For example, a driver who is looking for a parking slot simply drives around on the streets that are within walking distance from the destination, and parks at the first parking slot that is available when passed by. The area within which the consumer looks for a resource is referred to as the *search space*.

Information Guided Search. The second strategy is *information guided search*, or IGS. With this strategy, a consumer starts with a blind search. The search continues until either a valid resource is encountered (i.e. passed by in the road network), or some resource-report $a(R)$ is received. In the latter case, the consumer attempts to capture R (i.e. moves along the shortest path to R). If R is invalid when the consumer reaches it, then the consumer discards $a(R)$, returns to the closest point in the search space, and continues the blind search. Clearly, if a valid resource is passed by on the way to R, then the consumer captures it and the search ends. If another report $a(R')$ is received during the trip to R, and the relevance of $a(R')$ is higher than $\text{Rel}(a(R))$, then the consumer goes to R'. Thus, the relevance function plays an important role in the use of resource-discovery information.

4 Value of Resource Information

In this section, we evaluate how much time is saved when a consumer uses resource-reports to capture a competitive resource (resource-reports are disseminated by the PPB dissemination mechanism). First we describe the simulation method. Then we present the simulation results.

4.1 Simulation Method

Evaluation Metrics. We use the discovery time as the metrics for evaluating the benefit of the resource-discovery strategies. For a competitive resource, discovery means that the consumer captures the resource, i.e. it arrives at the resource while the resource is still valid. For example, discovering a parking slot means that the driver reaches the parking slot before it is occupied. The *discovery time* is the length of the time period starting when the consumer starts to search the resource type and ending when a resource of that type is captured. Traditionally, the effectiveness of a data dissemination algorithm is measured in terms of its throughput (how many resources are found) and the response time (i.e. the time it takes on average to find a resource). The resources addressed in this paper, whose state alternates between valid and invalid, enable us to combine the two measures into a higher level one, namely the discovery time.

Simulation Environment. We implemented our own simulation system in Java. First we describe the simulation of mobility and resources, and then we describe the simulation of wireless communication.

Simulation of Mobility and Resources. We synthetically generated and moved objects within a 1.2mile×1.2mile grid network. The distance between two neighboring grid points is 0.1 mile (approximately the length of one street block) (see Figure 1). Resources are generated at all non-border four-way intersections.

Each consumer o is introduced at a random location on the grid network. o is assigned a square as its search space, such that (i) the side length of the square is 0.6 mile; (ii) o is initially located on one of the four edges (i.e. north edge, east edge, south edge and west edge) of the square with equal probability; (iii) the square is aligned with the grid network such that o is as close to the middle of the edge as possible. The square is referred to as the *search square of o*. o moves along its search square to search resources either clockwise or counter-clockwise with equal probability. With IGS, consumers may leave the search square to capture resources that are inside or outside the square. o moves at a constant speed. The motion speed of o is randomly picked up from the interval [v-5, v+5] where v is a parameter. Initially, c consumers are introduced. Out of these consumers, fraction k use the IGS strategy (referred to as *IGS consumers*), and the others use the BS strategy (referred to as *BS consumers*). k is referred to as the *IGS consumer ratio*. Whenever an IGS (or BS) consumer captures a resource, and is thus eliminated from the system, a new IGS (or BS) consumer is introduced. Consequently, at any point in time there is a fixed number, c, of consumers in the system, fraction k using resource information.

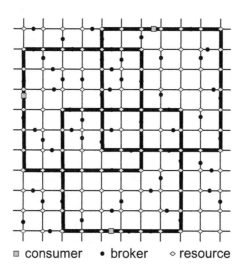

□ consumer   • broker   ◇ resource

Fig. 1. The grid network, resources, search square, brokers and consumers

There are g brokers per square mile. The mobility of each broker B is simulated as follows. We randomly choose two points on the grid network, and assign them as the start point and the first stop of B respectively. The path of B is the shortest path between the start point and the first stop. B moves along its path from the start point to the first stop at a constant speed. When the first stop is reached, another random point is chosen as the second stop of B, and B moves from the first stop to the second stop at the same constant speed. And so on. The motion speed of a broker is randomly chosen from the interval [v-5, v+5].

After a resource R is captured and thus becomes invalid, there is a time period until another resource is generated at the same intersection as R. This time period is referred as an *invalid duration*. The length of invalid duration follows an exponential distribution with mean q.

We use equation (1) with $\alpha = \lambda$ and $\beta = \lambda / v'$ as the relevance function, where v' is the motion speed of the consumer, and $\lambda = 2 \cdot c \cdot v / l$; $l = 31.2$ miles is the total length of all the edges in the grid network, c is the number of consumers, and v is the average speed of consumers. Observe that in computing β we use the actual speed of the consumer (namely v'), which is randomly distributed around the mean v, whereas in computing λ we use the mean v. When computing the relevance, we use the *route-distance* as the distance metric. The *route-distance* between two locations on the grid network is the length in miles of the shortest path between them on the grid network.

We argue in the appendix that with our simulation setup the arrival of consumers at a resource approximates a Poisson process with intensity λ. Furthermore, we traced in simulations the arrival of consumers at each resource and found that the arrival process indeed approximates a Poisson process with intensity λ. Thus, according to Theorem 1 the relevance function gives the probability that the resource is valid when the consumer reaches it.

Simulation of Communication. We assume that each moving object allocates only fraction a of the available short-range bandwidth to the simulated resource type. a is a parameter and is referred to as the *bandwidth allocation*. When computing the broadcast period as described in section 3.1, we use the data of 802.11b, and therefore the length of a time slot is 20μs. The data transmission speed is chosen to be 5.5Mbps. The transmission range is 150 meters. The size of each resource report is 32 bytes. The node density varies from 150 to 450 objects/mile^2, depending on the broker density g and the number of consumers c. The broadcast size varies from 1 to 121. All the parameters for the simulation system are illustrated in Table 1.

Our simulation system omits detailed representation of protocol layers and radio propagation. It models the reliability of communication by each neighbor correctly receiving a broadcast with certain probability. We consider two factors, i.e. (i) signal collisions due to hidden nodes; (ii) deteriorative channel conditions due to relative motion. To model the communication failures caused by signal collisions, we adopt the analytical model proposed in [1]. The analytical model computes the probability that a broadcast message is received by all of the sender's neighbors without suffering any collisions. Such a broadcast is referred to as a *successful broadcast*. In our simulation system, if a broadcast is not successful, then none of the sender's neighbors receives the broadcast message.

A successful broadcast is correctly received by each neighbor with certain probability depending on the relative speed of the sender and the receiver. The probability is referred to as the *reception probability*. We adopt the empirical results of [5] to determine the reception probability. Specifically, given the relative speed s, the ratio between the 802.11b throughput under s and that under relative speed 0 is obtained from [5]. This ratio is taken to be the reception probability.

Table 1. All parameters and their values

Parameter	Symbol	Unit	Value
Mean of invalid duration	q	minute	10, 15, 20, 25, 30
Broadcast size	M	report	1, 5, 10, 30, 50, 70, 90, 110, 121
Transmission range	r	meter	150
Motion speed	v	miles/hour	10, 20, 30, 40, 50
Number of consumers	c	objects /mile^2	50, 100, 150, 200, 250
IGS consumer ratio	k		0 to 1 with increment 0.1
Broker density	g	objects /mile^2	0, 50, 100, 150, 200
Data transmission speed	b	bits/second	2×10^6
Medium access time slot	τ	second	20×10^{-6}
Medium access control header	h	byte	47
Report size	S	byte	32
Bandwidth allocation	a		0.001, 0.002, 0.01, 0.1, 1

In summary, Each Simulation Run is Executed as Follows. At the beginning of the simulation run, 121 resources are generated, each at one four-way intersection. c consumers and $g \times 1.2 \times 1.2$ brokers are introduced at time 0 (remember that the total area simulated is 1.44 square miles) at random locations. Fraction k of the consumers are IGS consumers and the others are BS consumers. Resources and brokers periodically broadcast reports according to the PPB dissemination mechanism described in section 3.1. Each broadcast is correctly received by a neighbor with certain probability as described above. The sending and receiving of each broadcast is completed instantaneously (i.e. they take 0 time). The simulation run terminates after twenty simulated hours, out of which the first 500 seconds is the warm-up time period for the system to stabilize.

During each simulation run, the discovery time of each consumer is collected. The resource-discovery times of all the IGS consumers and the discovery times of all the BS consumers are averaged respectively. In the conducted simulation runs, the ratio between the 95% confidence interval and the simulation result (i.e. the average discovery time) ranges from 4% to 19%, with the average ratio being 6.6%.

4.2 Simulation Results

Impact of the Broadcast Size on IGS (Figure 2). Figure 2 shows that increasing the broadcast size does not improve the performance of IGS. In other words, with the PPB algorithm, broadcasting only the top one report is as good as broadcasting the whole database (121 reports). This is because PPB chooses the broadcasted reports based on their spatio-temporal relevance which reflects the benefit of the reports. The fact that broadcasting the top one report is enough is a nice property. It indicates that PPB is efficient in bandwidth consumption, and that it is drastically different than flooding that would broadcast all the reports in the database.

Overall Comparison Between IGS and BS. Figures 3 to 8 show the performance of IGS and BS under different parameter setups. There are three curves in each figure. Two of them represent the discovery times of IGS and BS collected in the same simulation run. The third curve, referred to as *benchmark BS*, represents the discovery time of BS under the same parameter setup, except that the consumer ratio $k = 0$. Thus benchmark BS represents the performance of BS when there are no IGS consumers in the system. From Figures 3 to 8 we can see the following. (i) IGS consistently outperforms both BS and benchmark BS. Sometimes IGS reduces discovery time by 70% compared to BS. (ii) Benchmark BS is always better than BS. This is because the IGS consumers capture resources faster than the BS consumers in the same system, which makes the BS consumers spend more time on searching than if there are no IGS consumers.

IGS Consumer Ratio (Figure 3). The discovery time of IGS increases as the IGS consumer ratio increases. This is because as the IGS consumer ratio increases, more consumers use reports. Thus for each individual IGS consumer, the chance to capture a reported resource decreases. In other words, in competitive situations the value of resource information decreases as more consumers have access to this information. Further observe that the discovery time of BS also increases as the IGS consumer ratio increase. This is because the more IGS consumers, the more likely it is that a resource is captured by an IGS consumer, and thus the less chance for a BS consumer to capture a resource.

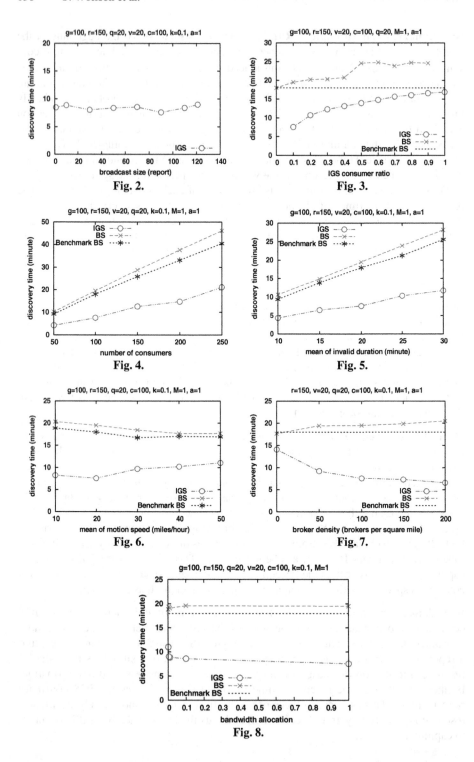

Fig. 2.

Fig. 3.

Fig. 4.

Fig. 5.

Fig. 6.

Fig. 7.

Fig. 8.

Number of Consumers (Figure 4). The discovery time of IGS and that of BS both increase as the number of consumers increases. However, the curve of IGS is flatter than that of BS. In other words, IGS is less sensitive to the increase of competition introduced by the increase of the number of consumers. This suggests that resource information is especially valuable in the areas where consumers are dense (such as downtown), i.e. competition for resources is fierce.

Mean of Invalid Duration (Figure 5). The discovery time of IGS increases as the mean of invalid duration increases. So does the discovery time of BS. However, the discovery time of BS increases faster than that of IGS. In other words, IGS is less sensitive to the increase of competition introduced by scarcity of resources. Thus, again, the value of information increases as competition for resources increases.

Mean of Motion Speed (Figure 6). Observe that an increased mean motion speed has a negative impact on IGS. This is somehow surprising because a higher speed is supposed to enable a consumer to capture a resource faster. However, higher mobility also leads to more deteriorative channel conditions and thus lower broadcast reception probability. Thus IGS consumers are less advantageous against BS consumers.

Broker Density (Figure 7). The discovery time of IGS decreases as the broker density increases. Intuitively, the increase of the broker density generates two contrary effects on performance. On the one hand, the reliability of broadcast decreases due to higher contention and more deteriorative channel conditions. On the other hand, each successful broadcast is likely to reach more objects. Figure 7 shows that the positive effect outweighs the negative one. Thus as the broker density increase, the newly generated reports are propagated more quickly and reach the consumer sooner, giving the consumer a higher probability of capturing a resource. In other words, the faster information spreads, the higher its value.

Bandwidth Allocation (Figure 8). Figure 8 plots the performance of IGS as a function of the bandwidth allocation for a particular parameter configuration. The discovery time of IGS is higher with partial capacity than that with the full capacity, but still lower than that of BS. Particularly, the discovery time of IGS increases from 7.5 minutes to 9 minutes as the bandwidth allocation (fraction) decreases from 1 (corresponding to 5.5Mbps baseline bandwidth) to 0.002 (corresponding to 11Kbps baseline bandwidth), and to 11 minutes as the fraction decreases to 0.001 (corresponding to 5.5Kbps baseline bandwidth. The reason for the increased IGS discovery time is that with the reduced bandwidth the broadcast period increases (to 5 seconds with 11Kbps and 10 seconds with 5.5Kbps). Further observe that the performance of IGS degrades very slowly as the bandwidth allocation decreases. This suggests that the bandwidth consumption of the PPB algorithm for one resource type is far below the full network capacity and therefore it is able to support many resource types and other network applications.

5 Relevant Work

A lot of works have been done in peer-to-peer data dissemination in MANET's (see e.g. [8, 10, 11, 13]). Most of these works are concentrated on how to disseminate resource information, whereas we study *how much* benefit the resource information may generate. In technical report [3], Goel et al. propose an architecture for dissemination of traffic information in mobile P2P environments and evaluate the benefit of traffic information in terms of the reduction of travel time. Their approach is geared to traffic information. For example, vehicles generate traffic reports only when the expected travel time on the road segment differs significantly from the travel time actually experienced by the vehicle, whereas we consider general spatio-temporal resources. Furthermore, they do not study how to use the resource information, whereas we do so in this paper.

This paper differs from our prior work [2] on the same topic mainly in three aspects. First, we make more realistic assumptions. For example, in [2] we assume that there is a single consumer. Second, we use peer-to-peer broadcast for reports dissemination whereas [2] uses pair-wise interactions. Finally, in this paper we use the relevance function to prioritize the communicated resource reports.

This paper differs from our prior work [14] in that in [14] we compare PPB with the client/server model whereas in this paper we compare PPB with other algorithms.

6 Conclusion and Future Work

In this paper we studied resource information for the discovery of competitive physical resources in mobile environments. First, we introduced a model of resource discovery information. Then we considered an information dissemination mode, namely *Peer-to-Peer Broadcast* (PPB). We determined that PPB results in reduced discovery time compared to the case where no information is used. Sometimes the discovery time is cut by 70%. We studied the impact of various parameters on the value of resource information (i.e. the amount of discovery time saved by using the information). The results show that in PPB mode, the value of resource information increases as the contention on resources increases. In addition, in PPB mode the resource information is more valuable when the broker density and the transmission range are large. However, resource information is less useful as more consumers use it. We also determined that the motion speed has little impact on the value of resource information.

A lot remains to be done in the future. For example, when-to-broadcast and what-to-broadcast in PPB need further study. Ranking of reports across different resource types including non-competitive resources needs to be addressed. Incentive mechanisms that stimulate brokers to participate in report dissemination are worth studying. How to integrate vehicular networks with cellular network is also worth studying.

References

1. J. Choi, J. So, and Y. Ko. Numerical Analysis of IEEE 802.11 Broadcast Scheme in Multi-hop Wireless Ad Hoc Network, *The Inter. Conf. on Information Networking*, Jan. 2005.
2. O. Wolfson, B. Xu, and H. Yin. Dissemination of Spatial-Temporal Information in Mobile Networks with Hotspots. *DBISP2P*, 2004.
3. S. Goel, T. Imielinski, K. Ozbay and B. Nath. Grassroots: A Scalable and Robust Information Architecture. Technical Report DCS-TR-523, CS Dept., Rutgers University, 2003.
4. B. Xu, A. Ouksel and O. Wolfson. Opportunistic Resource Exchange in Inter-vehicle Ad-Hoc Networks. *MDM* 2004.
5. J. Singh, N. Bambos, B. Srinivasan, and D. Clawin. Wireless LAN performance under Varied Stress Conditions in Vehicular Traffic Scenarios. *IEEE VTC*, 2002

6. S. Das, H. Pucha, and Y. Hu. Ekta: An efficient dht substrate for distributed applications in mobile ad hoc networks. WMCSA 2004.
7. Y. Hu, S. Das, and H. Pucha. Exploiting the Synergy between Peer-to-Peer and Mobile Ad Hoc Networks. In HotOS-IX, 2003.
8. W. Zhao, M. Ammar, E. Zegura. A Message Ferrying Approach for Data Delivery in Sparse Mobile Ad Hoc Networks. Mobihoc, Tokyo Japan, May 2004.
9. C. Frank and H. Karl. Consistency Challenges of Service Discovery in Mobile Ad Hoc Networks. MSWiM 2004.
10. F. Perich, A. Joshi, T. Finin and Y. Yesha. On Data Management in Pervasive Computing Environments. IEEE Trans. Knowledge and Data Engineering, 16(5), May 2004.
11. K. Rothermel, C. Becker and J. hahner. Consistent Update Diffusion in Mobile Ad Hoc Networks. Technical Report 2002/04, CS Department, University of Stuttgart, 2002.
12. C. Perkins and R. Koodli. Service Discovery in On-demand Ad Hoc Networks. *IETF Internet Draft*, October 2002.
13. M. Papadopouli and H. Schulzrinne. Effects of Power Conservation, Wireless Coverage and Cooperation on Data Dissemination among Mobile Devices. MobiHoc 2001.
14. O. Wolfson, B. Xu and H. Yin, Reducing Resource Discovery Time by Spatio-Temporal Information in Vehicular Ad-Hoc Networks (poster paper). *Proceedings of the Second ACM International Workshop on Vehicular Ad Hoc Networks (VANET)*, Cologne, Germany, September 2005.

Appendix

In this appendix we justify the fact that in our experiments the IGS strategy uses the relevance definition given in Equation (1). To do so, we show that the conditions of Theorem 1 are satisfied by our experimental setup. More specifically, we argue that in our simulations the arrival of consumers at a resource R approximates a Poisson process with intensity $\dfrac{2 \cdot c \cdot v}{l}$.

A Poisson process having intensity λ is a sequence of events such that[2]:

1. The numbers of events that occur at time 0 is 0.
2. The process has stationary[3] and independent[4] increments.
3. The probability that exactly one event occurs in a sufficiently small time interval of length δ, is $\lambda \cdot \delta$.
4. The probability that two or more events occur in a sufficiently small time interval is 0.

Now we show that in our simulations the arrivals of consumers at a resource R (each such arrival is an event) roughly satisfy the above properties. First, since each consumer o is introduced at a random location, the probability that o is introduced at the home of R is zero. Thus the number of consumers that arrive at R at time 0 is 0.

---

[2] Probability and Mathematical Statistics, Z. Sheng et al. (eds), Third Edition, Higher Education Press, China, 2001.

[3] An event sequence has *stationary increments* if the number of events during a time period depends only on the length of the time period and not on its starting point.

[4] An event sequence has *independent increments* if the numbers of events which occur in disjoint time intervals are independent.

Second, since the number of consumers in the system is fixed, the number of consumers that arrive at R during a time period depends only on the length of the time period, and not on its starting point. Thus the arrival process can be considered to have stationary increments. Furthermore, since the consumers move independently, the number of consumers that arrive at R during a time interval is independent of the number of consumers that arrive at R during any other disjoint time interval. Thus the arrival process can be considered to have independent increments.

Third, consider a sufficiently small time interval $[t, t+\delta]$. The probability that exactly one consumer arrives at R is the probability that at time t there is exactly one consumer within distance $v \cdot \delta$ from R, and moving towards R.

Now let us estimate the latter probability. Since consumers are introduced at random locations and they move at random directions, at time t the c consumers can be considered uniformly distributed in the grid network. Let the total length of all the edges in the grid network be l. Since R is located at a four-way intersection, the probability that at time t there is exactly one consumer within distance $v \cdot \delta$ from R is

$$c \cdot \frac{4 \cdot v \cdot \delta}{l} \cdot \left(\frac{l - 4 \cdot v \cdot \delta}{l}\right)^{c-1}.$$ (The second factor is the probability that a specific consumer is at the required distance, and the third one is the probability that all the others are not there). Because δ is sufficiently small, this is close to $\frac{c \cdot 4 \cdot v \cdot \delta}{l}$. The consumer within distance $v \cdot \delta$ may either move toward or away from R at time t, with equal probability. Thus the probability that at time t there is exactly one consumer within distance $v \cdot \delta$ from R, and moving towards R, is

$$\frac{c \cdot 4 \cdot v \cdot \delta}{l} \cdot \frac{1}{2} = \frac{2 \cdot c \cdot v}{l} \cdot \delta.$$ In other words, according to condition 3 $\lambda = \frac{2 \cdot c \cdot v}{l}$.

Finally, since consumers are introduced at random locations and they move at random directions, the probability that two or more consumers arrive at R within a sufficiently small time interval is negligible.

In summary, in our simulation setup the arrival of consumers at a resource approximates a Poisson process with intensity $\lambda = \frac{2 \cdot c \cdot v}{l}$.

Geo-Mobile Queries: Sketch-Based Queries in Mobile GIS-Environments

David Caduff[1] and Max J. Egenhofer[2]

[1] Department of Geography, University of Zurich – Irchel,
Winterthurerstr. 190, CH-8057 Zurich, Switzerland
caduff@geo.unizh.ch
[2] Department of Spatial Information Science and Engineering,
5711 Boardman Hall, University of Maine, Orono, Maine
max@spatial.maine.edu

Abstract. Traditional GIS tools are well suited for desktop workstations, but need to be adapted in order to satisfy the requirements of mobility. We propose a concept for sketch-based spatial querying in mobile GIS environments. This concept combines newest techniques for spatial querying and mobile technologies. Such a combination is beneficial because it allows formulating queries by drawing the desired spatial configuration on touch-sensitive screens, thus avoiding typing complex statements in some SQL-like query language. Client-server architectures in mobile environments are characterized by low and fluctuating bandwidth, and by frequent disconnections. We discuss client-server strategies in mobile environments and suggest an adaptive client-server architecture for geo-mobile querying. It is shown that adaptation to the mobile environment is necessary in order to ensure efficiency of geo-mobile queries.

Keywords: mobile, wireless GIS, geo-mobile, sketch-based queries.

1 Introduction

The combination of mobile appliances and wireless technology allows transferring certain portions of GIS technology from the desktop into the users' hands. One of the key operations in GISs is the retrieval of spatial information. Conventional query languages, such as the SQL, use text-based statements. While text-based query statements work well within data domains where data can easily be stored in tables, they lack expressiveness and flexibility within more complex domains, such as images, maps, or other spatially related, multi-dimensional data [1-3]. Images and especially maps, however, are an integral part of most GISs and, therefore, query methods for GISs need to be sufficiently expressive and efficient.

The use of handheld devices, such as cellphones, PDAs, or sub-notebooks as tools for querying spatial data in mobile environments, is becoming increasingly popular [4]. For spatial queries in mobile environments, particular attention needs to be paid to query languages that are responsive to bandwidth fluctuations, frequent disconnections, and various constraints of the mobile device, such as limited input bandwidth.

K.-J. Li and C. Vangenot (Eds.): W2GIS 2005, LNCS 3833, pp. 143–154, 2005.
© Springer-Verlag Berlin Heidelberg 2005

Recent research activities in visual information retrieval systems investigated novel techniques to query spatial data more efficiently [5, 6]. Visual information retrieval systems stress the use of visual tools to formulate a query. Unlike the SQL-based approach, these systems focus more directly on the end result, since an example of a user's query can be used as a formulation of a query statement. This paper studies visual information retrieval techniques, specifically sketch-based queries systems [5, 7, 8] in the context of mobile GISs. We will term this type of queries *geo-mobile queries*. As a framework and foundation, we use a sketch-based user interface for information retrieval systems [5, 6, 9], which allows users to formulate a query in form of a sketch that represents the spatial scene users want to find in a spatial database.

GIS applications on PDAs are unlikely to have all relevant data sources readily available in the device; hence, another critical aspect of information retrieval in mobile GIS environments is the response time. In addition, the use of handheld devices as spatial-query-by-sketch interfaces underlies the many restrictions of mobile appliances and wireless technology, such as interface restrictions, limited bandwidth, and power supply. One goal of this paper is to investigate the interplay between mobile clients, wireless networks, and static servers, and prove the practicability of Spatial-Query-by-Sketch [5] in dynamic use configurations. The main goal of this paper, however, is to extend the theoretical foundation of sketch-based querying [5, 6] from static to mobile environments.

The result of this investigation is a client-server architecture for geo-mobile querying that implements application adaptation in order to overcome the limitation of mobile environments. The investigation of the workflow and dataflow for sketch-based information retrieval systems in client-server architectures demonstrates the suitability of handheld devices as appropriate tools for performing geo-mobile queries. It is shown that adaptation to the mobile environment is necessary in order to ensure efficiency of geo-mobile queries.

2 Approach

Client-server architectures in mobile environments differ from the classical, wired architectures in many aspects [10]. The first part of this paper is concerned with identifying constraints of mobility that affect both, system and user behavior, so that properties of geo-mobile query systems can be defined. In the second part, these properties are applied to designing an adaptive client-server architecture that allows efficient geo-mobile querying of spatial data under varying conditions of the mobile environment.

Adaptation in a mobile client-server environment consists of three main steps: (1) resource monitoring, (2) an adaptation strategy, and (3) the adaptation process [11, 12]. Resource monitoring is concerned with identifying vital resource parameters for the application, while the adaptation strategy defines how these parameters influence adaptation for a specific system. Finally, the adaptation process controls the functionality of the application. Adaptation includes both the client and the server; therefore, we use a *mobile sketch*, which is derived from the sketched spatial scene and contains additional information about the client for guiding the adaptation process. The mobile sketch propagates the level of adaptation from the client to the server and contains a symbolic representation of the sketched scene, which is used for completion of the query process. We focus on the query formulation, because the resulting concepts and findings are generic and, therefore, valid for a wide range of applications. The presentation and analysis of the results, on the other hand, are application-specific and, therefore, should be investigated separately.

3 The Geo-Mobile Query-by-Sketch Architecture

The architecture of the geo-mobile query-by-sketch application is based on application-aware adaptation [12, 13] and the extended client-server model [10, 11, 14]. Since client and server share the responsibility of executing spatial queries, the adaptation logic resides on both, client and server. The idea of this client-server adaptation strategy is that the application on the mobile client is able to react to changes of the resources in the mobile environment. The request for adaptation is then propagated to the server in order to adjust the server's functionality.

3.1 The Mobile Client

The mobile client is the central part of the query system. It provides the interface that users use to draw the spatial configurations. The sketch is either drawn using a pen on a touch-sensitive screen or some other input device that allows freehand drawing of sketches. In addition to the user interface, the mobile client also hosts the adaptation logic. The architecture of the mobile client consists of the operating system running on top of the hardware, a middleware layer that acts as a mediator between system resources and the applications, and the geo-mobile querying application.

The role of the operating system and the middleware layer is to monitor scarce resources, and to respond to external events. The resource monitor keeps track of the resources, allocates the available resources among competing applications, and notifies the applications of changes to these resources. Complementary, the role of the application is to adapt to changing conditions by using the information and resources provided by the resource monitor. The application reacts to the changes by switching to a different level of functionality that guarantees best performance.

The change in resources affects both the user interface and the generation of the query statement. The user interface adapts to the change by enabling or disabling a specific set of functions for the current level of adaptation, while the query statement is issued in form of a mobile sketch. The mobile sketch is a digital representation of the user input, that is, the sketched scene, and reflects the effects of adaptation to available resources in terms of informative content and metadata of the sketched scene. The data transfer between client and server and the request for adaptation on the server is based on a transfer mechanism that utilizes the mobile sketch as control protocol.

3.2 The Server

The server is the core of the retrieval mechanism and is responsible for processing the query against the database. The role of the server in the adaptation process is passive because the client monitors the mobile environment and decides the extent of adaptation. For every query statement (i.e., mobile sketch) transmitted, the server identifies the level of representation and executes the appropriate tasks.

The query process is partitioned in such a way that the steps on the client and the steps on the server are complementary and result in a digital sketch that can be processed against a database. For instance, a mobile client with poor resources parses the user input, creates the mobile sketch, and transmits it instantly to the server. The server resumes the querying process and generates the objects, creates the digital sketch, processes the query against the database, and finally prepares the result for presentation to the user.

Sketch-based queries typically generate a set of results, which the server prepares for presentation to the user. The presentation of the result is based on a set of parameters of the mobile environment in order to guarantee efficient result browsing. Such parameters include screen size of the mobile client, color depth, etc. These parameters are captured in form of a user profile on the client and transmitted to the server.

3.3 Functional Partitioning

Functional partitioning is the process of decomposing an application's functionality into non-divisible pieces, called functional objects, and to allocate the objects to system components [13]. For our purpose, we desist of the system-allocation step of the functional partitioning process and replace it with a data flow analysis, that is, we merely use functional partitioning to define the modules (i.e., functional objects) of the system at a high level. This approach supports allocation of functionality to system components based on interaction and communication, which is an important aspect of mobile client-server applications [15].

The purpose of the data flow analysis is to show movement of information at a high level between a system and its environment, as well as data movement at a lower level between the individual modules of the system. The main objective of the data flow analysis of Spatial-Query-by-Sketch is to document how information flows within the system and to define the boundaries of the single modules of the system in order to design a plan on how to partition the client and the server. The tasks of the Spatial-Query-by-Sketch system are specified in Egenhofer [5] and Blaser [6]. The granular objects we investigate are sketch parsing, object processing, digital sketch generation, and query processing (Fig. 1).

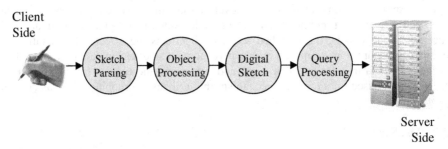

Fig. 1. The functional objects of Spatial-Query-by-Sketch

The main purpose of the first functional object, sketch parsing, is to generate a simplified stroke from the user input. This operation reduces the amount of data, and consequently the costs of transmission. Therefore, it needs to be located on the client and a data flow analysis becomes needless. Similarly, the purpose of the query-processing object is to assess the similarity between the digital sketch and a set of sketches in the database. This comparison is based on geometric -, topologic -, metric -, and direction similarity [16]. As a result, the query processing is a CPU- and memory-intense task that necessitates according infrastructure.

These considerations leave two functional objects left for the data flow analysis, that is, the object processing and the generation of the digital sketch. The simplified strokes from the sketch parser are the input for the second functional object, the object processing. The object processing analyses the stroke and yields a command that is instantly executed, or a data object (i.e., ASCII text, symbol, line, or region) that is added to the digital sketch. In addition, the process extracts the kernel and centerline of the objects and adds them to the digital sketch. Kernel and centerline are vital components of the digital sketch and are needed during the evaluation of the spatial relations (i.e., topology, direction, and metric), as well as during the query processing.

The second functional object that is relevant for the data flow analysis is the generation of the digital sketch. The first step in this process generates the association graph that defines the set of binary spatial relations among the sketched objects. The association graph generation is a computing intense task and the resulting binary relations together with the contained information (i.e., topology, direction, and metric) attribute considerably to the digital sketch in terms of memory consumption. A large digital sketch results in increased traffic between client and server, and thus contradicts the general principle of reducing data flow between the two parties. This observation advocates placing the generation process for the digital sketch on the server, if the available resources on the mobile client are insufficient.

The data flow analysis produces a coarse plan on how to map the functional objects onto system components. The first important discovery of the analysis is that two functional objects, sketch parsing and query processing, need to be assigned to the client and to the server, respectively. The second discovery is that the two other functional objects, (i.e., the object processing and the generation of the digital sketch) are responsible for data exchange between client and server and need to be carefully partitioned (Fig. 2).

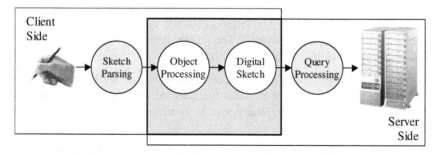

Fig. 2. Allocation of functional objects to system entities

In order to glue the functional objects together in a distributed system, an efficient data exchange mechanism is required. This mechanism and the refinement of the function allocation are investigated in the next section.

4 The Mobile Sketch

The result of the first three steps of the Spatial-Query-by-Sketch is a digital representation of a spatial scene consisting of spatial objects (points, lines, and regions) and the binary spatial relations among these objects. This digital representation of the sketched scene is called the *digital sketch* and is used to perform queries against the spatial database.

The main component of our approach is the mobile sketch. The mobile sketch is similar to the digital sketch as it is essentially a digital representation of the user's mental map of a spatial scene. Additionally, we extend and enable the mobile sketch to coordinate the workflow between client and server. The mobile sketch reflects important characteristics that are required to derive the digital sketch on the server, which is the final, meaningful representation of a sketch used for querying spatial databases [6].

4.1 Components of the Mobile Sketch

The mobile sketch is an abstraction of the digital sketch since its main goal is to efficiently capture the vital properties of the sketch at different levels of object representation. The main objective of this approach is to reduce the amount of data transmitted between client and server. The structure of the mobile sketch consists basically of four distinct sections. The following is a high level specification of the different sections.

Mobile Sketch Signature: A mobile sketch begins with a signature containing general information such as creation time, document size, and history. The most important information conveyed by the mobile sketch signature, however, is the level of representation of the mobile sketch. This information enables the server to perform the remaining steps that are necessary to create the digital sketch.

Hardware Profile: This profile contains system-specific information describing the properties of the mobile client. For instance, mobile clients may differ in terms of screen size, color depth, and resolution. This information is crucial for effective presentation of the query results on the mobile client.

User Profile: The user profile contains preferences that are set by the user on the mobile client. Such information includes the selected association graph model for the digital sketch, weights for binary spatial relations, and thresholds for result presentation.

Data Section: The data section reflects the sketch that the user draws on the touch-sensitive screen. Unlike the other three sections, which remain essentially the same for all adaptation levels, the content of this section may change depending on the chosen level of representation of the mobile sketch.

The purpose of the four sections of the mobile sketch is to enable the server to complete the generation of the digital sketch, support the query process, and supply parameters for a valuable presentation of the results. The next section discusses the generation scheme used to create the mobile sketch.

4.2 Mobile Sketch Generation Scheme

The scheme used to generate the mobile sketch may be described as a lossy compression technique applied on the digital sketch. Lossy compression techniques involve a compression such that if expanded less information may be available then what was in the original [17]. In return, such techniques generally obtain much higher compression ratios than is possible with lossless compression. Unlike most compression techniques, however, no decomposition and no compression algorithms are required to create multiple representations and reduce the amount of data of the mobile sketch. The degree of complexity (i.e., the actual object representation) of the mobile sketch is directly dependent on the number of steps involved in the creation of the sketch. This approach reduces not only the amount of data, but also the required infrastructure to create the mobile sketch. Therefore, it is the ideal approach for an adaptive application on a mobile client.

The sketch generation scheme is based on the functional objects of the query process: sketch parsing, object processing, and digital sketch generation. The general idea is that each of the three functional objects generates a mobile sketch at a different computational level, as depicted in Fig. 3. The mobile client selects an appropriate level of adaptation based on the available resources in the mobile environment, that is, the application running on the handheld device determines what steps are ideally performed on the mobile client given the set of parameters for the actual mobile environment. Accordingly, the selected level of adaptation defines the level of representation of the mobile sketch, since only the selected steps of the query process are executed. After the mobile sketch is generated, it is sent to the server where the generation of the mobile sketch is completed. Subsequently, the mobile sketch is converted into a digital sketch that can be used for the query against the database.

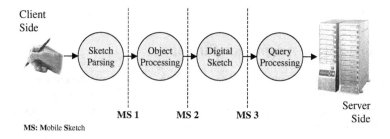

Fig. 3. Generation scheme for the multiple representations of the mobile sketch

4.3 Levels of Representation

The mobile sketch produced by the generation scheme may reflect any of the three different levels of representation. The term multiple representations in GISs refers to changes in geometric and topological structure of a digital object that may occur with the changing resolution at which that object is encoded for computer storage, analysis and depiction [18]. Accordingly, level of representation in our context does not refer to spatial details, since the sketched scene is the same for both, mobile sketch and digital sketch. Instead, it refers to qualitative and quantitative aspects (i.e., objects type, binary relations) of the mobile sketch compared to the digital sketch. The following description of the representation levels explains these differences.

MS 1-Simplified Line Strokes: Simplified line strokes are the lowest representation possible in a mobile sketch. Simplified line strokes basically consist of connected, time-stamped points (i.e., x- and y-coordinate, and creation time) as drawn by the user on the touch-sensitive user interface. Consequently, this level of representation requires the least powerful infrastructure and produces the smallest amount of data.

MS 2-Geographic Objects: This representation reflects the user input in terms of geographic objects (i.e., lines and regions), ASCII text, or symbols. The geographic objects consist of interconnected line segments and a set of properties. However, this level of representation contains no information about spatial relations among the sketched objects. The significant difference compared to the lowest representation level is the higher degree of computing resources required to process user input and to generate the objects and its properties.

MS 3-Digital Sketch: This level of representation corresponds to the digital sketch, as used for the query processing. It consists of a set of distinguishable sketched object and the corresponding spatial relations between them. The attributes and properties of the single object are the same as in the previous representation. The generation of the association graph of binary spatial relations and the assessment of topological, metrical, and directional attributes requires appropriate CPU and memory resources, and is therefore executed only if the resources are available. Furthermore, the amount of data increases drastically with the addition of the binary relations.

The mobile sketch facilitates an adaptive geo-mobile system architecture that guarantees both, an appropriate level of workload on the client and an amount of data that corresponds to the available network bandwidth. In order to achieve such adaptation to the mobile environment, we need to define a strategy that guides the adaptation.

5 Mobile-Aware Adaptation Strategy

Mobile-aware adaptation involves dynamic partitioning of the functionality between mobile host and server. By varying the partition of duties, however, we also vary the functionality of the user interface and above all, the quality of data produced on the mobile host. Consequently, adaptation involves the trading of data quality and user experience for resource consumption. The proposed architecture captures this notion of data degradation through three different levels of representation of the data produced on the mobile client (i.e., the mobile sketch).

5.1 Complementary Distribution of the Query Process

The representation levels define the degree to which data delivered to the server requires further processing. The lowest representation level results when resources on the mobile client are scarce and thus, full server support is required. The second level of representation applies when processing power, memory, and energy supply are abundant, but wireless communication with the server is not reliable or not existent. Finally, the application on the mobile client produces the highest level of representation if both, the handheld device and the wireless network provide sufficient resources. Fig. 4 illustrates the distributed query process and the three possible scenarios.

The choice of an appropriate adaptation level is based on predefined policies. Adaptation policies capture different system behavior in a flexible and customizable manner. The policies govern a discrete adaptation algorithm, which allows applications to move up along step or staircase shaped utility functions, rounding off the assigned value to the lower discrete adaptation level. The adaptation algorithm is discussed in the next section.

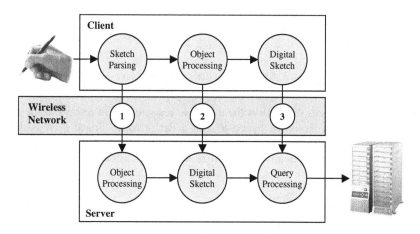

Fig. 4. Mobile-aware adaptation strategy

5.2 Adaptation Policy

In order to adapt to a changing environment, a system must evaluate its present situation and try to change the situation to another configuration that guarantees acceptable performance. Therefore, the role of the adaptation policy is central to capturing the application specific responses to resource availability. Due to the difficulty in obtaining an analytic expression that takes into account all possible parameters (e.g., CPU cycles, memory I/O operations, and jitter); profile-based modeling is used to approximate the mapping of the available resources to the application functionality.

We propose a profile-based, discrete adaptation policy, which allows applications to move up along step or staircase-shaped utility curves, rounding of the assigned parameters to the lower discrete parameter value (Fig. 5). Discrete adaptation requires complete increments of single steps to support multiple representations. It considers the portion of a step to determine a discrete representation for the mobile sketch.

The user profile defines the relation between the single steps of the utility curve, that is, it defines the thresholds that guide the transition from one step of the utility curve to the next. We utilize a compression factor (i.e., low, middle, high) to divide the resource in three sections, each representing a representation level for the mobile sketch. The compression factor divides the resource in a 1:2:3 (i.e., low: middle: high) ratio. The application adapts the thresholds for the steps every time the user changes the compression factor.

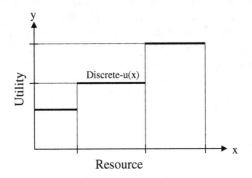

Fig. 5. Example of a discrete utility curve

We define two spaces that reflect the available resources with respect to the multiple representations; a Resource Space *R*, and a Performance Space *P*. *R* is dimensioned by resource characteristics in the mobile environment, which define the operational spectrum of the application. We utilize a two-dimensional resource space that

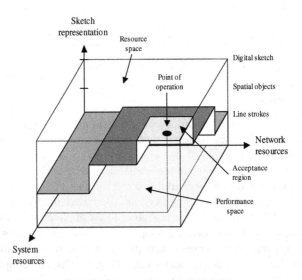

Fig. 6. Discrete adaptation model

includes system characteristics (i.e., CPU power and memory) and network properties (i.e., bandwidth and latency). Each axis reflects the resources assigned to the application by the middleware.

P is dimensioned along user-oriented parameters and includes three acceptance regions (i.e., representations of the mobile sketch). The Acceptance Region for a specific representation AR, of P is defined as the region in which the application is considered to be working properly with the current parameters. The adaptation model is illustrated in Fig. 6.

The application adapts its functionality every time it detects changes in the parameters received from the resource monitor. In addition, three protocols guide adaptation in case of abrupt changes of the wireless connection (i.e., a Disconnected Protocol, a Weak Connection Protocol, and a Connected Protocol). The disconnected protocol redirects the user input into a file that is stored locally. As soon as the connection is reestablished, the Connection Protocol or Weak Connection Protocol checks for such files and prepares them for transmission to the server.

6 Summary and Future Work

This paper investigates the implications of mobility on sketch-based information retrieval systems. Important issues in this context include challenges related to mobile technology, wireless communication, and the architectural structure of information retrieval systems in such environments. The main objective of this paper was to identify the major factors that influence the extension of sketch-based query techniques from static to dynamic mobile environments. The paper follows a top-down approach in that it first identifies characteristics of mobile computing and the challenges involved therein and creates an architectural framework that permits efficient sketch-based querying in mobile GIS environments.

Our work introduces a new adaptive approach for geo-mobile querying about which many questions remain unanswered and many variations and extensions remain to be explored. One important aspect of geo-mobile querying is context. Three types of context that need to be addressed by future research are spatial context dependency, context dependency of application adaptation, and task-based context dependency.

References

1. Egenhofer, M., Why not SQL! International Journal of Geographical Information Systems, 1992. **6**(2): p. 71-85.
2. Egenhofer, M., Deficiencies of SQL as a GIS Query Language, in Cognitive and Linguistic Aspects of Geographic Space: An Introduction, D.M. Mark and A.U. Frank, Editors. 1991, Kluwer Academic Publishers: Dordrecht, Boston and London. p. 477-492.
3. Egenhofer, M. and A.U. Frank, Query Languages for Geographic Information Systems. 1991, National Center for Geographic Information and Analysis: Orono, ME.
4. Artem, G., Management of Geographic Information in Mobile Environments, in Department of Computer Science and Information Systems. 2000, University of Jyväskylä: Jyväskylä, FIN. p. 107.

5. Egenhofer, M. Spatial-Query-by-Sketch. in VL '96: IEEE Symposium on Visual Languages. 1996. Boulder, CO: IEEE Society.
6. Blaser, A.D., Sketching Spatial Queries, in Spatial Information Science and Engineering. 2000, University of Maine: Orono, ME. p. 199.
7. Saund, E. and T.P. Moran. A perceptually-supported Sketch Editor. in Proceedings of the ACM symposium on User interface software and technology. 1994. Marina del Rey, CA USA.
8. Haarslev, V. and M. Wessel. Querying GIS with Animated Spatial Sketches. in IEEE Symposium on Visual Languages. 1997. Capri, Italy: IEEE Computer Society Press.
9. Blaser, A.D., Prototype Application Sketcho! 1999, University of Maine, Department of Spatial Information Science and Engineering and National Center for Geographic Information and Analysis: Orono, ME. p. 25.
10. Satyanarayanan, M. Fundamental Challenges in Mobile Computing. in Symposium on Principles of Distributed Computing. 1996.
11. Jing, J., A. Helal, and A. Elmagarmid, Client-Server Computing in Mobile Environments. ACM Computing Surveys, 1999. 31(2): p. 117-157.
12. Katz, R.H., Adaptation and Mobility in Wireless Information Systems. IEEE Personal Communications, 1994. 1(1): p. 6-17.
13. Satyanarayanan, M., et al., Application-Aware Adaptation for Mobile Computing. 1995, School of Computer Science, Carnegie Mellon University: Pittsburgh, PA. p. 7.
14. Rao, S.K., An Architecture for Adaptable Wireless Networks, in Department of Electrical Engineering and Computer Science. 2000, Massachusetts Institute of Technology. p. 65.
15. Imielinski, T. and B.R. Badrinath, Mobile Wireless Computing: Challenges in Data Management. Communications of the ACM, 1994. 37(10): p. 18-28.
16. Blaser, A.D. and M.J. Egenhofer. A Visual Tool for Querying Geographic Databases. in Advanced Visual Interfaces - AVI2000. 2000. Palermo, Italy.
17. Sayood, K., Introduction to Data Compression. 2 ed. 2000, San Diego, CA: Academic Press, A Harcourt Science and Technology Company.
18. Buttenfield, B.P., NCGIA Research Initiative 3 - Multiple Representations. 1993, National Center for Geographic Information and Analysis: Buffalo. p. 27.

Adaptive Path Finding for Moving Objects

Qiang Wu[1], Bo Huang[1], and Richard Tay[2]

[1] Department of Geomatics Engineering
[2] Department of Civil Engineering,
University of Calgary, AB T2N 1N4, Canada
huang@geomatics.ucalgary.ca

Abstract. Finding the fastest route in dynamic transportation networks aids navigation service considerably. Existing approaches are either too complex or incapable of handling complex circumstances wherein both the location of a mobile user and the traffic conditions change incessantly over time. In this paper, we propose an incremental search approach based on a variation of A*-Lifelong Planning A* (LPA*) to derive a dynamic fastest path, which continually adapts to the real-time traffic condition while making use of the previous search result. Our experimental results reveal that the proposed approach is a significant improvement over a conventional approach also using the A* algorithm.

1 Introduction

In recent decades, road transportation systems have undergone considerable increase in complexity and congestion proclivity. This presents a significant challenge to Location Based Service (LBS), especially with respect to navigation guidance. LBS is now capable of offering real-time information about traffic conditions and this information collected through loop detectors, probe vehicles and video surveillance systems can be very much up-to-date. Nevertheless, such information have not been exploited to the fullest extent as is evident from the lack of state-of-the-art systems to provide efficient service such as real-time en route navigation guidance [1].

Computation of the shortest path is one of the most fundamental problems in route guidance. Several algorithms have been presented since the classic shortest path algorithm proposed by Dijkstra in 1959 [2]. The original Dijkstra algorithm is less efficient as it explores too large unnecessary search area, thus leading to development of heuristic searches. Among the heuristic shortest path searches the A* algorithm [3] is commonly viewed as the most efficient. The equation "$f=g+h$", is a key element of A*. The variable g represents the cost of moving from the start node to another node in the network, h is the estimated cost to arrive at the goal node (or destination). A* employs this "heuristic estimate" that ranks each node by an estimate of the optimal route going through that node. This algorithm visits the nodes in order of this heuristic estimate and thus searches in the direction of the goal node. In such a way it avoids considering directions with non-favorable results and reduces computation time. Consequently the A* algorithm is an example of the best-first search.

Shortest path problems have been extensively studied in the past several decades. However, considering the search behavior in a dynamic environment, few of them are

K.-J. Li and C. Vangenot (Eds.): W2GIS 2005, LNCS 3833, pp. 155–167, 2005.
© Springer-Verlag Berlin Heidelberg 2005

capable of managing the circumstances in which the optimal route has to be fast re-planned and consequently adapt to the frequent environment change and the movement of objects. For example, from an airport to a conference center, although we can plan an optimal path prior to departure according to the current condition of the transportation network, usually it may not be the final path due to the fact that traffic condition changes continually during traveling. Hence we have to continually modify the plan and revise the path from current location to the destination based on the up-to-date traffic condition as informed by LBS. With these considerations, we propose a method to provide real-time en route navigation guidance based on a variation of the A* algorithm, i.e. Lifelong Planning A* (LPA*) [4]. The proposed algorithm is able to derive the shortest path for a moving object (e.g. a vehicle) adapting constantly to the dynamic change of transportation networks (i.e. the weight of a road link can change at regular time intervals) while utilizing the previous search result.

The remainder of the paper is organized as follows. Section 2 provides an overview of the shortest path algorithms, and Section 3 describes our proposed method based on LPA*. Section 4 evaluates the proposed algorithm and analyzes the experimental results, and finally Section 5 concludes the paper.

2   Shortest Path Algorithms

A network consists of nodes and links. Let us consider a weighted, directed graph $G = (N, L, W)$, where N is the node set, L is the link set, and W is the weight vector of links with non-negative cost values. Given n nodes$\in N$, the shortest path problem is to find a path of minimum weight between any two nodes, wherein the weight of the path is equal to the sum of the weights of the links it involves. In this paper, the weight of the shortest path between nodes v and w is the travel time taken for going through the path between nodes v and w. Although different research literatures tend to group the types of shortest paths problems in a varying manner, on the whole, between paths are typically calculated as one-to-one, one-to-some, one-to-all, all-to-one, or all-to-all shortest paths. This paper focuses on the one-to-one shortest path problem.

Shortest path computation has been a subject of extensive research over the past several decades. However, much of the available literature on shortest path algorithms seems to have focused on static networks that have fixed weights on the links. Clearly, these algorithms are not feasible for a dynamic traffic environment, in which the travel cost is time-dependent or randomly varying. However, a few early attempts on dynamic approaches can be found in [5-8]. The most notable algorithm relevant to this paper is LPA*, which deals with the fixed start and goal nodes. A brief description of this algorithm is provided below.

LPA* is an incremental version of A* that uses heuristics $h(s)$ to control its search. The first search of LPA* is the same as that of A*, but all subsequent searches are much faster as it reuses those parts of the previous search tree that are identical to the new search tree. The main principle of LPA* is described as follows. Assuming S denotes the finite set of nodes of the graph, $succ(s) \subseteq S$ denotes the set of successors of node $s \in S$. Similarly, $pred(s) \subseteq S$ denotes the set of predecessors of node $s \in S$. $0 < c(s, s') \leq \infty$ denotes the cost of moving from node s to node $s' \in succ(s)$ and $g(s)$ denotes the start distance of node $s \in S$, that is, the cost of a shortest path from s_{start}

to s. As for A*, the heuristics approximate the goal distances of the nodes s. They need to be consistent, that is, satisfy $h(s_{goal})=0$ and $h(s)< c(s, s')+ h(s')$ for all nodes $s\in S$ and $s' \in succ(s)$ with $s\neq s_{goal}$. LPA* always determines a shortest path from a given start node $s_{start}\in S$ to a given goal node $s_{goal} \in S$, knowing both the topology of the graph and the current link costs.

There are three estimates held by LPA* in its lifetime, the first one is the $g(s)$ of the start distance of each node s which directly corresponds to the g-values of A* and can be reused in the next search. The second one is the $h(s)$ of the approximate distance to s_{goal} with the same meaning of the h-value in A*, used to drive the search to the goal direction. Besides, LPA* also maintains another estimate of the start distances, namely rhs-values which are one-step look-ahead values based on the g-values and thus potentially better informed than the g-values. They always satisfy the following relationship: $rhs(s)=0$ when s is the start node or $rhs(s)=Min_{s'\in pred(s)} (g(s')+ c(s, s'))$ otherwise. A node is called *locally consistent* if its g-value equals its rhs-value. This concept is important as the local consistency check can be used to avoid node reexpansions. Moreover, the g-values of all nodes equal their start distances if all nodes are locally consistent. Actually, it is not necessary to make every node locally consistent in LPA*. Instead, it uses the heuristics $h(s)$ to converge the search and update only the g-values involved in the shortest path computation from s_{start} to s_{goal} [5].

LPA* maintains a priority queue that always contains exactly the *locally inconsistent* nodes. These are the nodes whose g-value potentially needs to be updated to make them locally consistent. The keys of the nodes in the priority queue correspond to the f-values used by A*, and LPA* always expands the node in the priority queue with the smallest key, similar to A* that always expands the node in the priority queue with the smallest f-value. The key $k(s)$ of node s is a vector with two components: $k(s) = [k1(s); k2(s)]$, where $k1(s) =Min(g(s), rhs(s))+h(s)$ and $k2(s) =Min(g(s), rhs(s))$. Obviously, $k1(s)$ corresponds directly to the f-values ($f(s) = g(s)+ h(s)$) used by A* because both the g-values and rhs-values of LPA* correspond to the g-values of A*, and $k2(s)$ corresponds to the g-values of A*. LPA* always expands the node in the priority queue with the smallest $k1$-value (f-value), like A* does, breaking ties in favor of the node with the smallest $k2$-value (g-value). The resulting behavior of LPA* is similar to that of A*. LPA* expands nodes until s_{goal} is locally consistent and the key of the node to expand next is no less than the key of s_{goal}.

As illustrated in Fig. 1, the goal is to find the shortest path from A to K in the graph. The left-upper graph shows the weight for each link. For illustration purposes, the start distance and heuristics are also provided in a bracket around each node. When LPA* performs the first search, it initializes the g-value and rhs-value of all nodes as infinity. Actually, it is not possible to initialize all nodes in a large map and hence each node is initialized whenever it is encountered during searching. In the following iterations, for each node a bracket is provided; the two values denote $k1$-value and $k2$-value respectively. The number above the bracket is the start distance (g-value). The single value in the bracket denotes the g-value of the nodes which is locally consistent. The black square indicates the node already visited in the current iteration. Here we use the Manhattan distance between any node and the goal node as heuristics for LPA*.

In iteration #1, the search expands from start node A, examines three successors B, E and D, assigns their keys, and inserts them into a priority queue according to their

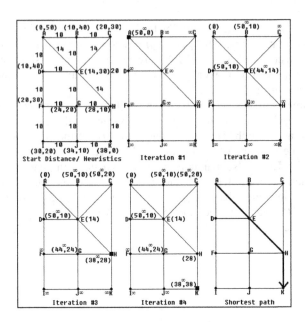

Fig. 1. LPA* first search

key order. Subsequently, from within the priority queue the node with the smallest priority is popped up, i.e. node E ($k1$=44). At this point in time, node E is locally consistent and has been popped from the priority queue. In the same way, the search expands to the nodes C, H, and G. In this iteration, rhs(C) has been updated by 20 because the least g-value of its neighbors is g (B) =10, and its parent assigned as B. Hence, we maintain the shortest path from the start node to each visited node. Finally, H ($k1$=38) is popped from the priority queue, the search terminates when node K is reached and it is locally consistent, any node expanded from K has no key less than that of K.

Fig. 2 demonstrates that the weight of any link may change arbitrarily. In this case, the weight of link EH increases by 10. To adapt to this change, we first check the estimates (g, rhs) of the nodes around the Link EH, which have the highest potential to be influenced by this change. In this case, they are nodes E and H. At this stage, node E is not affected by this change, but the start distance of node H changes (g(H)=38) and its rhs-value changes to 34 through update. Next, node K is updated and becomes locally inconsistent. Then, node G is popped from the priority queue. By expanding nodes G to H and J, the search results in the current shortest path without visiting many unnecessary nodes that are not affected by the changes. Consequently, LPA* can reuse the calculation result from the preceding search and facilitate fast route searching by incrementally updating the locally inconsistent nodes.

Although LPA* can manage dynamic environments efficiently, it cannot solve our problem in which the start node also changes continuously over time. The main advantage of LPA* is its capability to carry forward and reuse the start distance (g-value) in subsequent searches. While a mobile user is moving on a planned fastest path and desires to query on a new fastest path due to the changes in the traffic condition, LPA* will not be feasible for incremental search. This is because the startdistance (g-value) is no longer valid for the changed start point. Meanwhile, it is

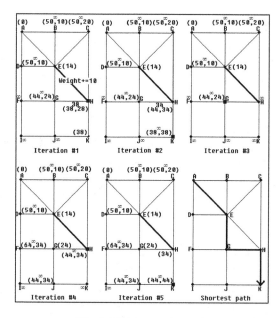

Fig. 2. LPA* second search

impossible to rebuild the *g*-value for these nodes, unless an independent search from the current start node is performed, which, however, dilutes the power of LPA*.

3 The Proposed Algorithm

3.1 Extended LPA* with Dynamic Start Point

Since the start distance (*g*-value) of nodes is of key importance in LPA*, the key problem turns to retaining the start distance of nodes obtained in the last search in order to take advantage of LPA*. Observing that the destination is always fixed while the start point changes, we modify the original LPA* in such a way: when a user is moving from node *v* to *w* (*v*, *w*∈ *S*), we can switch the search direction in computing the shortest path between them. Instead of searching from node *v* to *w*, we assign *w* as the source and perform the search from *w* to *v*. In this situation, the start node does not change, but the goal node keeps changing. Hence, the start distance of nodes can be carried forward and reused in subsequent searches. Clearly, with the goal (originally start node in LPA*, also current location of the moving object) changing, the heuristics of each node should be modified in accordance with different goal nodes. Note that, the weight of the opposite direction in the directed graph is adopted to ensure that the final shortest path leads from varying goal points to the fixed start node (actually destination) when calculating the start distance for each node.

We illustrate our approach with the same graph as shown in Figs. 1 and 2. Imagine that a mobile user would like to move from A to K. In the first search (Fig. 3), we follow the reverse direction from K to A and acquire the start distance of the involved nodes. As shown in Fig. 4, the mobile user starts moving on the planned fastest route derived in Fig. 3 from A. When the user reaches node E, he is informed with up-to-

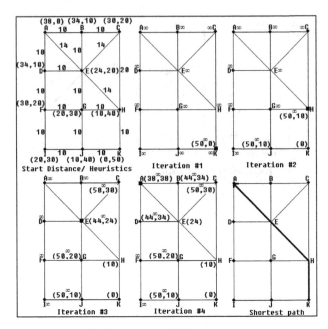

Fig. 3. Improved LPA* first search

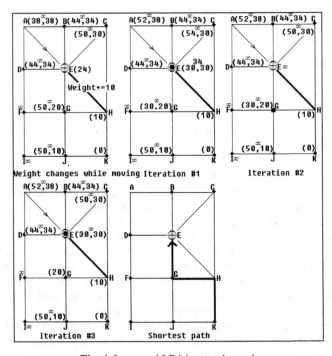

Fig. 4. Improved LPA* second search

date traffic information that there is a traffic jam in link EH. In this graph, it is represented as an increase in the weight of link EH by 10. To determine the fastest path in this case, we update the g-value and rhs-value for node E because its g-value comes from H. Clearly, it is locally inconsistent. Then node G is popped from the priority queue, and expands to E again, thus the new path is derived successfully.

The pseudocode of the algorithm is as follows:

```
//the following functions are used to manage the priority
queue:
U.TopKey() returns the smallest priority of all nodes in pri-
ority queue U. (If U is empty, then U.TopKey()returns [∞;∞].)
U.Pop() deletes the node with the smallest priority in prior-
ity queue U and returns the node.
U.Insert(s, k) inserts node s into priority queue U with
priority k.
U.Remove(s) removes node s from priority queue U.
Swap(s_start, s_goal) switch the start and goal nodes to perform
reversed search

Procedure CalculateKey(s)
{01} return [min(g(s), rhs(s)) + h(s);min(g(s), rhs(s))];

Procedure Initialize()
{02} U = ∅;
{03} for all s∈ S rhs(s) = g(s) = ∞ ;
{04} rhs(s_start) = 0;
{05} U.Insert(s_start, [h(s_start); 0]);

Procedure UpdateNode(u)
{06} if (u ≠ s_start) rhs(u) = Min_s'∈ pred(u)(g(s') + c(s', u));
{07} if (u ∈ U) U.Remove(u);
{08} if (g(u) ≠rhs(u)) U.Insert(u, CalculateKey(u));

Procedure ComputeShortestPath()
{09}    while (U.TopKey() `<CalculateKey(s_goal) OR rhs(s_goal)
≠ g(s_goal))
{10} u = U.Pop();
{11} if (g(u) > rhs(u))
{12}        g(u) = rhs(u);
{13}        for all s ∈ succ(u) UpdateNode(s);
{14} else
{15}        g(u) = ∞ ;
{16}        for all s ∈ succ(u) ∪ {u} UpdateNode(s);

Procedure Main()
{17} Initialize();
{18} Swap(s_start, s_goal);
{19} while (s_start ≠ s_goal)
{20}        ComputeShortestPath();
{21}        s_start =Top(Pathlist).next
{22}        Move to s_start
{23}        Detect the weight change in graph
{24}        If any change occurs
{25}            for all directed links (u, v) with changed
                link costs
{26}                Update the link cost c(u, v);
{27}                UpdateNode(v);
```

3.2   Constrained Shortest Path Search

To further enhance the efficiency of the proposed algorithm, we prune the search space of LPA* using an ellipse, thus applying an additional constraint. A similar approach was also used in [9] for a k-stops shortest path problem.

An ellipse represents the trajectory of all points whose distances to two specific points (i.e., the two foci of that ellipse) are fixed and equal to the length of major axis. All points within an ellipse are nearer to the two foci than those on or outside of the ellipse. In Fig. 5, given the network distance d between two nodes S and G, assuming d as the length of the major axis, and the positions of the two nodes S and G as the foci of the ellipse, we can assert that if there exists a shortest path existing between S and G, this path must be within the ellipse.

Proof: Let us assume that a shortest path from S to G exists and that there is a node V on this path, V lying outside the ellipse. Then |SV|+|VG|> d. Even if straight-line paths exist between S and V, and V and G, respectively, the length of this path must be greater than d. Therefore node V outside the ellipse cannot lie on the shortest path between S and G.

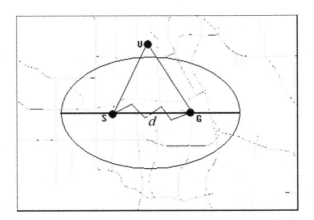

Fig. 5. Shortest path constrained by ellipse

Based on this observation, we can use the ellipse to prune the nodes in the searching process if a link is congested or blocked due to accidents. In such a case determining the size of the ellipse becomes an issue. From the first search of the improved LPA*, we know the entire shortest path from the start node to the goal node. While the weight of any link in this path increases and the mobile user tries to find an alternative fastest path, the network distance between S and G as in Fig. 5 can be used with the new weight value. By now, an ellipse can be defined using this network distance as the length of the major axis, employing G and current node S as the foci. Thus, if there exists a shorter alternative path, it must lie within the ellipse. Any node beyond this ellipse can be safely pruned from the search space, and so the efficiency of the LPA* can be improved using the constrained ellipse.

In the real implementation, a Minimum Bounded Rectangle (MBR) is used in lieu of the ellipse to simplify the calculations. As shown in Fig. 5, assuming that the two foci of the ellipse are $S(x1, y1)$ and $G(x2, y2)$, the half width of the major axis is a, the half height of the short axis is b, and the half of the distance between the two foci is c, the maximum and minimum x and y coordinates of the MBR can be calculated as follows:

$$\frac{[Cos\theta(x-x_c)+Sin\theta(y-y_c)]^2}{a^2}+\frac{[-Sin\theta(x-x_c)+Cos\theta(y-y_c)]^2}{b^2}=1 \tag{1}$$

where
$$\theta=\arctan(\frac{y_2-y_1}{x_2-x_1}) \qquad x_c=\frac{x_1+x_2}{2} \qquad y_c=\frac{y_1+y_2}{2}$$
$$c=\frac{\sqrt{(y_2-y_1)^2+(x_2-x_1)^2}}{2} \quad b=\sqrt{a^2-c^2} \tag{2}$$

and
$$x_m=x_c\pm\sqrt{a^2\cos^2\theta+b^2\sin^2\theta}$$
$$y_m=y_c\pm\sqrt{a^2\sin^2\theta+b^2\cos^2\theta} \tag{3}$$

In equation (3), the minus symbol is used to calculate the minimum x and y coordinates, while the addition symbol is used to calculate the maximum x and y coordinates. Using the ellipse to prune the nodes, our algorithm is modified as follows:

```
Procedure UpdateNode(u)
{05} if (!check(u,MBR)) return;
{06} if (u ≠ sstart) rhs(u) = Mins'∈pred(u)(g(s') +
c(s', u));
{07} if (u ∈ U) U.Remove(u);
{08} if (g(u) ≠ rhs(u)) U.Insert(u, CalculateKey(u));

Procedure Main()
{17} Initialize();
{18} Swap(sstart, sgoal);
{19} while (sstart ≠ sgoal)
{20}     ComputeShortestPath();
{21}     sstart =Top(Pathlist).next
{22}     Move to sstart
{23}     Detect the weight change in graph
{24}     If any change occurs
{25}         calculate_MBR(sstart, sgoal);
{26}         for all directed links (u, v) with changed
             link costs
{27}             Update the link cost c(u, v);
{28}             UpdateNode(v);
```

4 Computational Experiments

To test the above algorithm, we first need to obtain real-time traffic data. Real-time traffic simulation is performed using PARAMICS, a suite of high performance software tools used to model the movement and behavior of vehicles in urban and high-way networks. PARAMICS builds a complex picture of traffic conditions by accurate simulation of drivers and vehicles, and hence represents the vehicle flow realistically. PARAMICS also provides an Application Programming Interface (API) that facili-tates system customization to meet different needs. The simulation is performed using the real road network of Calgary, Canada (Fig. 6), which contains about 2000 nodes and 2500 links.

Fig. 6. Road map of Calgary

In our research, we compared the performance of our improved LPA* algorithm with the *static A** algorithm. The static A* algorithm searches the fastest path from the current location of the mobile user to the goal independently when traffic condi-tion changes, while the improved LPA* can partially reuse previous search results. To characterize the efficiency enhancement of our algorithm, we first selected a set of paths of different lengths. Then we utilized PARAMICS to simulate dynamic envi-ronment and made the weight of links changing with different proportions from 5% to 40%. For the improved LPA*, we tested its performance with and without the assis-tance of the constrained ellipse, respectively. To ensure consistent comparison, we used a binary heap to implement priority queue for both static A* and the improved LPA*. The number of nodes expanded is considered as a benchmark to test the effi-ciency. The first search of the LPA* is not involved in the comparison as it is the same as A*.

Table 1 shows the experimental results for different paths containing about 10 to 50 nodes in the final shortest path. In this test, only a few links were modified with a new weight value. Table 2 shows the experiment result in a dynamic environment that the weights of 10% links of the entire network were updated. Fig. 7 illustrates the node expansion in a dynamic traffic environment influenced by weight update with different percentages. The path contains about 40~50 nodes.

Table 1. Nodes expansion on different paths

Number of Nodes Approach	11	19	33	43	52
Static A*	34	75	156	284	497
Improved LPA* without constrained ellipse	7	20	32	73	128
Improved LPA* with constrained ellipse	5	16	25	55	98

Table 2. Nodes expansion in different paths with 10% links updated

Number of Nodes Approach	11	19	33	38	55
Static A*	32	78	165	280	512
Improved LPA* without constrained ellipse	9	28	37	72	134
Improved LPA* with constrained ellipse	6	19	26	59	104

It is observed that the improved LPA* approach notably outperforms the static A*. As is evident form Table 1, with the path length increases LPA* reduces the computational cost as compared with A*. In some instances, it can save up to 70~80% of the search cost. This has a significant implication on the navigation guidance service. The service provider may undertake considerable workload on the shortest path computation by using the static A* algorithm for a dynamic environment. Per se, the service quality is lower when the service provider faces a large number of clients. By reusing previous search results, the computational load is reduced significantly.

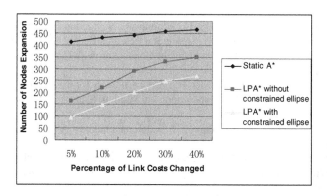

Fig. 7. Node expansion vs. links updated proportion

It can be found from Tables 1, 2 and Fig. 7, the improved LPA* with the assistance of constrained ellipse becomes more efficient without missing useful nodes. Although this does not signify an enormous improvement, it can still reduce 20~30% of the search cost.

Table 2 and Fig. 7 show that our approach works perfectly if the weight of links does not change widely. Under a worse scenario, i.e. a large proportion of the links is changed on their weights, the performance of the improved LPA* will be similar to A* as only little of previous search information can be reused.

5 Conclusion

This paper has presented a novel approach based on LPA* to sort out the dynamic shortest path problem for en-route navigation guidance in which the travelers can dynamically derive the fastest route. While dynamic shortest path algorithms do exist, they address the problems either with a fixed start node or by performing a shortest path search independently from the changed start node to the destination ignoring the previous search result.

LPA* combines the incremental search method and the heuristics notion to deal with the dynamic shortest path problem. Optimal solutions to a series of similar path planning problems can be found potentially faster than is possible by solving each independent path-planning problem from scratch using the static A*. LPA* utilizes the information from previous search episodes to accelerate subsequent searches. Nonetheless, this algorithm is not capable of solving our problem. Our research extends LPA* by reversing the search from the goal to the source and dynamically modifying the heuristics. The computational experiments show that our improved LPA* consistently outperforms independent searches using static A*.

Additionally, we employ a constrained ellipse to prune the search space. As a result, our improved LPA* can save up to 70~80% of the computational cost while compared with the static A*. Nevertheless, in our future works we intend to experimentally test our algorithm in different transportation networks.

References

1. Huang, B. and Li, H. G.: Developing Location-aware Navigation Guides That Use Mobile Geographic Information Systems. Transportation Research Record (2004) 108-113
2. Dijkstra, E. W.: A Note on Two Problems in Connection with Graphs. Numerische Math. (1959) 269-271
3. Hart, P. E., Nilsson, N. J., and Raphael, B. : A Formal Basis for the Heuristic Determination of Minimum Cost Paths. IEEE Transactions on Systems Science and Cybernetics (1968) 100-107
4. Koenig, S., Likhachev, M. and Furcy, D., Lifelong planning A*. Artificial Intelligence (2004) 1-2
5. Chabini, I.: A New Algorithm for Shortest Paths in Discrete Dynamic Networks. 8th IFAC/IFIP/IFORS Symposium on transportation systems, Tech Univ Crete, Greece, 16-18 (1997)

6. Cooke, K. L., and Hasley, E.: The Shortest Route through a Network with Time-dependent Intermodal Transit Times. Journal of Mathematical Analysis and Applications (1996) 493-498

7. Koenig, S., and Likhachev, M.: Incremental A*, Georgia Institute of Technology, Atlanta, GA 30312-0280 (2001)

8. Djidjev, H. N.: Improved Algorithms for Dynamic Shortest Paths, Computer Science Department, Rice University (1996)

9. Terrovitis, M., Bakiras, S., Papadias, D., and Mouratidis, K.: Constrained Shortest Path Computation. Proceedings of the 9th International Symposium on Spatial and Temporal Databases (SSTD), pp. 181-199, Angra dos Reis, Brazil, August 22-24, LNCS 3633, Spinger Verlag (2005).

Incremental Evaluation of Continuous Range Queries over Objects Moving on Known Network Paths

Dragan Stojanovic, Slobodanka Djordjevic-Kajan, and Bratislav Predic

Computer Graphics & GIS Laboratory,
Faculty of Electronic Engineering, University of Nis,
Aleksandra Medvedeva 14, 18000 Nis,
Serbia and Montenegro
{dragans, sdjordjevic, bpredic}@elfak.ni.ac.yu

Abstract. In this paper we address the problem and propose the method for continuous range query processing for mobile objects moving on known network paths. The method assumes that the objects know their destination in advance and move along the best/shortest path to it. The method is based on an available 2D indexing scheme (e.g. R* Tree) for indexing transportation network data. The network R* tree is extended to provide matching of queries and objects according to their locations on the network for stationary objects/queries or their network routes for mobile objects/queries and performing the filter step of the continuous query. The refinement step of the query processing methodology generates main memory data structures that represent temporal query result and support periodic, incremental evaluation to produce result updates.

1 Introduction

Advances in wireless communication technologies, mobile positioning and Internet-enabled mobile devices have given a rise to a new class of mobile applications and services, called Location Based Services (LBS). Such services, like automatic vehicle location, fleet management, tourist services, transport management, traffic control and digital battlefield are all based on mobile objects and the management of their continuously changing location data. The main problem and challenge in mobile, location-based services is how to efficiently handle different types of queries when both objects and queries can be mobile. The different types of location-dependent queries in LBS exist such as: range queries, k-nearest neighbor (k-NN) queries, reverse neighbor queries, distance joins, closest pair queries and skyline queries. Such queries are continuous in nature. Unlike snapshot queries that are evaluated only once, continuous queries require continuous evaluation as the query result becomes invalid with the change of the query's or the mobile objects' location. Any delay of the query response results in an obsolete answer. At any time there will be a number of continuous queries simultaneously running at the server which must be periodically and efficiently evaluated as queries and objects move.

Mobile objects in a real-world setting always move following a particular route, which represents a path in a transportation network [2]. Vehicles, trains, boats and passengers move following a particular network (roads, railways, rivers, pedestrian

K.-J. Li and C. Vangenot (Eds.): W2GIS 2005, LNCS 3833, pp. 168–182, 2005.
© Springer-Verlag Berlin Heidelberg 2005

tracks, air corridors, etc.). In addition to this, a mobile object in LBS, which can be a query object, a data object or both, always know their destination in advance. For example, taxi cabs, trucks, transport fleet, tourists, etc. start moving with predetermined objective and use LBS service to obtain the best/fast/ shortest paths to their destinations depending on the cost criteria (time, distance, etc.).

In this paper, we propose the method for continuous range query processing for mobile objects moving on a transportation network along the known network paths. The method is incorporated in the framework for mobile object data management called ARGONAUT [15]. The methodology is designed with the goal to provide efficient processing of continuous queries with respect to necessary CPU time and disk and main memory utilization using incremental evaluation and main memory data structures supporting periodic reevaluation of queries and generation of the incremental query result. As in SINA [12], the method updates the query result every T time units by computing and sending only updates, both positive and negative, of the previously reported answer. Thus, limiting the amount of data sent to the client issuing the query, the query processing methodology is made efficient in respect to a limited network bandwidth. The methodology deals with all combinations of objects and queries found in LBS. Thus, it is applicable to: stationary queries on moving objects (e.g., "Continuously report the cars that are within 3 miles of the gas station A"), moving queries on stationary objects (e.g., "Continuously report all Italian restaurants that are within 2 miles of my car location"), and moving queries on moving objects (e.g., "Continuously report all taxi cabs that are near (within 1 mile) of my location").

The rest of the paper is organized as follows: Section 2 surveys the previous work focusing on directly related topics. A section 3 describes the methodology and the algorithms for continuous range query processing. Section 4 provides a thorough experimental evaluation and Section 5 concludes the paper with some future directions.

2 Continuous Query Processing – Related Work

Continuous spatio-temporal query processing in a location-aware environment is an active area of research with many query processing methods, techniques and index structures proposed recently. In [14], velocity constrained indexing and query indexing (Q-index) has been proposed for efficient evaluation of continuous range queries with stationary query objects. According to proposed methodology, in-memory data structures and algorithms are developed and presented in [8]. Lazaridis et al. [11] define dynamic query as a temporally ordered set of snapshot queries. They specify the index structures for trajectories of moving objects and describe their efficient usage for evaluation of dynamic queries that represent predictable or non-predictable movement of an observer. The MQM method presented in [3] is also focused on continuous (monitoring) range queries. It is based on partitioning the query space into rectangular sub-domains, and assignment the resident domain to each mobile object in the system. A mobile object is aware only of the range queries intersecting its resident domain, and reports its current location to the server only if it crosses the boundary of any of these queries and participates in the query result.

To deal with mobile range queries over mobile objects, Gedik and Liu [5] propose the method and the system for distributed query processing, called *Mobieyes*. *Mobieyes* ships some part of the query processing to the mobile objects/clients while the server mainly acts as a mediator between moving objects. The workspace is partitioned using grid and the monitoring regions of the queries are maintained at the server. Their other work [6] focuses on efficient processing of moving continuous queries over moving objects. They propose a scheme called *Motion Adaptive Indexing* that enable optimization of continuous query evaluation according to dynamic motion behavior of the objects, and use the concept of motion sensitive bounding boxes (MSB) to model both moving objects and moving queries. Mokbel et al. in [12] present SINA, a method for processing continuous range queries over mobile objects at the server side. SINA is based on shared execution and incremental evaluation of continuous queries. Shared execution is achieved by implementing query evaluation as a spatial join between the mobile objects and the queries. Incremental evaluation means that the query processing system produce only the positive or negative updates of the previously reported answer, not the complete answer for every evaluation of the query. Hu et al. [7] propose a generic framework for monitoring continuous spatial queries over moving objects, both range and k-NN queries. Besides reducing the evaluation cost of continuous query processing, they also address the location update mechanism which is aware of currently running queries.

Two index structures for indexing the past trajectories of mobile objects in networks have been proposed. The Fixed Network R-Tree (FNR-Tree) [4] consists of a top level 2D R-Tree, whose leaf nodes contains pointers to 1D R-Trees. The 2D R-Tree is used to index the edges of the network, and for every leaf node of the 2D R-Tree, there is 1D R-Tree indexing the time interval of each object's movement inside the line segments of the network. The main disadvantages of this approach is very high number of entries and lots of updates in the index structures, as well as the limitation that an object cannot end or change its movement within the network edge, but only at nodes. The other index structure is proposed by Almeida and Gusting in [1] and is called Moving Objects in Networks Tree (MON-Tree). They describe two network models that can be indexed by the MON-Tree. The first model is edge oriented and represents the network by edges and nodes, and the second one is route oriented, represents the network by routes and junctions and is more suitable for transportation networks. The MON-Tree was experimentally evaluated against FNR-Tree and it showed better performance in answering range queries on complete moving object trajectories. In their tests, the MON-Tree indexing the route oriented network model showed the overall best results.

Some of previously mentioned methods, such as SINA [12] and [7] provide extensions for processing NN queries. Also, there is also a lot of work on continuous/monitoring NN queries and some examples are [18, 19]. The most related to our work are work on processing of stationary queries over stationary objects both referenced on the underlying network presented in [13] and the processing of mobile, continuous k-NN queries over stationary objects constrained by the spatial network using first order Voronoi diagrams, presented in works of Kolahdouzan et. al. [9, 10].

To the best of our knowledge, there is no reported work on query processing of continuous range queries over mobile objects whose motion is constrained by the transportation network, which know their destinations in advance and tend to reach them by the best possible (shortest, fastest, etc.) paths.

3   The Method and the Framework for Continuous Range Query Processing

The processing of the continuous range queries in mobile environment we developed as a part of ARGONAUT, a service framework for mobile object data management [15]. We base our approach on the application scenario appropriate in LBS for tourist and business guiding. In such scenario, when the mobile client registers to the service, he knows its destination, as well as point of interest/delivery he wants/have to visit on his trip. The service determines and returns to him the fastest/shortest route consisting of the connected network edges accessing the spatial network databases modeled using node-edge model. The location of the object in the geographic latitude/longitude format is obtained by a mobile positioning method (or generated by a simulator) and can be converted by the service in the format more suitable for transportation purposes: network edge and the distance from the beginning of the edge. The location of the mobile object can be calculated at any time instance according to its last location update, the time when the update occurred and the speed reported by the mobile object. The service also defines and sends to a mobile client an uncertainty threshold. The obligation of the mobile object is to send the location and speed update to the service if its current location is deviated from its calculated location on the proposed route by defined uncertainty threshold.

3.1   Methodology Overview

The ARGONAUT continuous range query processing methodology employs an incremental evaluation paradigm. The methodology is based on R* tree index structure for the filter step of query processing and generation of the candidate result set. The refinement step examines actual object/query spatial representation (i.e. location for stationary or route for mobile objects) and predicted temporal information for mobile objects/queries (i.e. the future object/query trajectory) to generate main-memory data structures representing temporal query result. Such data structures enable incremental evaluation of the query and periodical generation of the result updates.

For the purpose of query processing, we assume an available 2D indexing scheme in the underlying DBMS, like R* tree, for indexing segments of a transportation network. The ARGONAUT methodology for continuous range query processing extends the index in order to provide matching of the mobile/stationary objects/queries based on their spatial properties (location or route). Since both queries and objects are referenced and laid on network segments, they are indexed within the same index structure. The leaf nodes of the R* tree is appropriately modified to enable evidence of the both queries and objects, whether mobile or stationary. Each leaf node entry that has the form *<IDseg, MBR>* is extended with two new elements and is represented as quadruple *<IDseg, MBR, Olist, Qlist>* that contains the pointer to the list of objects' IDs (*Olist*) that move along (mobile objects) or reside on (stationary objects) particular network segment, and the pointer to the list of queries' IDs (*Qlist*) whose stationary or moving range intersects that network segment.

The insertion of the object into the index structure and the generation of the object list attached to the leaf node entries are performed according to the following rules:

- A stationary object ID is inserted in the *Olist* attached to the leaf node entry of the R* tree index that corresponds to the network segment at which such object resides.
- A mobile object ID is inserted the *Olist* attached to the leaf node entries of the R* tree index that correspond to the network segments which represents the part of the mobile object's route.

The insertion of the query in the same index structure is performed according to following rules:

- A stationary range query is inserted in the *Qlist* attached to the leaf node entry of the R* tree index if its range overlaps the MBR of the corresponding network segment.
- A mobile range query is inserted in the *Qlist* attached to the leaf node entry of the R* tree index if its route overlaps with MBRs of network segments. The route of the mobile query is defined by the reference mobile object and the query range.

Thus, the index structure performs the matching between mobile/stationary objects and mobile/stationary queries only according to their spatial properties and fulfillment of the spatial part of the query condition. Inserting the query into the index structure enables calculation the initial result set of the query (filter set). Since, the index structure maintains only spatial properties of the objects and queries, it is not selective enough, and thus the initial result set contains many false results. The ARGONAUT query processing methodology applies the refinement step to further refine the initial result set. It uses expected trajectories of mobile objects and mobile queries along with temporal information of the object/query motion and creates main memory data structures that support incremental evaluation. Such data structures represent temporal query result and record the set of mobile (stationary) objects that satisfies the query condition along with time periods (multi time periods) during which the query condition is satisfied. Such refinement step enables significant reduction of the CPU time needed for incremental query evaluation.

3.2 Data Structures

The two tables and associated lists are created in main memory by the refinement step and maintained in the ARGONAUT query processing system. *Continuous Range Query Table* (*CRQT*) stores information regarding continuous queries. A *CRQT* entry is described as (*QID, OID, range, resultSet*) and stores information regarding a continuous query. The table is indexed on the *QID* attribute which is the unique query identifier. *OID* is the identifier of the reference object of the query and *range* defines the shape of the spatial query range around the reference query object. *resultSet* is the initial query result set obtained by the filter step with additional, temporal information about satisfaction of a query created by the refinement step. The initial result set is a list of elements *CQResult* described as (*RID, OID, resPeriod, status*), where *RID* is the result identifier, *OID* is the unique identifier of the object which is the result of the query during period *resPeriod*, while its status in the query result is described by *status* attribute. The values of the *status* attribute are {*INIT_RESULT, NEW_RESULT, OLD_RESULT, NO_RESULT*}. Thus, an object has *INIT_RESULT* status when it will be the result of the query in some period(s) in the future. The status *NEW_RESULT* is associated to an object, when it becomes the new result of the query. The status *OLD_RESULT* is associated to an object when it is the member of the current query result, as well as was a member of the query result in previous evaluation of the query. An object has status *NO_RESULT* when it is not a member of the current query result, nor will be in the future, and will be removed from the result set. Because of time flow, an object as the initial (potential) member of the continuous query result changes its status in a strict sequence [*INIT_RESULT→NEW_RESULT→ OLD_RESULT*]$_n$→ *NO_RESULT*, where [ ]$_n$ indicates that the status sequence can be repeated if the resulting period of an object is a multi period (figure 1).

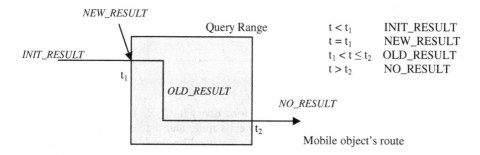

Fig. 1. Changing a mobile object status in a continuous query result with time

For each mobile object in the system, an in-memory *Mobile Object Table (MOT)* is created and maintained. The mobile object entry is described as (*OID, loc, time, speed, route, querySet*), where *OID* is the mobile object identifier, *loc* is the last received location update, *time* is the timestamp of the location update and *speed* is the last received speed update and the *route* is the pointer to the mobile object's route. For each mobile object an additional attribute *querySet* is registered, which represents the list of queries in which such object participates, either in a query result, or as a reference object of a query. Each query in this list is represented by *QueryRef* element which contains two attributes: *QID*, the query identifier, and *resID*, the reference to the appropriate *CQResult* element of this query maintained for the mobile object. If a mobile object is the reference object of a query this reference has *NULL* value.

3.3 Algorithms

The periodic, incremental evaluation of continuous range queries is performed by scanning and examination of *CRQT*, while location update for each mobile object requires scanning and updating both tables. The algorithms for creating those tables through refinement step are different for different types of continuous queries, i.e. mobile-stationary, stationary-mobile and mobile–mobile. The input argument of these algorithms is the set of object *OIDs* that represent the initial query results obtained by the filter step, by examination of the R* tree index. The algorithm for refinement of stationary query over mobile objects is shown on figure 2.

```
Procedure Refinement_SQMO (input: filterSet)
/* filterSet a set of OIDs */
Add new entry smquery in CQRT
for each mo.OID in filterSet
    if not exist mo in MOT then
         Add new entry mo in MOT
    else
         Find entry mo in MOT
    end if
    if mo.route intersects smquery.range then
              rp ∈ TimePeriod and rp ← when (mo.loc within smquery.range)
              if rp.end > currentTime then
              cqres ← new CQresult(RID, mo.OID, rp, INIT_RESULT)
                 smquery.resultSet.Add( cqres )
                 qr ← new QueryRef(smqery.QID, cqres.RID)
              mo.querySet.Add( qr )
              end if
    end if
end for
end procedure
```

Fig. 2. The algorithm for the refinement step for stationary query over mobile objects

The algorithm firstly adds a new entry for a query in *CQRT* table. The spatial relation *intersects* is examined on mobile object's route and the stationary query range. This step enables removing of false results obtained by the filter step. For those objects satisfying spatial relation *intersects*, the time period (multi time period) in which the mobile object is (was, will be) within the query range is calculated (*when* operator), based on current motion parameters (*speed, route*) of the mobile object and/or network data. The operators for spatio-temporal geometric calculations and topological relations in 3D/4D space+time (such as *intersects, within, when*, etc.) are developed and integrated in the ARGONAUT mobile object data management framework [16]. For objects whose resulting period ends somewhere in the future, the new *CQResult* and *QueryRef* elements are created and added to the lists of corresponding *CQRT* and *MOT* entries.

The refinement step for mobile query over stationary objects is performed by the algorithm in figure 3.

```
Procedure Refinement_MQSO (input: filterSet)
/* filterSet a set of OIDs */
Add new entry msquery in CQRT
for each o.OID in filterSet
    queryRoute ← buffer(msquery.OID, route, msquery.range)
    if queryRoute contains o.loc then
              rp ∈ TimePeriod and rp ← when (o.loc within msquery.range)
         if rp.end > currentTime then
              cqres ← new CQresult(RID, o.OID, rp, INIT_RESULT)
                 msquery.resultSet.Add( cqres )
                 qr ← new QueryRef(msqery.QID, NULL)
              Find mo in MOT with msquery.OID
              mo.querySet.Add( qr )
              end if
    end if
end for
end procedure
```

Fig. 3. The algorithm for the refinement step for mobile query over stationary objects

Again, the query is firstly registered in the *CQRT* and new entry is initialized. After that the containment relation (*contains* operator) is examined for each stationary object from the filter set and the polygonal area that is generated as the route of the mobile query (*buffer* operator). As in the previous algorithm, for those objects that are potential query results (relation *contains* is satisfied), the result period *rp* is calculated by applying *within* spatio-temporal relation to a stationary point and a mobile polygon geometries, and returning time period (multi time period) when this relation is satisfied (*when* operator) [16]. Only those objects whose result period ends in the future represent potential query result and corresponding elements are entered in *CQRT* and *MOT* tables.

For the mobile query over mobile objects the algorithm for the refinement step can not be as restrictive as previous refinement algorithms. Since both the query and objects are mobile, it is impossible to calculate exact result periods for each object in the filter set, and thus more processing must be transmitted to the incremental evaluation steps. The algorithm for refinement of mobile quieries over mobile objects is performed through steps shown on figure 4.

```
Procedure Refinement_MQMO (input: filterSet)
/* filterSet a set of OIDs */
Add new entry mmquery in CQRT
for each mo.OID in  filterSet
    if (not exist mo in MOT) then
            Add new entry mo in MOT
    else
        Find entry mo in MOT
    end if
    queryRoute ← buffer(msquery.OID, route, msquery.range)
    if mo.route intersects queryRoute then
        rp ← when (mo.loc within queryRoute)
        if rp.end > currentTime then
            cqres ← new CQresult(RID, mo.OID, rp, INIT_RESULT)
            mmquery.resultSet.Add( cqres )
            qr ← new QueryRef(msqery.QID, cqres.RID)
            mo.querySet.Add( qr )
        end if
    end if
end for
end procedure
```

Fig. 4. The algorithm for the refinement step for mobile query over mobile objects

After initialization of corresponding entries in *CQRT* and *MOT* tables, the intersection between mobile object's route (*polyline* geometry) and a query route (*polygon* geometry) is examined for each mobile object in the filter set. For those mobile objects that satisfy the intersection relation, the result period is calculated, as in Algorithm 1, considering mobile query as a stationary query with the range of a mobile query route. Because the relations (e.g. distance, within, etc.) between two moving objects are not linear it is impossible to exactly determine the resulting period for each mobile object – a potential result of the mobile query. The algorithm can determine only the part of the mobile object's route on which it may potentially be the result of the mobile query, as far as the mobile query is in the corresponding part of its route. Only those objects whose result period ends in the future represent potential query result and corresponding elements are entered in *CQRT* and *MOT* entries' lists. The corresponding *QueryRef* entry is put only in the *querySet* of the mobile objects which are included in the result set, but not in the *querySet* of the mobile objects which are query reference. Thus, the refinement step for the mobile queries over mobile objects is analogous with the refinement for stationary queries over mobile objects when the query range is represented by the buffer around query's route for specified range.

The incremental evaluation step is performed periodically and evaluates the temporal query condition. It determines the incremental query result in regard to the previous evaluation and result tha was sent to the mobile client. The incremental result represents the set of *IncResult* elements containing *OID* of the object and the Boolean attribute *resUpdate* indicating that the object becomes the part of the result of the query (*true* value), or that it is not the result any longer (*false* value). The incremental evaluation step is performed for all continuous queries installed in the system according to the algorithm shown on figure 5.

```
Procedure IncrEval_MS (output: incResultSet)
/* incResultSet of type set of IncResult */
for each cq in CQRT
    for each cqres in cq.resultSet
        if cqres.resPeriod contains currentTime then
            if cqres.status = INIT_RESULT then
                cqres.status ← NEW_RESULT
                ir ← new IncResult (cqres.OID, true)
                incResultSet.Add( ir )
            else
                cqres.status ← OLD_RESULT
            end if
        else if cqres.status = OLD_RESULT then
            if cqres.period is a TimePeriodSet and has periods in the future then
                cqres.status ← INIT_RESULT
            else
                cqres.status ← NO_RESULT
                ir ← new IncResult (cqres.OID, false)
                incResultSet.Add( ir )
                remove cqres from cq.resultSet
            end if
        end if
    end for
end for
end procedure
```

Fig. 5. Incremental evaluation of the set of continuous queries (mobile-stationary and stationary-mobile cases)

If a mobile object enters the query range several times during its motion (the result period is a set of time periods), after one period form the set passed, the object's status is *INIT_RESULT* again, till the beginning of the next period from the set. If the result period of an object passed, the negative query result update is generated and the corresponding element is removed from the query result set (*NO_RESULT* status). The incremental evaluation for the case of mobile queries over mobile objects must include an additional test whether current location of a mobile object lies within the current query range (figure 6).

```
Procedure IncrEval_MM (output: incResultSet)
/* incResultSet of type set of IncResult */
for each cq in CQRT
    for each cqres in cq.resultSet
            mo ← MO with cqres.OID
            if cqres.resPeriod contains currentTime and
                                        mo.currentLoc() within cq.currentRange() then
                if cqres.status = INIT_RESULT then
                    cqres.status ← NEW_RESULT
                    ir ← new IncResult (cqres.OID, true)
                    incResultSet.Add( ir )
            else
                    cqres.status ← OLD_RESULT
                    end if
            else if cqres.status = OLD_RESULT then
                    if cqres.period is a TimePeriodSet and has periods in the future then
                        cqres.status ← INIT_RESULT
                    else
                        cqres.status ← NO_RESULT
                        ir ← new IncResult (cqres.OID, false)
                    incResultSet.Add( ir )
                    remove cqres from cq.resultSet
                end if
            end if
        end for
end for
end procedure
```

Fig. 6. Incremental evaluation of the set of continuous queries (mobile-mobile case)

The functions, *currentLoc()* and *currentRange()* calculate the location/range of the mobile object/query at the current time, given the last received location and the speed of the object/query reference object, the time its location and speed updates was recorded and the route of a mobile object/query. As mentioned, a mobile object moves on its predefined route by its last reported speed. When its predicted location (obtained by the *currentLoc()* function) differs form its exact location by the specified uncertainty threshold, the object must send location and speed update, as well as the time of those updates. Upon receiving updates the server must scan the main memory data structures and update corresponding *MOT* entry, as well as all *CQRT* entries of the affected queries and their result sets (figure 7).

Update of the result periods of an object issuing location and speed updates at certain time instant is based on uncertainty threshold value ut, previous speed v_o, the new speed v_n, and the time t_n of the new update. The following expressions are used to update the resulting period rp of a mobile object (or every time period in the set of time periods) upon receiving location and speed update:

$$rp.start = \frac{v_o(rp.start - t_c) \pm ut}{v_n} + t_c \qquad rp.end = \frac{v_o(rp.end - t_c) \pm ut}{v_n} + t_c$$

The uncertainty threshold value in this formula is added if the mobile object is advanced in regard to its predicted location, and subtract if it is late in regard to its predicted location. Thus, the system provides up to date and accurate result set for every continuous range query it maintains according to location/speed updates of mobile objects.

```
Procedure Update_MDS (input: newloc, newspeed, newtime)
    Update MOT entry for mo.OID
    mo.loc ←   newloc
    mo.speed ←    newspeed
    mo.time ← newtime
    for each qr in mo.querySet
        cq  ←CQR with qr.qid
        if qr.resEntry != NULL then
            update(cq.resulSet, qr.resEntry)
        else
            for each  res in cq.resultSet
                update(cq.resultSet, all)
            end for
        end if
    end for
end procedure
```

Fig. 7. The algorithm for updating main memory data structures upon receiving location/speed update

4   Experimental Evaluation

We perform performance tests and obtain useful results showing that our methodology is applicable in the real world settings of scalable mobile and wireless location based services intended for monitoring and tracking mobile objects. We use the *MobiSim*, the generator of mobile objects on the spatial network to generate a set of mobile objects and mobile queries [17]. The *MobiSim* generator use similar approach as the Network-based Generator of Moving Objects [2], but it enables determination of the current location of a mobile object according to its last location and speed update. The generation of motion data is simulated in real-time for on-line processing. The input to the generator is the real road map of Nis (city in Serbia). The output of the generator is a set of mobile objects that moves on the road network, where some of them also represent the reference objects for continuous queries. All the experiments are conducted on Intel Pentium 4 CPU 3.0 GHz with 512 MB RAM running Windows XP Professional. ARGONAUT continuous query processing algorithms and main memory data structures are implemented using Microsoft Visual Studio C++ and STL collection classes for dynamic arrays and linked lists. Our performance measures are the CPU time needed for refinement step and the creation of main memory data structures, the CPU time for incremental evaluation and generation of incremental query results, and CPU time for updating of main memory data structures upon receiving location/speed update of a mobile object. Since the performance for the access and update of R* tree based index necessary for the filter step of our methodology is well known, we did not perform such experiments. We start our consideration using the set of objects produced by the filter step, which are the candidates for the final result set according to their spatial characteristics, i.e. location for the stationary objects/queries and route for mobile objects/queries. We perform the experiments for the 10000 mobile (stationary) objects and 1000 mobile (stationary) queries and measure the CPU time (in milliseconds) necessary for the refinement step of a continuous query and generation of necessary data structures in main memory for incremental evaluation which is performed periodically and produces incremental query answer (figure 8).

We change the maximal number of objects that are obtained by the filter step of the query processing methodology, and matching of objects and queries based on the R* tree index.

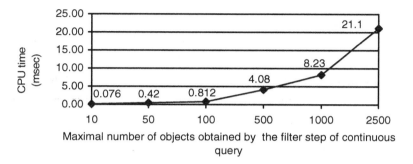

Fig. 8. The duration of the refinement step per query for 10000 MO/1000 CRQ

The experiments show that the refinement step needs very small amount of time, and that for 10000 mobile objects and 1000 continuous range queries, with the maximum of 2500 of all objects in the query filter set, the refinement needs 21.1 milliseconds on the target platform. The memory requirement for main memory data structures generated by the refinement step is given in the figure 9.

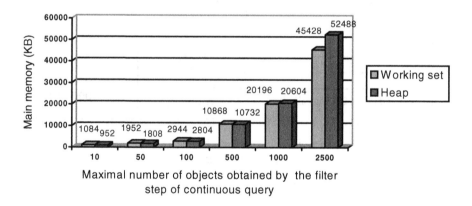

Fig. 9. The memory requirements of the main memory data structures for 10000 MO / 1000 CRQ

The total amount of main memory needed for main memory data structures for the 10000 mobile objects and 1000 continuous queries is about 44 MB of the working set and 51 MB for the heap. The incremental evaluation procedure needs to access the main memory data structures, examine the temporal satisfaction of the query condition and generate incremental result in regard to the previous evaluation of the query. In our experiments the duration of the incremental evaluation for 1000 continuous queries over 10000 objects, for different query ranges representing by the amount of objects selected in the refinement step is in order of millisecond to few tens of milliseconds (figure 10).

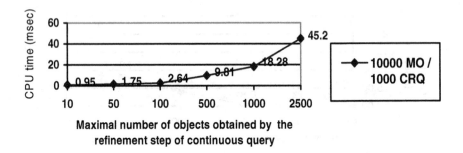

Fig. 10. The CPU time for incremental evaluation for mobile/stationary CRQ over station-ary/mobile objects

For mobile continuous queries over mobile objects, the examination of the additional condition is included in the incremental evaluation procedure, which examines satisfaction of query condition on the current location/range of mobile objects/queries. The experimental results for CPU time needed for refinement step in mobile objects/mobile queries case show an order of magnitude worse time than for the previous experiments (figure 11).

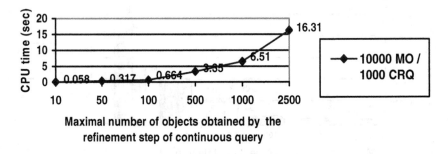

Fig. 11. The CPU time for incremental evaluation for mobile CRQ over mobile objects

According to algorithm on figure 7, a mobile object must update the resulting periods for all continuous queries in whose answer it participates according to its new location and new reported speed. When a mobile object is the reference object of a query (queries) the resulting periods of all results in the set must be updated accordingly. The experiments calculates the CPU time needed for updating the main memory data structures, for 10000 mobile objects and 1000 continuous queries, when the size of the filter set varies from 10 to 2500 objects (figure 12). The 500 mobile objects from the set are randomly selected to be the reference objects of 500 mobile continuous queries. Those objects can also be the members of the result sets of other mobile and stationary queries.

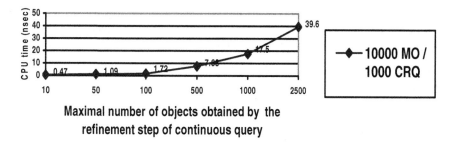

Fig. 12. The average CPU time needed for data structures update upon location/speed update of a mobile object

According to necessary CPU time and main memory storage, the ARGONAUT methodology and algorithms for pre-refinement of the filter query result provides excellent performance applicable in the real LBS applications. Based on created main memory data structures, the algorithm for incremental query evaluation shows excellent performance even in the case of mobile queries over mobile objects. To maintain main memory data structures up-to-date, the Argonaut methodology provides very efficient algorithm which needs few nanoseconds per mobile object which issues location update and which can be both the result of several queries and a reference object of a query.

5   Conclusion

This paper presents the ARGONAUT framework and methodology for evaluation of continuous range queries over mobile objects moving on a fixed network. The ARGONAUT methodology is based on both traditional disk based index structure (R* tree) and main memory data structures, and employs incremental evaluation paradigm to achieve scalability and efficient processing of continuous range queries. It introduces an additional step in traditional spatio-temporal query processing strategy, the pre-refinement step. We perform comprehensive experiments measuring necessary CPU times needed for the pre-refinement step, periodical refinement steps which generate incremental results and update of the main memory data structures due to location/speed updates of mobile objects. Also main memory requirements for pre-refinement data structures are examined. Such experiments show that the performance of the ARGONAUT query processing methodology is more than satisfactory for real world settings in applications for monitoring and tracking mobile objects and LBS.

As future work, we plan to continue working on continuous query processing over objects constrained by the underlying spatial network. We plan to extend our methodology for mobile objects/queries who know only part of their route in advance (or do not know it all), or their routes are changed dynamically according to traffic conditions (jams, accidents, etc.) or change of travel interests. This would require updates of both index structures and main memory data structures and improvement of query processing algorithms to support those changes. An interest direction will also be the development of distributed and mobile query processing methodologies which ship some part of query processing to the mobile clients/objects that has enough processing power and memory capacity to perform some part of the query processing algorithms and store data related to query results.

References

1. Almeida, V. T., Güting, R. H.: Indexing the Trajectories of Moving Objects in Networks. GeoInformatica 9(1) (2005) 33-60
2. Brinkhoff, T.: A Framework for Generating Network-Based Moving Objects. GeoInformatica Journal, Vol. 6, No. 2 (2002), 153-180
3. Cai, Y., Hua, K., Cao, G.: Processing Range-Monitoring Queries on Heterogeneous Mobile Objects. Mobile Data Management, Berkeley, California, USA (2004) 27-38
4. Frentzos, E.: Indexing objects moving on fixed networks. 8th Int. Symp. on Spatial and Temporal databases (SSTD), Santorini, Greece (2003) 289-305
5. Gedik, B., Liu, L.: MobiEyes: Distributed Processing of Continuously Moving Queries on Moving Objects in a Mobile System. EDBT, Heraklion, Greece (2004) 67-87
6. Gedik, B., Wu K-L, Yu, P., Liu, L.: Motion adaptive indexing for moving continual queries over moving objects. CIKM, Washington, DC, USA (2004) 427-436
7. Hu, H., Xu, J., Lee, D.L.: A Generic Framework for Monitoring Continuous Spatial Queries over Moving Objects. ACM SIGMOD, Baltimore, Maryland, USA (2005)
8. Kalashnikov, D., Prabhakar, S., Hambrusch, S.: Main Memory Evaluation of Monitoring Queries Over Moving Objects. Distributed and Parallel Databases: An International Journal, Vol. 15, No. 2 (2004) 117 – 135
9. Kolahdouzan, M. R., Shahabi, C.: Voronoi-Based Nearest Neighbor Search for Spatial Network Databases. VLDB (2004) 840-851
10. Kolahdouzan, M. R., Shahabi, C.: Continuous K Nearest Neighbor Queries in Spatial Network Databases. STDBM (2004).
11. Lazaridis, I., Porkaew, K., Mehrotra, S.: Dynamic Queries Over Mobile Objects. 8th International Conference on Extending Database Technology (EDBT), Prague, Czech Republic (2002) 269- 286
12. Mokbel, M., Xiong, X., Aref, W.: SINA: Scalable Incremental Processing of Continuous Queries in Spatio-temporal Databases. SIGMOD Conference, Paris, France (2004) 623-634
13. Papadias, D., Zhang, J., Mamoulis, N., Tao, Y: Query Processing in Spatial Network Databases. VLDB (2003).
14. Prabhakar, S., Xia, Y., Kalashnikov, D., Aref, W., Susanne E. Hambrusch: Query Indexing and Velocity Constrained Indexing Scalable Techniques for Continuous Queries on Moving Objects. IEEE Transaction on Computers, Vol. 51, No. 10 (2002) 1124-1140
15. Predic, B., Stojanovic, D.: A Framework for Handling Mobile Objects in Location Based Services. 8th AGILE Conference on Geographic Information Science, Lisbon, Portugal (2005) 419-427
16. Stojanovic, D., Djordjevic–Kajan, S.: Modeling and Querying Mobile Objects in Location based Services. Scientific Journal Facta Universitatis – Series Mathematics and Informatics, Vol. 18, No.1 (2003) 59-80
17. Stojanović, D., Djordjević-Kajan, S.: Generation of Mobile Objects Moving on a Transportation Network. Yu INFO, Kopaonik (2003)
18. Xiong, X., Mokbel, M. F., Aref, W. G.: SEA-CNN: Scalable Processing of Continuous K-Nearest Neighbor Queries in Spatio-temporal Databases. ICDE (2005) 643-654
19. Yu, X., Pu, K. Q., Koudas, N.: Monitoring K-Nearest Neighbor Queries over Moving Objects. ICDE (2005) 631-642

Using Styled Layer Descriptor (SLD) for the Dynamic Generation of User- and Context-Adaptive Mobile Maps – A Technical Framework

Alexander Zipf

i3mainz - Institute for Spatial Information and Surveying Technology,
Department of Geoinformatics and Surveying,
University of Applied Sciences FH Mainz,
Holzstrasse 36 - 55116 Mainz, Germany
zipf@geoinform.fh-mainz.de
http://www.geoinform.fh-mainz.de/~zipf/

Abstract. The well known OGC Styled Layer Descriptor (SLD) specification allows to specify the design of a map. On the other hand in LBS and UbiGIS maps need to be generated dynamically taking a lot of factors into account which describe the current user, situation and context. We present how to transform such user and context models with a base map represented as SLD resulting in an "adapted" SLD. Further we discuss how to apply these in order to generate SVG-based mobile maps. In order to generate base maps represented as SLD we developed a ArcMap2SLD-generator. This tool allows designing a map using ESRI ArcMap and automatically converting it into a valid SLD-file. This acts as a base for modifications using the mentioned user and context models. Using this SLD as parameter within WMS-requests results in an "adapted map". We explain this approach and discuss potentials and weaknesses.

1 Introduction

The OGC Styled Layer Descriptor (SLD) specification allows specifying the design of a map – in particular a map served by a SLD-WMS. It is getting more and more popular, but still has some weaknesses – especially for use in LBS (e.g. Brinkhoff 2005). On the other hand in LBS or UbiGIS maps need to be generated dynamically taking a lot of factors into account – in particular also attributes describing the current user, the situation and general context [9, 12, 21, 22, 23]. This is being adopted now more and more. An example application would be user-specific focus maps as introduced by [20]. Such a User and Context model can be represented also using XML, e.g. [18, 19] present XML schema for task-oriented mobile maps within a tour guide scenario. See [18] for adaptive mobile GI services based on Ontologies for pedestrian navigation. Now we have the task to use the information represented within these models to parameterize maps. This is done using the Styled Layer Descriptor (SLD) specification. But as this specification still lacks some expressiveness this still leads to problems. We present these after explaining the general idea of the necessary

K.-J. Li and C. Vangenot (Eds.): W2GIS 2005, LNCS 3833, pp. 183–193, 2005.

transformations in order to gain a valid SLD from the mentioned user and context models. Further we show how these then can be used in order to generate also SVG-based mobile maps [10] and what problems we encountered with that approach. A further section will introduce our ArcMap2SLD-Generator. This tool is helpful to generate a base map using ESRI ArcMap and then generate a valid SLD-file from that. The generated SLD in turn acts as a base for further modifications through the earlier mentioned user and context models. Using this SLD as parameter within a WMS request results in an "adapted map". We explain this approach and discuss the potentials and weaknesses.

2   User and Context Modelling for Adaptive GI Services

Since a few years it has become more and more accepted, that the design of electronic maps – in particular mobile maps - needs to consider a much broader range of influences than conventional maps in order to present just the right information needed in the current situation by the current user of such a map-based system (21, 22, 23). After focusing on technical limitations of mobile devices (storage, processing, interaction, display size, bandwidth etc.) the focus of research in mobile maps shifted recently to cognitive aspects (9, 21), e.g. navigation and wayfinding support [8, 11, 16]. Further examples for adaptive GI applications include e.g. the computation of routes based on context-related criteria [7] or user-aware spatial push of information [24].

In order to actually apply the ideas presented there to an automated system we need to consider three different main aspects:

- What are the indicators influencing the design of a map (which attributed describing the current task, user, situation etc. – we can refer to this as the *User Model* and *Context Model*. They (are sometimes combined) and deliver the structure and possible value domains describing the situation.
- How do these attributes actually influence the design of the map? For answering this we need to components: a.) knowledge about cognitive aspects how to present which information the best way to the user and b.) a mathematical or computational framework for actually applying this within a computerized system – telling how to calculate the values for the weighting the adaptation etc. See [25] for details.
- A technical framework how to apply this in a standards-based open system.

We will only very shortly introduce the state of art for the first two aspects and then will focus on proposing a generic technical framework that makes use of open GI standards only.

In spite of much research the terms context, situation and user model etc. are still quite vague. A range of definitions and proposals exist – mainly originating from work in Ubiquitous Computing, which also has been tried to adopt within the GI community. We do not consider that it is fruitful to argue about "THE RIGHT" model here (if one exists at all), but argue, that we need some interoperable way to transform between the different flavors of application and domain specific classifications. As one example we present a suggestion by [18] adapting ideas from [5 and 6] that was used for some research prototypes.

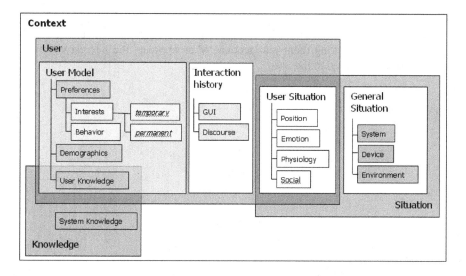

Fig. 1. Integrated User and Context model [18]

For further discussions of these topics see [4, 5, 6]. As such models are nowadays typically expressed using XML we can expect that there will be ways to transform these into the actually needed representation (or even a standard ontology, once a widely accepted one appears) quite easily (e.g. using XSLT). What we have to note here is that we do need not only theoretical construct, but really a formal representation of the relevant concepts, their value domains and relationships, e.g. using the OWL language. OWL allows to define and instantiate *ontologies*, which are explicit formal descriptions of concepts or classes in a domain of discourse, which express a shared specification of a conceptualization. OWL thus provides the possibility of expressing information associated with people, events, devices, places, time, and space etc. Moreover, it provides means for sharing such context knowledge, thereby minimizing the cost of sensing.

3 Applying User Modeling for Adaptive GI Services

As an important example we focus now on how to model the user within such an adaptive map-based system. [18] propose an ontology-based approach for their own realizations of adaptive GI services that employs different machine learning methods based on stereotype reasoning, domain inference etc. [3] in order to calculate dynamic user properties as for example the current interest of the user in specific types of objects. They present a XML schema (see figure 1) for a user model that consists of basic user properties (UserID, name, preferred language etc.).

It also includes demographic attributes and account data. But the most important property is the different *interests* of the user modelled as "*UMInterest*". This is described by name, description and further type definition. Within the *UMConfidence* property the probabilities (individual and normalized over all users) calculated by a software module, that calculates individual user preferences and their probabilities dynamically from the different data sources are stored as well as the algorithm used for this. This gives a measure for the validity of the calculated interest values. Storing this explicitly allows taking them into account when applying the interest values for adapting a service offered to the user.

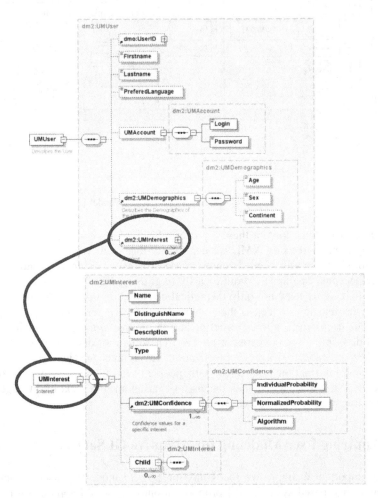

Fig. 2. User Model User XML Schema & UMInterest including confidence elements [18]

One of the dominant factors for adaptation is the task the user wants to perform - what does the user wants to do at all. As all parameters relevant for adaptation the relevant factors need to be represented formally within the system. Therefore we present shortly an example of an ontology for tasks the user wants to perform with a mobile map. The idea is that user activities can be described in an ontology. See figure 3 for a recent example of a task ontology that has been newly developed by [18] based on the ideas of [12].

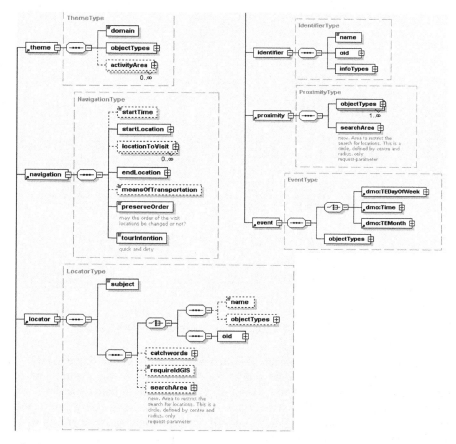

Fig. 3. Extract of XML schema of the "MapTask" model (see [18] extending work by [12]).

4   A Technical Framework to Generate User-Adapted SLDs

The OGC Styled Layer Descriptor Specification [26] defines an XML Schema to describe the appearance of the layers a map. The general model (simplified version) is depicted as UML class diagram in figure 4. A SLD document is a XML file that can be validated against this model. SLDs are getting more popular in Web Mapping applications with the growing availability for SLD support in WMS. But until recently these SLDs are more or less hand-made or application specific. But as SLDs provide the means to specify the look of map in a domain and vendor-neutral way it is a good choice for a formal representation of maps in general.

The question is now how to go beyond these hand-made SLDs and generate these in an automated way (using Open Standards predominantly). This is a technical question and can be solved easily. An example is given in section 4 where a SLD generator for ESRI ArcMap maps is presented. A more general way is to use different data sources (e.g. OGC Catalogs or WFS and their metadata – all of which are XML-based) in order to generate the XML-based SLD files from these using XSL

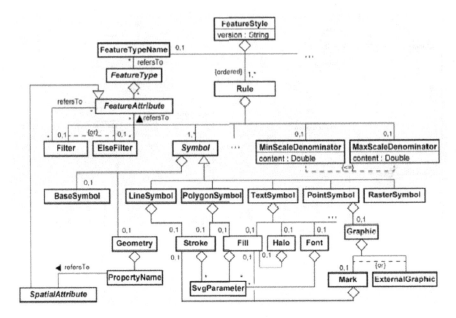

Fig. 4. Simplified Data Model of SLD according to (OGC 2003)

Transformations. A similar approach has often been used for converting e.g. GML to SVG (this would be only the right side (Case A) of figure 5 with a static gml2svg transformation script). But in both examples we would have to hard-code the styling information within the XSLT script. This is not desirable, as styling information should be separated from code. Therefore [10] present an innovative approach where also the transformation scripts are being dynamically generated using standards-based data sources like information e.g. from OGC WFS *DescribeFeatures* and *GetCapabilities* requests. But while in this approach even two XSL Transformations are generated dynamically, still the SLD is a static file (figure 5, left oval). Therefore we want to extend this approach by also eliminating the need to build this SLD by hand. Further we want to extend the approach and include user and context specific elements to generate adapted maps. In the following first a short introduction to the original transformation cascade is given and then of the extended approach to include user- and context parameters.

4.1 Generic Transformations in Order to Produce Maps

For a generic application the gml2svg transformation script cannot be a static document because both the structure of the GML data as well the styling of the presentation depend on the specific application. Therefore the script must be computed dynamically. As the presentation information is contained in an SLD document it is possible to generate the gml2svg script in another XSL transformation from the SLD document.

Figure 5 shows the three XSL transformations differentiating between 'runtime transformation' being executed after a specific query and 'parameterization transformation' which can be executed earlier. It shows the complete transformation cascade

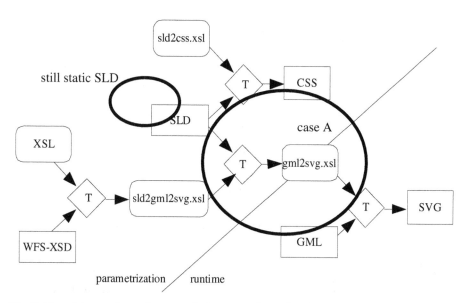

Fig. 5. Complete transformation cascade for a generic application-parameterized generation of SVG from GML data with styling information from an SLD document [10]. T stands for executing a XSL Transformation.

that needs be executed in order to display geodata from a WFS as an SVG document based on an XML schema from the WFS and an application-specific SLD document in a completely generic way.

4.2   Generating User Adaptive SLDs

In the following we want to extend this approach by also generating the still static SLD document also dynamically - taking user and context information into account. Here come the user and context models introduced earlier into play: First we need a base map, or more precisely a base SLD describing the not-adapted map. This can be generated from desktop GIS like ArcMap as explained later or from another SLD generator tool that certainly will appear soon. But certainly somewhere we need basic signature rules in some format for the first step. So let's take the mentioned base SLD: we then have the task to combine this base SLD with the user and context model. This can be achieved by generating a XSL transformation script from both the user and context model that transforms the base SLD into an adapted SLD. This generation of the transform script includes the knowledge of how to adapt a base SLD according to specific user and context values.

This approach leads to the incorporation of the adaptation knowledge into "hard coded" rules that generate the XSL. This is a situation that should also be improved. This means instead of writing the rules into the code it would be wishful to have some declarative language or representation that describes the adaptation rules in a language independent way. As such a declarative rule representation is not yet available we propose the future definition of such a rule base. The following figure shows the approach. The resulting "*Adapted SLD*" then can act as input for the transformation cascade introduced by [10].

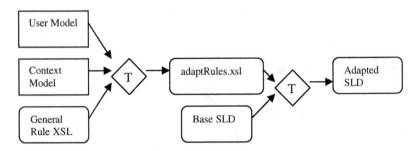

Fig. 6. Extension of the transformation cascade in order to generated an adapted SLD from User and Context Models and general rules how to apply these (specified in XSL)

5 Visual Generation of SLD-Files with Desktop GIS

Our application that generates the base SLD from existing maps in commercial Desktop GIS is introduced briefly. On the top left corner of the figure 7 one can see a screenshot of the ArcObjects application that analyses all layers and their according

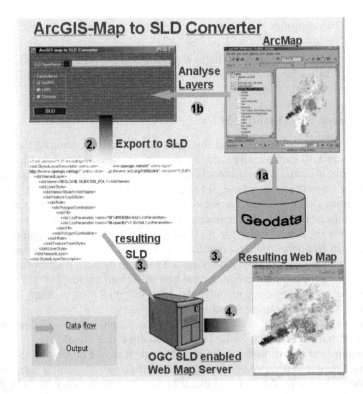

Fig. 7. Process of designing a map in ArcMap and exporting it to a SLD document, that can be used to configure WMS servers or to issue user-specific requests to SLD Web Map Services

renderer types and symbol definitions within an ESRI ArcMap map and transforms these into an SLD document that can act as input for an SLD WMS (e.g. UMN, degree, ArcIMS). We propose to use this base map SLD as a base for further modifications according to the user and context models introduced. The results of applying the generated SLD file to a WMS can be seen in figure 8, which compares the map to the original ArcMap display. One can recognize from figure 8 that it is still not possible to achieve 100% the same look using the WMS on the one hand and the original ArcMap map on the other, but a very good compromise can be achieved.

Some map server currently still offer even less support then the ones we used for all the parameters defined in SLD and therefore result in maps looking more differently. It is hopefully only a matter of time until this varying support of the SLD has reached a more stable situation and the different render engines produce very similar maps from the same SLD configuration. In order to achieve this also the SLD specification needs further extensions in order to clarify how to represent a range of symbolization issues.

6 Summary and Outlook

In this paper we have presented several novel ideas for generating adaptive GI services for mobile applications using dynamic personalization as well as context factors. Possibilities for future enhancements include first of all a more specific definition of the rules how to adapt the SLD in what way for specific parameters. It is an innovative approach of applying adaptation techniques like learning of user models in the domain of geographic information services that opens a new area of research within GIScience.

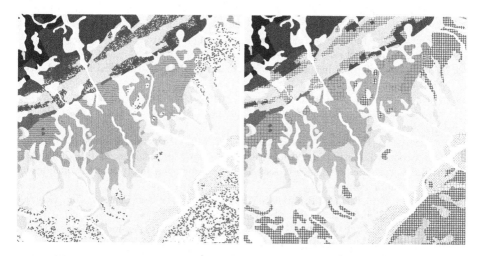

Fig. 8. Comparison of the resulting map from the dynamically generated SLD description renderend by UMN Mapserver by SLD (right side) and the original map in ArcMap (left side)

A lot of further work is necessary to develop a solid theory for this kind of adaptation to GI services. While we have shown that it is possible to adapt GI services dynamically to context and user properties in general - how to actually do this (what parameters to choose, how to weight them and what types of adaptation to realize) the best way in order to achieve optimal results - is yet open. This requires further empirical tests, evaluations as well as theoretical work.

Acknowledgements

I like to thank all former and current colleagues for their inspiration and help.

References

1. Agrawala, M. and Stolte, C. (2001). Rendering Effective Route Maps: Improving Usability Through Generalization. In SIGGRAPH 2001, Los Angeles, California, USA
2. Brinkhoff, T. (2005): Towards a Declarative Portrayal and Interaction Model for GIS and LBS. Proceedings 8th Conference on Geographic Information Science (AGILE 2005), Estoril, Portugal, 2005, pp. 449-458.
3. Fink, J. & A. Kobsa (2002): User Modeling in Personalized City Tours. Artificial Intelligence Review 18(1), 33-74
4. Chen, H. (2004): SOUPA - Standard Ontology for Ubiquitous and Pervasive Applications. http://pervasive.semanticweb.org/
5. Dey, A.K., Abowd, G.D.: Towards a Better Understanding of Context and ContextAwareness. In CHI 2000 Workshop on the What, Who, Where, When, and How of ContextAwareness.
6. Jameson, A. (2001): Modeling Both the Context and the User. Personal Technologies, 5, 1.
7. Joest, M. and Stille, W. (2002): A User-Aware Tour Proposal Framework using a Hybrid Optimization Approach. Agnès Voisard, Shu-Ching Chen (Eds.): ACM-GIS 2002, Proceedings of the Tenth ACM International Symposium on Advances in Geographic Information Systems, McLean, VA , USA.
8. Kray C. 2003: Situated Interaction on Spatial Topics. PhD. thesis, DISKI series vol. 274, AKA Verlag, Berlin, 2003.
9. Meng, L., Zipf, A. and Reichenbacher, T. (eds.) (2004): Map-based mobile services – Theories, Methods and Implementations. Springer Geosciences. Springer Verlag. Heidelberg.
10. Merdes, M., J. Häußler, A. Zipf (2005): GML2GML: Generic and Interoperable Round-Trip Geodata Editing using Standards-Based Knowledge Sources. AGILE 2005. 8.th AGILE Conference on GIScience. Association of Geographic Information Laboratories in Europe. Estoril. Portugal.
11. Raubal, M., Miller, H. and Bridwell, S. (forthcoming 2004): User Centered Time Geography For Location-Based Services. Geografiska Annaler B.
12. Reichenbacher, T. (2004), Mobile Cartography - Adaptive Visualisation of Geographic Information on Mobile Devices, PhD thesis, TU Munich.
13. Reuter, A., Zipf, A. (2005 in print): GIScience – Where Next? In: Fotheringham S. and Wilson, J.P. (eds.): Handbook of GIS. Blackwell Publishers.
14. W3C: Extensible Stylesheet Language, Version 1.0, W3C Recommendation, 2001.
15. W3C: Scalable Vector Graphics (SVG) 1.1 Specification, W3C Recommendation, 2003.

16. Winter, S., Raubal, M. and Nothegger, C. (2004): Focalizing Measures of Salience for Route Directions. In: A. Zipf, L. Meng and T. Reichenbacher (Editors). Map-based mobile services – Theories, Methods and Implementations, Springer. Berlin.
17. Zipf, A. and Krüger, S. (2001): TGML - Extending GML by Temporal Constructs - A Proposal for a Spatiotemporal Framework in XML. ACM-GIS 2001. The Ninth ACM International Symp. on Advances in Geographic Information Systems. Atlanta. USA.
18. Zipf, A and Jöst, M. (2005 accepted): Implementing Adaptive Mobile GI Services based on Ontologies - Examples for pedestrian navigation support. In: CEUS - Computers, Environment and Urban Systems - An International Journal. Special Issue on LBS and UbiGIS. Pegamon Press, Elsevier.
19. Zipf, A. und von Hunolstein S. (2003): Task oriented map-based mobile tourist guides.International Workshop: "HCI in Mobile Guides". at Mobile HCI 2003. Fifth International Symposium on Human Computer Interaction with Mobile Devices and Services. 8.-11.Sept. 2003. Undine. Itlay.
20. Zipf, A. and Richter, K.F. (2002): Using Focus Maps to Ease Map Reading. Developing Smart Applications for Mobile Devices. In: Künstliche Intelligenz (KI). Special issue: Spatial Cognition. 04/2002. 35-37.
21. Zipf, A. (2002): User-Adaptive Maps for Location-Based Services (LBS) for Tourism. In: K. Woeber, A. Frew, M. Hitz (eds.), Proc. of the 9th Int. Conf. for Information and Communication Technologies in Tourism, ENTER 2002. Innsbruck, Austria. Springer Computer Science. Heidelberg, Berlin.
22. Zipf, A. (1998): DEEP MAP - A prototype context sensitive tourism information system for the city of Heidelberg. In: Proc. of GIS-Planet 98. Lisboa, Portugal.
23. Zipf, A. (2000): DEEP MAP / GIS - Ein verteiltes raumzeitliches Touristeninformationssystem. Phd-Dissertation. Ruprecht-Karls-Universität Heidelberg.
24. Zipf, A. and Aras, H. (2002): Proactive Exploitation of the Spatial Context in LBS - through Interoperable Integration of GIS-Services with a Multi Agent System (MAS). AGILE 2002. Int. Conf. on Geographic Information Science of the Association of Geographic Information Laboratories in Europe (AGILE). 04.2002. Palma. Spain.
25. Zipf, A. (2003): Zur Bestimmung von Funktionen für die personen- und kontextsensitive Bewertung der Bedeutung von Geoobjekten für Fokuskarten. Symposium für Angewandte Geographische Informationstechnologie. AGIT 2003. Salzburg.
26. OGC Inc.: Styled Layer Description Implementation Specification, Version 1.0.0, 2002(a).

Delivering Personalized Context-Aware Spatial Information to Mobile Devices*

Joe Weakliam[1], Daniel Lynch[1], Julie Doyle[1],
Michela Bertolotto[1], and David Wilson[2]

[1] Department of Computer Science, University College Dublin, Dublin 4, Ireland
[2] Department of Software and Information Systems,
University of North Carolina at Charlotte, 9201 University City Blvd,
Charlotte, NC 28223, USA
{joe.weakliam, daniel.b.lynch, julie.doyle, michela.bertolotto}@ucd.ie,
davils@uncc.edu

Abstract. When attempting to locate specific spatial information on-line users face the burden of having to differentiate between relevant and extraneous spatial content. This problem is more evident in the mobile environment where users are impeded by several device limitations. One way of overcoming this is to automatically profile users' spatial content preferences by recording all interactions users have with maps and monitoring users' movements in the field as they interact with maps. We describe a multimodal mobile GIS that implicitly records all user movements, as well as interactions between users and maps, to dynamically recommend information and to infer persistent spatial information preferences. A search engine, prefetching context-aware information, is incorporated to enhance the users' experiences. Modeling preferences in this manner allows us to recommend personalized context-aware spatial content to users whenever they request maps. A specific case study has been developed around subjects working on surveying tasks where spatial information is required in the field.

1 Introduction

Several well-documented problems become evident in GIS when users request specific spatial information online. Many applications delivering spatial infor-mation in the form of maps do not account for user spatial interests and simply present users with maps containing default content. This is unacceptable es-pecially when users request spatial information in the field where information overload becomes critical. Mobile devices are well known for their limitations (e.g processing power, screen size) and delivering maps containing superfluous detail results in both unnecessarily long downloading times and the obfuscation of map interaction goals. Several mobile GIS applications propose overcoming these drawbacks by soliciting the user for input [1][2] each time the user re-quests spatial information. Although some degree of personalization is provided,

---

* The support of the Informatics Research Initiative of Enterprise Ireland is gratefully acknowledged.

K.-J. Li and C. Vangenot (Eds.): W2GIS 2005, LNCS 3833, pp. 194–205, 2005.
© Springer-Verlag Berlin Heidelberg 2005

this solution is not practical as the user is continually pestered to input detail pertaining to current interests where interacting with mobile devices can be an arduous task.

In existing GIS applications users have the potential to interact with maps in a variety of contrasting ways when locating content satisfying their goals, e.g. a tourist searching for points of interest, a professional seeking directions to their destination, etc. Users have the option of browsing the map through panning, zooming, and toggling features on or off. Various aspects of map content can be highlighted by performing specific spatial queries. Clients can also record personal experiences describing different areas and features of the map by posting annotations. Monitoring all these implicit interactions between users and maps provides an invaluable means for modeling user preferences. There is no burden on the user to supply explicit input related to their current interests which is paramount when interacting with mobile devices. Information describing user preferences can simply be extracted from the interaction detail recorded using data mining and collaborative filtering techniques.

Many GIS applications exist that deliver both semantic information and spatial content to clients upon receiving requests for map content. However, many of these Location-based Services (LBS) return information based on location and possibly profile detail, and thus no information related to future destinations of a user is provided. Incorporating a user's trajectory, together with location and profile detail, offers increased scope for recommending even more pertinent information, as data related to a user's future movements can be dynamically transmitted. Prefetching relevant data before a user reaches a particular location is extremely useful when transmitting information to mobile devices due to device constraints. Also, few LBS exist allowing clients to annotate the physical space around them. Those applications that do provide this functionality, however, associate annotations with physical locations as opposed to map features. Linking annotations to features allows detail related to spatial content preferences to be extracted from annotation content when users browse or create annotations.

We have developed a multimodal mobile GIS called CoMPASS (Combining Mobile Personalized Applications with Spatial Services) [3] on a Tablet PC. CoMPASS delivers personalized context-aware information to users with contrasting requirements. In this paper, we describe a case study outlining how information is delivered to surveyors who require specific information in the field. As CoMPASS caters for multimodal input, surveyors are able to interact using pen or voice-based input, depending on what best suits their needs for a particular task in a particular context. This is crucial as input modalities such as a mouse or keyboard may be unfeasible or inappropriate in the field. In such environments pen and speech based input may enhance a user's experience as users can locate and record task-relevant information simply by issuing basic voice commands. All movements and interactions between the surveyor and the map are captured implicitly at the interface and are used to dynamically recommend content. Relevant information regarding persistent spatial preferences is extracted from recorded interaction detail to create surveyor profiles. CoMPASS improves the quality of dynamic information searching by basing the search process on several parameters, i.e. surveyor location, trajectory, map content, and profile information.

This paper is structured as follows. Section 2 describes related research in the areas of mobile GIS, multimodal interaction, implicit profiling, and information retrieval, all of which are incorporated into the CoMPASS application. We introduce the CoMPASS system in section 3 detailing the integration of various system components and how we provide personalized context-aware spatial information to surveyors in the field. Section 4 provides an evaluation of our application with results showing how relevant preferences are established. We conclude in section 5 and propose future research topics.

2   Related Work

There are many LBS developed for the mobile environment. FLAME2008 [1] is a mobile GIS that is being developed for the Bejing Olympics in 2008 and proposes delivering personalized situation-aware information to clients using LBS. However, the architecture of FLAME2008 is based on the user supplying explicit input related to interests whereas CoMPASS requires no input from users. Hinze and Voisard [4] describe an event notification system that delivers various information to mobile devices based on location, time, profile of end users, and their history. Whereas many systems only consider the user location when recommending content to clients, the work in [4] also takes time and user interests into context. CoMPASS goes one step further by recommending information based on current location, trajectory, profile, and content present in the map.

Graffiti [5] is an application allowing users to collectively define what is relevant about a particular location by posting electronic notes. GeoNotes [6] is another LBS, similar to Graffiti, in that both are context-aware applications incorporating the notion of social navigation, i.e. the social and subversive qualities of content created by users may be more interesting than content created by administrators. There are two fundamental differences between these 2 systems and CoMPASS: (1) map feature detail is used in the search mechanism of CoMPASS when recommending information to clients, and (2) CoMPASS incorporates a trajectory model providing more accurate result sets and introducing the concept of positional relevance to the search process. In Genie [7] a strategy for intelligently precaching information is proposed. Genie returns information on the attractions a tourist might visit in their vicinity. A precaching system is especially relevant to mobile applications due to restrictions on processing power and bandwidth limitations and thus we integrate precaching of information in CoMPASS. One major difference between Genie and CoMPASS is that precaching in CoMPASS is based in large part on the trajectory of the user as opposed to in Genie where it is based solely on the user's current location.

CoMPASS uses the idea of implicit profiling when building models of user preferences. Implicit profiling is the notion of monitoring users' implicit interactions when for example, browsing the Web, and then ascertaining preferences in specific content based on the interactions. Cheese [8] is an intelligent interface that monitors all mouse movements on a Web page to infer user interests. With Cheese it was found that certain common mouse behaviors are useful for content providers when increasing the effectiveness of interface design. Kelly [9] deems three sources of implicit feedback to be most significant when establishing user interest in Web pages: reading time per document, scrolling, and interaction. The following hypotheses are outlined in [9]: users spend more time (1) reading, (2) scrolling within, and (3) interacting with, documents they find relevant. CoM-PASS utilizes concepts prevalent in implicit profiling to ascertain user interests in aspects of spatial and semantic information when users browse maps.

The use of multimodal interfaces allows for the simplification of user interaction with an application. In [10] Oviatt et al discuss the advantages of multimodal interfaces and the use of speech and pen-based input as individual modalities and combined modalities is described. An evaluation of speech and pen-based interactions is provided in [11]. Compared with speech-only interaction it was shown that during visual-spatial tasks with users, multimodal pen/voice interaction can result in 10% faster task completion time, 36% fewer task-critical content errors, and 50% fewer spontaneous disfluencies. In [12], a mobile architecture for pedestrian navigation is outlined incorporating the fusion of different modes of input such as speech, gesture and keyboard/mouse as well as sensors. The aim of [12] is to increase speech recognition rates in environments where noise levels are high and user contexts are continually changing. We incorporate pen- and speech-based input in CoMPASS allowing surveyors to interact with the personalized maps in a manner they prefer.

3   The CoMPASS System

In this section we introduce and describe CoMPASS. Figure 1 shows the system architecture. CoMPASS is based on a 3-tier architecture comprising a deployment layer (interface), a services layer (providing personalization and context-aware information), and a server layer (containing profiles and spatial data). The system architecture and associated functionality are described in the following sections within the context of the surveyor case study considered in this paper.

3.1   Deployment Layer

The deployment layer forms the system interface and has two main functions: display the (vector) map content and capture all explicit and implicit actions executed by surveyors. Using vector data allows for map content to be divided into distinct map layers where each layer corresponds to a specific map feature. This enables the capture of detailed information each time the surveyor interacts with the map, as each action can be associated with a particular feature or set of features. As CoMPASS caters for multimodal interaction, surveyors can interact with the maps using either pen-based or voice-based input. Actions executed by surveyors at the interface are divided into 2 categories: (1) standard map

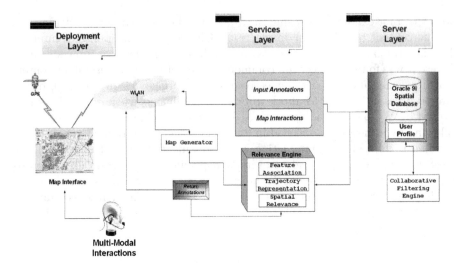

Fig. 1. CoMPASS System Architecture

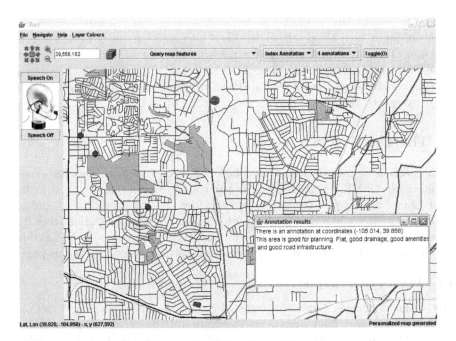

Fig. 2. CoMPASS ScreenShot

actions involving map features and specific map regions, e.g. pan, zoom, highlight feature, etc; (2) annotations browsed and created. Map feature content displayed is determined by detail contained in surveyors' profiles, whereas annotations displayed are determined by several criteria including the surveyors' location and trajectory (GPS), profile information, and feature content currently present in the map.

Figure 2 shows a sample screenshot of the CoMPASS interface displaying both map feature content and annotations based on one particular surveyor's context, i.e. their current location, trajectory, and profile. The interface has been developed using an open source, Java-based toolkit called OpenMap^{TM}[13]. In the case of Figure 2, the surveyor is trying to locate potential sites for developing an apartment complex. Notable geographic factors determining suitable locations include drainage, aspect, infrastructure, and local amenities. Several annotations, relevant in terms of the surveyor's current context and created by other similar system users, are returned by the system (these are represented by dark points on the map). In figure 2 the surveyor has opened up one specific annotation to see what information it contains. Annotations can take the form of text, image, audio, or video files.

3.2   Services Layer

Whenever the surveyor interacts with the map content on the Tablet PC, several items related to the current state of the map and the surveyor's current context are recorded in log files. If a standard map action is executed the following is recorded:

- The action executed (pan, highlight feature, etc.).
- The map feature(s) upon which the action was executed.
- The number of the action executed.
- The time at which the action was executed.
- The boundary of the resulting frame generated by the action.
- The map feature(s) intersecting the map frame produced by the action.

Capturing this detail implicitly enables us to infer persistent surveyor interest in particular map features, e.g. one surveyor highlights perennial shorelines whenever he requests maps. If a surveyor opens an annotation to access its contents we record the following:

- The id of the user viewing the annotation.
- The rating assigned to the annotation by the viewer.
- The feature(s) described by the annotation.

If the surveyor creates their own annotation then the following detail is captured by CoMPASS:

- The id of the user creating the annotation.
- The current location of the user.
- The time and date the annotation was created.
- The map feature(s) linked to the annotation.

Recording this detail from surveyors' interactions with annotations allows us to ascertain more information about surveyors' preferences. Personalized context-aware information is then recommended based on detail extracted from the log files.

When prefetching annotations to recommend to surveyors, CoMPASS makes use of location and trajectory information. Buffered surveyor locations provide the basis for the CoMPASS trajectory model and enables us to introduce positional relevance when searching for and prefetching succinct annotations. A search boundary is created mirroring the surveyor's movements within which annotations are considered to have positional relevance. The direction and velocity of the surveyor dictates the size and shape of this search boundary. Using the trajectory model to predict the user's future movements enables us to return relevant annotations before the user reaches a particular location. When prefetching annotations, if a surveyor explicitly turns off a map feature, an assumption is then made that they are not interested in either the feature or any information associated with the feature. Annotations, therefore, can be associated not only with a physical location, but also with specific map content.

3.3   Server Layer

This component stores the spatial data, annotations created by surveyors, and surveyor profile information. Vector data from Tiger/Line 2000 files [14] and stored in a remote database is used to render the maps. Recorded interaction information from map sessions is analyzed with relevant preferences inserted into the surveyor profiles. When determining surveyor interests regarding map feature content, CoMPASS uses data mining [15][16] to spot patterns in individual and group surveyor behavior. Clustering and association rule mining are used to extract trends in the surveyors' browsing behavior from the log files.

Interest map frames are extracted from log file information when inserting detail into the surveyor profiles. A map frame is the current visible state of the map after the execution of a map action. Interest frames are determined based on the following criteria: (a) the time interval between two consecutive map actions exceeds a threshold value, and (b) the first map action is performed on only a single map feature, e.g. highlighting a feature. Each interest frame can be viewed as a vector object with the following associated attributes:

1. *frame_time*: the time interval before the surveyor performs the immediate succeeding action.
2. *frame_area*: the area of the frame.
3. *frame_boundary*: the outer boundary of the frame (latitude/longitude).
4. *frame_features*: all the map features toggled on and intersecting the outer frame boundary when the frame was recorded.

A score is also associated with each frame where the score is calculated as follows:

$$frame\_score = frame\_features * frame\_area * 1/frame\_time \qquad (1)$$

Clustering interest frames allows us to spot trends in individual user behavior or with group behavior. The clustering process can be tested with different pairs of input attributes, e.g. *frame_score* and *frame_time*, or *frame_time* and *frame_area*, to obtain contrasting result patterns. Examining the content of generated clusters reveals patterns in attributes of the interest frames belonging to each cluster, e.g. the sets of map features and the areas of the map that similar users focus on. It is also possible to cluster interest frames based on different sets of input map features in order to ascertain clusters of users based on map feature content. As a result of the clustering process, specific map feature content is then recommended to users belonging to the same cluster. This means that CoMPASS is capable of accommodating users with contrasting goals and requirements, i.e. not just surveyors. We intend to extend the data mining functionality of CoM-PASS to facilitate the clustering of users based on actual session information. A session definition ('tag'), describing the core focus of each user session, will be created based on the most significant interest frames of that session. Users will then be clustered based on session 'tags' and map feature content can then be recommended to all members of the one cluster.

Association rule mining is the discovery of association rules in large databases. We also use the concept of association rule mining for establishing trends in how users interact with various map features whenever they request maps and for grouping users with similar feature interests together. Similarity measures between map features can be calculated based on feature presence in session map frames. Map features that are highly similar are inclined to appear in map frames together, i.e. feature A and feature B are similar if frames containing feature A also contain feature B. If 2 features are found to be similar then the system can recommend both if recommending one as being an interest feature.

4   Evaluation

We ran two experiments to evaluate the effectiveness of CoMPASS when recommending personalized context-aware information to users. The primary objective was to show that both individual and group interests in spatial content could be ascertained by simply monitoring implicit interactions and movements of participants in the experiment, in this case subjects simulating surveyors in the field. Three participants took part in the experiment. As detailed vector data in Ireland is proprietary, we are reliant on source data from US Tiger files, which necessitated the simulation of each surveyor's movements and actions in the field. Mapping tasks were assigned to participants for each map session where the task ultimately determined what feature(s) was the focus of the session. When assigning tasks it was necessary to vary the task sequences during the course of the experiment whilst maintaining some degree of consistency among the map content involved. Data from 80 sessions involving the three participants was gathered. A predetermined set of 80 mapping tasks was drafted whereby each of the 3 users was assigned the exact same task sequences for each of the first 40 sessions and for the remaining 40 sessions the task sequences were varied.

Figure 3 shows the results of the first experiment and displays a graph of session number vs. mean similarity score for 3 different pairs of features for each participant. The pairs of features chosen were deemed significant for surveyors locating suitable sites for development, i.e. shorelines/rivers for drainage, high-

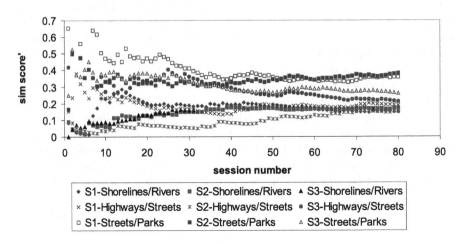

Fig. 3. Feature similarity scores

ways/streets for infrastructure and streets/parks for facilities. The similarity score between any 2 features is calculated by measuring the Manhattan distance between them.

$$sim_{AB} = \frac{f(A \cup B)}{f(A)}. \tag{2}$$

In (1) $f(A \cup B)$ is the frequency of map frames containing both feature A and B and $f(A)$ is the frequency of map frames containing only feature A. A distance measure of 0 reveals that the two features are exactly similar, i.e. if one feature is present in a map frame then we can be certain that the other feature is also present in that frame. A Manhattan distance of 2 between two features indicates that the features are completely dissimilar. In figure 3 we can see that the three participants interacted with each pair of features roughly in the same manner, as the similarity scores between each pair of features suggests, e.g. the mean similarity score between perennial shorelines and rivers is 0.15, 0.17, and 0.16 for surveyors S1, S2, and S3, respectively. This is what we would expect as each surveyor was instructed to locate potential development areas of the map and naturally would have switched these features on when determining optimum sites. If these features were therefore present in the majority of map frames together, then we could conclude that not only are they relevant in terms of each surveyor's individual preferences, but they are also relevant in terms of group preferences, i.e. all surveyors. These results show that as user profiles evolve over the course of tasks, they tend to converge on task-relevant features. The mean similarity between predetermined task-relevant features reveals how this is measured and shows how map personalization is provided at the feature level.

Each interest frame has several associated attributes (see section 3.3) namely the frame boundary, disclosing detail related to map regions, and frame features, storing features falling within the interest frames. Figure 4 shows the results of the second experiment. The graph shows that some surveyors, when zooming in directly on specific areas of the map, did not feel the need to reduce the level of map content below a certain level, i.e. there are on average between 6 and 13 features, out of a total set of 30, present in interest frames recorded by CoMPASS. We discovered that these particular features were directly related to the surveyors' tasks, i.e. features recorded included road features (infrastructure), hydrographic features (drainage), and amenity features (shops, schools, hospitals). This confirms that all surveyors interacted with the maps in a similar fashion resulting in the toggling on of particular features related to locating suitable sites for potential development.

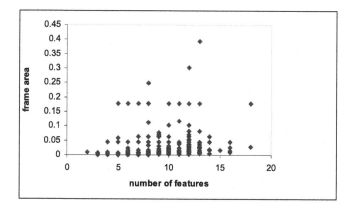

Fig. 4. Clustering of interest frame vectors

Figure 4 also enables us to extract detail regarding regions of the map of most interest to surveyors. Looking at the graph we can see a cluster of vectors where the area < 0.05 and number of features < 8. Examining the content of these vectors revealed that areas visited by different surveyors overlapped. This is exactly what we expected as surveyors with the same task sequences selected similar areas of the map as suitable sites for development. We can draw the following conclusions from the second experiment: (1) there are common task-relevant feature sets within map areas, (2) different users will focus on the same task-relevant map areas, and (3) personalization at the area level can be effective.

5   Conclusions and Future Work

Mobile interactive map applications must be able to take advantage of locational context while minimizing mobile platform limitations such as bandwidth and screen size. In contrast to typical current GIS applications, CoMPASS streamlines mobile mapping interactions by providing personalized map content based on user modelling. CoMPASS user models are implicitly derived from normal user interactions (pen or voice based), eliminating the impractical requirement of explicit profile maintenance by end users. CoMPASS delivers map and locational content based on a combination of the current user model and spatial context (location and trajectory). This paper has provided an overview of CoMPASS and a user evaluation case study for surveying tasks. The evaluation demonstrates that the user modeling mechanism captures task-relevant context that can provide better quality map interactions both in terms of features and regions. Future work includes both finer-grained feature personalization, extended evaluations of user models and trajectory context, and expanding case study domains. There is also a need to address the possibility of storing some profile information at the client so that the profile can be updated dynamically as the user interacts with maps. In this way, trivial interactions with users can be processed on the mobile client while more complex processing can be handled at the server.

References

1. N Weisenberg, A Voisard, and R Gartmann. Using ontologies in personalized mobile applications. In *Proceedings ACMGIS'04*, pages 2–11, Washington DC, USA, November 2004.
2. C Rinner and M Raubal. Personalized multi-criteria decision strategies in location-based decision support. In *Journal of Geographic Information Sciences 11*, pages 61–68, In Press.
3. J. Weakliam, D. Lynch, J. Doyle, M. Zhou, E. MacAoidh, M. Bertolotto, and D. Wilson. Mapping spatial knowledge for mobile personalized applications. In *Proceedings KES'05*, Melbourne, Australia, 2005, In press.
4. A. Hinze and A. Voisard. Locations- and time-based information delivery in tourism. In *Proceedings of the 8th International Symposium on Advances in Spatial and Temporal Databases*, pages 489–507, Santorini Island, Greece, 2003.
5. J. Burrell and G. K. Gay. Collectively defining context in a mobile, networked computing environment. In *Extended Abstracts, CHI'01, ACM Press*, 2001.
6. Petra Fagerberg. Social awareness in a location based information system. pages 149–156, November 2002.
7. M. O'Grady and G. P. O'Hare. Just-in-time multimedia distribution in a mobile computing environment. *IEEE MultiMedia*, 11(4):62–74, 2004.
8. F. Mueller and A. Lockerd. Cheese: Tracking mouse movements on websites, a tool for user modeling. In *Proceedings CHI'01*, Seattle, Washington, 2001.
9. D. Kelly and N.J. Belkin. Reading time, scrolling and interaction: Exploring implicit sources of user preferences for relevance feedback during interactive information retrieval. In *Proceedings of the 24th Annual International Conference on Research and Development in Information Retrieval*, pages 408–409, USA, 2001.
10. S. Oviatt, P. Cohen, L. Wu, J. Vergo, L. Duncan, B. Suhm, J. Bers, T. Holzman, T. Winograd, J. Landay, J. Larson, and D. Ferro. Designing the user interface for multimodal speech and pen-based gesture applications: State-of-the-art systems and future research directions. In *Human-Computer Interaction, 15(4)*, pages 263–322, 2000.

11. S. Oviatt. Multimodal interactive maps: Designing for human performance. *In Human-Computer Interaction (special issue on Multimodal Interfaces)*, 12:93–129.
12. R. Wasinger, C. Stahl, and A. Kreuger. Robust speech interaction in a mobile environment through the use of multiple and different input types. In *EuroSpeech 2003 - InterSpeech 2003, the 8th European Conference on Speech Communication and Technology*, pages 1049–1052, 2003.
13. Openmap. http://openmap.bbn.com/.
14. Tiger files. http://www.census.gov/geo/www/tiger/.
15. J Han, M Kamber, and AKH Tung. Spatial clustering methods in data mining: A survey. In *In H. Miller and J. Han (eds.), Geographic Data Mining and Knowledge Discovery*, Taylor and Francis, 2001.
16. K. Koperski and J Han. Discovery of spatial association rules in geographic information databases. In *Proceedings SSD'95*, pages 47–66, Portland, Maine, USA, 1995.

A Hybrid Approach for Spatial Web Personalization

Yanwu Yang and Christophe Claramunt

Naval Academy Research Institute BP 600, 29240, Brest Naval, France
{yang,claramunt}@ecole-navale.fr

Abstract. In the context of Web personalization, Markov chains have been recently proposed to model user's navigational trails, in order to infer user preference and predict future visits through computation of transitional probabilities. Based on these principles, the research introduced in this paper develops a hybrid Web personalization approach that applies k-order Markov chains towards an integration of spatial proximity and semantic similarity for the manipulation of geographical data on the Web. This framework personalizes Web navigational experiences over spatial entities embedded in Web documents. A reinforcement process is also introduced to evaluate and adapt interactions between the user and the Web on the basis of user's relevance feedbacks. An illustrative case study applied to spatial information available on the Web exemplifies our approach.

1 Introduction

Web personalization attempts to overcome the information overload, navigation problems and cognition mismatch between Web authors and end users. This implies Web designers to approximate user preferences with elicitation approaches, and to offer appropriate personalisation processes to adapt Web structures and contents according to user profiles and expectations. The problem to deal with is not to develop searching mechanisms such as well known keywords-based facilities, but rather to develop inference mechanisms that monitor user actions on the Web, infer user preference and personalize Web accesses. This requires to consider more deeply the way that spatial information, entities and relationships are embedded within Web pages, and the semantic exhibited by the information content of these Web pages [1], a step towards the semantic Web [2] [3].

In the context of Web personalization, many research proposals have been oriented towards the modeling and prediction of user's behaviors on the Web [4] [5]. In particular, Markov chains have been applied for the predictive modeling of contiguous visit sequences on the Web [6]. Our research is oriented to data personalization in the particular context of spatial information available on the Web. Spatially enhanced information retrieval and search engine on the Web recently attract wide research efforts [7] [8]. Nonetheless, and to the best of our knowledge, a few researches have been oriented to the modelling of user's interests and preference, and inference of personalized services when manipulating spatial information on the Web. Personalization services are expected to reduce information flows, adapt information delivery to user's needs and interests, thus improving his/her satisfaction.

K.-J. Li and C. Vangenot (Eds.): W2GIS 2005, LNCS 3833, pp. 206–221, 2005.

In a previous work, we introduced a personalization framework for the manipulation of spatial and semantic information personalization on the Web [9]. The proposed framework monitors user's manipulation of spatial entities and reference locations available on a given Web site, and recommends the most appropriate spatial entities given the user preferences the system is able to infer. User's interests and preference are derived from the assumption that the higher the number of closer spatial entities of similar interest to a given spatial entity of interest, the higher the value is given to this entity. The personalization process is supported by a competitive back propagation neural network that derives class preference patterns, and qualifies spatial entities of interest.

The research presented in this paper extends our previous work by integrating user's navigational trails within the user preference elicitation and personalization processes. We introduce a hybrid personalization approach and reinforcement process that facilitate user's navigations and interactions with spatial entities embedded in Web pages. The approach combines semantic similarity, spatial proximity, and k-order Markov chains to predict the next spatial entity which is likely to be in interaction with a given user. The semantic similarity reflects to which degree a spatial entity is close to another in the semantic domain, while the spatial proximity gives a contextual form of inverse distance between two spatial entities. Markov chains implicitly monitors and records user's trails on the Web, and derives navigational patterns and knowledge in order to predict user's interactions on the Web. A reinforcement process complements the approach by adapting the interactions between the user and the Web, that is, a sequence of iterative negative/positive rewards evaluated on the basis of user's relevance feedbacks to personalized presentations.

The remainder of this paper is organized as follows. Section 2 briefly describes the main principles of current personalization techniques and their applications on the Web. Section 3 introduces the modeling principles behind the presentation of spatial entities over the Web. Section 4 develops the hybrid Web personalization approach. Section 5 develops a reinforcement process to adapt transition probabilities. Section 6 illustrates the framework using an experimental personalization process. Section 7 gives some conclusive remarks and discusses some research perspectives.

2   Web Personalization

Personalization techniques on the Web attempt to overcome the information overload, to remove irrelevant information, and to increase utility and user's satisfaction by providing the user with effective services tailored to his/her specific needs. Among many personalization tools, recommender systems and Web personalization are amongst the most successful systems applied so far to improve information services and searching engines on the Web [10]. A personalization process can be categorised according to three main components, namely a *personalization goal*, a *user preference elicitation process* and a *personalization engine* (Figure 1).

A *personalization goal* is generally considered as a way of positively increasing the utility of the information delivered and user's satisfaction. A *user preference elicitation* over a given domain knowledge requires either observing user's choice behaviors, or directly interacting with the user with predefined questions. The range of techniques used varies from the implicit tracking of user actions to explicit user's feedbacks on the information provided. Evaluating user preference is often derived by explicit information such as direct user feedbacks, keywords based evaluation of user's interests, and implicit user feedbacks such as analysis of reading times, frequency of document downloads and page browsing [11] [12]. A *personalization engine* supports personalizing activities, services and attitudes to a specific individual or group taking into account the personalization goal and user preference. Personalization engines usually correspond to a set of computational components that take user profiles and logs as inputs and as outputs a series of information items (e.g. Web pages or components) that might be of interest to the user.

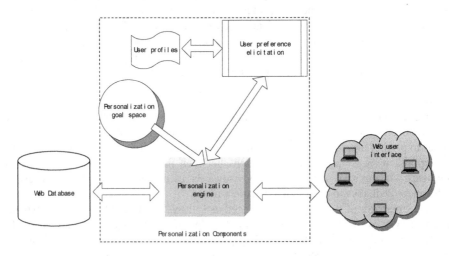

Fig. 1. Personalization components

Web personalization favours the presentation of Web information, content and structure according to user's explicit or implicit preferences. Two orthogonal filtering dimensions are often applied in Web personalization techniques: content-based filtering and collaborative filtering. Content-based filtering is oriented towards the personalization of Web pages and information retrieval processes, based on the analysis of Web document similarities and user's personal profiles. Collaborative filtering takes as inputs user's explicit (or implicit) ratings on items of interest and generates recommendations according to user preference similarities using proximity or correlation measures. However, and despite recent developments of Web personalisation techniques over conventional applications, there is still a need for capturing more complex relationships and patterns [13]. With the emergence of the semantic Web [2] [3], incorporating semantic knowledge and domain ontology into personalization processes should at least influence the next generation of Web personalization systems. Applied to the spatial domain, the semantic Web should include spatial ontologies, qualitative reasoning and representation of spatial knowledge on the Web [14].

3 Spatial Entities on the Web

A reasonable proportion of Web resources can be mapped to some degree to geo-referenced entities associated to a given location. Statistics collected by search engines and systems on the Web found that spatial information is pervasive on the Web, and that many queries contain spatial information [15]. However, current Web pages and interfaces are not completely adapted to the manipulation and personalisation of geo-referenced information. Modelling and identifying semantic and spatial relationships amongst entities embedded in Web documents is still a challenging task.

A spatial entity usually materializes a real world or virtual object. Different classes of spatial entities of interest (e.g. sightseeing places, hotels, universities) are commonly embedded in multi-media Web documents, either in textual or map forms. Maps favour the representation and display of spatially referenced data to the users, whereas other media forms such as text prevalent in Web documents serve as supplementary means to describe some semantic and spatial contents. Spatial entities represented on maps explicitly denote their locations and their geographical distribution. They can be linked to some semantic documents that can describe additional semantic properties. Maps on the Web are so far provided by either graphic files or interactive maps software. The latter provides an effective way to dynamically present spatial information on the Web. Interactive maps allow the user to have an access to various levels of manipulation and interaction, thanks to some customized user interfaces [16] [17]. For instance, the image of a spatial entity can be linked to an interactive map viewer, thus allowing the users to perform some map-oriented operations and hyperlink interactions (e.g. clicking on the map to view additional information on a spatial entity).

Let us represent a given set of spatial entities E explicitly embedded in a Web pages as $E = \{e_1, e_2, ...e_p\}$ where p is the cardinality of the set. Spatial entities materialised on the Web and associated by hyperlinks form a graph that relates them in the Web space. We assume that a spatial entity is likely to possess a semantic content and some spatial properties: $e = (spatial(e), semantic(e))$ where $spatial(e)$ denotes the spatial component and $semantic(e)$ the semantic component of the spatial entity e. The spatial component describes the location of a spatial entity as an abstract data type and as, $spatial(e) = (x, y)$ where (x, y) denotes the coordinates of the spatial entity e in a two dimensional space. The semantic component can be considered as an h-dimensional vector that specifies the semantic parameters of a given spatial entity: $semantic(e) = \{w(c_1, e), w(c_2, e), ... w(c_h, e)\}$ where h is an integer that denotes the number of semantic parameters; $w(c_i, e)$ gives the relevance of the spatial entity e associated to a semantic class c_i. A semantic class corresponds to a categorization of entities that share some semantic properties. Relevance values are membership values given by the unit interval [0,1], they qualify the membership degree of an entity with respect to a given semantic class C_i.

We do not consider the case, which is far beyond the objective of our research, of spatial entities textually and implicitly embedded on the Web as this leads to explore and develop Web data extraction and classification algorithms. Instead we consider situations where spatial entities are explicitly embedded within a Web page (Figure 3). User's navigational behaviors are recorded using historical Web logs. The basic element of such a log information is a page-view, that is, a "Visual rendering of a Web page in a specific client environment at a specific point in time" as stated by the W3C

Web Characterization Activity (http://www.w3.org/WCA/). At the user level, navigation is triggered by a session. A user session is a sequence of user page-views made during a single visit by a given user. At a finer level of granularity, a transaction denotes a meaningful subset of page-views within a user session. According to [18] [19] these notions are defined as follows:

Definition 1: Spatial Entity-Oriented User Session

A *spatial entity-oriented user session s* is a n-dimensional ordered vector $s = <e_1, e_2, ...e_n>$ that materializes a sequence of spatial entities accessed by a given user on the Web.

Definition 2: Spatial Entity-Oriented Transaction

A *spatial entity-oriented transaction t* is a m-dimensional vector $t = <w(e_1, s_1), w(e_2, s_2), ...w(e_m, s_m)>$ that materializes a semantically related subset of a user session, and where each spatial entity e_i is associated with a weight s_m, that denotes its semantic and spatial importance with respect to the user's interests.

4 Markov Chains Personalization

Markov chains are used extensively to predict the next state of a system given a sequence of previous states. A Markov chain can be represented by a tuple with three parameters $<S, T, \lambda>$. $S = \{s_1, s_2, ..., s_n\}$ corresponds to the state space, namely the set of all possible states for the Markov chain; T is a transition probability matrix, where each entry t_{ij} represents the transition probability from a_i to state a_j; λ corresponds to the initial distribution of the states in S.

The state space of a Markov chain depends on the number of sequences of previous states available to predict the next state. A 0-order Markov chain is an unconditional base-rate probability of x_n denoted as $p(x_n) = Pr(X_n)$. In a 0-order Markov chain, states are independent of each other. A first-order Markov chain only considers one-step transition probabilities $p(x_2|x_1) = Pr(X_2 = x_2|X_1 = x_1)$, that is, the probability of the next state given the immediately previous state. In a first-order Markov chain, each transition corresponds to a state. A k-order Markov chain considers the conditional probability by looking at the last k states to compute the predictions, $p(x_n|x_{n-1}, ..., x_{n-k}) = Pr(X_n = x_n|X_{n-1}, ..., X_{n-k})$. The state-space of a k-order Markov chain contains all possible sequences of *k* states.

The dimensionality of a Markov chain has a direct influence on the exhibited properties and performance of a given sequence. Lower-order Markov chains cannot successfully predict the next state of a given sequence because they don't consider far enough past states for a valid discrimination. High-order Markov chains result in high state space and low coverage, and sometimes even worse prediction accuracy due to the high number of sequential states (Deshpande and Karypis 2000). It has been observed, in an empirical analysis of data (Pitkow and Pirolli 1999), that using a 4th order Markov chain is an optimal option upon an assumption that the benefit of making a correct hit equals the cost of marking an incorrect prediction.

Sarukkai [20] introduced Markov chains for link prediction and path analysis to dynamically model URL access patterns, and to predict the next Web page accessed by the user. Padmanabhan and Mogul [4] used n-top Markov models to improve prefetching strategies for Web caches. Pitkow and Pirolli [21] explored the predictive capabilities of user paths and identified user access patterns on the Web. They introduced Longest Repeating Subsequence (LRS) models to predict World Wide Web surfing. LRS models reduced predictive model size and complexity by nearly a third while retaining predictive accuracy. In order to improve prediction accuracy, and at the same time to maintain a low state complexity, Deshpande and Karypis [22] proposed a class of Markov models based on some prediction algorithms called *selective Markov models*. This Markov model is obtained by selectively eliminating a large fraction of the states of the All-K^{th}-Order Markov model. Empirical results show that the performance of selective Markov models is superior to that obtained by higher-order Markov models to predict Web accesses.

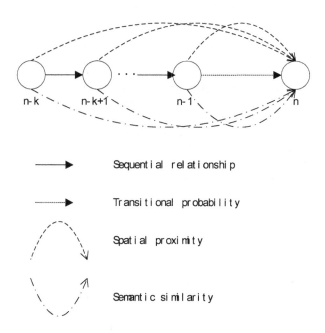

Fig. 2. Spatial entities relationships within k-order Markov chains

Web personalization based on Markov chains predicts the next Web page a given user is most likely to visit by matching the user's current access sequence with historical Web access patterns. The entities extracted and identified from various Web documents constitute the state space. A state is defined as a Web entity, while a transition denotes a hyperlink from one entity to another. Markov chains use a sequence of Web page-views/entities the user accesses as inputs, with the goal of building Markov chains to predict the page-view/entity the user is most likely visit next. The predictive process corresponds to matching user's current navigation trails with historical Web access sequences, and determination of the next visit with transitional probability.

We retained a hybrid Web personalization approach that integrates k-order Markov chains with a combination of semantic similarity and spatial proximity criteria (denoted as *SemSpa similarity*). The intuition behind is as follows

> Given a sequence of *k* previously visited spatial entities $<x_{n-k}... x_{n-1}>$ on the Web, with consideration of conditional transition probability from $<x_{n-k}... x_{n-1}>$ to x_n, and *SemSpa* similarity between $<x_{n-k}... x_{n-1}>$ and x_n, the Web personalization engine predicts the n_{th} spatial entity which is likely to be visited by the user (Figure 2).

Figure 2 illustrates the principles of a k-order Markov chain that reflects a sequence of spatial entities of interest on the Web. Content-based relationships between the spatial entities are evaluated by a combination of spatial proximities and semantic similarities. This is supported by a stepwise approach that measures semantic and spatial similarities between a sequence of spatial entities on the one hand, and a candidate entity on the other hand. The initialisation of the predictive Markov chain is decomposed into three steps as follows:

1) Determine the *SemSpa* similarity between each spatial entity in a k-sequence of user interactions with spatial entities embedded on the Web, and a candidate spatial entity embedded or connected by a hyperlink to the last page accessed in this k-sequence.
2) Similarly, compute the *kSemSpa* similarity between the spatial entities in a given k-sequence and a candidate spatial entity.
3) Compute the *kSemSpaM* similarity, a combination of *kSemSpa* similarity and transitional probability in a given k-order Markov chain.

1) Semantic and Spatial Similarity Between Two Spatial Entities
The first step of this approach is to determine the *SemSpa* similarity. This is given by a combination of semantic similarity and spatial proximity values between a spatial entity in a k-sequence x_i, and a candidate spatial entity x_j. The *SemSpa* similarity is given as follows

$$SemSpa(x_i, x_j) = \sqrt{(1 + Sem(x_i, x_j)) \times Spa(x_i, x_j)} \tag{1}$$

where $Sem(x_i, x_j)$ denotes the semantic similarity, and $Spa(x_i, x_j)$ the spatial proximity between x_i and x_j.

The most common approach used to compute a degree of similarity between two vectors in Web information retrieval is the standard cosine similarity. Accordingly, and in order to deal with membership degrees of spatial entities, we applied the adjusted cosine similarity introduced by [23] to determine the semantic similarity between two entities x_i and x_j. The semantic function $Sem(x_i, x_j)$ is given as

$$Sem(x_i, x_j) = \frac{\sum_{h=1}^{m}(x_i^h - \overline{x^h}) \times (x_j^h - \overline{x^h})}{\sqrt{\sum_{h=1}^{m}(x_i^h - \overline{x^h})^2 \times \sum_{h=1}^{m}(x_j^h - \overline{x^h})^2}} \tag{2}$$

The domain of the semantic function is given by the unit interval [0, 1]. A semantic parameter x_i^h reflects the membership degree of a spatial entity x_i with respect to a predefined semantic class c_h. The m semantic classes are defined upon the requirement of the application. Membership degree values are given by fuzzy quantifiers bounded by the unit interval [0,1]. $\overline{x^h}$ is the average value of the semantic parameters of the spatial entities with respect to a given semantic class c_h. The value domain of $Sem(x_i, x_j)$ is given by the interval [-1, 1].

The spatial function $Spa(x_i, x_j)$ is specified by the contextual proximity $p(x_i, x_j)$ introduced in [9]. The contextual proximity denotes the closeness of two spatial entities taking into account the overall distribution and context of the underlying spatial structure. The higher $p(x_i, x_j)$ the closer x_i to x_j, the lower $p(x_i, x_j)$ the distant x_i to x_j, and *vice versa*. The spatial function is given as

$$Spa(x_i, x_j) = P(x_i, x_j) \tag{3}$$

The contextual proximity is an asymmetric value, it is bounded by the unit interval [0,1], and given as

$$P(x_i, x_j) = \frac{1}{1 + RD(x_i, x_j)^2} \tag{4}$$

where x_i is the entity under consideration, $RD(x_i, x_j)$ is the relative distance from x_i to x_j.

The relative distance is given as

$$RD(x_i, x_m) = \frac{d(x_i, x_m)}{\dfrac{1}{p-1} \displaystyle\sum_{m=1, m \neq i}^{p} d(x_i, x_m)} \tag{5}$$

where $d(x_i, x_j)$ stands for the Euclidean distance between x_i and x_j, p is the number of entities in the set $X=\{x_1, x_2, \ldots x_p\}$.

2) Semantic and Spatial Similarity Between Spatial Entities in k-Sequence and a Candidate Spatial Entity

The second step of the hybrid approach is to determine the *SemSpa* similarity between a sequence of k spatial entities $<x_{n-k} \ldots x_{n-1}>$, and a candidate spatial entity x_n. As Web surfers may have two or more kinds of interests in mind, their interests may change from time to time when they are browsing on the Web. The latter is so-called "concept drift" [24], an issue beyond the scope of traditional Web personalization applications. In order to address the "concept drift" issue, we introduce a discount rate γ to adapt semantic similarity and spatial proximity values, on the basis of an assumption that following the user's navigational trails, "nearer" entities are more related than distant ones. The *kSemSpa* similarity is computed using a discount rate γ that refines the *SemSpa* similarity value between each spatial entity embedded in a sequence $<x_{n-k}...$ $x_{n-1}>$ and x_n. The *kSemSpa* similarity is given as follows

$$kSemSpa(< x_{n-k},...,x_{n-1} >,x_n) = \sum_{k=1} \gamma^{k-1} SemSpa(x_{n-k},x_n) \qquad (6)$$

where γ is a discount rate parameter, $0 \ulcorner \gamma \ulcorner 1$, that recursively decreases the *SemSpa* similarity between each spatial entities in a historical sequence $<x_{n-k}... x_{n-1}>$ and x_n with the historical length. The historical length denotes the number of steps from a given spatial entity x_i in a sequence $<x_{n-k}... x_{n-1}>$ to a spatial entity x_n.

3) Combination of k_SemSpa Similarity and Transitional Probability
The third step of the hybrid approach is to combine the *kSemSpa* similarity with the transitional probability exhibited by the k-order Markov chain $<x_{n-k}... x_{n-1}>$ in order to predict the n_{th} candidate spatial entity. The *kSemSpaM* value is given as

$$kSemSpaM(< x_{n-k},...,x_{n-1} >,x_n) = \sqrt{Pr \times kSemSpa}$$

$$\text{with } Pr = p(x_n | x_{n-1},...,x_{n-k}), \qquad (7)$$

$$kSempa = kSemSpa(< x_{n-k},...,x_{n-1} >,x_n)$$

where $p(x_n | x_{n-1},...,x_{n-k})$ is the transitional probability of the k-order Markov chain, statistically collected from the Web logs that record user's previous behaviors on the Web.

5   Reinforcement Process

Interactions between the user and the personalization engine form an iterative process when he/she is surfing on the Web. These interactions consist of two kinds of process. First, the Web system provides personalized information services according to his/her interests. Secondly, the user gives some relevance feedbacks through various behaviors. User's relevance feedbacks reflect his/her attitudes to the personalized results. We take into account this component to adjust the transitional probability of the k-order Markov chains $p(x_n | x_{n-1},...,x_{n-k})$, using a reinforcement process. The reinforcement process is a learning process based on the observation of user's feedbacks to the predictive result provided (i.e., the n_{th} spatial entity). Possible forms of user's feedbacks to the n_{th} state is valued by two alternative Boolean values *satisfied* and *unsatisfied*. In the former situation, the user is likely to visit the recommended n_{th} spatial entity; while in the latter, the user will follow some other hyperlinks. The reinforcement process gives either positive or negative rewards. The reinforcement process is given as

$$Pr \leftarrow Pr \pm \eta \times r \qquad (8)$$

where η is the learning rate, r the reinforcement reward.

The value of η may be slightly smaller than 1 when learning begins, and then slowly decreased to 0 as learning progresses. A simple approach is to make use of τ, the number of user accesses, to adjust these values dynamically. Then $\eta = \dfrac{\alpha}{\tau}$, α is the reinforcement factors with $0 < \alpha < 1$, and is initialised once. The reinforcement reward r is given as

(for positive reinforcement)
$$r = (1 - Pr) \times (1 - kSemSpaM)$$
(for negative reinforcement) $\qquad (9)$
$$r = (1 - Pr) \times kSemSpaM$$

Then the reinforcement process is given as

(for positive reinforcement)
$$Pr \leftarrow Pr + \frac{\alpha}{\tau}(1 - Pr) \times (1 - kSemSpaM)$$
(for negative reinforcement) $\qquad (10)$
$$Pr \leftarrow Pr - \frac{\alpha}{\tau}(1 - Pr) \times kSemSpaM$$

The transactional probability from a Web entity/page-view to the next in sequential Web data mining is statistically calculated from Web logs that record user's historical navigation trails. The reinforcement process introduced is dynamic and provides a mechanism for conditional transition probability according to user's feedbacks to the personalized results. Probabilities of transitions (Pr) with a few hits converge toward a null value, while those with many hits converge toward the unit value.

6   Case Study

In a previous work, we introduce a prototype experiment applied to the city of Kyoto [9]. In order to apply the concepts introduced in this paper, we extend this prototype towards the personalization of navigational trails over spatial entities embedded on the Web. Historical and sightseeing places are modeled as spatial entities. The Web system encodes the sightseeing places as spatial entities to support Web-based travel planning for the user. The main interface is enriched with image schemata and affordance concepts (Figure 3), based on the assumption that the user have little knowledge on the given city [9]. These spatial entities contain semantic attributes, and are distributed in space (Figure 8). Each spatial entity embedded on the Web map interface is presented by a symbol or an image, and associated to additional textual information that allows the user to actively interact with the Web interface. The personalization results are presented to the user in various formats and an interactive map with hyperlinks to Web resources of interest.

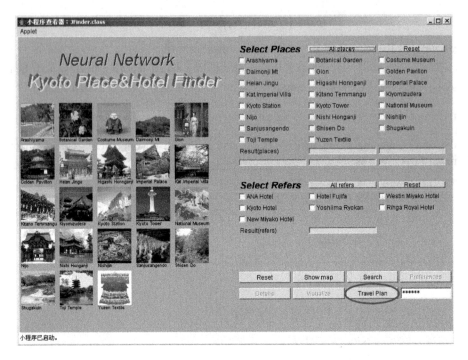

Fig. 3. The main interface

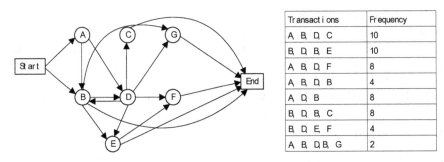

Transactions	Frequency
A, B, D, C	10
B, D, B, E	10
A, B, D, F	8
A, B, D, B	4
A, D, B	8
B, D, B, C	8
B, D, E, F	4
A, B, D, B, G	2

Fig. 4. Navigation trails and transactions

Without loss of generality, let us consider a set of Web transactions as presented in Figure 4 (right). The set of Web transactions records user's navigational trails involving seven spatial entities that represent some historical and cultural interests. These entities include A (Kitano Temmangu), B (Nijo), C (Higashi Honnganji), D (Yuzen Textile), E (Arashiyama), F (Costume Museum) and G (Nishijin), represented as a labeled directed graph (the left of figure 4). We use a third-order Markov chain to model these transactions. Through some appropriate Web usage mining processes, the set of user's transactions is transformed to a set of transactions represented as a 3-order Markov chains (Figure 5). The left part of these transactions forms the state space, while the transitional probabilities constitute the transitional probability matrix.

Transactions	Frenquency	Transitional probability
A, B, D --> C	10	5/12
A, B, D --> F	8	1/3
A, B, D --> B	6	1/4
B, D, B --> E	10	5/12
B, D, B --> C	8	1/3
B, D, B --> G	2	1/12
B, D, B --> END	4	1/6
D, E, F --> END	8	1.0
B, D, E --> F	4	1.0
D, B, C --> END	8	1.0
A, D, B --> END	8	1.0
B, D, F --> END	8	1.0
D, B, E --> END	10	1.0
B, D, C --> END	10	1.0
D, B, G --> END	2	1.0

Fig. 5. Transaction, frequency and transitional probability for 3-order Markov chains

Suppose a specific user is browsing entity D after visiting A and B successively. The Web personalization component takes the transaction $A \rightarrow B \rightarrow D$, and the semantic and spatial criteria into account to predict users next visits. Possible candidate entities are C, F, B, and transitional probabilities from $A \rightarrow B \rightarrow D$ are 5/12, 1/3, 1/4 respectively. Computed results of *kSemSpa* are presented in the results exhibited by Figure 6 with $\gamma = 2$:

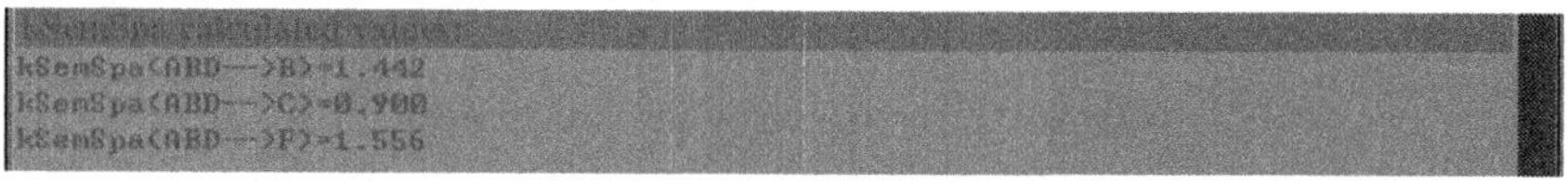

Fig. 6. Computed results of *kSemSpa*

Computed results of *kSemSpaM* are (Figure 7)

Fig. 7. Computed results of *kSemSpaM*

The Markov chain evaluation recommends the spatial entity which is most likely to be "visited", the entity F in the example above (Costume Museum). Personalization results are illustrated in Figure 8. The recommendation reflects the fact that most previous users with similar trails visit entity F, and F has relative strong relationship

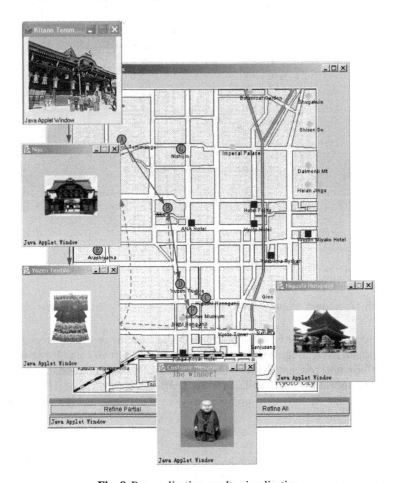

Fig. 8. Personalization results visualization

with previous three entities accessed by the user. Consequently the transitional probability from the sequence <A, B, D> to F, that is, $p(F \mid A, B, D)$ is positively reinforced if the user follows the personalized result, which shows user's feedback as *satisfied*; otherwise, as an example, if the user goes to visit the entity C, that is, in the case of *unsatisfied* feedback, then $p(F \mid A, B, D)$ is negatively reinforced and $p(C \mid A, B, D)$ positively.

The hybrid Web personalization approach uses navigational knowledge and profiles extracted from the users' historical trails on the Web, and then ameliorates them with spatial proximity and semantic similarity responsible for content-based filtering of spatial information entities. This avoids the defects of using each of the two individually. The reinforcement process is used to update the navigational knowledge through unobtrusively observing user's implicit feedbacks.

Whether a user is physically located and acts or not in the city represented on the Web has an influence on the levels of perception and interaction in the environment. The former preferably refers to mobile environments where the user interacts with the environments through portable and embeddable devices. The latter denotes conventional interactions between the user and a Web information space using a client "table" computer. Navigations on the Web constitute sequences of Web pages that can be recorded by Web logs. The main application scenarios we consider at the moment to apply the framework include Web-based travel planning and Location-aware mobile services. Our Current developments are oriented towards the first scenario, that is, an attempt to provide a prototype framework for Web-based travel planning in a "Web urban space". Based on this framework, inference rules can be modelled to identify user's interests and preference, and then personalize user's travel and experience when interacting with spatial entities embedded on the Web. Without loss of generality, the framework can be also applied to location-aware mobile environments with some minor adaptations.

7   Conclusion

The research presented in this paper introduces a hybrid Web personalization approach that combines Markov chains with spatial and semantic similarity, and a reinforcement process in order to model and predict user navigational trails when interacting with spatial information materialized on the Web. The personalization process is based on an integration of two orthogonal dimensions that facilitate the approximation of user preferences, that is, semantic similarities and spatial proximities between spatial entities embedded in Web pages. Markov chains integrated with these relationships allow the system to recommend spatial entities that are of interest for the user. A reinforcement process, based on the monitoring of user actions and relevance feedbacks, complements the personalization mechanisms by employing a learning component. The potential of the approach is illustrated by an exemplified case study. The approach and the underlying modelling concepts can have a several direct or indirect impacts on the benefits of a given Web site. Direct as deriving preference patterns might help Web designers to refine the design of their Web interfaces and tailor the content of Web pages, indirect as categorising users might also have several "marketing" implications for the Web page owners. Further work concerns experimental validation of the personalisation model and reinforcement process, and development of knowledge-based mechanisms that implicitly derive class preferences with flexible learning process, and closer integration of the Markov model and the reinforcement learning process.

Acknowledgement

We would like to thank the three anonymous reviewers for their valuable comments.

References

1. Dai, H. and Mobasher, B. Using ontologies to discover domain-level Web usage profiles. In 2nd Semantic Web Mining Workshop at ECML/PKDD02 (2002)
2. Semantic Web Activity of the World Wide Web Consortium. http://www.w3.org/2001/sw

3. Berners-Lee, J., Hendler, J. and Lassila, O. The Semantic Web, Scientific American, vol. 184, no. 5, (2001) 34-43,
4. Padmanabhan, V. and Mogul, J. Using Predictive Prefetching to Improve World Wide Web Latency. In Proc. of the ACM SIGCOMM '96 Conf. on Applications, Technologies, Architectures, and Protocols for Computer Communication, (1996) 22-36
5. Mobasher, B., Cooley R. and Srivastava, J. Automatic personalization based on Web usage mining, Communications of the ACM 43(8), (2000) 142–151
6. Pirolli, P. L. and Pitkow J. E. Distribution of surfers' paths through the World Wide Web: empirical characterization. World Wide Web. 2 (1-2), (1999) 29-45
7. Jones, C. B., Purves, R., Ruas, A., Sanderson, M., Sester, van Kreveld, M. and Weibel, R. Spatial information retrieval and geographical ontologies an overview of the SPIRIT project. SIGIR 2002, 387-388
8. Larson R.R. and Frontiera, P. Ranking and Representation for Geographic Information Retrieval. Presented at SIGIR 2004 Workshop on Geographic Information Retrieval. Sheffield, UK, July 29, (2004)
9. Yang, Y. and Claramunt, C. A Flexible Competitive Neural Network for Eliciting User's Preferences in Web Urban Spaces, in Fisher P (eds.), Developments in Spatial Data Handling, Proceedings of the 11th International Spatial Data Handling Conference, Springer-Verlag, 23-25 August, University of Leicester, (2004) 41-57
10. Shahabi, C. and Chen, Y. Web Information Personalization: Challenges and Approaches, The 3nd International Workshop on Databases in Networked Information Systems (DNIS 2003), Aizu-Wakamatsu, Japan, September (2003) 5-15
11. Oard, D.W. and Kim, J. Modelling Information Content Using Observable Behaviour. In Proceedings of the 64 Annual Meeting of the American Society for Information Science and Technology, USA, (2001) 38-45.
12. Kelly, D. and Teevan, J. Implicit Feedback for Inferring User Preference: a Bibliography. SIGIR Forum 37(2), (2003) 18-28
13. Berendt, B., Hotho, A. and Stumme, G. Towards Semantic Web Mining, In I. Horrocks & J. Hendler (eds.), The Semantic Web - ISWC 2002 (Proceedings of the 1st International Semantic Web Conference, June 9-12th, 2002, Sardinia, Italy). LNCS 2342, Heidelberg, Germany: Springer (2002) 264-278
14. Egenhofer, M.J. Toward the Semantic Geospatial Web, In Proceedings of the Tenth ACM International Symposium on Advances in Geographic Information Systems, McLean, Virginia (2002)
15. Silva, M. J. Martins, B., Chaves, M. and Cardoso N. Adding Geographic Scopes to Web Resources, Ana Paula Afonso ACM SIGIR 2004 Workshop on Geographic Information Retrieval, Sheffield, UK, June (2004)
16. Open GIS Consortium, Inc. (OGC). Open GIS Web Map Server Interface Implementation Specification (Revision 1.3.0). Wayland, Massachusetts: Open GIS Consortium, Inc. http://www.opengeospatial.org/specs/ (2004)
17. Open GIS Consortium, Inc. (OGC). Open GIS Web Feature Service Implementation Specification (Revision 1.1.0). Wayland, Massachusetts: Open GIS Consortium, Inc. http://www.opengeospatial.org/specs/ (2005)
18. Cooley, R., Mobasher, B. and Srivastava, J. Data Preparation for Mining World Wide Web Browsing Patterns, Knowledge and Information Systems, Vol. 1, No. 1, (1999) 5-32
19. Mobasher, B. Web usage mining and personalization. Chapter in Practical Handbook of Internet Computing, Munindar P. Singh (ed.), CRC Press (2004)
20. Sarukkai, R. Link Prediction and Path Analysis Using Markov Chains, Computer Networks, vol. 33, n. 1-6, (2000) 377-386

21. Pitkow J. and Pirolli, P. Mining longest repeating subsequence to predict wolrd wide Web surfing. In Second USENIX Symposium on Internet Technologies and Systems, Boulder, C0 (1999)
22. Deshpande, M. and Karypis G. Selective Markov models for predicting Web page accesses, ACM Trans. Internet Techn. 4(2), (2004) 163-184
23. Sarwar, B., Karypis, G., Konstan, J. and Riedl, J. Item-based collaborative filtering recommendation algorithms. In Proceedings of the 10th International WWW Conference, Hong Kong (2001)
24. Webb, G., Pazzani, M.J. and Billsus, D. Machine Learning for User Modelling. User Modelling and User–Adapted Interaction, (11), (2001) 19–29

Connectivity Inferences over the Web for the Analysis of Semantic Networks

Roderic Béra[1] and Christophe Claramunt[2]

[1] Department of Geomatic Engineering,
University College, London, UK
rbera@ge.ucl.ac.uk
[2] Naval Academy Research Institute, Lanvéoc-Poulmic,
BP 600, 29240 Brest Naval, France
claramunt@ecole-navale.fr

Abstract. The World Wide Web constitutes a large information space and a promising support for the development of data inference, analysis and mining mechanisms. The research presented in this paper introduces a modelling approach that derives a social network and computes some of its emerging properties, from the semantics exhibited from a domain knowledge embedded in a series of Web pages. The framework is applied to the research communities related to a series of conferences in a given domain, and the university connections materialised by the researcher trajectories over time. The properties of the social network are analysed using graph-based measures, and a novel geographical dispersion coefficient.

1 Introduction

The generality of the notion of connection offers many opportunities to explore the properties and the semantics exhibited by a given social system. The concept of connection is local, but can act as a primitive relationship to infer and construct a semantic network from which properties can be studied using graph-based measures, from local to global levels depending on the types of properties one is interested to study. A connection between two entities can be not even explicit as in the case of a binary relationship, but also implicit and the result of a mediation between them. A mediation is an interaction between two entities through a third one. Examples of mediation and relationship between spatial entities are processes, exchanges, attractions, flows and trajectories that link them with respect to a given phenomenon of interest. These mediations can be either geographically derived from the geometry, or inferred using inference mechanisms from which the structure of the phenomenon of interest emerges. When the semantic properties of interest are implicit and hidden in an information space, a challenging problem is the construction of the semantic network. This implies to delimit the boundaries of the information space, the entities and elements of interest, and the relationships that connect them, and computational resources to infer and analyse these constituents.

The semantic web is a good example of information space where emerging structures and patterns can be inferred and analysed [1]. The Web constitutes a semantic network whose structure can be studied in order to identify emerging

K.-J. Li and C. Vangenot (Eds.): W2GIS 2005, LNCS 3833, pp. 222–234, 2005.

properties such as hubs, local authorities and remarkable patterns. Amongst many semantic properties that can be studied, the relationship between the properties a social network exhibits, and the way this network is distributed in space, is one aspect that deserves more research attention. This should help to understand the role of space in a given social network, and for instance to which degree network properties are correlated to spatial properties.

The objective of the preliminary research presented in this paper is to infer and analyse the structure and properties of a semantic network, and exploration of spatial and network correlation measures, virtually derived from the relationships embedded and hidden in the World Wide Web. This requires to delimit a domain of study, the explicit components of the semantic network of interest, and the relationships that constitute the mediations and connections between them. We selected as a case study the semantic network formed by the scientific community of spatial reasoning intimately related to Geographical Information Science. This research network is commonly considered as supported by two major conferences of the field: the series of Conference on Spatial Information Theory (COSIT) and that of Geographical Information Science (GIScience). The information inputs are materialised by the Web sites of the last edition of these conferences, that is, in 2004 and 2005, respectively. The components that constitute the elements of the network to infer are researchers having papers presented at these conferences, and a mediation given by their academic trajectories along universities. This information is derived and computed from the short biographies as they appear in the researchers' Web pages hyperlinked to the conference Web sites. This supports derivation of a semantic network whose properties are analysed using graph measures and geographical-based correlations.

The remainder of the paper is organised as follows. Section 2 surveys related work in the inference of spatial relationships over the semantic web. Section 3 introduces the principles of our modelling and computational approach. The case study is developed in Section 4. Finally, Section 5 draws some conclusions and outlines further work.

2 Related Work

Inferring information from the Internet has been an active area of Web engineering research over the past few years. While initial efforts were orientated to the analysis of the content of Web pages, search engines are getting more sophisticated where current search engines and algorithms associate the analysis of Web documents with Web structure and usage [2]. Combination of Web pages content and structure is the main idea behind the well known Google page rank algorithm [3], and Kleinberg's algorithm based on the reduction of the search space and a graph-based analysis of the resulting Web links structure to derive Web site hubs and authorities [4]. Several related approaches such as stochastic analysis of Web communities [5] and cluster matrix analysis [6] have been introduced to analyse Web page contents and structure. Mining Web usage is a complementary inference mechanism that integrates users' behaviour in the information search process [7], [8], [9].

Nowadays, the content of the Web information space is getting extremely rich and diverse, thus stimulating the exploration of novel data inference mechanisms. In particular, a lot of geographically-related information is implicitly present over Web page contents but techniques to make this implicit are still lacking. In [10] Web pages are considered as a sort of human representation of a geographical space. The authors analysed the way places and landmarks are related in Web pages using spatial prepositions that denote proximity relationships and their distortion. Semi-automated and spatial indexing methods have been developed by the Kyoto Database Laboratory to classify Web pages per region at different levels of detail [11], [12], [13]. Locality of Web pages, that is, the relationship between a predefined region and locations of interest are inferred from the analysis of Web page contents and strengths of link connections to similar Web pages.

Retrieving spatially- and temporally-related geographical information over the Web has been applied using Web textual extraction mechanisms [14]. In [15], a preliminary experimentation is developed to study to which degree the Web can be used to support automation and development of pedestrian urban navigation. Web personalisation of maps by creating and maintaining user profiles and the analysis of user interactions [16], and the elicitation of user preferences in the search for places of interest in a Web geographical environment [17] are other approaches where geographical knowledge can be derived from the combined manipulation of Web content and usage.

3 Modelling Principles

3.1 Model Basics

Without loss of generality, let us introduce the modelling principles of our approach applied to a case study. The modelling approach is designed on top on a Web information space, which is delimited by a specific and chosen subset of the World Wide Web, from which some entities of interest are identified, and connected using a mediation relationship[1]. The semantic network is inferred and derived using a sequential process that successively identify the boundaries and the content of the Web information space, and network nodes and links. The main principles of this inference process are described hereafter.

The information space considered, that is, a subset of the World Wide Web, is potentially made of several types of data such as textual, graphical, as well as image and video, information structurally embedded in Web pages organised locally in a hierarchy of Web pages. Web pages connected using hyperlinks form a sort of semantic network. We make the difference between reference Web pages from which the analysis start with, and neighbouring Web pages connected to them using hyperlinks. A connection materialised using an hyperlink represents a relationship between two Web pages, and their information content. The nature of the hyperlinks are either specific or categorised according to some semantic criteria (e.g. a list of people in a given page where every actor's name is hyperlinked to its personal Web page). Categorised hyperlinks can be used to represent the primitive elements of a semantic network. In the context of our study, categorised hyperlinks are represented

---

[1] These entities have a spatial semantic in the context of our study but a-spatial entities can be considered as well.

by the authors' names extracted from the list of accepted papers available on both conference Web sites, and their hyperlinks to their respective Web pages. In short the Web information space derived is given by the conference Web sites, and the hyperlinks to the program committee Web pages.

The objective of the second step of the inference process is the *delineation of the elements and nodes of the semantic network*. The universities derived from the academic trajectories of the program committee members provide the elements to consider for the identification of the network nodes, these academic trajectories the mediation between the universities. For example, the event of an academic who got her/his PhD at the University College in London and successively moves to the University of Nottingham and the University of Edinburgh is represented by a subgraph whose nodes are these three universities, and links connections between these universities.

3.2 Computational Principles

The semantic network is modelled as a hypergraph. In a hypergraph, several edges can connect two given nodes, this not being allowed in a graph. This allows to emphasize multiple connections between universities. More formally such a hypergraph is denoted as a pair $G(N,E)$ where N is the finite set of universities, E the finite set of connections between these universities inferred from the researchers' trajectories. A node is denoted as n_i, a link between two semantic network nodes n_i, $n_j \in N$ as a pair (n_i, n_j).

Several local and global graph-based values can be computed from local to global measures. Local measures include the degree (i.e. number of nodes connected to a node) and the clustering coefficient of a node. The clustering coefficient evaluates the extent to which the neighbours of a node i are also linked one to another. The closer to 1 its *clustering coefficient*, the more clustered a node. Shortest path measures such as the *average path length*, *total depth* and *closeness centrality* are other global measures which are computed using the whole graph [18]. Several centrality measures based on shortest paths have been also introduced in the graph literature, they are based on the average distance between nodes or the ratio of shortest paths a node lies on. A representative measure of centrality is the *betweenness centrality* $C_b(i)$ of a given node i defined as [19], [20]

$$C_b(i) = \sum_{k \neq j \neq i} \frac{S_{jk}(i)}{S_{jk}} \, , \tag{1}$$

where S_{jk} denotes the number of shortest paths from j to k and $S_{jk}(i)$ the number of shortest paths from j to k that i lies on. Other forms of global measure are given by the number of paths between two nodes i and j, or accessibility of a node [21], or contextual distances [22]. For the purpose of our study, properties of the emerging semantic network are evaluated using the *degree* and the *betweeness centrality* as indicators of the local and global properties of the network, respectively.

These graph measures are complemented by a geographically-related measure that correlates the structural and geographical properties of the semantic network. From a semantic network $G(N, E)$, we first define the geographically-based subsets of N that group the nodes of N according to their membership to a given classification and partition of the underlying space (e.g. defined at a scale relevant to the phenomenon studied). This allows us to analyse to which degree links in the semantic network correspond to links within a same class of the given partition of space. This gives an evaluation of the degree of dispersion in the underlying geographical space of the semantic network.   More formally, with respect to a given classification $C = \{ c_1, c_2, ..., c_p \}$ forming a partition of N with $p>1$, let us define for each node n_i of a class c_j of N a geographical dispersion value $dv(n_i)$ given as follows

$$dv(n_i) = \frac{\left| n_i \rightarrow \right|}{\left| N - c_j \right|} - \frac{\left| n_i \leftarrow \right|}{\left| c_j \right|} \quad , \tag{2}$$

where $\left| n_i \leftarrow \right|$ gives the cardinality of the set of links that connect n_i to nodes that belong to the same class c_j of n_i, $\left| n_i \rightarrow \right|$ the cardinality of the set links that connect n_i to nodes that do not belong to the same class c_j of n_i. $dv(n_i)$ values are given by the interval $[-1,+1]$, values that tend to -1 (alternatively $+1$) denote a lower (alternatively higher) geographical dispersion of the links of n_i, values that tend to 0 denote a balanced geographical distribution of the links of n_i.

The overall coefficient of geographical dispersion of the semantic network nodes is given by

$$dv(N) = \sum_{i=1}^{|N|} dv(n_i) = \sum_{i=1}^{|N|} \left(\frac{\left| n_i \rightarrow \right|}{\left| N - c_j \right|} - \frac{\left| n_i \leftarrow \right|}{\left| c_j \right|} \right) . \tag{3}$$

Applied to the case study, the analysis of the graph and geographical-based emerging properties of the semantic network should help to qualify the degree of integration of the research community from the information implicitly available over the Web information space. Amongst the patterns and trends to explore, we can mention the key university players in the research area of interest, connections between these universities, and degrees of compactness versus spread of the research community, clusters, and peripheries.

4   Case Study

The case study investigated is that of a semantic space connecting researchers to a conference, and their academic trajectories. Two related conferences have been selected, namely, COSIT 2003 and GIScience 2004 as they appear relatively central in the field of geographical information science, and well documented on the Web. Only full papers of these conferences were considered, that is, 26 for COSIT, and 25 for GIScience, out of 60 to 80 submissions so that both samples can be considered of comparable size and acceptance rate. We also made the assumption that no further normalisation of the dataset is needed in order to correct possible size effects. These conferences allow us to delimit the population of interest, and the connections between them, from the conferences' Web pages. Figure 1 summarises the main principles of our approach. It shows the set of actors that constitute the relevant population, i.e., full paper authors. Each researcher has an academic history, for a great majority of them accessible on the personal Web pages, from which connections, that is, graph edges between the universities of his academic trajectory, form the edges of the semantic graph, the nodes being these universities. Significant academic changes considered are those substantial change in the university employing the actor. The universities and the links that relate them constitute the social network interfacing the Web semantic space and the geographical space, through the universities' geographical locations.

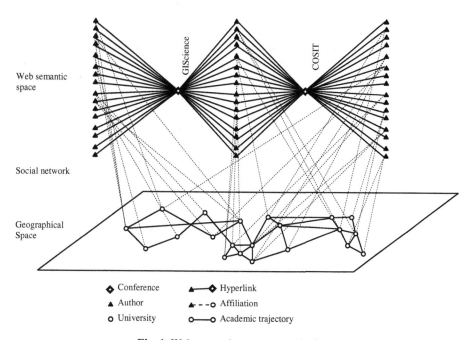

Fig. 1. Web semantic vs. geographical space

The approach considers trajectories as made of a form of cumulative links between universities. This has been preferred to that, more intuitive, of the depiction of the trajectories as chains of subsequent employments in different universities. We assume that researchers have a history, and once they have been working somewhere, interacting with colleagues and students, they build links to the university which, we believe never disappear completely. Coming back to the example of the academic staff moving from the University College London to the University of Nottingham, and then to the University of Edinburgh, this means that once in Edinburgh, the actor's history is such that he can somehow be considered a link between University College and Nottingham, between Nottingham and Edinburgh, but also between UCL and Edinburgh. Nevertheless, these links may not be considered equivalent and can be discriminated by a trajectory-based distance attribute. For example, the academic trajectory depicted above sets a distance of 1 from UCL to Nottingham as well as from Nottingham to Edinburgh, but the distance between UCL and Edinburgh is 2. A consequence is that on the graph of universities single researchers' influence can still be seen, as a presence of cliques of universities if all links are displayed, and the academic moves themselves are the links having a one-step distance.

The network of universities derived from the two Web conference sites has several emerging characteristics (figure 2). The main component of the graph connects most of the universities, with highly connected and attractive nodes reflecting key players. This is the case for instance of the University of California at Santa Barbara (UCSB), the State University of New York, Buffalo (SUNY Buffalo) or the University of Melbourne. Other highly attractive nodes are related to the academic changes of a very mobile researcher, who connects 6 universities together (i.e., SUNY at Buffalo, the University of Leipzig and Saarland University, Schaan, Sheffield, and Manchester). Also, some vertices are highly connected but appear quite repulsive, as is the case of the Technical University in Vienna (TUW), if we consider that all the links but one diverge from TUW. This is due to the fact that many junior researchers,

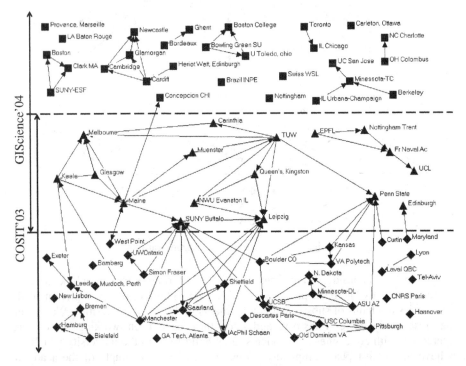

Fig. 2. COSIT 2003 and/or GIScience 2004 university networks (roles in COSIT 2003 only as diamonds, GIScience 2004 only as squares, role in both as triangles)

getting their doctoral diploma at TUW move to other sites, providing an important "input" to the research network. Aside this main component, only few and small isolates are present (with one to four vertices, or even five, in the case of that composed of the universities of Glamorgan, Cambridge, Newcastle, Cardiff, and Heriott Watt University in Edinburgh). The connectivity characteristics of COSIT 2003 are different from those of GIScience 2004. Whereas in COSIT the graph is strongly dominated by its main component (made of 33 nodes), GIScience is less structured with respect to the academic trajectories, with more small components. This suggests that the academic trajectories played a smaller role in the elaboration of the conference or in the constitution of the GIScience community, and the fact that most of these components are composed of North American universities suggest that another mechanism, geographically connected is at work. Also it is worth noticing that in the main component of the graph (figure 2), all of them except one (Concepcion University in Chile) are involved in COSIT 2003, whereas only a third of the total were involved in GIScience. Figure 3 shows the different universities of the same graph with respect to their respective countries.

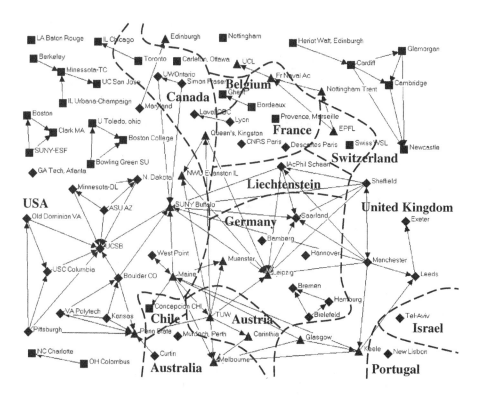

Fig. 3. Universities network vs. countries

These emerging trends can be analysed using graph-based measures. Figure 4 presents *betweenness centralities* that exhibit the graph's global structure. The main component of the graph is presented since it contains the greatest variability of degree and global structure. Similar analyses can be applied to the other components of the graph. The "key players" of the semantic network clearly appear to be (in order or prevalence) SUNY Buffalo, UCSB, the University of Maine, and TUW.

The information extracted from the main structural component of the network can be completed using additional information such as thematic or spatial attributes. In order to analyse the relationship between space and the universities network, the geographical dispersion index previously introduced is applied. The underlying partition is given by the countries where the universities are located in (figures 5 and 6). A highly negative geographical dispersion reflects an university whose connections are preferably national, while a large positive geographical dispersion is the case of an university preferably in relationship with international counterparts. For instance, within the US the most important node is UCSB, a highly connected node, that also attracts exclusively research actors from the US. There are only a few international links between nodes with negative geographical dispersion values (ranging from -0.004 to -0.487).

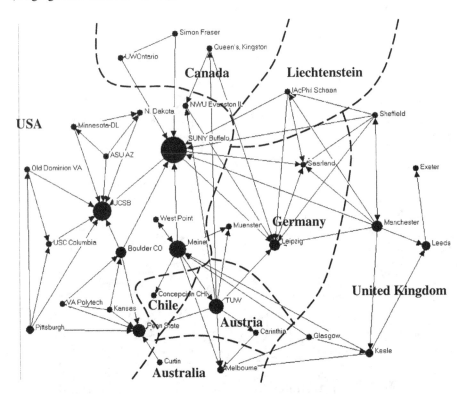

Fig. 4. Betweenness centrality in the main component of the network. Nodes' sizes are proportional to undirected centrality values

Positive values of the geographical dispersion are shown on figure 6 using proportional node circles. It appears that universities of "small" countries (or more precisely countries hosting few universities active in our field of interest) are relatively well represented as these are more likely to interact with universities of other counties. In the most populated class (USA), the ones appearing are SUNY Buffalo and the University of Maine, which also appear to be two of the most important nodes according to the *beetweenness centrality*. The magnitudes have been emphasised with respect to figure 5, as all positive values of the geographical dispersion index are low (from 0.01 to 0.04) Only a few nodes (by comparison with the number of nodes of a given geographical class) act as entry points in countries having globally low geographical dispersion (i.e., USA and UK). Nodes from other countries tend to be connected mainly with the USA and/or the UK.

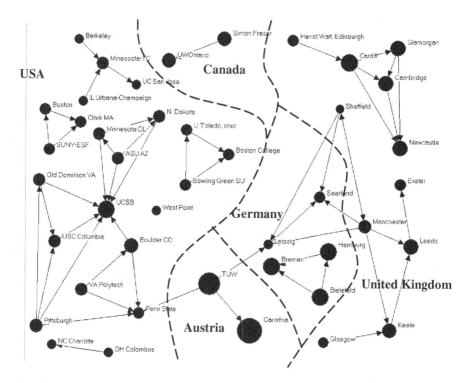

Fig. 5. Nodes with negative geographical dispersion index. Small nodes are the most negative

The geographical dispersion index allows us to analyse the types of connexions between the different universities. For instance, it appears that UCSB plays a key role in the USA from a national point of view, as it tends to be connected exclusively to other US universities. This is not the case of SUNY Buffalo or the University of Maine as both share almost exclusively connections with non-US universities. This highlights a difference in policy (conscious or not) of academic appointments and the university attractivity abroad. For example the departments involved in the above mentioned conferences are mainly North-American and European, and North

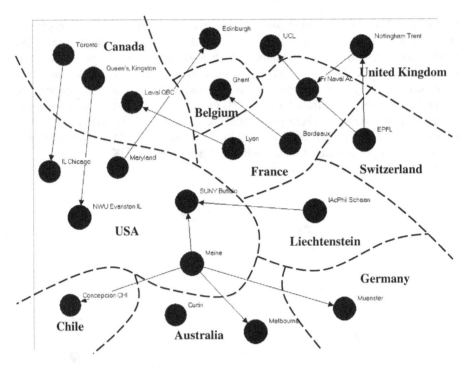

Fig. 6. Nodes with positive geographical dispersion index

America appears more attractive to European academics than the reverse. Nevertheless, and for diverse reasons – of which one can imagine that geographical remoteness plays a role – the East Coast of the USA drags most of the European, who might feel not too far away from home, as they are just "on the other side of the pond".

5 Conclusion

The approach introduced by this paper provides a preliminary contribution towards the inference and exploration of semantic and spatial relationships over the Web information space. The modelling framework infers and derives a social network from the information on a domain knowledge embedded over the Web. Graph and geographical-based operators support a structural and spatial analysis of the network properties. Combination of betweeness centrality and the geographical dispersion measure introduced give some encouraging results. The emerging properties exhibited show that the Web is an information space that offers many opportunities for generating and studying social networks. Further work concerns the systematic exploration of graph and network-based measures, and further exploration of combination of network and geographical analysis. In order to be applied to large scale, our approach should be combined with information extraction mechanisms.

References

1. Berners-Lee, J., Hendler, J. and Lassila, O., 2001 *The Semantic Web*, Scientific American, vol. 184, no. 5, pp. 34-43.
2. Madria, S. K., Bhowmick, S. S., Ng, W. K. and Lim, E. P., 1999, Research issues in web data mining. In *Proceedings of the 1st International Conference on Data Warehousing and Knowledge Discovery*, pp. 303-312.
3. Brin, S. and Page, L., 1997, The anatomy of a large-scale hypertextual Web search engine. In *Proceedings of the 7Th International WWW Conference*, Brisbane, Australia, pp. 107-117.
4. Kleinberg, J. M., 1999, Authoritative sources in an hyperlinked environment. *Journal of the ACM*, 46(5), 604-632.
5. Greco, G., Greco, S. and Zumpano, E., 2002, A stochastic approach for modelling and computing web communities. In *Proceedings of the 3rd International Conference on Web Information Systems Engineering*, IEEE Press, Singapore, pp. 43-52.
6. Hou, J. and Zhang, Y., 2002, A matrix approach for hierarchical web page clustering based on hyperlinks. In *Proceedings of the 3rd International Workshops on Web Information Systems Engineering*, IEEE Press, Singapore, pp. 207-216.
7. Lawrence, S., 2000, Context in Web search. *IEEE Data Engineering Bulletin*, 23(3), 25-32.
8. Xue, G.-R., Zeng, H.-J., Chen, Z., Ma, W.-Y. and Lu, C.-J., 2002, Log mining to improve the performance of site search. In *Proceedings of the 3rd International Workshops on Web Information Systems Engineering*, IEEE Press, Singapore, pp. 238-245.
9. Stojanovic, N., Stojanovic, L. and Gonzalez, J., 2002, On enhancing searching for information portal by tracking users' activities. In *Proceedings of the 3rd International Workshops on Web Information Systems Engineering*, IEEE Press, Singapore, pp. 246-255.
10. Tezuka, T., Lee, R., Kambayashi, Y. and Takakura, H., 2001, Web-Based Inference Rules for Processing Conceptual Geographical Relationships. In *Proceedings of the 2nd International Conference on Web Information Systems Engineering (WISE'01)*, Kyoto, Japan, pp. 14-21.
11. Yamada, N., Lee, R., Kambayashi, Y. and Takakura, H., 2002, Classification of web pages with geographic scope and level of details for mobile cache management. In *Proceedings of the 3rd International Workshops on Web Information Systems Engineering*, IEEE Press, Singapore, pp. 22-29.
12. Inoue, Y., Lee, R., Takakura, H. and Kambayashi, Y., 2002, Web locality based ranking utilizing location names and link structure, In *Proceedings of the 2nd International Conference on Web Information Systems Engineering*, IEEE Press, Kyoto, pp. 56-63.
13. Lee, R., Shina, H., Takakura, H., Kwon, Y. J. and Kambayashi, Y., 2003, optimisation of geographic area to a web page for two-dimensional range query processing. In *Proceedings of the 3rd International Workshop on Web Information Systems Engineering*, IEEE Press, Roma, pp. 9-17.
14. Tezuka, T. and Tanaka, K., 2004, Temporal and spatial attribute extraction from web documents and time-specific regional web search system. In *Proceedings of the 4th International Workshop on Web and Wireless Geographical Information Systems*, Internet Information Retrieval Research Center, Hankuk Aviation University, South Korea, pp. 78-89.
15. Tomko, M., 2004, Case study: assessing spatial distribution of web resources for navigation services. In *Proceedings of the 4th International Workshop on Web and Wireless Geographical Information Systems*, Internet Information Retrieval Research Center, Hankuk Aviation University, South Korea, pp. 90-104.

16. Doyle, J., Han, Q., Weakliam, J. and Bertolotto, M., 2004, Developing non proprietary personalised maps for web and mobile environments. In *Proceedings of the 4ᵗʰ International Workshop on Web and Wireless Geographical Information Systems*, Internet Information Retrieval Research Center, Hankuk Aviation University, South Korea, pp. 287-302.
17. Yang, Y. and Claramunt, C., 2004, User preference elicitation and refinement in web geographical information systems. In *Proceedings of the 4ᵗʰ International Workshop on Web and Wireless Geographical Information Systems*, Internet Information Retrieval Research Center, Hankuk Aviation University, South Korea, pp. 27-44.
18. Sabidussi, G., 1966, The centrality index of a graph, *Psychometrika*, 31:581-603.
19. Freeman, L. C., 1977, A set of measures of centrality based on betweenness, *Sociometry*, 40:35-41.
20. Brandes, U., 2001, A faster algorithm for betweenness centrality, *Journal of Mathematical Sociology* 25(2):163-177.
21. Batty, M., 2004, *Distance in space syntax*, Working Paper, n° 80, Centre for Advanced Spatial Analysis, UCL, London.
22. Béra, R. and Claramunt, C, 2003, Relative adjacencies in spatial pseudo-partitions, *Conference on Spatial Information Theory (COSIT '03)*, W. Kuhn, M. Worboys, and S. Timpf (eds.), *Lecture Notes in Computer Science* 2825, Springer, Ittingen, Switzerland, pp.218-234.

Trajectory-Based Presentation of Heterogeneous Spatio-temporal Content

Taro Tezuka and Katsumi Tanaka

Graduate School of Informatics,
Kyoto University
{tezuka, tanaka}@dl.kuis.kyoto-u.ac.jp

Abstract. This paper discusses the dynamic presentation of heterogeneous spatio-temporal content along a trajectory. Applications based on this scheme provide users with the ability to view target information and its surrounding context together in an opportunistic manner. We discuss various types of triggers contained in a trajectory that induce dynamic changes in content. We describe different implementations based on this scheme.

Keywords: Trajectory-based presentation, Spatio-temporal data, Content integration, Opportunistic browsing, Heterogeneous media.

1 Introduction

Trajectory-based presentation of heterogeneous spatio-temporal content enables dynamic visualization of spatio-temporal content. A series of content items can be presented in opportunistic manner, without requiring continuous action from the user. It is a push-type media similar to TV and radio, rather than the conventional usage of the World Wide Web. Today's Web users must continuously send queries to the system, such as clicking hyperlinks or typing search keywords. These actions are sometimes bothersome, especially when the desired activity is solely the browsing of information. By implementing a trajectory-based presentation interface, Web content can be browsed with less effort, which is helpful especially for children, the elders, and untrained users.

In this paper, we discuss the components of trajectory-based presentation. We also describe various implementations under this scheme, mainly focusing on geographic applications.

The rest of the paper is organized as follows. We discuss related work in Section 2. In Section 3, we describe the scheme for trajectory-based presentation. In Section 4, we discuss triggers that could be used to switch content. In Section 5, we present application examples. Section 6 is the conclusion.

2 Related Work

Trajectories are often associated with moving objects. There are a number of works concerning moving objects and moving queries, since it has many applications including location based services, traffic monitoring, enhanced 911 services, keeping track of criminals or wild animals, to name a few [1][2].

K.-J. Li and C. Vangenot (Eds.): W2GIS 2005, LNCS 3833, pp. 235–245, 2005.
© Springer-Verlag Berlin Heidelberg 2005

Erwig et al. discussed spatio-temporal data types that could be stored in databases [1]. Objects were modeled as entities in three or higher dimensions. Moving point type was defined as a mapping from time to point, while moving region type was defined as a mapping from time to region. Forlizzi et al. extended such data types into a formal model [3].

Prabhakar et al. used the maximum possible speed of moving objects to delay updating of the index and increase computational efficiency [4].

Zhang et al. discussed location-based spatial queries for mobile clients moving around in space [5]. The proposed method employs validity region to reduce frequent updates of closest neighbors. Tao et al. discussed the assignment of closest neighbors to every point on a line segment [6]. They proposed the concept of time-parameterized queries, which divides the line segments into parts by calculating *influence points*, where another point gets closer to the line segment.

Mokbel et al. discussed an algorithm for evaluating concurrent continuous spatio-temporal queries [2]. Moving objects and moving queries under the incremental evaluation paradigm.

Ishikawa et al. proposed a function to search information along trajectories for car navigation systems [7]. The work was based on the location and velocity of the moving object at each point.

One of the functions of a trajectory-based query is that it enables opportunistic browsing. The effect of such browsing has been discussed in various studies. Nadamoto et al. implemented the Web Carousel, where Web pages can passively be browsed under hardware limitations such as those of mobile devices [8]. Henzinger implemented a system that searches web contents based on caption data provided with TV broadcasts [9]. Ma described a query-free Web browsing system for spatially and temporally restricted content [10].

There is also much work on the implementations of Web-based regional information systems [11][12][13]. Most of these systems, however, do not have trajectory browsing of regional information.

Integration of video data with maps has been discussed in some studies [14][15][16]. The usability of map interfaces was also discussed in several studies [17][18][19].

3   Trajectory-Based Presentation of Content

Most digitized map applications today are built on the query-and-response model. Under this model, the map interface is used either to acquire user queries or to present responses to queries. These are query-driven systems. In contrast, we discuss maps that change spontaneously. We propose a trajectory-based presentation interface. The system presents dynamically changing regional information without waiting for user queries.

Because point, path, and region queries do not have temporal extensions, a user must continuously send queries in order to change the content. Trajectory queries are different from other spatial query types in that they have both spatial and temporal extensions. Following the user's trajectory, the content can dynamically change depending on different types of triggers.

Triggers are the cue to change the content. The aim of using the triggers in our presentation system is to deduce the user's intention that is not explicitly specified. Various types of triggers can be used to induce change in the content. These various types of triggers are discussed in the next section.

Heterogeneous content, including the map and the content with spatio-temporal attribute, is integrated through the trajectory-based presentation system.

Although in this paper we discuss map-based presentation interfaces only, another group of interfaces involves mobile and ubiquitous devices. Moving objects generate trajectories as it move along. For example, a trajectory can be retrieved from a global positioning system (GPS) attached to a mobile device.

The common definition of a trajectory is a point traveling in space over a course of time. However, in an expanded definition, regions, instead of points, can travel in space. In this case, the size or the shape of the region may change. We consider this expanded definition in this paper also.

4   Content Change Triggers

For the trajectory-based presentation of content, triggers to change the content are fundamentally necessary. Triggers are events that induce changes of the content to be presented. In this section, we describe various types of the triggers that could be used for a trajectory-based presentation interface.

4.1   Distance-Based Triggers

Content may be associated to a specific point in space. When it is, as the focus moves along the trajectory, the content can change depending on the distance.

If the object closest to the trajectory changes based on the distance from the focus of the trajectory, then the distance at a certain moment is used. This is a spatial distance.

There is also case where the direction of the movement is also considered? Suppose that the trajectory is heading a certain direction. Then it is suitable to use spatio-temporal. In this case, the nearest object from a certain point on the trajectory can be defined based on the spatio-temporal distance. Using Euclidean distance, the distance d in space-time can be represented using an arbitrary coefficient k as $d = \sqrt{(x - x')^2 + k(t - t')^2}$. The coefficient k determines the significance of the time factor in measuring spatio-temporal distances. This relationship is shown in Fig. 1.

[D] Distance-based triggers
[ST-D] Spatio-temporal distance-based triggers.

4.2   Curvature-Based Triggers

Characteristic curvatures on the trajectory can also be used as triggers. Different measures from trajectories can be used as triggers for switching content. For example, a rapid change in the position of focus or a change in speed indicate changes in the user's intention. The content located in the direction in which the focus is now heading may then be presented.

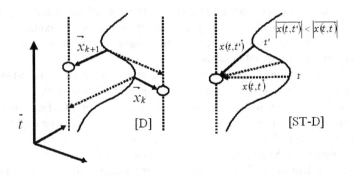

Fig. 1. Distance-based triggers

The spatial and temporal sizes of the trajectory, x and t, give scale to what the user is interested in. The speed, v, of the trajectory, and the acceleration, a, also characterize curvatures.

[T] Size of temporal extension. Expresses the extent of the user's interest.
[X] Size of spatial movement. Expresses the extent of the user's interest.
[V] Velocity. Indicates the level of the user interest in a point.
[A] Acceleration. Indicates the change in the user's interest.

4.3 Zoom-Based Triggers

In a zoomable map interface, changes of scale can act as triggers. A change in scale indicates that the user intends to obtain information not available at the present scale. Because zoom and motion are two distinct actions, they can be combined. Zoom can go in or out. Different combinations of zoom actions and trajectories are indicated in Fig. 2. A region moves along the time axis instead of a point.

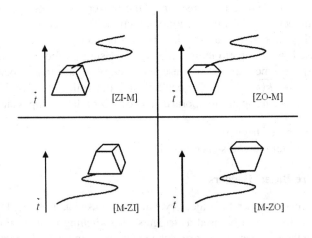

Fig. 2. Zoom and trajectory combinations

[ZI-M] Motion after zooming in.
[ZO-M] Motion after zooming out.
[M-ZI] Zoom in after motion.
[M-ZO] Zoom out after motion.

For ZI-M and ZO-M, a further distinction is made depending on whether the motion goes out of the original area or not. In the following expressions, A_i indicates a region at certain point in time, either before or after the zoom or motion.

[ZI-MI] $\forall x \in A_{i-1}.x \in A_{i+1} \wedge Z = (A_{i-1}, A_i) \wedge A_i \subset A_{i-1} \wedge M = (A_i, A_{i+1})$
[ZI-MO] $\nexists x \in A_{i-1} \wedge x \in A_{i+1} \wedge Z = (A_{i-1}, A_i) \wedge A_i \subset A_{i-1} \wedge M = (A_i, A_{i+1})$
[ZO-MI] $\forall x \in A_{i-1}.x \in A_{i+1} \wedge Z = (A_{i-1}, A_i) \wedge A_{i-1} \subset A_i \wedge M = (A_i, A_{i+1})$
[ZO-MO] $\nexists x \in A_{i-1} \wedge x \in A_{i+1} \wedge Z = (A_{i-1}, A_i) \wedge A_{i-1} \subset A_i \wedge M = (A_i, A_{i+1})$

Combinations of zooming actions and movements are indicated in Fig. 3.

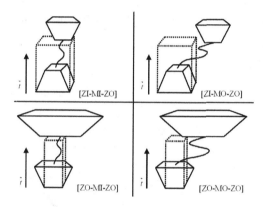

Fig. 3. Pairs of zoom/trajectory movements

The user's intention is different for each pair of zooms and motions. For example, when a user performs [ZO-MO-ZI], he/she wanted to move a great distance. On the other hand, in [ZO-MI-ZI], the user did not actually move very far and zoomed in again.

A zoomable trajectory, J, is defined as a finite series of zooms and motions.

$J = (S_0, S_1, ...S_n)$
$S_i \in \{ZO(A_i, A_{i+1}), ZI(A_i, A_{i+1}), MO(A_i, A_{i+1}), MI(A_i, A_{i+1})\}$
$A_i = (x_{1,i}, y_{1,i}, x_{2,i}, y_{2,i})$

5   Applications

In this section, we describe applications of trajectory-based presentation interfaces. As described in the previous sections, the types of trajectory-based presentation interfaces are numerous, so the examples below are not exhaustive.

5.1 Dynamic Map Interface on the Web

The first application is a regional Web browsing system with an automatic progression mechanism. In this system, the user either draws an arbitrary trajectory over the map interface or imports recommended trajectory information. Then the map starts automatic motion along the trajectory. The system continually shows Web pages related to the significant place name closest to the map center. The system is implemented as a meta-search system, using the Google Web API [23].

Users can view Web content along a specified trajectory without continuous action such as clicking hyperlinks or sending keywords to search engines. We named the system the Train Window system. It is based on a regular GIS, a digitized residential map provided by Zenrin, Ltd. [22].

The user can zoom in/out of the map area during browsing. The scale of the map reflects the user's intended level of detail. If the map is zoomed out, the user wants to see an overview of the region. In this case, the map shows only the place names with high significance. The displayed Web pages are those related to the most significant landmarks in the area. If the map is zoomed in, the user wants to get more detailed information on the region, so landmarks with less significance are shown, along with corresponding Web pages (Fig. 4).

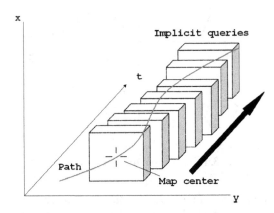

Fig. 4. Implicit search by automatic motion

The basic steps for browsing Web content using the Train Window system are illustrated in Fig. 5. The steps are as follows.

Definition: *Train Window System.*
INPUT: An arbitrary area, $A(0)$, chosen by the user.
INPUT: A trajectory, J, connecting two arbitrary points on the map.
OUTPUT: Show the area, $A(t)$, by changing t, at a given speed $\delta t/\delta T$, where δt is a system time and δT is a real time.
Find the content item, C, that is linked to point x and closest to $center(A(t))$.
OUTPUT: The content item C.

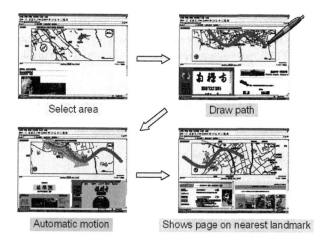

Fig. 5. Automatic motion interface for Train Window System

In the Train Window system, the trajectory data can be imported from various sources. For example, the user can import a series of coordinates obtained using GPS. This enables the system to keep track of real world movement and visualize it on the map. Using GPS, the system can obtain Web pages related to a commuting route. Travelers can also visualize their routes on the map and retrieve relevant Web pages along the trajectory, thereby adding to their knowledge about the places that they have just visited. Train Window thus enables trajectory-oriented travel planning. Users can virtually move along travel routes instead of selecting from a list of points of interest.

5.2 Visualization of Temporal Changes in City Activities

The second application is a system that visualizes temporal change in city activities. Today, the World Wide Web contains a large amount of information on shop hours.

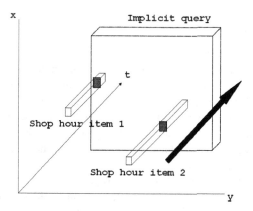

Fig. 6. Visualization of temporal changes

The system extracts pairs of shop hours and locations through text pattern mining. The address information is converted to coordinates based on GIS. The title of the page is extracted from the HTML for each match. Each pair is stored into the database prior to use.

The user specifies an arbitrary region on the map interface. Then the map presents changes of city activities over time. Thus, the changes in the daily activities in a city are visualized (Fig. 6).

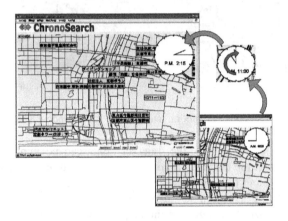

Fig. 7. Visualization of temporal changes in ChronoSearch

The system not only provides the user with the ability to search spatio-temporally specific information, but also visualizes how the city activities change as time passes. An example of a city's extracted activities is shown in Fig. 7.

We developed the ChronoSearch, a system for extracting and presenting spatial and temporal information from the Web. The details of the system are described in our previous paper [21].

5.3   Integration of Video Archives and Map

The third application is the integration of a map with video archives. The aim of this application is to map TV programs or other video content to geographic locations and enable users to view video data as related to specific regions along a trajectory.

To map video content to coordinates, we used caption data attached to TV broadcasts. The method we used to collect video caption data is described by Yumoto et al. [20]. The system parses caption data and place names contained in a regular GIS are extracted. The set including the place name, the URI for the video clip, and the offset in the video clip are stored in the database (Fig. 8).

The browsing of video content based on a trajectory-based query is shown in Fig. 9. As the user or the system changes the selected region on the map interface, the query analyzer observes the place name that is closest to the map center and checks to see if it is contained in the database. If it is, the player starts the video from the point where the place name appears.

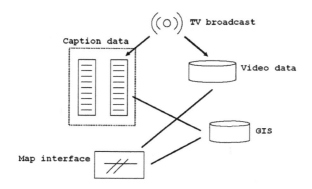

Fig. 8. Video archive linked to map interface

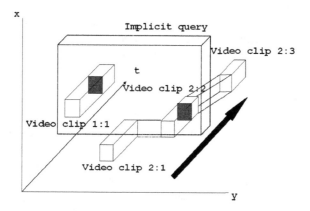

Fig. 9. Implicit search of video clips

6   Conclusion

We discussed trajectory-based presentation interfaces, which change their area and content based on trajectories given by the user. This scheme enhances user experiences of digitized maps.

Various types of trajectory-based presentation interfaces are possible, and we described a few. Spatio-temporal content such as Web content and video archives are mapped to geographic locations and presented along the user-specified trajectory.

Trajectory queries are useful for providing information to mobile device users. We discussed only applications that could be used for both desktop and mobile devices. In the future, we will consider discussing applications of trajectory-based queries specific to mobile devices.

More advanced combinations of zoom and map area changes are another interesting field to explore (Fig. 10). Because few map interfaces have such functions yet, we did not them.

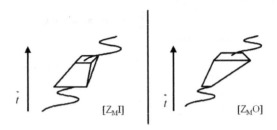

Fig. 10. Zooming while moving

$[Z_M I]$ Zooming in while moving.
$[Z_M O]$ Zooming out while moving.

Our future work will include elaborate discussion of the advantages and disadvantages of trajectory-based presentation interfaces. Different implementations must be compared, and the advantages of trajectory-based presentation interfaces over query-driven map interfaces must be quantified and measured.

Acknowledgments

This work was supported in part by the Japanese Ministry of Education, Culture, Sports, Science and Technology under a Grant-in-Aid for Software Technologies for Search and Integration across Heterogeneous-Media Archives, a Special Research Area Grant-In-Aid For Scientific Research (2) for the year 2005 under a project titled Research for New Search Service Methods Based on the Web's Semantic Structure (Project No, 16016247; Representative, Katsumi Tanaka), and the Informatics Research Center for Development of Knowledge Society Infrastructure (COE program of the Japanese Ministry of Education, Culture, Sports, Science and Technology).

References

1. M. Erwig, R. H. Guting, M. Schneider and M. Vazirgiannis, Spatio-temporal data types: An approach to modeling and querying moving objects in databases, GeoInformatica, Vol. 3, No. 3, pp. 269-296, 1999.
2. M. F. Mokbel, X. Xiong and W. G. Aref, SINA: Scalable incremental processing of continuous queries in spatio-temporal databases, Proceedings of the 2004 ACM SIGMOD International Conference on Management of Data, pp. 623-634, Paris, France, 2004.
3. L. Forlizzi, R. H. Guting, E. Nardelli and M. Schneider, A data model and data structures for moving objects databases, Proceedings of the 2000 ACM SIGMOD International Conference on Management of Data, pp. 319-330, Dallas, Texas, 2000.
4. S. Prabhakar, Y. Xia, D. Kalashnikov, W. Aref and S. Hambrusch, Query indexing and velocity constrained indexing: Scalable techniques for continuous queries on moving objects, IEEE Transactions on Computers, Special Issue on DBMS and Mobile Computing, Vol. 51, No. 10, 2002.

5. J. Zhang, M. Zhu, D. Papadias, Y. Tao and D. L. Lee, Location-based spatial queries, Proceedings of the 2003 ACM SIGMOD International Conference on Management of Data, pp. 443-454, San Diego, California, 2003.

6. Y. Tao, D. Papadias and S. Qiongmao, Continuous nearest neighbor search, Proceedings of the 28th International Conference on Very Large Data Bases (VLDB2002), pp. 287-298, Hong Kong, China, 2002.

7. Y. Ishikawa, Y. Tsukamoto and H. Kitagawa, Implementation and evaluation of an adaptive neighborhood information retrieval system for mobile users, Proceedings of the Third International Workshop on Web and Wireless Geographical Information Systems (W2GIS2003), pp. 17-26, Rome, Italy, 2003.

8. A. Nadamoto, H. Kondo and K. Tanaka, WebCarousel: Restructuring Web search results for passive viewing in mobile environments, Proceedings of the Seventh International Conference on Database Systems for Advanced Applications (DASFAA 2001), Hong Kong, China, 2001.

9. M. Henzinger, B. W. Chang, B. Milch and S. Brin, Query-free news search, Proceedings of the Twelfth International World Wide Web Conference (WWW2003), pp. 1-10, Budapest, Hungary, 2003.

10. Q. Ma, Query-free Information Retrieval Based on Saptio-temporal Criteria and Content Complementation, Doctoral Dissertation, Graduate School of Informatics, Kyoto University, 2004.

11. K. Hiramatsu, K. Kobayashi, B. Benjamin, T. Ishida and J. Akahani, Map-based user interface for Digital City Kyoto, Proceedings of the Tenth Annual Internet Society Conference, Yokohama, Japan, 2000.

12. S. Yokoji, K. Takahashi, N. Miura and K. Shima, Location oriented collection, structuring and searching methods of information, *Information Processing Society of Japan Journal*, Vol. 41, No. 7, pp. 1987-1998, 2000.

13. T. Sagara, M. Arikawa and M. Sakauchi, Spatial information extraction system using georeference information, *Information Processing Society of Japan Journal:Database*, Vol.41, No.SIG6(TOD7), pp. 69-80, 2000.

14. Y. Theodoridis, M. Vazirgiannis and T. Sellis, Spatio-temporal indexing for large multimedia applications, Proceeding of the Third IEEE Conference on Multimedia Computing and Systems, pp. 441-448, Hiroshima, Japan, 1996.

15. N. Neves, J. Silva, P. Gonalves, J. Muchaxo, M. Silva and A. Camara, Cognitive spaces and metaphors: a solution for interacting with spatial data, New University of Lisbon, 1998.

16. M. E. Donderler, E. Saykol, O. Ulusoy and U. Gudukbay, BilVideo: A video database management system, IEEE Multimedia, Vol. 10, No. 1, pp. 66-70, 2003.

17. D. Mark and A. Frank (Eds.), User Interfaces for Geographic Information Systems: Report on the Specialist Meeting, Santa Barbara, CA: National Center for Geographic Information and Analysis, Report 92-3, 1992.

18. W. Kuhn and M. Egenhofer (Eds.), Visual Interfaces to Geometry, Report on a Two-Day Workshop at CHI'90, National Center for Geographic Information and Analysis, Santa Barbara, California, 1991.

19. T. Bruns and M. Egenhofer, User interfaces for map algebra, *Journal of the Urban and Regional Information Systems Association*, Vol. 9 No. 1, pp. 44-54, 1997.

20. T. Yumoto, Q. Ma, K. Sumiya and K. Tanaka, A dynamic content integration language for video data and Web content, Proceedings of the Fourth International Conference on Web Information Systems Engineering, pp. 83-92, Rome, Italy, 2003.

21. T. Tezuka and K. Tanaka, Temporal and spatial attribute extraction from Web documents and time-specific regional Web search system, Web and Wireless Geographical Information Systems, Lecture Notes in Computer Science 3428, pp. 14-25, Springer-Verlag, 2005.

22. Zenrin Co., Ltd., http://www.zenrin.co.jp/

23. Google Web API, http://www.google.com/apis/

Interoperable Geographic Information Services to Support Crisis Management

Artur Rocha[1], Bojan Cestnik[2,3], and Marco A. Oliveira[1]

[1] INESC Porto, R. Dr. Roberto Frias 378, 4200-465 Porto
{artur.rocha, mao}@inescporto.pt
[2] Temida d.o.o., SI-1000 Ljubljana, Dunajska cesta 51,
bojan.cestnik@temida.si
[3] Jozef Stefan Institute, SI-1000 Ljubljana, jamova 39

Abstract. In this article we focus on interoperable geographic information (GI) services from the crisis management perspective. Based on Open Geospatial Consortium [10] standards and initiatives, we present the building blocks of the interoperable solution for supporting crisis management that is proposed as a result of the EU sponsored project, MEDSI [1]. In particular, we focus on the application and operationalization of several OGC standards, some adopted and some still under discussion, such as WMS, WFS, WMC, SLD and SMS, as well as their integration and cooperation within a single software framework.

1 Introduction

Nowadays, we face a considerable increase in the complexity of the living environment of the western world. This trend is particularly evident in the domain of critical infrastructures. One of its negative consequences is manifested by the fact that the society has become more vulnerable. For that reason, advancing the field of crisis management for protecting critical infrastructures has been recognized as one of the top priorities in European countries [20].

One of the main concerns when responding to a crisis is how to facilitate the integration of information from various sources through different media in a meaningful way. Here, the crucial task is how to obtain timely and accurate geospatial information to quickly visualize and understand the context of emergency situations. To effectively handle this task, Open Geospatial Consortium [10] (OGC) established standards for Geographic Information (GI) processing. Among others, they promote standards like Web Map Server [9] (WMS) to retrieve geographic information in image format and Web Feature Server [12] (WFS) to retrieve GI in vector format through the use of Geography Markup Language [5] (GML). Furthermore, OGC also proposes standards that cover the display of symbols in WMS, like Styled Layer Descriptor [4], which can be found by means of a Style Management Service [6] and standards that cover the storage of a description of the requests of one or more maps from one or more map servers in a portable, platform-independent format - Web Map Context Documents (WMC) [13]. Although the adoption of the OGC standards by

K.-J. Li and C. Vangenot (Eds.): W2GIS 2005, LNCS 3833, pp. 246–255, 2005.
© Springer-Verlag Berlin Heidelberg 2005

GIS software providers has been a slow process, these standards are widely accepted by the GI community and represent a firm foundation for constructing distributed GI-based software systems.

The incorporation of state of the art information technology advances in the field of supporting and enhancing decision-making capabilities in crisis management represents one of the key aspects of EU sponsored project MEDSI. Since good technology is always built on the foundation of good technology, we made a commitment to apply and operationalize the standards and initiatives of OGC to propose a modern interoperable infrastructure for supporting crisis management within MEDSI. By enforcing the OGC standards, MEDSI intends to exploit in particular the interoperability issues raised by the multiplicity of formats and heterogeneous ways to access various sorts of data.

To promote the protection of critical infrastructures as one of its key areas, OGC has established a specific line of action for the Critical Infrastructure Protection Initiative [11]. MEDSI has adopted this experience by incorporating many of the premises and concepts of this initiative. By building upon their work, MEDSI expects to be able to contribute for accelerating the launch of the assets of the European management decision support for critical infrastructures.

The resulting MEDSI framework was tested on realistic user scenarios, like, for example, fire and explosion of hazardous materials in an industrial area, and river flooding. The scenarios allow MEDSI partners to validate not only the suitability of the proposed architecture but also the application of instantiated MEDSI system in a real user environment. Potential users of the proposed software framework are private and governmental organizations, including city management, regional management, central institutions and agencies, international crisis management organizations, public safety and security forces, and intelligence services.

In the paper we first present the proposed MEDSI framework for supporting crisis management decisions. Then, we give an overview of technological platform. Next, the functionality of the framework is demonstrated in supporting collaborative crisis management and symbology. We conclude by calling attention to the most important points presented in this paper.

2   Crisis Management Support

Given the broad scope of the concept "Critical Infrastructure" and the wide variety of potential users for MEDSI system (local, regional, national or transnational level), it was obvious from the feasibility and scalability point of view that a distributed network of self-contained cells would have to be put in place. Moreover, these cells, which can vary in size and geographic distribution, need to be self-sufficient in the protection of the infrastructure they are aimed to protect, while they also should be able to cooperate in case of broader emergency situations [Figure 1].

Also, the central role of GI together with the ability to swiftly exchange the most updated representations of geographical data (maps) among crisis management actors was a premise in the inception of MEDSI. This assumption remains true not only for exchanges between MEDSI cells, but also inside the scope of a single cell, instantiated in a crisis management center.

Originating from these premises and being aware of the interoperability issues arising when trying to use together several heterogeneous GIS software and data sources, we have decided to enforce the use of OGC Web Services (OWS) for all sorts of GI access and exchange in MEDSI.

Users of MEDSI system have the capability of finding the appropriate GI sources by means of a catalogue service where the Web Services providing the relevant geodata have been previously registered.

It should be stressed that the services providing GI may be available not only inside the crisis center, where typically resides information like local aerial photos, streets, buildings, available resources, etc., but also from external providers like up to date satellite photos, sensor/weather data or even the most updated "map" of an endangered facility, made available upon request [figure 1].

Although this paper will not focus on the specific use cases implemented in MEDSI, it's worth mentioning that it consists of a rich client application capable of providing support to domain-specific tasks such as risk analysis, crisis plans, standard operation procedures, etc. In other words, MEDSI handles a set of specific domain objects, some of them comprising associated geometries, and it tries to do so maintaining the lowest possible coupling with the datasource level. For the GI realm, this means that MEDSI domain objects can be accessed through a WFS interface. As such, it is possible that another web service

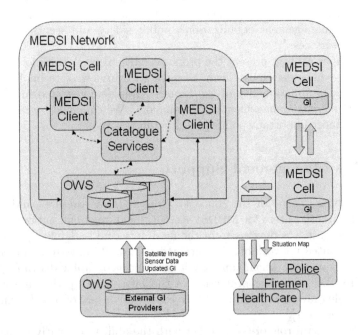

Fig. 1. Organizational view of MEDSI

makes a "request" to the WFS for its schema in order to be able to interoperate with it.

As outputs from MEDSI system, the most recent "situation maps" are produced to generate reports and updates to the units operating in the crisis scene, as well as for leading updated information to the several actor responsible for taking decisions in a crisis situation.

Moreover, it's worth mentioning that due to the ability of exchanging "Context Documents" amongst crisis management actors, these can interact in a much more efficient way as they are able to see exactly the same "map representation" (as if using paper based maps), but with the possibility of continuing to browse afterwards like in any on-line map.

3 Technology Overview

MEDSI comprises several modules supporting crisis management specific tasks ranging from Analysis and Planning to Simulation, Decision Support, Resources Management and also some horizontal types of functionalities like messaging and reporting.

These modules which implement the main specific functionalities will not be detailed under the scope of this paper, however they have the particularity of being connected to the GI infrastructure in one way or another. First because objects addressed in the crisis management domain correspond directly to a geographical feature. And second, because although sometimes no direct mapping is feasible, the geographical representation of involved areas provides a meaningful context to understand and respond to a crisis situation or help revealing a potential threat.

A special attention has also been paid to symbology, given its high expressiveness which helps the user to quickly absorb a significant level of information, provided that the used symbols are commonly understandable.

In this section we describe the technological platform being built for MEDSI project focusing mainly on the GI infrastructure.

As previously said, MEDSI has chosen to use in its prototype WMS as a portrayal service for displaying maps in image format and WFS for data services returning GML, which is then rendered in vector format. Because aerial photographs provide a high level of understandability even for users not familiarized with cartography, a Web coverage Service (WCS) [7] was also used in MEDSI prototype realization.

Although other services such as Web Terrain Server (WTS) [2] could also have been used for enhanced terrain visualization, the aforementioned ones have been deemed adequate for establishing a proof of concept.

As the first step in the prototype implementation, the consortium has configured several geographical data sources, in different technologies capable to output GI under the form of WMS and WFS. MEDSI has successfully configured and tested interoperable access to several platforms providing GI by means of web services. From then the consortium has been seamlessly using both open source geodata sources such as Deegree [14], UMN map server [17] and Geoserver [18], but also popular proprietary solutions such as Geomedia Web Server [16] and ESRI ArcIMS [15] through their respective WMS and WFS connectors.

A catalogue service has also been deployed [8] and enhanced with the capability of classify these GI services according to a proposed ontology to facilitate finding of the appropriate data sources.

On MEDSI client side, we used an Open Source GI viewer [19] able to view WMS which we extended to support WFS accesses as well as other functionalities required for proper integration with other implemented modules.

A catalogue browser is also used in the client for finding the needed data sources. Some editing and annotation functionalities, along with some basic spatial analysis have also been used to provide added value to MEDSI client [figure 2].

Although the resulting prototype has proved itself as a reliable, highly customizable and interoperable framework for accessing distributed geographical information, other functionalities have been identified as a prerequisite for supporting a collaborative approach to decision support in crisis management.

One of such functionalities is the ability to store and further reproduce the status of a GI view, i.e. the set of map requests that originated that same view. Saving and reproducing map context information is essential to support any underlying workflow mechanism and also to create personal views for each user profile or for each type of crisis.

Furthermore, a gazetteer service [3] can be used to find a geographic feature by its name (e.g. a street) returning a new geographical extent to update the present context.

Other important factor to support collaboration is the ability of crisis management actors within a cell to be able of visualizing geographic information

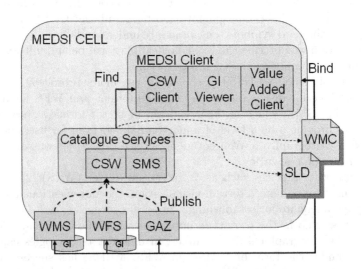

Fig. 2. OGC Web Services at use in MEDSI

from other cells, e.g. points of interest, according to their own used symbology, leading to the requirement of changing symbology in runtime.

4   Supporting Collaboration

A successful collaborative approach starts with the definition of each actor's roles and needs. In this sense, MEDSI allows the definition of a set of user profiles associated with the actors' application needs and preferences. Depending on the type of crisis, the user may also have a pre-defined set of default information needs.

The collaborative nature of MEDSI framework has turned the requirements concerning workflow mechanisms and broadcast of situation maps a priority.

From the GI infrastructure point of view, this builds up to the need of loading, saving and exchanging map contexts, containing the necessary information used to recreate the exchanged "map view".

Despite its limitation of binding only with OGC Web Map Service interface, OGC Web Map Context Documents (WMC), or simply contexts [13] were used as a starting point to fulfill these requirements.

A context is some sort of "memento" for maps, comprising the description in a portable, platform-independent format of the grouping of one or more map requests from one or more map services for storage in a repository or for transmission between clients [13].

As such, the consortium has implemented a specific framework component for loading and saving WMC documents (XML), as well as a repository for storing and retrieving them which also provides an ad-hoc workflow mechanism allowing the exchange of contexts between users and/or groups of users.

Figure 3 depicts a situation map being sent from the Head of a Crisis Management Center (HC) to the Analysts Team (AT) for further task execution. The analysts will then receive a notification that a new context document awaits them and upon opening it, their "map viewer" will be directed to the area specified by the HC, i.e. the client will perform the same map requests necessary to reproduce the same situation map.

In another example of usage inside a specific MEDSI Cell, a context document resulting from pre-planning tasks can be bound to a crisis ontology, so that when a specific crisis situation occurs, the most suitable "map context" (servers, layers, extents, etc) will be automatically loaded.

Context documents are also used to support the broadcast of livesituation maps, either between cells or to external actors, such as Firemen. This is important when dealing with information that is constantly evolving during the crisis, enabling the receivers to access the most up to date information or simply a more relevant view over the same geodata.

Either supported by a traditional workflow engine or simply by means of ad-hoc workflow support, WMC documents have an important role in enabling collaborative distributed decision support for GI-based applications such as MEDSI.

Although the current software infrastructure serves as proof of concept for collaboration by enabling the mechanisms to store and find context documents,

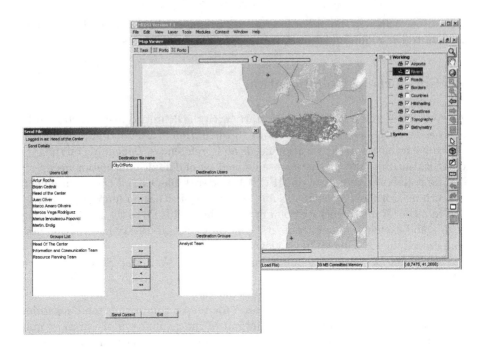

Fig. 3. Web Map Context Document - Sending

broader usage could probably benefit from a Web Catalogue Service, eventually leading to a spatial extension to Universal Description, Discovery and Integration (UDDI).

Since Web Map Context Documents have the limitation of only binding with WMS interfaces, empowering its usage will require further extensibility in order to bind with other OGC interface specifications such as WFS.

5 Symbology

A collaborative approach to crisis management requires establishing a common "language" for team communication. Symbology takes an essential role for quick visual identification of the most important spots within the crisis geographical extent. Within MEDSI project we have established a framework for the generation of symbols from a structured definition containing the symbol description.

Styled Layer Descriptor[4] is a language that can be used to customize the output of WMS and WFS on the client side, as it defines styles for presenting different map layers. A symbol for denoting a specific phenomenon on the map is first dynamically constructed from an icon selected from the symbology repository and augmented with dynamic information from the data base. Then, the necessary SLD file is built and placed in a location accessible from the web.

Since the SLD location (URL) is a paramenter in a WMS request, new WMS requests using the stylesheet (SLD) at that location will display the updated symbols on the map. In such a way, symbols can be displayed with dynamical attributes of the portrayed entity.

On the other hand, since for each WMS entry in the catalogue service MEDSI defines a collection of possible SLDs, it is possible to have a different set of symbols for each "user community", which facilitates communication while they don't agree on a common set.

Style Management Service (SMS) manages objects that represent styles and symbols and provides the means to discover, query, insert, update and delete these objects. Styles provide the mapping from feature types and feature properties and constraints to parameterized symbols used in drawing maps. Typically, SMS is realized by means of a catalogue service and provides a way of finding an appropriate SLD for displaying symbols on a WMS. By the same token, both technologies are used also within MEDSI framework.

6   Lessons Learned

MEDSI has decided to follow the path of OGC Web Services for its own GI infrastructure, while aiming to support a distributed and collaborative approach to Crisis Management. This has proved a strong asset concerning the aspect of solving interoperability issues that necessarily arise when using distributed heterogeneous systems and data sources.

By enforcing the use of standards like WMS and WFS to help solving issues resulting from the definition of a distributed architecture, MEDSI has aligned itself with the European and International tendencies on building common Spatial Data Infrastructures, which can help solving relevant problems such as the ones involved in the protection of critical infrastructures.

The definition of a solid application layer for a specific domain, over a set of distributed geodata sources in the form of web services has brought MEDSI before the need of complementing the standard interfaces for accessing data with many other abstractions and mechanisms to provide the necessary functionalities while keeping independence from the information sources.

An example of these abstractions was a kind of context information that could be used to save, exchange and restore the status of a composed GI view. The Web Map Context documents (a position paper by the time we started) was identified as the vehicle to store and transport this information across the network, thus enabling collaboration.

Symbology can be seen as lingua franca for interpreting emergency maps, however different communities may use different symbols to represent the same concepts. Dynamic binding of Styled Layered Descriptions (SLD) to map services (WMS) has helped overcome this issue.

On the other hand, the low-coupling between maps services and symbols and the fact that they can be loaded in run-time has helped MEDSI taking the dynamic aspects of symbology a step further into augmenting symbols with database information for better and faster map interpretation.

Acknowledgement

The work reported in this article is a result of the research project "MEDSI IST-2002-506991" funded by the Commission of European Communities. We are grateful to all the MEDSI Consortium members for their contributions to the project.

References

1. Bojan Cestnik, Artur Rocha, and Martin Endig. Emergency response through collaborative crisis management. In *Proceedings of Eastern European eGov days 2005*, Budapest, Hungary, March 17-18 2005.
2. Open Geospatial Consortium. Web terrain server, version 0.3.2. Available in World Wide Web, August, 24 2001. http://portal.opengeospatial.org/files/?artifact_id=1072.
3. Open Geospatial Consortium. Gazetteer service profile for a wfs, version 0.0.9. Available in World Wide Web, September, 03 2002. https://portal.opengeospatial.org/files/?artifact_id=7175.
4. Open Geospatial Consortium. Styled layer descriptor implementation specification, version 1.00. Available in World Wide Web, August, 19 2002. https://portal.opengeospatial.org/files/?artifact_id=1188.
5. Open Geospatial Consortium. Geography markup language, version 3.0. Available in World Wide Web, January, 29 2003. https://portal.opengeospatial.org/files/?artifact_id=7174.
6. Open Geospatial Consortium. Style management services for emergency mapping symbology, version 1.00. Available in World Wide Web, January, 20 2003. http://portal.opengis.org/files/?artifact_id=7470.
7. Open Geospatial Consortium. Web coverage service, version 1.0. Available in World Wide Web, October, 16 2003. https://portal.opengeospatial.org/files/?artifact_id=3837.
8. Open Geospatial Consortium. Catalog service specification, version 2.0. Available in World Wide Web, August, 02 2004. http://portal.opengeospatial.org/files/?artifact_id=5929&version=1.
9. Open Geospatial Consortium. Web map service specification, version 1.3. Available in World Wide Web, August, 02 2004. http://portal.opengeospatial.org/files/?artifact_id=5316.
10. Open Geospatial Consortium. Available in World Wide Web, 2005. http://www.opengeospatial.org.
11. Open Geospatial Consortium. Critical infrastructure protection initiative. Available in World Wide Web, 2005. http://www.opengeospatial.org/functional/?page=cipi.
12. Open Geospatial Consortium. Web feature service specification, version 1.1. Available in World Wide Web, May, 03 2005. https://portal.opengeospatial.org/files/?artifact_id=8339.
13. Open Geospatial Consortium. Web map context documents, version 1.1. Available in World Wide Web, May, 03 2005. https://portal.opengeospatial.org/files/?artifact_id=8618.
14. Deegree. Available in World Wide Web, 2005. http://deegree.sourceforge.net/.

15. ESRI. Gis standards and it interoperability. Available in World Wiede Web, 2005.
    `http://www.esri.com/software/standards/`.
16. Intergraph. Geomedia. Available in World Wide Web, 2005. `http://www.intergraph.com/geomedia/`.
17. University of Minnesota MapServer. Available in World Wide Web, 2005.
    `http://mapserver.gis.umn.edu/`.
18. The GeoServer Project. Available in World Wide Web, 2005.
    `http://geoserver.sourceforge.net/`.
19. The JUMP Project. Available in World Wide Web, 2005. `http://www.jump-project.org/`.
20. J. Solana. A european route to security. The International Herald Tribune, December 12 2003. Also published in other international newspapers.

Web GIS Management and Risk Evaluation of a Road Slope Using a Terrestrial LiDAR

Youngjoo Kwak[1], Yonggu Jang[2], and Injoon Kang[1]

[1] GSIS(GeoSpatial Information System) Lab,
Pusan National University 30 Jangjeon-dong
Geumjeong-gu Busan 607-735, South Korea
{maestro99, ijkang}@pusan.ac.kr
http://home.pusan.ac.kr/ ijkang
[2] LBS Research Center, KICT, 2311, Daehwa-Dong ilsan-Gu,
Goyang-Si Gyeongi-Do, South Korea
wkddydrn@kict.re.kr

Abstract. Recently, slope failures are disastrous when they occur in mountainous areas adjoining highways. The accidents associated with slope failures have increased due to rapid urbanization of mountainous areas. Therefore, the inspection of slopes is conducted to maintain road safety as well as road function. In this study, we apply a remedy which is comparing existent descriptions to advanced technology using GIS. We utilize a terrestrial LiDAR, an advanced method, to generate a precise and complete road slope model from an expert point of view. In result, we extract hazardous slope information from external measurements referring to the evaluation criteria of external slope stability. We suggest not only the database but also the method of road risk evaluation based on internet GIS.

1   Introduction

Korea is topographically and meteorologically prone to natural disasters. In addition to extraordinary weather, localized heavy rain is an irregular occurrence. Roads in Korea are frequently damaged by rain, wind, flood and extreme temperatures. Recently, slope failures are disastrous when they occur in mountainous areas adjoining highways. The accidents associated with slopes failures have increased due to rapid urbanization of mountainous area. Therefore, the inspection of slope is conducted to maintain road safety as well as road function. The Ministry of Construction & Transportation is also trying to study and develop a prediction model as a failure mechanism[1].

In this study, we apply to the remedy which is comparing existent descriptions to advanced technology using GIS. We utilize a terrestrial LiDAR, an advanced method, to generate precise and complete road slope models from an expert point of view. The study site is located in Kyeng-sang province, Korea's Highway 24th has experienced slope failures caused by heavy rains and typhoons in the last year. As a result, we extract hazardous slope information from external measurements referring to the evaluation criteria of external slope stability. We

K.-J. Li and C. Vangenot (Eds.): W2GIS 2005, LNCS 3833, pp. 256–266, 2005.
© Springer-Verlag Berlin Heidelberg 2005

suggest not only the database but also the method of road risk evaluation based on internet GIS.

2   The Management of Hazard Slope

2.1   Failure Pattern of the Rock Slope

An embankment slope is a long term natural stability process in which a natural slope or material's quality management is possible. However a cut slope is a spontaneous ground structure which is imposing an artificial transformation. It is difficult to stabilize because of weathering and scouring, a deterioration phenomenon. Therefore, continuous maintenance and management are essential. Depending on the situation, failure and disaster an strike in many ways. In case of earthy material erosion to cut slopes, it causes a surface collapse that is influenced by the action of surface water or underground water. According to structural quality of discontinuity in rock slopes, landslides can occur in the various ways. Rock slope failure is classified that is presented by Varnes in the following Table 1[2].

Table 1. Failure pattern

Failure pattern		Example	
Fails		Rock Fall	
Topples		Rock Topple	
Slides	Rotational Slides	Rock Slump	Few Units
	Translational Slides	Rock Block Slide	
	Translational Slides	Rock Slide	Many Units
Lateral Spreads		Rock Spread	
Flows		Rock Flow	
Complex		Multiple Retrogressive and Successive Slide	

(1) Circular Failure

When the material is very weak, as in a soil slope, or when the rock mass is very heavily jointed or broken, as in a waste rock dump, the failure will be defined by a single discontinuity surface but will tend to follow a circular failure path. This type of failure has been treated in exhaustive detail in many standard soil mechanics.

(2) Plane Failure

Plane failure occurs when a geological discontinuity such as a bedding plane, strikes parallel to the slope face and dips into the excavation at an angle greater than the angle of friction.

(3) Wedge Failure

When two discontinuities strike obliquely across the slope face and their line of intersection in the slope face, the wedge of rock resting on these discontinuities will slide down the line of intersection, provided that the inclination of this line is significantly greater than the angle of friction.

(4) Toppling Failure

Toppling failure involves rotation of columns or block of rock about some fixed base and the simple geometrical conditions governing the toppling of a single block in and inclined surface. Toppling failure occurs open cut and joint gradient on its opposite.

2.2   Disaster Prevention Inspection

Inspection is conducted to accurately establish the conditions of earth structures, such as cut slopes and embankments, under management and their surrounding areas. Disaster prevention inspection is a detailed inspection which is conducted by specialist engineers to check the topographical and geological conditions of a slope, the effect of existing countermeasures and the history of disasters[3].

2.3   Discontinuity Inspection Using Terrestrial LiDAR

Measuring data of a LiDAR system was converted from a time lag to distance with an emitting and reflecting laser. Time-of-Flight is composed of a main apparatus, receiving apparatus, time measurement. After the receiving laser is measured with a time lag, distance is calculated by the following equation (1)[4].

$$Distance = C \times \frac{(t_1 - t_0)}{2} \tag{1}$$

$$C \; : \; \text{The speed of light,}$$

$$t_1 - t_0 \; : \; \text{Phase Difference of laser pulse}$$

Error of Time-of-Flight techniques usually happened as followed: General measurement 5mm, a precision of measurement 1mm. Because of the special quality time lag, it is characteristic that accuracy falls in near distances. Triangulation technique emits laser beam to target, and laser spots are recorded using a CCD camera. The laser spot's location and the inner emit angle of the recorded laser beam were geometrically measured by the main apparatus and the CCD camera's Base. Distance is calculated by the following equation (2).

$$Z = \frac{f_0 \times d}{p + f_0 \tan \theta} \tag{2}$$

$$X = Z \tan \theta \tag{3}$$

$$p \; : \; \text{Position in laser spot's screen}$$

$$f_o \; : \; \text{Focus of lens}$$

$$d \; : \; \text{Distance of CCD and main apparatus of laser}$$

After calculating the correct vector value from two internal reflectors, coordinates x, y and z are created in 3D space in a computer. 3D coordinates

Fig. 1. Terrestrial LiDAR

are numerical values which are related to each other. They are relocated and transferred to cyberspace.

The Composition of the LiDAR equipment is as follows: Head apparatus of precision LiDAR, AC power source or a battery charger, PC- notebook, observation distance is 1.5 200m, density is 0.25mm@50M, real numerical values are 800 2,000 points/second, accuracy is point ¡Max 6mm@50M, modeling ¡Max 2mm@50M.

3   Application to Slope Investigation

3.1   Study Site

A public office of Jin-young National Highway, a group within the Ministry of Construction & Transportation, has made an analysis of rock slope failure which occurred by natural disaster. In summer, the main causes of slope failures are typhoons and rainfall. After a good grasp of failure mechanisms, we extracted the failure factor from the standard for risk management. Accordingly, the National highway 24th presents a study site from the Miryang-Sannae Myon to Ulju-Sangbuk Myon. Slope failures frequently occur due to its local geological and topographic features and climatic conditions in the nearby mountainous area.

After being extracted by examining contours using a digital map on a scale of 1:5,000, a 3D model is established from a DEM; with primary topographic attributes, such as mean elevation. It makes a selection as a failure model in intensive occurrence sites. This study site is composed of granite, weathered rock and plutonic/hypabyssal rock. This rock slope is growing crust caused by progress of stratification and lamination which is the main characteristic of the surface of a slope[5]. The Rock slope was evaluated according to the flowchart shown in Figure 3.

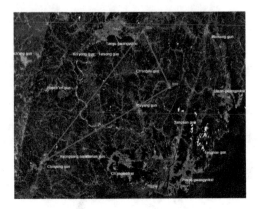

Fig. 2. The Field Site of this study

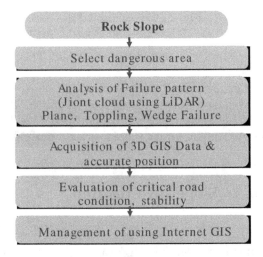

Fig. 3. The flowchart of this study

3.2   Slope Inspection of a Discontinuity Plane

Generally, a discontinuity plane is analyzed by direct measurement by using a clinocompass. However, it is impossible to measure as the slope is very high and accessibility is difficult. Therefore, stability estimations are very difficult because of considerable error. The maximum distance of LiDAR precision is 200m, so that it is useful for inspections of discontinuity planes on inaccessible sites[6].

Using a terrestrial LiDAR, we can make out items which are analyzed in an elevation and gradient caused by more accurate 3D coordinates. When engineers construct highways, this system is useful and efficient. Figure 4 shows face mapping accomplished by such an investigation. Experts provided us utilizing data as well as converting data using GIS. Figure 5 shows a form of point cloud which involved x, y and z information. With Cyclone software, it is possible to revolve

Fig. 4. Slope Face Mapping (dir/dip)

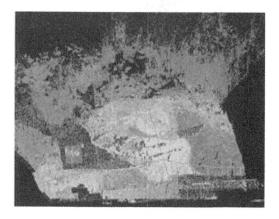

Fig. 5. Point Cloud

in a free direction and a 3D section can be expressed because it can observe 3D direction and various points of view.

Figure 6 shows the surface of a slope that is processed by with Cyclone software. To conclude, it is a result of analyzing discontinuity, specifically about discontinuity's arrangement. Thus we can presume the discontinuous direction of the inner part. We can utilize the discontinuity as an estimated GIS data. Coordinates data are composed of a point clouds and need to be put in mass storage. Thus, these data represent general-purpose 3D data using a Microstation program.

We can understand the direction of a slope plane in scanning results. Generally, plane direction can be expressed by dip and dip direction. Careful analysis of synthesized plane direction shows the development of a slope's discontinuity. Measurements of discontinuity are efficiently analyzed by using Clino-compass by an expert and by using terrestrial LiDAR. The second section and third section are also decided to the gradient and gradient direction through a select principal joint.

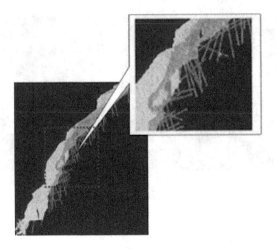

Fig. 6. Surface of Discontinuity (Part 1)

Table 2. Dir/Dip of Discontinuity   (unit:°)

No.	dir/dip	No.	dir/dip	No.	dir/dip	No.	dir/dip
1	215/84	9	176/81	⋯	⋯	33	183/82
2	127/82	10	192/79	⋯	⋯	34	187/89
3	182/80	11	182/81	⋯	⋯	35	168/78
4	224/88	12	183/78	⋯	⋯	36	173/79
5	207/82	13	18976	⋯	⋯	37	113/74

3.3   Determination of GCP on a LiDAR System Using a GPS

Relative positioning occurs when two receivers are used simultaneously to observe satellite signals and to compute the vector joining the two receivers. In relative positioning, the position of one point on earth is determined relative to the position of a known point, whereas in point positioning, the position of the occupied point is directly determined. Relative positioning can provide better accuracies because of the correlation possible between measurements simultaneously made over time to different satellites by two or more receivers[7][8].

The GCP (ground control point) is determined by differencing positioning. The types of surveying are those in which code pseudo-range measurements or carrier measurements are made at a base station, and then used to correct measurements made at another survey station. In this study, a base station is an unattended GPS station, TEGN in Tea-gu City and JINJ in Jin-ju city. The survey station is a site CP1 located at a rock-slope. Figure 7 shows a control survey configuration in the process of spectrum survey software. Thus, we calculate the coordinates x and y of the control point.

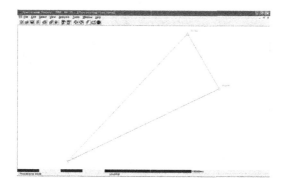

Fig. 7. Post Processing Network

Table 3. Control Point   (unit:m)

No.	X	y
Site CP1	200083.19	232737.41
TEGN	26766.61	182123.52
JINJ	186711.14	113428.22

3.4   Evaluation of Collapse Risk

We suggest more detail than present analysis of road slopes. In order to devise a better method, we divided a whole slope into 3 parts caused by discontinuity and features. We analyzed typical discontinuity distributed throughout 3 parts on the model slope. Typical discontinuity is the most dangerous discontinuity and it is possible for each part to collapse. By using a Lambert projection, we can make possible to judgments and inferences. Table 4 shows input data and output data for processing a Lambert projection. We can estimate the possibility of plane failure according to the direction shown in Figure 8.

Table 4. Lambert projection (Prat 1)

Slope	Rock	slope	dip/dip direction			ϕ
			J1	J2	J3	(°)
20.0	20.0	50/182	79/183	83/121	29/192	30
Plane·Toppling Failure			Wedge Failure			

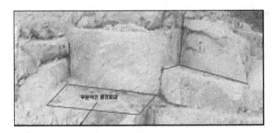

Fig. 8. A strike and dip direction(Part 1)

3.5   Application of Web GIS Database

Existing slope management systems are mostly composed of mapping systems based on the web[9]. Figure 9 shows an existing slope management system and the slope's location along the road. On the web, it shows linked text-information of the slope. On the other hand, we need more information as well as geological and other attribute data.

We convert existing data into GIS DB data, after we connect to the internet. Figure 10 shows a risk management of a partial shape on a road slope. We suggest more detail than present analysis on road slopes. In order to devise a better method, we divided a whole slope into 3 parts caused by discontinuity and features. A management system is loaded to an information file (*.shp *.dbf) which is a slope stability analysis, critical road condition and road damage evaluation. It progresses to decision-making using a GIS function based on the Internet. GIS environments consist of ArcGIS9, ArcIMS and establish a GIS data table of slope information.

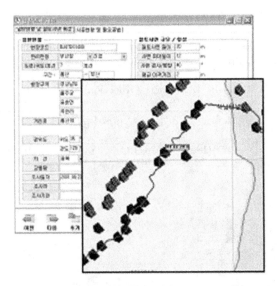

Fig. 9. On going Cut Slope Management System

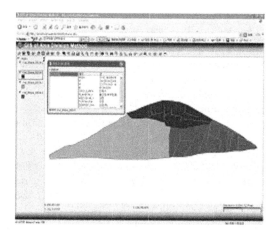

Fig. 10. The partition of shape based on internet GIS

4 Conclusion

Regarding disaster prevention inspection of road slopes, we attempted to evaluate what is the most dangerous slope. This study can be summarized as follows:

1) We inspected a discontinuity of inaccessible rock slopes using a terrestrial LiDAR System. Next, slope stability was evaluated by a Lambert projection of preliminary analysis. This system is more accurate than present methods of investigation. We could obtain large amounts of data at one time.
2) We had to convert the relative coordinate system into an absolute coordinate system applying Differential GPS. The LiDAR System has 3 dimensional relative coordinates. Thus, we applied an absolute coordinate system on the model slope. This 3D data makes best use of digital maps and diversity application from a GIS point of view. So, we suggested a new method for hazardous slope evaluation and improved the position of this slope. Moreover, we added to the contents of face mapping for on going Cut Slope Management System.
3) In this study, we developed basic function and risk management of a partial shape on road slopes based on the Internet. It is important for quantitative risk evaluation of road slopes. The Management System will be developed to allow for more accurate decision-making using GIS function based on the Internet in the years ahead.

Acknowledgement

The authors are grateful for the help extended and supported by the Ministry of Construction & Transportation in this study.

References

1. KICT and Korea Infrastructure Safety & Technology Corporation. Development of operation of road cut slope management system in 2003. Technical report, Ministry of Construction & Transportation., 2004.
2. E. Hoek and J. W. Bray. *Rock slope Engineering*, pages 29–34. Institution of Mining and Metallurgy, revised third edition, 1997.
3. PWRI. Estimation of cut slope using gis. Technical report, Joint-Research Report, Public Works Research Institute, 2004.
4. Taeyoung Jung. Studies about joint measurement of the rock slope using 3d laser scanner. In *Korea Society of Civil Engineering*, pages 1363–1368, 2004.
5. Youngjoo Kwak and Injoon Kang. Risk analysis and consideration of a cut slope on highway using gis. In *Journal of the Korean Society for GeoSpatial Information System*, pages 11–18, 2004.
6. Hongsung Gyun, Kim Young Sool, and Lee Hoe Kwan. When measurement and registration about reduction error using laser scanner. In *Korean Society of Precision Engineering*, volume 20, pages 197–204, 2003.
7. Injoon Kang. *Surveying & GeoSpatial Information Engineering*, pages 520–534. Moonwoodang, 2001.
8. Injoon Kang. Accuracy study of field dgps using. In *Korean Society of Surveying, Geodesy, Photogrammetry and Cartography*, pages 73–78, 2005.
9. Chunsik Kim and Kwangwo Lee. The development of a real-time manless-guard system for the management of a road slope and a forecast-alarm. In *Korea Society of Civil Engineering*, volume 24, pages 1–10, 2004.

SAMATS - Triangle Grouping and Structure Recovery for 3D Building Modeling and Visualization

Joe Hegarty and James D. Carswell

Digital Media Centre, Dublin Institute of Technology, Aungier St., Dublin 2, Ireland
joe@dmc.dit.ie, jcarswell@dit.ie

Abstract. Location based and spatial technologies research for the web has endless application for mobile/position content delivery (m-commerce or p-commerce). By exploiting the inherent location-based intelligence of the underling spatial component, relevant examples can include geometrically accurate and photo realistic virtual representations for: property assessments; land/marine information systems; routing information; on-line shopping; cultural heritage/tourist information/sites; etc. A major challenge for this technology is its reliance on professional developers when creating the virtual worlds used for web-based navigation of these services. This paper describes SAMATS, a Semi-Automated Modeling And Texturing System, which has the capability of producing geometrically accurate and photorealistic VR building models for web-based p-commerce applications from a set of geo-referenced terrestrial images. This paper describes the second of three main components that comprise the full functionality of the complete SAMATS implementation. It focuses on the triangle grouping and structure recovery steps, while providing an overview of SAMATS' other components.

1 Introduction

2D and 3D information visualization using VR modeling is becoming an important area of e-commerce research for today's web-based location based services (LBS) applications. Examples of exploiting VR navigation for both cultural heritage and environmental applications can be found in [1,2,5]. However, producing visually convincing VR models for these LBS applications requires expert VR knowledge on the part of the system developers. This research investigates building reconstruction technology for creating geometrically accurate, photorealistic 3D models from terrestrial digital photography for use in LBS applications that non-expert VR developers can exploit. It is envisioned that the resulting 3D model output from this work be web-enabled and made available to subsequent LBS research endeavors (e.g. for archaeologists, town planners, tourism, e-Government, etc.). Being able to produce 3D VR building models using terrestrial imagery allows all users to exploit the future commercialization potential of web-based LBS.

In the literature, it can be seen that many previous and contemporary modeling systems require manual correspondences to be made across the image set in order to accurately determine the models 3D structure. For example, Ullman (1976) was among the first to investigate the principle of modeling structure from motion and

K.-J. Li and C. Vangenot (Eds.): W2GIS 2005, LNCS 3833, pp. 267–280, 2005.
© Springer-Verlag Berlin Heidelberg 2005

along with Taylor and Kriegman (1995) require manual correspondences to be made. [12,13] Debevec et al (1996) approached the problem differently by creating a modeling and rendering system that allows the user to create models using a set of block primitives and by setting constraints on these primitives.

More automated modeling approaches are seen to involve the modeling of roofs from aerial imagery. However, models produced in this way fail to capture building façades accurately. Countering this, Lee et al [8,9,10] have looked into the merging of façade textures from ground based imagery with models produced from aerial imagery. Results closer to our approach can be found in [3] where a large set of 3D building models is constructed by using spherical mosaics produced from accurately calibrated ground view cameras fitted with a GPS device. Although highly automated, this system was limited to modeling simple shaped buildings by simply identifying the rooflines and extruding walls downwards. [14] Still closer is an example of extracting building and window edges which, like SAMATS, determines correspondences automatically, although a rough model of the structure being modeled is required in order for this system to work. This approach differs from SAMATS as we do not require such a model to be available a-priori.

SAMATS uses a novel approach to creating building models without the need for manual correspondences to be made. The ability of SAMATS to remove the manual correspondence step found in most modeling approaches is achieved by having all images geo-referenced in the same reference frame. However, the acquisition of geo-referenced terrestrial images is still a bottleneck that does not have a straightforward solution. It is a process that requires knowing both the X,Y,Z ground coordinates of the camera station plus the orientation of its field of view. SAMATS does not solve the difficulties in acquiring geo-referenced imagery - it only investigates the usefulness of such imagery in the overall modeling process.

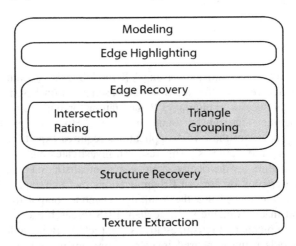

Fig. 1. SAMATS system diagram. The highlighted steps are the focus of this paper

Modeling and rendering in SAMATA is a 2 stage process. The first stage is broken into 3 steps – namely: building edge highlighting; building edge recovery; and building reconstruction (i.e. structure recovery). This paper focuses on the triangle grouping and structure recovery steps in the modeling stage of SAMATS, but for completeness gives an overview of the other components. For a detailed description of the edge highlighting component and the intersection rating component refer to [6]. For all other components refer to [7]. Figure 1 shows a systems overview of SAMATS.

2 Modeling

This section describes the process used to model the geometry of a building from a set of geo-referenced images using only simple edge highlighting by the user. The basic concept behind the modeling process is as follows; if one has two images of a scene taken from different locations, and the exact position and orientation of the camera is known for each image (i.e. the exterior orientation parameters $X_o, Y_o, Z_o, \Omega, \Phi, K$) then the exact location of any point visible in both images can be determined. This configuration is illustrated in figure 2. The modeling process outlined in this section extends this idea by using planar triangle intersections to find edges rather than line intersections to find points. The modeling process can be split into three main steps; Edge Highlighting, Edge Recovery and Structure Recovery.

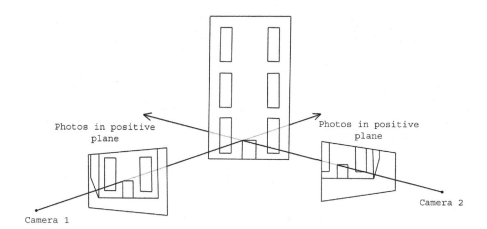

Fig. 2. Line projection used to determine a point in 3-space

2.1 Edge Highlighting

Edge highlighting is the only manual step performed by the user in the SAMATS modeling process. Primary lines and secondary lines are used to highlight edges in the images. Primary lines are used to recover the position of building edges directly, determining the core structure of the model. They are responsible for the creation of every vertex in the final model. A secondary line is used to connect these primary lines together and must have each of its endpoints connected to one or more primary lines.

The reason the entire model is not defined by primary lines is because it is difficult to recover some edges given the input data. Primary lines are well suited to recovering the position of vertical edges because it is possible to create arbitrarily large angles of intersection about the vertical edge axis. However, for horizontal edges near camera level it is not possible to create arbitrarily large intersection angles, making it difficult to recover the horizontal edges accurately since slight inaccuracies in the camera's interior or exterior orientation parameters results in large errors in estimated edge location.

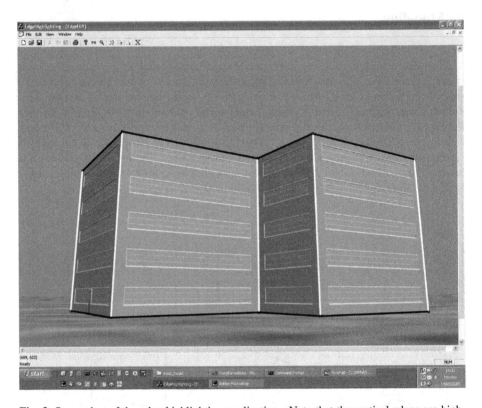

Fig. 3. Screenshot of the edge highlighting application. Note that the vertical edges are highlighted using white primary lines while the horizontal roof tops and building footprints are highlighted using black secondary lines.

Secondary lines work by connecting primary lines, where the use of a primary line would be prohibitive due to insufficient intersection angle between the triangle planes. Since primary lines will generally be used to recover the vertical edges of buildings, secondary lines should then be used to highlight the horizontal wall bases (building footprints) and roof tops, which indicates to the system that these edges should be connected without invoking the same recovery technique used for the primary edges.

Primary edge must be highlighted in at least three images, this is a requirement of the automated correspondence algorithm. It can be advantageous to define a primary edge in more than three images when trying to recover edges that are poor primary edge candidates. Secondary edges need only be defined in a single image. Figure 3 shows a screenshot of the edge highlighting application.

2.2 Edge Recovery

After the primary edges have been manually highlighted, six automated steps are performed to recover the final edges; Line Projection, Triangle Intersection, Correspondence Recovery, Edge Averaging, Vertex Merging, and Secondary Edge Recovery. Each of these steps is described next.

2.2.1 Line Projection

The first step in determining the positions of the primary edges is to project the 2D primary lines to form 3D triangles. The interior and exterior orientation parameters of the camera are used to project the primary lines from the cameras position out to infinity. This is performed for every primary line in each image.

2.2.2 Triangle Intersection

Once every 2D primary line has been transformed to a 3D triangle, the next step is to determine the intersections between the triangles. Every triangle stores a list of the triangles it intersects.

2.2.3 Correspondence Recovery

Generally each triangle intersects many other triangles even though only a small number of the triangle intersections have both their primary lines highlighting the same edge. Most 3D modeling systems resolve this problem by performing manual correspondences between the lines so that lines which highlight the same building edge are grouped together. Once the lines are converted to triangles the only valid intersections are between members of the same group. This can be a very time consuming process. SAMATS improves on contemporary techniques by performing this correspondence automatically in three steps; Intersection Rating, Triangle Grouping and Group Merging.

2.2.3.1 Intersection Rating

The process of intersection rating requires every triangle to rate each of the triangles it intersects to determine which of the intersecting triangles represent the same primary edge as itself. This automated rating process exploits the condition that there must be at least three primary lines, and hence triangles, for each primary edge. Each intersecting triangle is not rated on the coverage of the intersection line it makes, but rather on the similarity of its intersection line with others.

At the end of the intersection rating step, the list of intersecting triangles for each triangle will have a rating. Also, since the rating system is based on comparing intersection lines, a reference to the triangle responsible for the rating is also stored. For example, triangles t_i t_j and t_k all intersect each other. If t_j is the best rated intersecting triangle of t_i, and it was a comparison between the intersection lines l_{ij}, l_{ik}, and l_{jk} which were responsible for this rating, then a reference to t_k will be stored along with this rating for t_j in t_i's intersecting triangles list.

2.2.3.2 Triangle Grouping

After the intersection rating step, for every triangle t_i, every intersecting triangle t_j will have a rating assigned to it. Also, the t_k responsible for each t_j rating will be stored along with the rating. This information can then be used to group triangles together, with each group representing a primary edge.

Essentially, the grouping process is performed in two steps. Firstly, the GSS (Group Scope Set) of each triangle is determined. The GSS for a triangle t_i is a list of triangles which contains the triangle itself (in this case t_i), the GSS for $\underline{t_j}$ (the best rated t_j) and the GSS for $\underline{t_k}$ (the t_k for $\underline{t_j}$). The GSS can only hold a single instance of any triangle. This ensures that the recursive triangle grouping algorithm terminates. Not every triangle will have the same size GSS. The size of these sets will vary depending on the number of triangles used to represent each primary edge as well as the relationship between their intersection lines.

The simplest case arises when a primary edge is represented by three triangles. In this configuration each triangle t_i refers to the other two as either its $\underline{t_j}$ triangle or as its $\underline{t_k}$ triangle. In such a situation all three triangles have identical GSS containing the three triangles, see figure 4.

Fig. 4. Three triangles, all with the same GSS   **Fig. 5.** Four triangles, all with the same GSS

If there are more than three triangles representing a primary edge there can be three broad types of set configuration. One configuration involves four or more triangles that represent the same primary edge with every triangle having identical GSSs, see figure 5. Another configuration involves four or more triangles that represent the same primary edge but with only a subset of triangles having identical GSSs, while the other triangle(s) have GSSs containing the subset of triangles plus additional triangles. This results in the real group consisting of four or more triangles although the GSSs of some of the triangles will only have a subset of these triangles, see figure 6. The final configuration involves six or more triangles that represent the same primary edge but with each triangle having one of two or more GSSs. In this configuration each group is solved independently and then the groups are merged as a post-process, see figure 7. Any combination of the above configurations can also occur together.

The second step in the grouping process is to use the GSSs to group the triangles into groups. The grouping algorithm runs in two phases. In phase one only triangles that have three triangles in their GSSs are processed. Each triangle as well as its GSS members are assigned a new group. The first phase solves either fully or partially the configurations shown in figures 4, 6, and 7. At the end of this phase the majority of triangles will have been assigned a group. Only triangles which have a configuration similar to that shown in figure 5 or unreferenced triangles like those shown in figure 6 remain. In phase two these remaining triangles are assigned a group. If a triangle refers to triangles in an existing group (figure 6), it is added to that group provided that its rating in this group is within some minimum threshold. If a triangle's GSS has triangles which have not yet been grouped, a new group will be created for these triangles (figure 5). It may not be possible to assign a group to every triangle for a number of reasons. For example, the user may not have used three primary lines to highlight a particular primary edge. Also there may be too great an error to group some primary lines together either due to an error in the camera's interior and/or exterior orientation parameters or an error in primary line placement by the user. In such cases these triangles are marked as invalid.

 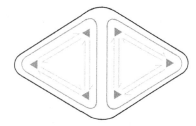

Fig. 6. Four triangles, three of which have the same GSS. The unreferenced triangle has a GSS containing all four triangles.

Fig. 7. Six triangles forming two separate GSSs. The black line represents the group after merging.

2.2.3.3 Group Merging

The final step in the grouping process is group merging. This is required because sometimes a primary edge may be represented by 6 or more triangles, which form 2 or more self-contained groups with no inter-group referencing (figure 7). If the groups were left the way they were, there would be 2 primary edges representing the same building edge instead of just one. The merging step simply compares each group to each other group by first comparing the highest ranked members of each group to each other. If it is found that the ranking between these triangles is within some threshold, the algorithm goes on to test every combination of group members together to guarantee that they; a) all intersect, and b) the lowest ranking observed is within some minimum threshold. If these two criteria are met, the two groups are merged.

2.2.4 Edge Averaging

Once all triangles have been assigned a group the primary edges must be determined for each group. This is simply the weighted average of all the intersection lines between all group members.

2.2.5 Vertex Merging

During the edge averaging step, each primary edge will be created totally independently from all other primary edges. In most cases this is acceptable since the majority of primary edges are not connected to any other primary edge. Sometimes however primary edges are connected. This is indicated in the edge highlighting step by having two or more primary lines share the same endpoint.

All primary edges that are connected need to have their connected endpoints coincident. This is achieved by creating a mapping between every primary line and every primary edge, and also between every primary line endpoint and every primary edge vertex. Once the mappings have been made, we can see if any of the primary lines share the same endpoints, which maps to primary edges sharing the same vertex. Once the vertices are identified they are set to the average of their positions.

2.2.6 Secondary Edge Recovery

Secondary edges are determined using the same mapping information obtained during the vertex merging step. First the secondary lines endpoints are determined. Then the corresponding vertices are determined for these endpoints and a new group is created for each secondary line using these vertices as the secondary edges endpoints. The outline of the model should be complete. See figure 8 for a screenshot of the recovered primary and secondary lines of the building shown in figure 3.

2.3 Structure Recovery

Even though the outline of the model has been determined there is still no surface data associated with the model. The model is only defined in terms of vertices and lines, and not in terms of surfaces and the triangles that make up each surface. Recovering this structural information is broken into three steps; Surface Determination, Surface Aligning, and Surface Triangulation.

Fig. 8. Screenshot of the recovered building from figure 3. Note that the location of the camera from figure 3 is highlighted. The projection of the 5 primary lines are clearly shown.

2.3.1 Surface Determination

Surfaces are determined by treating the model as a graph, with the models vertices representing nodes in the graph and the primary and secondary edges representing the edges in the graph. Each surface corresponds to a cycle in the graph, but not every cycle in the graph corresponds to a surface, as illustrated in figure 9.

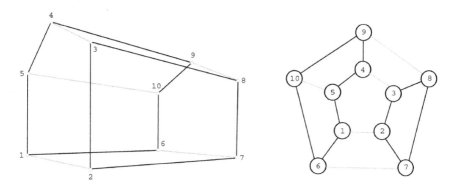

Fig. 9. The black outlines represent cycles in the graph. One of the cycles represents a surface (2-3-8-7), while the other does not.

There are two main assumptions made in order to determine the surfaces from the vertices and edges; the model must be closed and the number of surfaces associated with each vertex is equal to the number of edges connected to it. Surfaces are then determined by finding the shortest cycles in the graph where all the vertices are co-planar.

2.3.2 Surface Aligning

Once all the models surfaces have been determined, the normal vector for each surface must be determined. The first step is to determine the adjacency of the surfaces, i.e. which surfaces are adjacent to each other. This is performed because surfaces are aligned in pairs. Once the surface adjacencies have been determined one of the surfaces is flagged as the master surface, while all other surfaces are flagged as slave surfaces. First all slave surfaces that are adjacent to the master are aligned, becoming themselves masters in the process, then all slave surfaces adjacent to these new master surfaces are aligned, becoming masters themselves. The process continues recursively until all surfaces have been flagged as masters. The aligning step uses the fact that adjacent surface pairs are attached along one of their edges. This edge can act like a hinge between the two surfaces making it possible to rotate one of the surfaces about this hinge so that the two surfaces are co-planar. If then the surfaces are transformed so that they are perpendicular with the z-axis with the hinge between them aligned with the x-axis, we notice that the interior of one surface is above the hinge while the interior of the other surface is below the hinge.

Using this fact each surface pair is aligned by transforming both the master surface and the slave surface so that their surface normals are aligned with the z-axis and the edge vector between them is aligned with the x-axis. Then each surface is checked to see if its interior is above or below the hinge edge. If both surfaces are on the same side of the hinge edge they are misaligned so the normal of the slave surface is

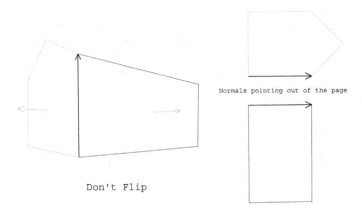

Fig. 10. The surfaces are on opposite side of the edge vector. Therefore the surfaces are correctly aligned.

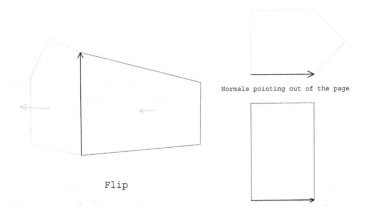

Fig. 11. The surfaces are on the same side of the edge vector. Therefore the normal of the slave surface needs to be inverted.

flipped. If the two surfaces are on opposite sides, the two surfaces are already aligned, see figures 10 and 11.

Even though the models surfaces have been determined at this stage there maybe a serious problem with the models normals, they may all be pointing inwards instead of outwards. This is due to the fact that a random surface was chosen as the master surface at the beginning of the surface aligning step but it was not determined whether or not this normal points inwards or outwards. Luckily this is not a serious problem since all we have to do to rectify the situation is flip all the surface normals.

2.3.3 Surface Triangulation
Once each surface has been determined and aligned, each surface must be decomposed into triangles. The surfaces in the model can be either convex or concave although the surfaces should not contain holes. There are many factors that can be

used to determine how a surface should be decomposed; minimize the number of triangles created, try to keep all triangles equilateral, try to keep all triangles close to equal area. The algorithm used to triangulate each surface can be found in [11]. This algorithm does not take any of these factors into consideration however. First each surface is orientated so that it is perpendicular with the z-axis. The z-coordinate is then ignored and the triangulation process treats the surface as if it was a 2D surface.

3 Texture Extraction

Coming into this section, we have a geometrically accurate model of the building. However, there exists data contained in the image set that has not yet been used to

Fig. 12. Final packed texture of the example scene. Textures packed large to small from top to bottom, left to right. The black gaps in the middle are for the roof and floor triangles which have no texture information from the image set. Also note the color clamping from the border of each triangle, most noticeable for the door at bottom row middle column.

increase the models realism, the buildings façades. The SAMATS texture extraction process takes the façades from the images and applies them to the model. An overview of this component is presented next. For a more detailed explanation of the Texture Extraction component refer to [7].

3.1 Overview

The aim of the texture extraction process is to produce a 3D model with photorealistic textures. The texture extraction process can be broken into a number of steps. Firstly, the number of images that will contribute to each triangle is determined using back-face culling. There can be any number of contributing images, with each image's contribution first being stored in a temporary texture before they are all blended together per-pixel based on the camera-surface distance and orientation. Occlusion maps are used to prevent incorrect façade data being stored with each triangle. All triangles are then packed into a single large texture retaining the relative size of each triangle, thus creating an authalic texture map. The texture coordinates for each triangle are then set to sample the correct region of the texture map, with the texture then being assigned to the model. Figure 12 shows the final packed texture for the example scene and figure 13 shows a screenshot of the final model created.

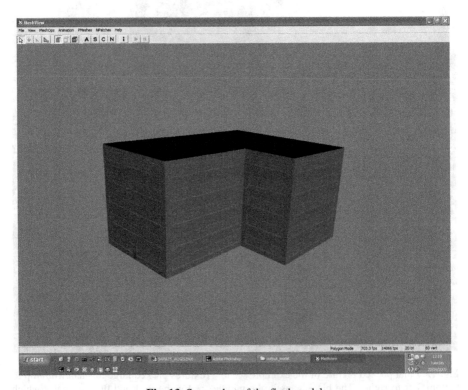

Fig. 13. Screenshot of the final model

4 Conclusions

This research shows that given sufficient geo-referenced terrestrial imagery, user input to the modeling process can be reduced significantly. In SAMATS, user input is required for the edge highlighting step but since no correspondence is required this step could potentially be automated using edge detection and a set of heuristics to guide the choice between using primary lines or secondary lines.

To date, SAMATS has only been tested on synthetic images where the exact EO and IO parameters of the camera are known. Achieving such precision in the real world would prove difficult without specialized equipment. As such, new techniques for the non-expert will be required to facilitate the gathering of the geo-referenced images required by SAMATS in order for this system to be utilized effectively in the real world. As the user friendliness and functionality of today's GPS enabled digital imaging technology improves over time this constraint may no longer apply - making the acquisition of accurate geo-referenced imagery as easy as regular imagery.

SAMATS has shown the ability to model rectangular and triangular roofed structures very well; however SAMATS does have trouble modeling certain other structures. For example, SAMATS has no special ability to model curved surfaces accurately where cylindrical column must be replaced by rectangular columns. Another difficulty that can arise is SAMATS' inability to handle partially highlighted edges making it difficult to model buildings in tightly confined spaces. However, in many cases SAMATS is proving very effective as a 3D modeling and visualisation tool for the non-expert when developing applications of web-based VR LBS.

References

1. J.D. Carswell, A. Eustace, K. Gardiner, E. Kilfeather. An Environment for Mobile Context-Based Hypermedia Retrieval, in 13th International Conference on Database and Expert Systems Applications (DEXA2002); IEEE CS Press; Aix en Provence, France; September 2002
2. J.D. Carswell, M. Bertolotto, N. Mandrak. Applications of Mobile Computing for Fish Species at Risk Management: in Proceedings of International Conference on Environmental Informatics of International Society of Environmental Information Sciences (ISEIS2004); Regina, Canada; August 2004
3. S.R. Coorg. Pose Imagery and Automated Three-Dimensional Modeling of Urban Environments. PhD thesis, MIT Ph.D. Thesis, 1998.
4. P.E. Debevec, C.J. Taylor, and J.Malik. Modeling and Rendering Architecture from Photographs: A hybrid geometry- and image-based approach. In SIGGRAPH '96 Conference Proceedings, 11-20, 1996.
5. K. Gardiner and J.D. Carswell. Viewer-based Directional Querying for Mobile Applications: International Workshop on Web & Wireless Geographical Information Systems (W2GIS2003); IEEE CS Press; Rome, Italy; December 2003
6. J. Hegarty and J.D. Carswell. SAMATS – Edge Highlighting and Intersection Rating Explained. Proceedings of 2nd International Workshop on CoMoGIS, 314 – 323, 2005.
7. J. Hegarty. SAMATS – Semi-Automated Modeling And Texturing System. Masters Thesis, Dublin Institute of Technology.

8. S.C. Lee, S.K. Jung, and R. Nevatia. Integrating Ground and Aerial Views for Urban Site Modeling. In Proceedings of International Conference on Pattern Recognition, 2002.

9. S.C. Lee, S.K. Jung, and R. Nevatia. Automatic Integration of Façade Textures into 3D Building Models with a Projective Geometry Based Line Clustering. Computer Graphics Forum, 21(3):511-519, 2002.

10. S.C. Lee, S.K. Jung, and R. Nevatia. Automatic Pose Estimation of Complex 3D Building Models. Proceeding of the 6th IEEE Workshop on Applications of Computer Vision, 2002.

11. J. O'Rourke. Computational Geometry in C (Second Ed.). Cambridge University Press, 1998.

12. C.J. Taylor and D.J. Kriegman. Structure and Motion from Line Segments in Multiple Images. PAMI, 17(11):1021-1032, November 1995.

13. S.Ullman. The Interpretation of Structure from Motion. Proceedings of the Royal Society of London, 1976.

14. S. Zlatanova and F.A. van den Heuvel. Knowledge-based Automatic 3D Line Extraction from close range images. Web – http://www.gdmc.nl/zlatanova/thesis/ html/refer/ps/ SZ_FH_Corfu.pdf

Surface Modelling for GPS Satellite Visibility

George Taylor, Jing Li, David Kidner, and Mark Ware

GIS Research Centre, School of Computing,
University of Glamorgan, CF37 1DL, Wales, UK
{jli, gtaylor, dbkidner, jmware}@glam.ac.uk

Abstract. This paper describes an automated method for predicting the number of satellites visible to a GPS receiver, at any point on the earth's surface at any time. Intervisibility analysis between a GPS receiver and each potentially visible GPS satellite are performed using a number of different surface models and satellite orbit calculations. The developed software can work with various ephemeris data, and will compute satellite visibility in real-time. Real-time satellite availability prediction is very useful for mobile applications such as in-car navigation systems, personal navigations systems and LBS. The implementtation of the method is described and the results are reported.

1 Introduction

The use of Global Navigation Satellite Systems (GNSS), such as the United States' Global Positioning System (GPS), GLONASS the Russian equivalent and the proposed European Galileo system, on the surface of the Earth, can sometimes be severely compromised by limited satellite visibility and unwanted reflections of signals (multipath). If insufficient satellites are visible (normally fewer than four), a 3D location cannot be computed. Hence, there is a requirement to test for continuity, reliability and accuracy of GNSS to provide positioning information, at various times and places. This is especially true for many transportation applications such as land surveying, fleet management, speed limitation, and vehicle navigation. Although many GPS manufacturers supply project-planning packages as part of their GPS receiver systems, all assume a locally flat Earth where simple elevation masks can be manually added for individual obstructions around a point location. These packages are useful but limited to static point positioning applications with limited, unrealistic obstructions, and more importantly, without analysis of multipath. They require extensive manual user input to define the geographical terrain surrounding point locations. They are of little or no use as a test bed for transport applications of GNSS, because in these cases the nature and distribution of obstructions are changing constantly.

Over the last decade, with the increased availability of high-resolution laser scanning surface models and technological advances in digital photogrammetry, the accuracy of GPS satellite availability prediction has been improved dramatically through tight integration with digital surface models, especially in urban areas. The limitations such as the lack of terrain information in the traditional GPS mission planning software has become apparent, and has led to decreased accuracy, efficiency

K.-J. Li and C. Vangenot (Eds.): W2GIS 2005, LNCS 3833, pp. 281–295, 2005.

and productivity for the surveyor. A number of researchers have proposed methods to address this issue. Boulianne et al. [1] suggested a new photogrammetric method of generating obstruction diagrams based on floating cones injected into the stereo model to reduce the amount of work in field and photogrammetric survey. Similarly, Walker and Sang [2] used the elevation mask angles that were derived from a photogrammetrically created digital terrain model. The conclusion drawn in their work is that accurate DTM information is invaluable to the users of high precision RTK (Real Time Kinematic) GPS in harsh environments. Moreover, in recent years, LiDAR (light detection and ranging) has become more accessible than ever to the GIS community. Its high density and accuracy is well suited for satellite visibility modelling. Verbree et al. [3] reconstructed building models from LiDAR point clouds with the aid of ground plan maps. The building polygons were split into segments such that the LiDAR point cloud within each segment can be represented by predefined roof structures like a flat roof, gable roof or hip roof. The reconstructed building model was then used to predict the signal coverage of GPS/Galileo in a dense built-up area in Delft. The simulation results for the fifty observer points show that the availability of the GPS and Galileo is nearly 100% (i.e. no less than four satellites in view). However, the result was not verified with real observations. In addition, a concern is that fitting LiDAR points into segmented ground plans for rooftop reconstruction may have a bearing on the prediction accuracy. In fact, in terms of real time simulation of GPS availability, a number of technical issues including coordinate transformation of satellites positions from WGS84 to a local datum or vice versa, the use of a range of ephemeris (e.g. almanac, broadcast and precise ephemeris), the choice of terrain data, line of sight (LOS) analysis in a GIS and the validation and verification of the prediction results should be addressed.

The work described in this paper aims to identify the accuracy and complexity of 3D digital feature and terrain models required for GPS availability modelling. Furthermore, a real-time GPS mission planning package based on ESRI's ArcGIS9 has been developed to simulate satellite availability, as a vehicle travels along a road in urban areas. For example, a particular bus route at specific times of the day can quickly be analysed to determine if GPS is a feasible option for an arrival/schedule information system. A variety of LOS, terrain modelling and coordinate transformation techniques are presented in detail in the following sections.

2 Experimental Methodology

Since all the 2D map and terrain data used in this project are based on the British National Grid (OSGB36), vehicle and satellite positions have to be transformed from WGS84 to OSGB36 prior to LOS analysis in a GIS. In general, transformation between different 3D Cartesian coordinate systems can be computed through the well-known 3D conformal transformation (i.e. three rotation parameters, three translation parameters and one scale factor). In order to achieve a better accuracy, the National Grid Transformation and Geoid Model OSTN02 / OSGM02 were used to convert WGS84 3D Cartesian coordinates to easting, northing and orthometric height (i.e. the height above mean sea level) and vice versa.

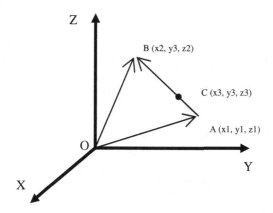

Fig. 1. LOS vector scaling in WGS84 Cartesian coordinate system

As stated by the Ordnance Survey, the horizontal transformation accuracy has been improved from 0.2m to 0.1m RMS and the vertical accuracy has been improved from 0.05m to 0.02m RMS compared to the previous models OSTN97 / OSGM91 [4]. For real time simulation, the coordinate transformation was computed on the fly and embedded into the developed mission planning software package. However, a problem remains in that the OSTN02 / OSGM02 does not function with the WGS84 coordinates of the satellites in space, since they are obviously outside the transformation area (i.e. outside the UK). Hence, the satellites have to be moved down their line of site, until they are in the sky above the test area, prior to the conversion to the local grid at each epoch (second). A similar approach was taken by Vrhovski [5]. A brief description of the LOS vector scaling between satellite and receiver positions in WGS84 is presented as follows:

As shown in Fig.1, A represents a receiver position on the ground. B is a satellite in space. The scaled satellite coordinates of C along the LOS vector $\overrightarrow{AB}$ are unknown, but can be computed by equation 1, provided that the length of the vector $\overrightarrow{AC}$ in equation 2 is known and predetermined by a user.

$$\overrightarrow{OC} = \left(\overrightarrow{OB} - \overrightarrow{OA}\right) \times scalar + \overrightarrow{OA} \tag{1}$$

where

$$scalar = \frac{\left\|\overrightarrow{AC}\right\|}{\left\|\left(\overrightarrow{OB} - \overrightarrow{OA}\right)\right\|} \tag{2}$$

Note that, intuitively, the closer the objects are, the more likely they are to produce obstructions. However, care has to be taken when choosing the predetermined length of the vector $\overrightarrow{AC}$, as features on the surface model that block the LOS between observers and satellites could be bypassed if the length of the vector $\overrightarrow{AC}$ is too short (e.g. a distant hill). The satellite positions are computed from Receiver Independent Exchange (RINEX) navigation file in which broadcast ephemeris is available.

2.1 Height Data

As mentioned earlier, one of the objectives of this research is to investigate the accuracy and complexity of 3D digital surface models required for GPS availability modelling. A range of height data and 2D plan map were used and evaluated with respect to the prediction accuracy. Table 1 shows a summary of the height data used in this research. It is seen clearly in Fig. 2 that far more fine details can be picked out with 1m LiDAR when compared with 5m Radar data. In addition to the height data, 2D Building Polygons of the testing area, derived from Ordnance Survey Master Map, were incorporated into the LiDAR data to enhance the performance of visualization and LOS analysis (Fig. 3). The absolute positional accuracy of OS Master Map at 1:1250 is less than ±1.1*m* [4].

Table 1. Summary of elevation data evaluated in this research

Product	Abbreviation	Horizontal Resolution (m)	Vertical Accuracy (m)	Format
LiDAR DSM first pulse return (InfoTerra)	1m LiDAR DSM FP	1	0.15	Points
LiDAR DTM last pulse return (InfoTerra)	1m LiDAR DTM LP	1	0.15	Raster
Airborne IFSAR DSM (NextMap)	5m RADAR DSM	5	1-1.15	Raster

2.2 Digital Photogrammetry Versus LiDAR

Photogrammetry is a traditional technique for measuring 3D coordinates of objects from a pair of overlapping photographs. In recent years, the rapid development of digital photogrammetry (i.e. softcopy photogrammetry) has led to increased productivity of generating topographic maps and digital elevation models (DEMs). However, LiDAR tends to replace this traditional terrain data acquisition technique due to the fact that it can offer higher productivity, it is cheaper and its accuracy is improving.

At present, 1m spacing LiDAR data have been made readily available to academia while higher resolution models (e.g. 25cm) are currently in development. In this paper, two surveying techniques are merged to produce more realistic digital surface models for GPS satellite visibility analysis. It is anticipated that photogrammetry can compensate for the lack of detailed break lines in LiDAR data.

For this experiment, a state-of-the-art photogrammetric system from Z/I Imaging was used to measure all the building roofs in 3D stereo from scanned aerial

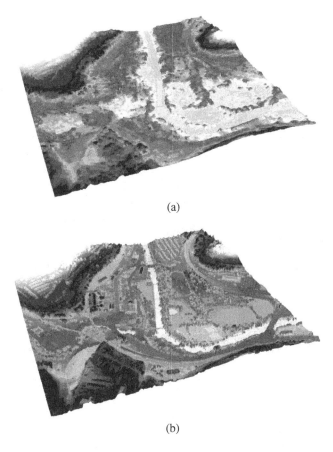

(a)

(b)

Fig. 2. (a) 5m Radar DSM. (b) - 1m LiDAR DSM FP

photographs. The photos used here have 25cm ground resolution and pixel size of 20microns. Having performed interior, relative and absolute orientations, the summary statistics page, Fig. 4, shows a variety of parameters to indicate the quality of the model. Note that the Sigma value on the top right corner is the computed standard deviation in the least squares adjustment. It is the single most important statistics for overall analysis of the results. As a rule of thumb, for a 20 micron image, the acceptable IO, RO and AO limit Sigmas (i.e. interior , relative and absolute orientation) were set to one second pixel of the scan resolution in microns (i.e. 10 microns). Hence, it can be seen from Fig. 4 that a Sigma value of 6.4 microns is below 10 microns and therefore a successful solution. In addition, it is also important to know the ground-coordinate statistic for all the control points used in the project. Theoretically, a minimum of about two horizontal and three vertical ground-surveyed photo control points should be used per stereo model. However, redundant control points may lead to higher accuracy and better averaging in the least squares adjustment.

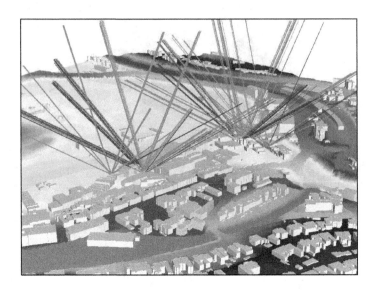

Fig. 3. LOS to GPS satellites

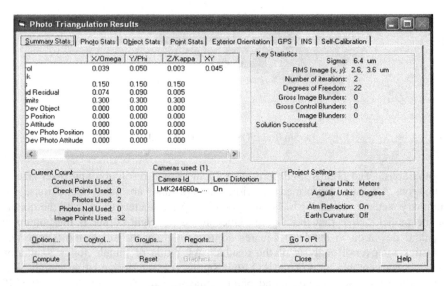

Fig. 4. Summary statistics page

Fig. 5 shows the fit to control points. The combined 3D ground residual errors V(XYZ), which are the differences between the computed control point coordinates and the measured ones, are all less than 10 centimeters (cm). Thus, a satisfactory solution is achieved. Six 3D control points were collected by dual frequency phase static GPS and their configuration is shown in Fig. 6.

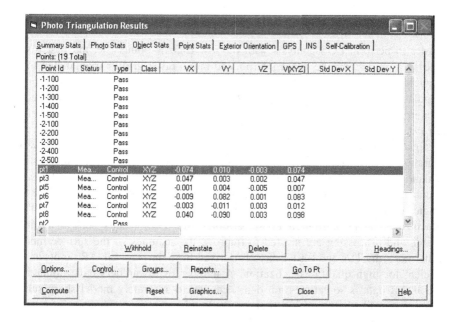

Fig. 5. Control (Object) statistics tabbed page (meters)

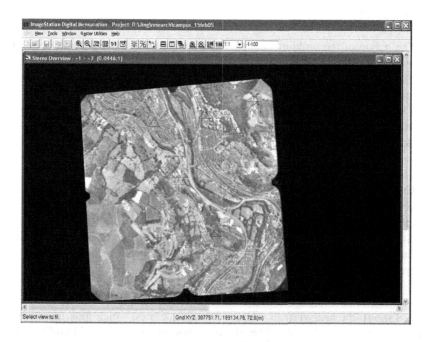

Fig. 6. Six control points used in the project

2.3 Digital Surface Modelling and LOS Analysis

In order to perform LOS analysis with the raw LiDAR points (i.e. the first row in Table1), Point data can be either interpolated into a raster grid or triangulated into a Triangulated Irregular Network (TIN) using the interpolation algorithm and Delaunay triangulation provided by ArcGIS9 3D Analyst. It should be noted that the effect of the interpolation algorithm and various LOS algorithms based on TIN and Grid have been extensively researched over the last ten years. See [6] and [7] for a through investigation of this issue. The interest here is particularly focused on how the integration of LiDAR and digital photogrammetry affect LOS results in real time simulation of GPS availability. Examining the TIN and Raster surface models reveals inaccuracies in some building representations, such as sloping walls and erroneous triangles on rooftops that fail to represent the correct shape of roof structure. These artifacts may all be attributed to the errors in the LOS results such that further research and processing are needed to improve the accuracy of the surface models. Furthermore, the TIN and Raster directly derived from the Raw LiDAR points are not sufficient for high quality visualization. A number of researchers have pointed out that LiDAR data is sometimes not dense enough to accurately model sharp surface discontinuities like break-lines ([8] and [9]). In this case, supplementary information from other sources such as 3D break-lines compiled photogrammetrically can be incorporated into the LiDAR data through the well-known constrained Delaunay triangulation.   The steps taken to combine photogrammetry with LiDAR are explained as follows:

1. The height of the building foundation is computed by taking the average of all the bare-earth LiDAR points that fall into each building footprint.
2. The height computed from Step 1 is assigned to each photogrammmtrically created building footprint.
3. Clean up the LiDAR DSM FP (see Table 1) points that fall inside the building footprints.
4. Add the building footprints to the LiDAR DSM FP data to create flat building foundations. The heights associated with the building footprints are computed in Step 1 and 2.
5. Create a 1cm buffer around each of the building footprints. This is because conventional TIN model is 2.5D, which means that two different heights are not allowed at the same X, Y position.
6. Add the photogrammmtrically created rooflines to the model computed in Step 4 through Constrained Delaunay Triangulation that guarantees that no triangles can cross the rooflines.

The resulting model from the above procedure is shown in Fig. 7.

Fig. 8 shows the near-vertical walls and roof structures, which look more realistic than the original LiDAR data. The 3D line work are collected in MicroStation and stored in a Computer Aided Design (CAD) design file (i.e. a DGN file).

Fig. 7. TIN created from photogrammetry and LiDAR

Fig. 8. Near-vertical walls and roof structures

It should be noted that the above-mentioned approach has its limitations. For example, too many vertices are added to the building edges to enforce near-vertical walls. It is also difficult to model complex man-made objects like holes and bridges without a true 3D data structure. Tse and Gold [10] extended the TIN to represent tunnels and bridges by introducing a subset of CAD-type Euler Operators in conjunction with a Quad-Edge data structure. For this experiment, the accuracy is the major concern, thus the simple Constrained Delaunay Triangulation suffices.

In terms of satellite visibility analysis, the sensitivity of LOS to GPS satellites was found to be very high. For example, a person turning around on a spot will gain and lose satellites. Therefore, it is beneficial to add building polygons to LiDAR data for visual inspection of LOS results as shown in Fig. 3 (green LOS vector indicates a satellite visible). In Fig.3, Building polygons were extruded using the estimated height from 1m LiDAR DSM FP (See Table1). The resulting extruded buildings were then put back onto the 1m LiDAR DTM LP (i.e. the bare-earth model) to form one single surface model. The LOS algorithm was modified accordingly.

The LOS is first checked on the bare-earth LiDAR model, if it is unobstructed, a search is conducted to find all the intersection points with all the building polygons that are projected onto a plane. After adding the actual heights to the intersection points, the slope between the receiver and each intersection point is computed. The LOS is considered blocked if the slope is greater than that from the receiver to satellites. This approach may be extended to work with other 3D vector data format such as CAD data.

3   Field Test and Results

Two field tests were conducted to evaluate the LOS results on a variety of digital surface models. The first one aims to test a large number of DGPS points in a dynamic mode. The second places more emphasis on photogrammetrically created buildings for comparison with LiDAR DSM FP in terms of LOS accuracy.

3.1   Test 1

To test the accuracy of the developed mission planning package, GPS Coarse Acquisition (C/A) code observation data were collected using Leica 500 series geodetic GPS receivers in a dense built-up area near the University of Glamorgan in Wales (see Fig. 9). Simultaneously, a GPS base station was set up on the roof of the School of Computing to record base station data. Unfortunately, the Real Time Kinematic (RTK) data was not available due to the poor coverage of the GPS signal in the testing area, which has very narrow streets with tall buildings on either side.

All available satellites visible to both receivers were used in the position solution computation. This number varied throughout the route from none to eight. Differential GPS points (DGPS) were computed; these are assumed to represent ground truth. It can be argued that the more accurate RTK positions should be used. However, at this initial stage of the experiment, it is interesting to see how the performance of the real time simulation varies with inaccuracies in DGPS positions.

There were a total of 767 DGPS points available throughout the route. The percentage error in the modelled number of satellites visible at each epoch is computed as follows:

$$\% \text{ error} = \frac{\text{error in the number of satellites modelled as visible}}{\text{number of satellites actually visible}} \times 100 \qquad (3)$$

Note that the percentage error takes two scenarios into account:

1. The modelled number of visible satellites is greater than that of satellites actually visible.
2. The modelled number of visible satellites is less than that of satellites actually visible.

The success rate equals the number of epochs modelled correctly divided by the number of total epochs. Table 2 shows the results for 767 DGPS points.

Fig. 9. All GPS positions used in Test1

Table 2. Results for 767 DGPS points

Type of DSMs	Success rate	Mean error in the modelled number of visible satellites	The mean error as a percentage
5m RADAR DSM	312/767	2.7 satellites	46%
1m LiDAR DSM FP	510/767	0.43satellites	8%
Bare-earth LiDAR + extruded building polygons	497/767	0.46 satellites	9%

3.2 Test 2

In order to test how differently the LiDAR and photogrammetry models perform in terms of LOS analysis, 20 high accuracy Kinematic GPS points were collected on the campus placing greater emphasis on photogrammetrically created building polygons. (see Fig. 10). The results for the twenty Kinematic GPS points are shown in Table3.

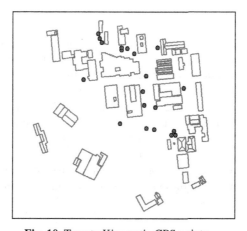

Fig. 10. Twenty Kinematic GPS points

Table 3. Results for 20 Kinematic points

Type of DSMs	Success rate	Mean error in the modeled number of visible satellites	The mean error as a percentage
5m RADAR DSM	1/20	4.85 satellites	82%
1m LiDAR DSM FP	7/20	0.75satellites	13%
1m LiDAR + Photogrammetry	6/20	0.8 satellites	14%

4 The Analysis of the Results

Test1, Table2 shows that 1m LiDAR data is significantly better than 5m Radar (by almost 200 points modelled correctly out of 767 points). Therefore, low resolution DSMs should not be used in GPS mission planning especially in dense built-up areas, as buildings close to the receiver are not adequately modelled. The prediction accuracy of LiDAR data is quite satisfactory although errors exist. In fact, a perfect representation of urban areas is not possible, as the errors caused by the laser instrument, GPS/INS and coordinate transformation all propagate through into the final LOS results. Test1 also proved that real-time satellite availability modelling can be done with a large number of known observation points over a very short time interval. Test2 aims to reveal differences in how the two surveying techniques affect the LOS results. As illustrated in Fig. 11, the simulated number of satellites matches up quite closely with that of the observed satellites. In Fig.11, the X axis is the GPS seconds in time. The Y axis represents satellites PRN number that is unique to each of the satellites. It can be seen that there is one point difference between photogrammetry and LiDAR shown in Table3.

Having carefully examined this one point difference visually, it transpires that the discrepancy is caused by building eaves measured by photogrammetry that block the LOS to one satellite. This can be clearly seen from Fig. 12. The picture on the left is the photogrammetrically created building model. The right one is the original 1m LiDAR DSM. This is because, for that particular building, the building eaves are overhanging by almost one meter such that the building footprints cannot be seen on the Stereo model and consequently caused the error in the LOS analysis. In practice, for mapping users, building eaves are usually classified as building footprints

Apart from this artifact, the photogrammetric model lines up with the original LiDAR model quite closely in a vertical range of 10cm, which indicates that both LiDAR and Photogrammetry can offer a very high accuracy. However, digital photogrammetry is less productive than LiDAR due to the time and effort involved at the terrain data acquisition stage, especially for a very large area where the heights of terrain features vary over a wide range. In addition, the automatic elevation collection tool may not perform well in those areas so that significant manual editing is required to capture the 3D break lines.

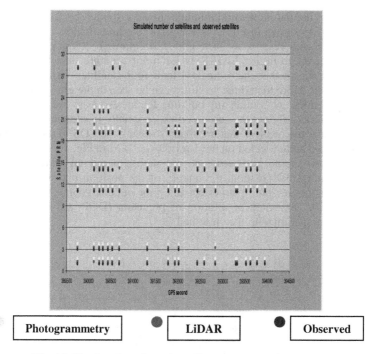

Fig. 11. Simulated number of satellites and observed satellites

Fig. 12. Photogrammetry vs LiDA

5 Viewshed Analysis

The purpose of creating a viewshed for the satellites above a particular elevation mask angle at a specific time is to assist in GPS mission planning for a very large area. Viewsheds may be created from grid-based and TIN models of the terrain. For this project, a grid-based model is used, as Grids lend themselves to particularly simple methods of deriving the viewshed, although they are limited by the resolution of the grid itself [11]. As shown in Fig.13 and Fig. 14, the line of sight scaling process has to be computed with respect to each grid cell centre. It is quite obvious that the viewshed computed from 1m LiDAR is far more accurate than that of 5m Radar DSM. Fig. 13 shows that there are less than four satellites visible in those areas highlighted in red. More than three satellites can be seen in the green areas. In Fig. 14, 5m Radar DSM does not contain any building features so as to make all the satellites visible. This is obviously not the case in cities, especially in situations where there are tall buildings near the receiver that are likely to block the LOS to the satellites. This fact is best proved and reflected on the 1m LiDAR DSM in Fig. 13.

Furthermore, it should be noted that, although a minimum of four satellites are required to obtain a 3D position, the quality of the position may not be necessarily good due to the possible multipath effect and poor satellite geometry (i.e. high PDOP values). Therefore, a variety of dilution of precision (DOP) values should also be computed in conjunction with the viewshed.

Fig. 13. Viewshed computed from 1m LiDAR DSM

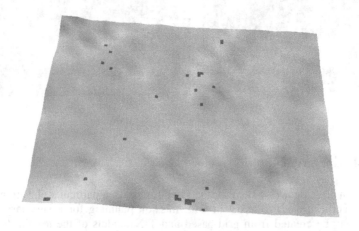

Fig. 14. Viewshed computed from 5m Radar DSM

6   Conclusion

The real time simulation and modelling of GPS availability has been conducted in a dense built-up area. The initial testing results have been presented. The newly developed mission planning software tool has implemented a variety of techniques including LOS scaling, coordinate transformation, LOS analysis, and is capable of working with various forms of digital surface models (e.g. vector, raster and TIN). It has been shown that LiDAR is the most appropriate data set for modelling and predicting GPS satellites availability in terms of reliability, productivity and accuracy. Future wok will focus on modelling the uncertainty in the LOS analysis with respect to GPS satellites and multipath effects in different terrain environments.

Acknowledgments

The authors express thanks to the Ordnance Survey for providing OS Master Map data and InfoTerra for the LiDAR data used in this work.

References

1. Boulianne, M., Santerre, Rock., Gagnon, P. and Nolette, C.: Floating lines and cones for use as a GPS mission planning aid, Photogrammetric Engineering & Remote Sensing, Vol. 62 No. 3, (1996), 311-315
2. Walker, R., and Sang, J.: Mission planning for high precision RTK GPS surveying using accurate digital terrain information, Proceedings of ION GPS 1997 Conference, Kansas City, Missouri, USA, (1997)
3. Verbree, E., Tiberius, C. and Vosselman, G.: Combined GPS-Galileo positioning for location based services in urban environment, proceedings of the location based services & telecartography symposium, (2004), 99-107
4. Ordnance Survey: A guide to Coordinate Systems in Great Britain, http://www.gps.gov.uk/guidecontents.asp, accessed on 23 Feb 2005, (2004)
5. Vrhovski, D.: Satellite visibility in simulating urban satellite positioning-based road user charging, proceedings of ION GPS/GNSS 2003, Portland, Oregon, USA, (2003)
6. Dorey, M.: Digital elevation models for intervisibility analysis and visual impact, Unpublished Ph.D. thesis, University of Glamorgan, Pontypridd, Wales, UK, (2002),
7. Kidner, D.B.: Higher order interpolation of regular grid digital elevation models, International Journal of Remote Sensing (in press).
8. Schickler, W. and Thorpe, A.: Surface Estimation Based on Lidar, 2001 ASPRS Annual Conference, St. Louis, Missouri, (2001)
9. Thompson, G, F., and Manue,D,F.: Issues and answers in quality control of LiDAR DEMs, North Carolina floodplain mapping program, (2001), 119-122
10. Tse, R. and Gold, C.: A proposed connectivity-based model for a 3D cadastre. Computer, Environment, and Urban Systems, Vol. 27, (2003), 427-445
11. Jones, C.B.: Geographical Information Systems and Computer Cartography (book), Longman (Pearson Education), (1997)

The Effect of Resident-Perceived Neighborhood Boundary on the Equity of Public Parks Distribution: Using GIS

Chun-Man Cho[1] and Yun-Soo Choi[2]

[1] Korea Research Institute for Human Settlements,
1591-6 Kwanyang-dong Anyang-si, South Korea
cmcho@krihs.re.kr
[2] Department of Geoinformatics, University of Seoul,
90 Jeonnong-dong, Seoul, South Korea
choiys@uos.ac.kr

Abstract. Because of the ready availability of various data at residence level, census tracts have been the spatial units most commonly selected. In some cases, municipally defined service districts have also been selected, and they are, in fact, only the aggregates of several neighboring census tracts. The problem encountered in the current study is that Census-based Neighborhoods such as census tracts and the aggregations of census tracts frequently do not correspond with commonly recognized neighborhoods experienced informally in daily life. The primary purpose of this study was to investigate the effects of Resident-perceived Neighborhood Boundaries (as the alternative unit of analysis to conventionally-used Census-based Neighborhood Units) on the accessibility to public parks based on equity consideration. The result indicates that when Resident-perceived Neighborhood Boundaries are adopted, there is no significant change the equity of accessibility to public park distribution among neighborhoods of different social strata.

1 Research Background

One of the most important issues in the study of Urban-Service Distribution is the choice of unit of analysis on services allocation. In practice, public services affect and benefit groups of people collectively, and they show many of the characteristics of public goods [1]. So, some groupings of residents tend to be the unit of analysis in public services distribution [2]. Plus, because most prior research of services distribution has focused on place prosperity through geographically distributed services rather than demographically targeted services, geographic groupings of residence units have been the most commonly used spatial units [2].

Meanwhile, mainly because of the ready availability of various data at the level of residence units, census tracts have been the groupings that are most commonly selected, and in some cases, municipally-defined service districts such as postal codes, municipal utility districts, police patrol districts, school districts, and voting districts have been also selected as part of those popular groupings [2][3][4]. However, these are, in fact, the aggregates of several neighboring census tracts.

K.-J. Li and C. Vangenot (Eds.): W2GIS 2005, LNCS 3833, pp. 296–307, 2005.
© Springer-Verlag Berlin Heidelberg 2005

Hence, the use of census data at census tract level has been dominantly recognized as an important component of many activities in public or private services delivery [3]. In his neighborhood identification study, Martin [3] mentioned the role of census tract data in neighborhood delineation saying that, "conventionally, quantitative neighborhood delineation involves the use of multivariable data for small areas, usually drawn heavily on census tracts, augmented by other data sources."

2 Problem Statement

The problem encountered in the current study is the fact that census-based neighborhoods such as census tracts and the aggregation of census tracts may reflect many important features of urban social fabric, but frequently they do not correspond with the commonly recognized neighborhoods experienced informally and do not match local residents' perceptions of their neighborhoods as social areas [3][5]. Pacione [6] commented that "the neighborhood remains a meaningful territorial component of urban life for most people and a planning ideal in many parts of the world." In addition, many a neighborhood effect research acknowledges that arbitrarily census-defined, or administrative neighborhood boundaries are not always real neighborhood boundaries that reflect actual residents' activities across the neighborhood [4].

In practice, much empirical neighborhood research supports the argument that the Resident-perceived Neighborhood Boundaries and Census-based Neighborhood Units may show quite a difference in terms of area, shape and its scale [4][7][8][9][10][11].

3 Objectives of the Study

This study discovered how the boundary difference between traditionally used Census-based Neighborhoods (i.e., Census Tracts, Block Groups, School Districts, Police Patrol Districts, Zip Code Areas, Voting Districts, Neighborhood Plan Areas, and Neighborhood Association Areas) and Residents-perceived Neighborhoods affects the equity in the distribution of public parks among neighborhoods of different social strata in terms of accessibility.

In planning, the distribution of public resources according to locational equity can be defined in different ways, but there have been at least four separate criteria for defining equity in distribution [12]: (1) equality; (2) need; (3) demand; and (4) market efficiency. While the relationship between equity and accessibility can be interpreted in different ways, accessibility has been widely adopted as an indicator of equity in most studies [13]. And, accessibility to public services across socio-economically and demographically diverse groups has been a way of determining the equity of urban public services distribution [12][13][14][15].

Considering the obvious characteristics of class and racial segregation in U.S. cities, when we measure service outcomes such as public services satisfaction and allocation, there has been a need for proxies for social class and racial groupings of persons [2]. As mentioned, conventionally, researchers and planners used to depend on Census-based Neighborhood boundaries such as census tracts or the aggregations of adjoining census tracts as the surrogates for those class and racial groupings because census variables at the level of census tract are considered to be good explanatory factors to capture the socio-economic characteristics of the residents.

Conventionally, as the literature indicates, most services distribution studies used census-based modifiable areal units. As the current study hypothesized, the choice of Residents-perceived Neighborhood Boundaries as the alternative analysis unit to traditionally used Census-based Neighborhood Units may affect the accessibility measures and decisions about equitable distribution of public services in urban areas. In keeping with Talen [16] who emphasized the importance of residents-perceived accessibility to public services, an objective of the current study is to see how the adoption of Resident-perceived Neighborhood Boundaries as the alternative unit of analysis alters accessibility measures and the degree of pre-established equity in public services distributions among neighborhoods of different social strata.

So, the research question is whether or not the adoption of Resident-perceived Neighborhood boundaries as the unit of analysis will significantly change the pre-established equity in the distribution of public services in terms of accessibility.

4 Proposed Methodology

4.1 Target Population

The target population for this study is the urban neighborhood residents of Travis County. The study area was the city of Austin, Texas. The reasons for choosing this area are as follows. First, there is a great deal of spatial data available. The city provides numerous GIS database warehouses on-line and on the web, enough to carry out the current research (ftp://issweb.ci.austin.tx.us/pub/coa_gis.html). Second, city-wide, neighborhood planning has been very active since the Austin City Council adopted the Dawson Neighborhood Plan on August 28, 1998. Also, the city's Planning, Environmental & Conservation Services Department has taken the initiative to work with neighborhood representatives to produce a neighborhood plan. Subsequently, a lot of city background information regarding public services in relationship to neighborhood planning is available [17].

4.2 Study Area Sampling

As well as the cluster sampling, the current study utilized "stratified random sampling" which uses information known about the total population prior to sampling to make the sampling process more efficient. First, all elements of the total census tracts (N=181) of Travis County were distinguished according to their values on relevant characteristics. In doing so, Race (i.e., white, black, and hispanic), and Median Household Income (i.e., high, medium, and low income levels based on 2000 census data) formed the sampling strata [18]. Next, census tracts were sampled randomly from within these strata. And, finally, census block groups are randomly selected from those census tracts chosen. (See Table 1)

Table 1. Distribution of Sampled Block Groups

Race	Income Level	Census Track	Block Group	Population	Race (%)	Median Household Income ($/year)
White	High	18.28	1	1,830	82.50%	75,436
White	High	16.03	5	1,318	95.68%	79,179
White	Medium	18.17	2	1,285	89.10%	61,838
White	Medium	24.24	2	2,716	61.93%	41,250
White	Low	17.47	3	1,672	66.57%	50,391
Hispanic	Medium	20.03	4	1,957	53.29%	38,636
Hispanic	Low	18.12	3	1,750	76.06%	29,909
Hispanic	Low	18.06	3	3,224	52.85%	27,188
Black	Medium	21.09	2	1,570	59.60%	31,553

4.3 Survey on Perceived Neighborhood Boundaries

The survey instrument was used to gather residents' neighborhood boundary perceptions. For the objectives of this study, the technique initially used by Lee [7] would be the most appropriate for eliciting a perceived map of neighborhood. This technique enables the standardization of map data for GIS analysis, so the residents are provided with a street map to outline neighborhood boundaries instead of drawing their neighborhood and its elements freehand on a blank sheet of paper [10].

First, household members were asked to describe their neighborhood in terms of its important elements and boundaries, then they were asked to draw boundaries of their own neighborhood on the street map of the census tract. The census tract maps were printed so that the block group for the specific respondent appeared in the center of the map and the surrounding 8-mile radius was printed around it [4]. This map size is small enough to fit on an 11" by 17" piece of paper and show sufficient detail [4]. To help the residents orient, street names were on the map, along with a few landmarks, such as main streets, and waterways [4].

4.4 Operationalization of Accessibility Measure

It is true that different accessibility measures may produce different spatial patterns of accessibility and, depending on the concept of access, the distributional equity of public services may vary [12][15]. The choice among them depends on the relevant policy questions [13]. Accordingly, the current study considered the characteristics of public service (i.e., Austin public parks) under study, and the features that each of the five most widely used accessibility models: four distance-based models of Gravity Model, Minimum Distance Model, Travel Cost Minimization Model, Container Approach [15]; and Covering Objectives Model [13][19][20]. The Gravity Model was employed for the current study to measure accessibilities of public parks in Austin. This measure, called also the spatial interaction model, is one of the simplest, yet most widely used models [21].

4.5 Data Sources and Preparation

The City of Austin has comprehensive data sources that make it possible to conduct accessibility and public services utilization studies at a census-based level. The data sets utilized for the current study are from six major sources (see Table 2).

The primary data sets are mainly GIS TIGER lines and their pertinent attribute tables are from the official website of Austin (www.ci.austin.tx.us). To enable spatial statistics to be used for analyzing socio-spatial equity, the data for each census unit had to be explicitly associated with that spatial unit in the GIS database. The configuration of the census areas in the census geography is recorded on the U.S. Bureau of the Census's TIGER (Topologically Integrated Geographic Encoding and Referencing) file. The boundary files of the census units are available from selected generalized extracts from the Census Bureau's TIGER geographic database designed for use in a Geographic Information System (GIS) or similar mapping system, or these files can be downloaded through the ESRI (Environmental Systems Research Institute)'s ArcData Online website (www.esri.com). The spatial and statistically available attribute data were then joined together to form single tables of information within ArcView software.

The second data source is the 2000 Census from the U.S. Bureau of the Census. The Census data to be utilized in the analysis of the equity of the public parks were obtained from two sources: SF1 (Summary File 1) and SF3 (Summary File 3). Most of socio-demographic data for stratifying census tracts and other census units were from the SF1 of Census 2000. These were then disaggregated to the level of census block, the smallest census unit available. The remaining economic data, such as median household income, were from the SF3 of Census 2000.

Table 2. Data Types and Sources

Sources	Data	Type	Format
Travis Central Appraisal District (TCAD)	Parcel GIS Attribute Table (owner's name & address)	Table	.dbf file
	City Boundary (full)	Polygon	.shp
	Public Parks (city)	Polygon	.shp
	School Districts	Polygon	.shp
	Police Patrol Districts	Polygon	.shp
	Zip Code Areas (postal areas)	Polygon	.shp
Austin GIS data set	Voting Districts	Polygon	.shp
	Neighborhood Plan Areas	Polygon	.shp
	Neighborhood Assn. Areas	Polygon	.shp
	Address Points	Point	.shp
	Street Center-lines	Line	.shp
	Austin Parcel Data	Polygon	.shp
	County Boundary	Polygon	.shp
2000 Census Tiger data	Census Tract Boundary	Polygon	.shp
	Block Groups Boundary	Polygon	.shp
2000 Census SF1	Socio-demographic data	Table	.dbf file
2000 Census SF3	Economic data	Table	.dbf file
	Resident-perceived Boundaries	Polygon	.shp
Mail-Out Survey	Parks Utilization Data	Table	.dbf file
	Socio-demographic Info.	Table	.dbf file

The third source of the data for this study is the official website of the city of Austin [17]. The website provided administrative boundaries, the locations of the public parks, street center lines, address points, and administrative services area boundaries, such as police patrol districts, neighborhood plan areas, neighborhood associations areas, zip code areas, voting areas.

The fourth data source was the mail-out survey conducted during August and November of 2003. The survey questionnaire was composed of an introduction letter, questions about neighborhood perception, public parks utilization, and the respondents' background information as well as an actual map of the recipient's living area and the Austin public parks inventory for reference.

4.6 Accessibility Measuring Method

The spatial distance may be calculated in various ways such as 'straight-line distance (i.e.,"as the crow flies")', 'network distance', 'travel-time distance', and so on. The current study used 'network distance', which is measured by finding the shortest path applied to the actual street network lines. For this task, Network Analyst, an extension utility for Arcview software, was utilized. Also, the Avenue script was used for measuring the basic network distance between each park centroid location. The center of each neighborhood unit was obtained from ESRI online support center (http://arcscripts.esri.com/details.asp?dbid=11572). By simulating the situation closer to the actual travel time of neighborhood residents between supply location and demand location rather than using straight-line distance measure, the accessibility measurement based on network distance is generally accepted as a better approach in accessibility studies [15].

Meanwhile, the process of measuring the network distance between each neighborhood and public park is not possible without having the centroid points of each neighborhood and public park. For this important process, the SpaceStat extension for Arcview was used [22], and the detailed procedure conformed to the instructions in "Spatial Data Analysis with SpaceStat and ArcView Workbook (3rd Edition)." Figure 1 below shows the distribution of sampled block groups and park centroids.

4.7 Finding Consensus of Perceived Neighborhood Boundary

Ideally, the residents of a neighborhood would have the perceptions of their neighborhood boundary perfectly overlapping one another, but in reality, it is almost impossible to find even two residents who have identical neighborhood boundary perceptions. Throughout the literature there have been many efforts to discover how neighborhood residents perceive and draw their neighborhood boundaries. Originally, Lee [7] initiated the utilization of residents' perceived neighborhood maps as a method of defining a neighborhood. He considered an urban neighborhood as a socio-spatial schema, a sort of mental representation of physical-socio space. He developed an index with relation to urban planning, called "N.Q. (neighborhood quotient) [7]. Inspired by his methodology of neighborhood residents' environmental perception, Golledge and Spector [9] explored the residents' perception of local environments and experiences, and Aiken and Prossor [23] used neighborhood maps to investigate the characteristics of residents' spatial knowledge of neighborhood. Until recently there was no study that emphasized the importance of finding consensus of perceived neighborhood boundaries among residents of the same neighborhood environment. The literature considered perceived neighborhood as an individual experience, not a group experience that is possible to be achieved by consensus.

The current study dealt with the 70% consensus area as the resident-perceived neighborhood boundary for each census-based block groups as in the study by Coulton, et al. [4].

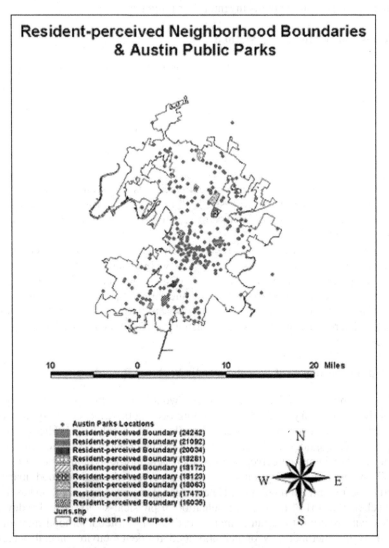

Fig. 1. Distribution of Sampled Blocks & Park Centroids

4.8 How to Get Perceived Neighborhood Boundaries

In finding the consensus of resident-perceived neighborhood boundaries, the Spatial Analyst program was used as one of the Arcview 3.0 extensions. Arcview Spatial Analyst provides a useful way to represent and analyze the geographic objects such as temperature, climate, and elevation that are distributed in a continuous manner across a surface. Instead of digitizing them in the form of shapes such as point, lines and polygons, it divides the whole surface and the shapes are turned into a matrix of identically-sized square cells, so-called grids [24].

Working with objects as numbers in cells is working with the raster data model, so the Arcview Spatial Analyst does not work with points, lines and polygons that are useful geographic objects for the vector data model. That is, each cell possesses a number that stores the geographic object's value at that exact location of the cell. In Spatial Analyst, the raster data sets themselves are called grids. Figure 2 below shows one of the nine overlapped views of Resident-perceived Neighborhood maps.

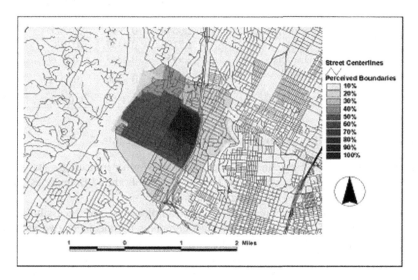

Fig. 2. An Overlapped View of Resident-perceived Neighborhood (BG-16035)

5 Analysis Results

5.1 Descriptives of Accessibilities by Neighborhood Units

Before considering the equality of park services distribution, the accessibility indices were measured using the gravity model. Table 3 below shows the descriptive statistics of accessibilities by neighborhood units, indicating whether there is any significant difference in accessibility measurements between Resident-Perceived Neighborhood Boundaries and the rest of eight, census-based, neighborhood units.

First of all, Table 3 doesn't show whether the means of accessibilities by neighborhood units are significantly different, but, in terms of arithmetic difference, the means of accessibilities measured based on Census Tracts (0.0063) and Block Groups (0.0084) are closer to that of Resident-Perceived Neighborhood Boundaries than those measured by Voting Precincts (0.0212), Police Patrol Districts (0.0735), Postal Areas (0.0186), and Neighborhood Plan Areas (0.0231), while accessibilities by School Districts (0.2074), Neighborhood Association Areas (0.1172) showed the least similar accessibility measures to those by Resident-Perceived Neighborhood Boundaries .

Table 3. Descriptives of Accessibilities by Neighborhood Units

		Mean	S.D.	Mean Difference with RPNB
Resident-Perceived Neighborhood Boundaries (RPNB)		2.7379	0.3806	0
Census-based Neighborhood Boundaries	Census Tracts	2.7316	0.3667	0.0063
	Block Groups	2.7463	0.3757	(0.0084)
	Voting Precincts	2.7167	0.3395	0.0212
	Police Patrol Districts	2.6644	0.2993	0.0735
	Postal Areas	2.7193	0.4457	0.0186
	School Districts	2.9453	0.5347	(0.2074)
	Neighborhood Association Areas	2.8551	0.3496	(0.1172)
	Neighborhood Plan Areas	2.7167	0.3395	0.0212

5.2 Test of Accessibility Differences by Neighborhood Units

There is a need for investigating whether the accessibility indices are statistically significantly different between Resident-Perceived Neighborhood Boundaries and the rest of the Census-based Neighborhood Boundaries.

Table 4 below shows the result of paired-samples t-test of accessibilities by neighborhood units. The paired samples t-test compares the means of two variables, and compares the difference between the two variables for each case, and tests to prove if the average difference is significantly different and if the difference is significantly bigger than zero. The paired t-test is generally used when measurements are taken from the same subject before and after some manipulation as a treatment. The current analysis considered the accessibility measurements based on different neighborhood units as a treatment. In this sense, the paired samples t-test was employed for accessibility comparisons among neighborhood units.

As Table 4 indicates below, at the $p < 0.05$ level, this paired samples t-test analysis indicates that a significant correlation exists between each pair of variables (accessibilities by RPND and by each census-based neighborhood unit). In detail, Pearson's correlations between accessibilities by Resident-Perceived Neighborhood Boundary and by each census-based neighborhood boundary mostly exceeded 0.80 which is normally considered a very high correlation. But, relatively, correlations with School Districts and Neighborhood Association Areas were somewhat low, ranging between 0.761 to 0.769. Although this paired samples t-test shows strong correlations of accessibility mean values, the t-values, whether plus or minus, only indicate whether accessibility by RPNB is bigger than that by a paired census-based neighborhood unit.

As significance of all eight t-values are over 0.05, precluding the significance at the $p < 0.05$ level, it indicates that it is not significant whether the mean accessibility by RPNB is bigger or smaller than that by a census-based neighborhood unit, and they are different case by case. As a result, there was no significant difference found between accessibilities by Resident-Perceived Neighborhood Boundaries and those by census-based neighborhood units.

Table 4. Paired Samples T-test of Accessibilities between by RND & by Census-based Units (Note: RPNB = Resident-perceived Neighborhood Boundaries, CTR = Census Tracts, BG = Block Groups, VP = Voting Precincts, PPD = Police patrol Districts, PA = Postal Areas, SD = School Districts, NAA = Neighborhood Association Areas, NPA = Neighborhood Plan Areas. / * statistically significant at 0.05 level.)

		Mean	N	S.D.	Correlation	Sig.	t	df	Sig.
Pair 1	RPND	2.738	9	0.381	0.986	0.000	0.299	8	0.772
	CTT	2.732	9	0.367					
Pair 2	RPND	2.738	9	0.381	0.987	0.000	-0.41	8	0.692
	BG	2.746	9	0.376					
Pair 3	RPND	2.738	9	0.381	0.942	0.000	0.491	8	0.636
	VP	2.717	9	0.339					
Pair 4	RPND	2.738	9	0.381	0.846	0.004	1.08	8	0.311
	PPD	2.664	9	0.299					
Pair 5	RPND	2.738	9	0.381	0.924	0.000	0.321	8	0.756
	PA	2.719	9	0.446					
Pair 6	RPND	2.738	9	0.381	0.761	0.017	-1.789	8	0.111
	SD	2.945	9	0.535					
Pair 7	RPND	2.738	9	0.381	0.769	0.016	-1.406	8	0.197
	NAA	2.855	9	0.350					
Pair 8	RPND	2.763	5	0.301	0.947	0.015	1.097	4	0.334
	NPA	2.715	5	0.304					

6 Conclusions

The investigation in the current study asked if there was any significant difference between accessibility measurements by Resident-Perceived Neighborhood Boundaries and Census-based Neighborhood Units. The result showed that there was no statistically significant difference in accessibility indices by whatever neighborhood units they were measured. Therefore, it is reasonable to conclude that the adoption of Resident-Perceived Neighborhood Boundary as the alternative unit of analysis to traditionally used Census-based Neighborhood Units doesn't affect the equity of accessibility to public Parks in the city of Austin.

The results of the current study give very important information to current practitioners and policy makers regarding public parks allocation. Coulton, et al. [4]

suggested that if researches and policies rely only on census-based definitions, they may misunderstand neighborhood effects because residents' activities are not accurately represented within census boundaries. But, as this study concludes, as the unit of analysis for park services allocation, in spite of the probable investment of time and efforts, residents' commonly agreed neighborhood boundaries do not contribute to making differences in park services allocation. Hence, conventionally used Census-based Neighborhood Units are still time-saving and cost-effective unit of analysis for park services allocation.

The current study utilized the structured questionnaire in the form of a survey by which the neighborhood residents in the study area passively contributed to the data gathering regarding their perception of neighborhood boundaries, as well as basic socio-demographic information. The survey method is an efficient study method in the sense that it systematically collects data from a broad spectrum of individuals and social settings. Though most widely utilized in social studies, survey research is carried on in spite of many drawbacks such as dependence on maximizing the response rate for the generalizability of the study results, a longer time period than other study methods and the process of data coding into statistical tools, even after full returns at successful rates.

In the present information age, as an alternative research method, the adoption of WebGIS (Web-based Geographic Information System) can be proposed in public services allocation. WebGIS refers to the existing and emerging computer technology of realizing spatial mapping and GIS functionality on the Internet. The use of interactive web mapping technology is expected to enable WebGIS to play a crucial role for the enhancement of the public participation in planning sphere. As Chang [25] argued, together with the advantages of the Internet, GIS could be useful in allowing many more grassroots organizations to have access to GIS functionality, and it may enhance public participation in the planning decision making process. It is entirely possible that a WebGIS will play an important part in the development of PPGIS (Public Participation GIS) [26]. Though discussed in a different term, 'resident-generated GIS', Talen [27] also emphasized the future role of GIS as an important method of enhancing public participation in the planning process.

References

1. Ostrom, V.: The Intellectual Crisis in Public Administration, University of Alabama. The University of Alabama Press (1974)
2. Rich, Richard C.: Analyzing Urban-Service Distributions. Lexington, MA, D.C. Health and Company (1982) 10
3. Martin, D.: Automatic Neighborhood Identification from Population Surfaces. Computer, Environment and Urban Systems 22, 2 (1998) 107-120
4. Coulton, Claudia J., Jill Korin, Tsui Chan, Marilyn S.: Mappping Residents' Perceptions of Neighborhood Boundaries: A Methodological Note. American Journal of Community Psychology 29, 2 (2001) 371-382
5. Sawicki, David S., Patrice F.: Neighborhood Indicators; a Review of the Literature and an Assessment of Conceptual and Methodological Issues. APA Journal, spring (1996) 165-183

6. Pacione, M.: Neighborhoods and Public Service Boundaries in the City: A Geographical Analysis. Geoforum 13, 3 (1982) 237-244
7. Lee, T.: Urban Neighborhood as a Socio-spatial Schemata. Human Relationships 21 (1968) 246-268
8. Lee, T.: A Theory of Socio-spatial Schemata. In Humanscape: Environments for people, edited by Kaplan S., Kaplan R., N. Scituate, MA, Duxbury Press (1978)
9. Golledge R. G., Spector, A. N.: Comprehending the Urban Environment: Theory and Practice. Geographic Analysis 10 (1978): 403-426
10. Mutter, L. R.: The Application of a Cognitive Mapping and User Analysis Methodology to Neighborhood Park Service Area Delineation. Master's Thesis, Texas A&M University (1985) 54-60
11. Gale, N., Golledge, R. G., Halperin, W. C., Conclelis H.: Exploring Spatial Familiarity. The Professional Geographer 42 (1990) 299-313
12. Talen, E.: Visualizing Fairness: Equity Maps for Planners. Journal of the American Planning Association 64, 1 (1998) 22-38
13. Lindsey, G., Maraj, M., Kuan, S.: Access, Equity, and Urban Greenways: An Exploratory Investigation. The Professional Geographer 53, 3 (2001) 332-346
14. McLafferty, S.: Urban Structure and Geographical Access to Public Services. Annals of the Association of American Geographers 72, 3 (1982) 347-354
15. Talen, E., Anselin, L.: Assessing Spatial Equity: An Evaluation of Measures of Accessibility to Public Playgrounds. Environment and Planning A 30 (1998) 595-613
16. Talen, E.: Constructing Neighborhoods from the Bottom Up: the Case for Resident-generated GIS. Environment and Planning B: Planning and Design 26 (1999) 533-554
17. Austin City Connection: The Official Website of the City of Austin - Texas, accessible at http://www.ci.austin.tx.us
18. White, Michael J.: American Neighborhoods and Residential differentiation. New York, Russell Sage Foundation (1987)
19. Nicholls, S.: Measuring the Accessibility and Equity of Public Parks: A Case Study Using GIS. M.S. Thesis, Texas A&M University (1999)
20. Sui, D.: GIS, Environmental Equity Analysis, and the Modifiable Areal Unit Problem (MAUP). In Geographic Information Research: Trans-atlantic Perspectives, edited by M. Craglia and H. Onsrud. Bristol. PA, Talor & Francis (1999) 41-54
21. Pacione, M.: Access to Urban Services – the Case of Secondary Schools in Glasgow. Scottish Geographic Magazine 105 (1989) 12-18
22. Anselin, L.: Spatial Data Analysis with SpaceStat and ArcView Workbook (3rd Edition), Department of Agricultural and Consumer Economics, University of Illinois (1999) 17
23. Aitkin, S. C., Prosser, R.: Residents' Spatial Knowledge of Neighborhood Continuity and Form. Geologographical Analysis 22 (1990) 301-326
24. Ormsby, T., Alvi, J.: Extending Arcview GIS – Teach Yourself to Use ArcView Extensions. ESRI Press (1999)
25. Chang, K. P.: The design of a web-based Geographic Information System for Community Parcicipation. Master's Thesis, University of Buffalo (1997)
26. Nyerges, T., Barndt, M., Brooks, K.: Public Participation Geographic Information Systems. Proceedings of Auto-Carto 13, Seattle-WA (1997) 224-233
27. Talen, E.: Constructing Neighborhoods from the Bottom Up: the Case for Resident-generated GIS. Environment and Planning B: Planning and Design 26 (1999) 533-554.

Author Index

Lecture Notes in Computer Science

For information about Vols. 1–3717

please contact your bookseller or Springer